PATERSON EWEN

SPONSOR'S FOREWORD

Paterson Ewen is one of Canada's great artists. His paintings touch us deeply with their sublime power and monumentality.

The Fraser Elliott Foundation is pleased to sponsor this book, which celebrates the achievements of a major contemporary artist in innovative ways. Here we have the life of the artist and his œuvre brought together in one volume by distinguished writers, critics and peers. Here we acknowledge the Art Gallery of Ontario's collection of Paterson Ewen's work, now the largest public holding and the study centre for his career. Here, too, we present the first in a series of books that will be published through the ongoing sponsorship of The Fraser Elliott Foundation, highlighting the œuvre of other major Canadian contemporary artists, as these collections are developed at the Art Gallery of Ontario into the twenty-first century.

We congratulate the artist, Paterson Ewen, and the Art Gallery of Ontario for bringing this project to fruition. We acknowledge with pride the significant contributions made by writers Michael Ondaatje and Ron Graham, Art Gallery of Ontario Chief Curator Matthew Teitelbaum, and artist Eric Fischl who have, with this book, provided a new model for art publishing in Canada.

Fraser Elliott
The Fraser Elliott Foundation
March 1996

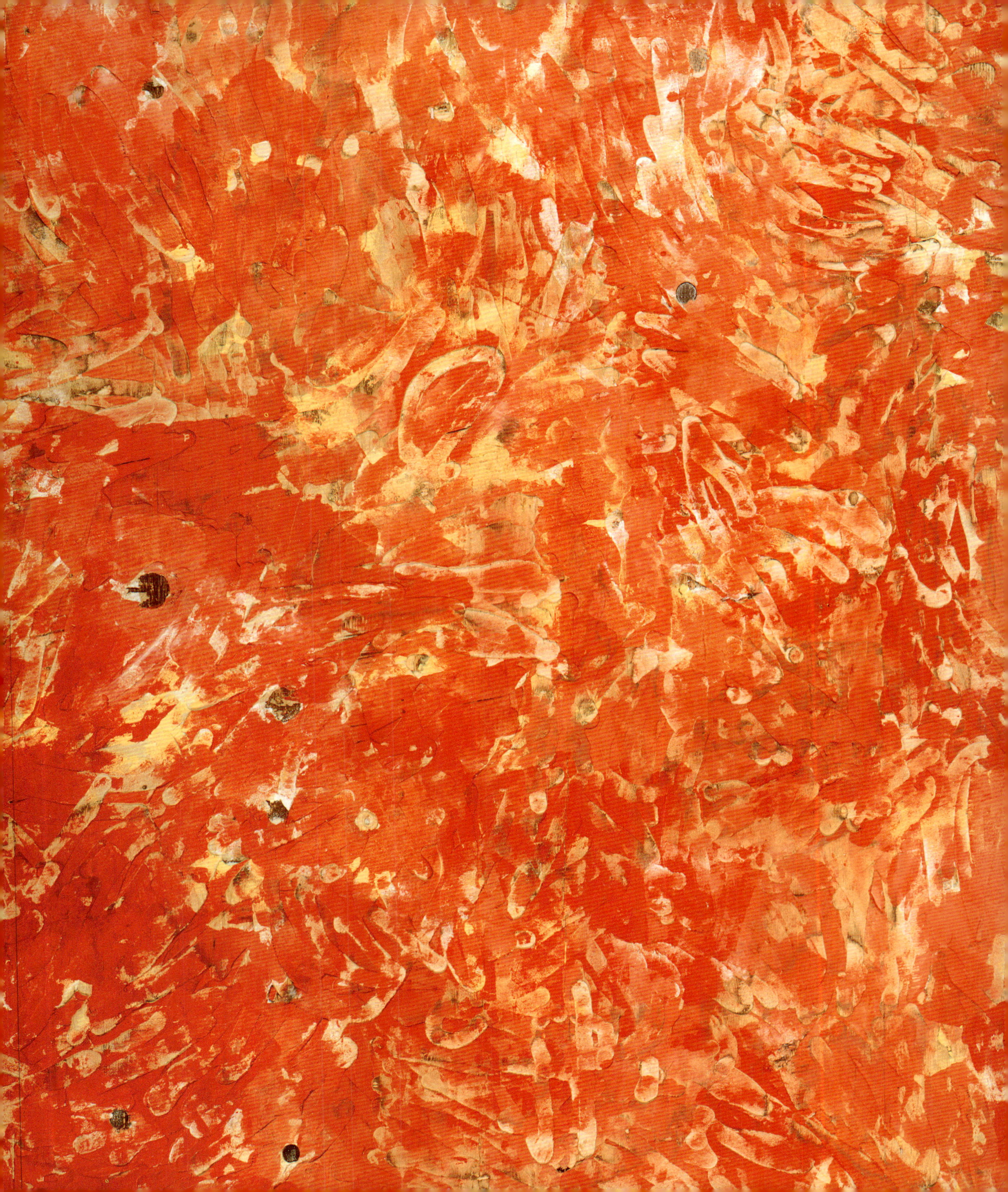

PATERSON EWEN

Edited by

MATTHEW TEITELBAUM

Introduction by

MICHAEL ONDAATJE

Essays by

RON GRAHAM

MATTHEW TEITELBAUM

Afterword by

ERIC FISCHL

DOUGLAS & McINTYRE / VANCOUVER *and* TORONTO
ART GALLERY OF ONTARIO / TORONTO

96 97 98 99 00 5 4 3 2 1

The Art Gallery of Ontario is funded by the people of Ontario through the Ministry of Culture, Tourism and Recreation. Additional operating support is received from the Municipality of Metropolitan Toronto, the Museums Assistance Program of the Department of Canadian Heritage and The Canada Council.

Produced in association with *The Fraser Elliott Foundation.*

Supported by a grant from the Exhibition Assistance Program of The Canada Council.

This book is published on the occasion of *Paterson Ewen: Earthly Weathers/Heavenly Skies,* the exhibition organized and circulated by the Art Gallery of Ontario, Toronto, and sponsored by W. Bruce C. Bailey, Chairman, Bailey & Company Inc., Toronto, with the support of The Fraser Elliott Foundation.

Douglas & McIntyre
1615 Venables Street
Vancouver, British Columbia V5L 2H1

CANADIAN CATALOGUING IN PUBLICATION DATA

Ewen, Paterson, 1925–
Paterson Ewen

Co-published by Art Gallery of Ontario.
Catalogue of an exhibition held at the Art Gallery of Ontario, September 1996.

ISBN 1-55054-514-0

1. Ewen, Paterson, 1925– —Exhibitions. I. Graham, Ron, 194–
II. Teitelbaum, Matthew. III. Art Gallery of Ontario. IV. Title.
ND249.E94 4 1996 759.11 C96-910388-3

Editing by Saeko Usukawa
Design by Barbara Hodgson
Printed and bound in Canada by Hemlock Printers Ltd.
Printed on acid-free paper ∞

The publisher gratefully acknowledges the assistance of The Canada Council and of the British Columbia Ministry of Tourism, Small Business and Culture.

All dimensions of works of art are given in centimetres; height precedes width.

Frontispiece:
SURFACE OF THE SUN
(detail) 1993
Acrylic on gouged plywood
226.1 x 228.6
Art Gallery of Ontario

Cover painting by
Paterson Ewen
HALLEY'S COMET AS SEEN BY GIOTTO (detail)
1979
Acrylic and fluorescent paint on galvanized steel and gouged plywood
229.0 x 244.0
Art Gallery of Ontario

PATERSON EWEN DEDICATES THE EXHIBITION

Paterson Ewen: Earthly Weathers/Heavenly Skies

TO MARY ALISON HANDFORD

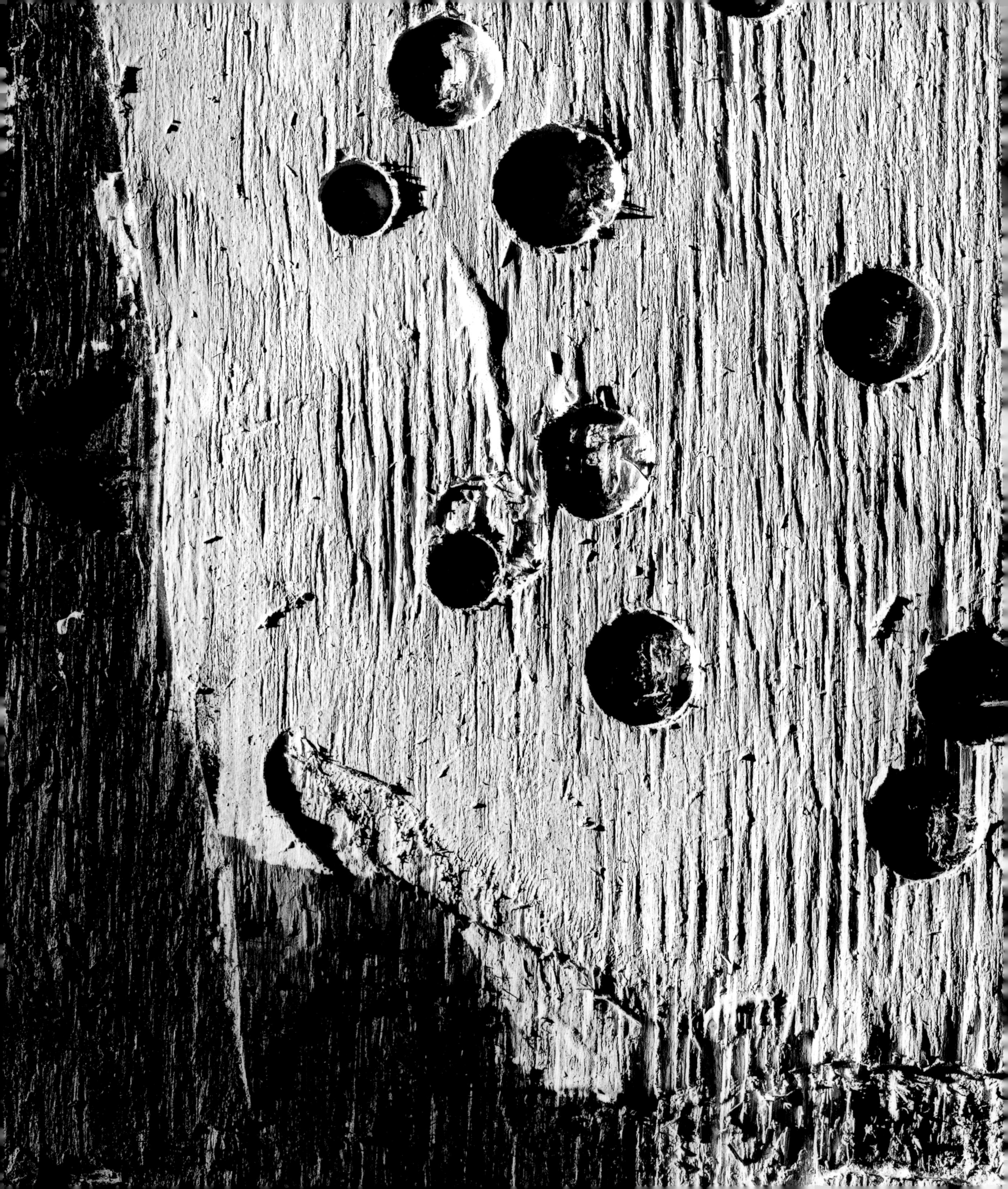

CONTENTS

DIRECTOR'S FOREWORD

Although the land both is the subject of and yields materials for Paterson Ewen's later landscapes, the powerful, kinetic elegance of these works sets them apart from other efforts to chronicle our surroundings using natural elements. Ewen's accomplishments over the forty years of this survey are extraordinary by any measure, and we are grateful to have had the opportunity to organize this compelling project.

The combined wisdom of Michael Ondaatje, Ron Graham, Eric Fischl, and our Chief Curator, Matthew Teitelbaum, makes this an important and memorable volume. Their insights into the life and œuvre of Paterson Ewen add significantly to our understanding of this seminal artist's achievements.

We deeply appreciate the support of The Fraser Elliott Foundation in making this publication possible. In addition to the Foundation, I wish to thank Paterson Ewen and those who have made his work available to a larger public by contributing to the Art Gallery of Ontario. Paterson Ewen's rhythmic elegies deserve our continued scrutiny and appreciation, and we have much to learn from this retrospective.

Maxwell L. Anderson
Director
Art Gallery of Ontario

ACKNOWLEDGEMENTS

It is a pleasure to acknowledge the many individuals who have contributed to the realization of this celebration and exploration of the work of one of Canada's leading artists, Paterson Ewen. A number of collectors have generously donated paintings by Paterson Ewen to the Art Gallery of Ontario, and their willingness to share, with future generations, works that they have cared for is very much appreciated. They are: Ruby and the late Bruno Cormier, Ben and Yael Dunkelman, the Ramstein family, Geoffrey and the late Goldie Rans, Reed Paper Limited, and Alan and Alison Schwartz.

Crucial to the realization of this publication has been the support of The Fraser Elliott Foundation. Over many years, Fraser Elliott has made a remarkable contribution to the presentation and documentation of Canadian contemporary art, and we are grateful to him. The Foundation is joined in its support of the Art Gallery of Ontario by W. Bruce C. Bailey, Chairman, Bailey & Company Inc., Toronto, who, in an exemplary way, has sponsored the exhibition *Paterson Ewen: Earthly Weathers/Heavenly Skies*. His generous support, allowing the Gallery to present Paterson Ewen's work in the best way possible, is rooted in a commitment to Ewen's art. "I am delighted," said Bruce Bailey, "to sponsor the exhibition of Paterson Ewen, a towering figure in the history of art, who has particularly enriched Canadian culture through his interpretation of our dreams and myths. Mr. Ewen's startling originality, mastery of colour, utilization of unconventional materials and blending of abstraction and representation place him amongst the most important painters of the twentieth century."

At the Art Gallery of Ontario, a number of truly dedicated colleagues have helped to make this project what it is, and though too numerous to

Page vi:
ECLIPSE OF THE MOON
(detail) 1990
Acrylic on gouged plywood
266.8 x 297.6
Art Gallery of Ontario

Page 1:
TORNADO #3
1989
Watercolour on
handmade paper
74.2 x 100.7
Art Gallery of Ontario

mention, their contributions have made a tremendous difference. Of particular note is the care given to individual works of art by key members of our conservation staff, Barry Briggs, Margaret Haupt and Sandra Webster-Cook. The chronology began as an idea, a virtual treasure hunt for information. Michelle Jacques worked tirelessly in the archives at the beginning of the project; Laura Brown worked tirelessly in the archives, too, and saw the full project through to its final form. Laura gave the chronology its form and much of its life, with intelligence, commitment and not a little patience. I am grateful to both of them. With gratitude, I would also like to acknowledge Geoffrey Rans, who marked our friendship through a direct though gracious reading of my text.

At every step of the way, Mary Handford remained involved and supportive. I thank her for the many different ways she helped bring ideas and images together.

I learn from Paterson Ewen almost every time we talk and every time I look at one of his paintings. He has been generous with his time, caring about detail, and committed to sharing my ambition for what this project is, in all its aspects. My hope is that this publication will encourage further study of Paterson Ewen's art, as well as that of his colleagues, and bring renewed attention to the pleasures of Canadian art.

Matthew Teitelbaum
June 1996

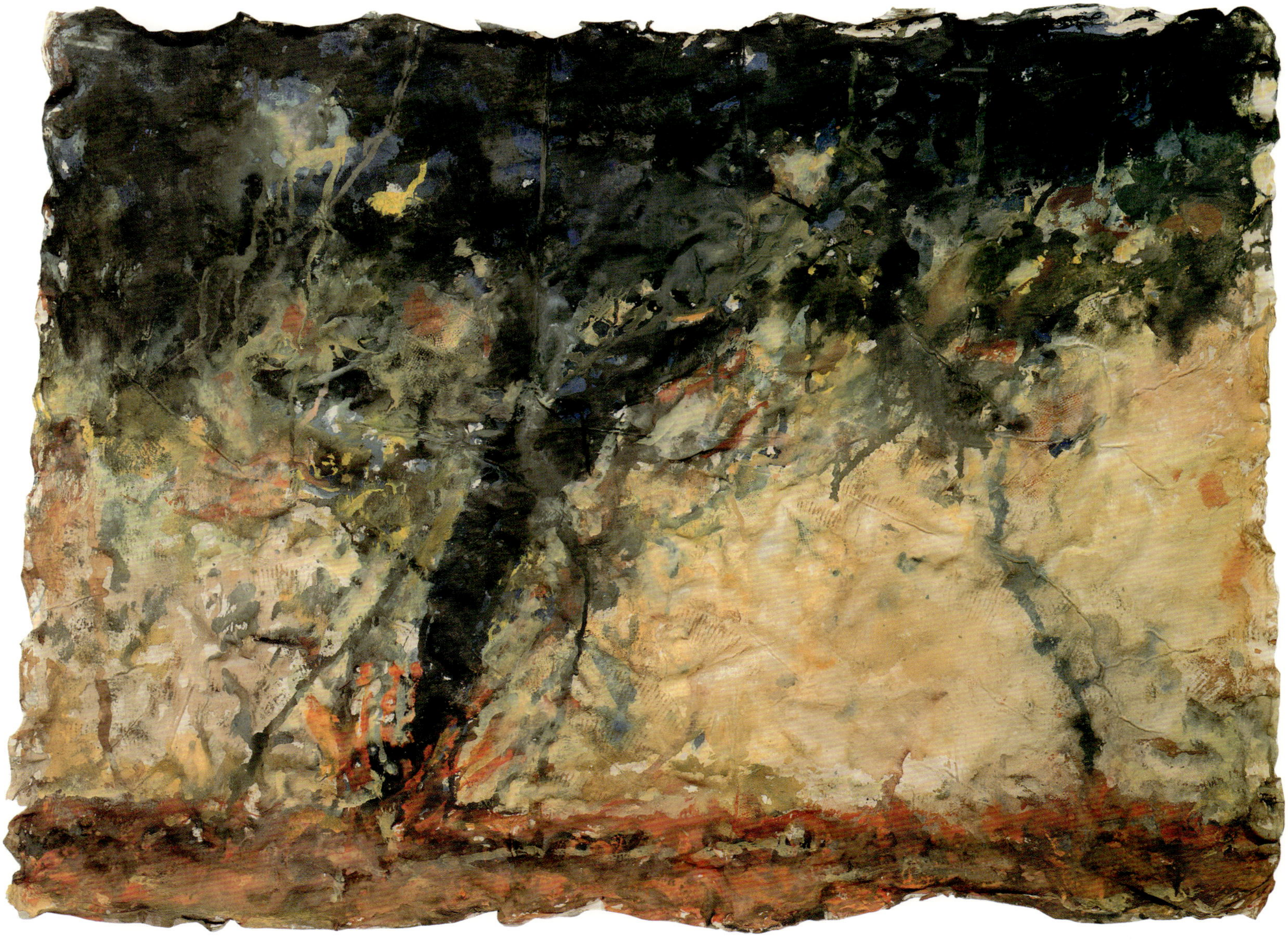

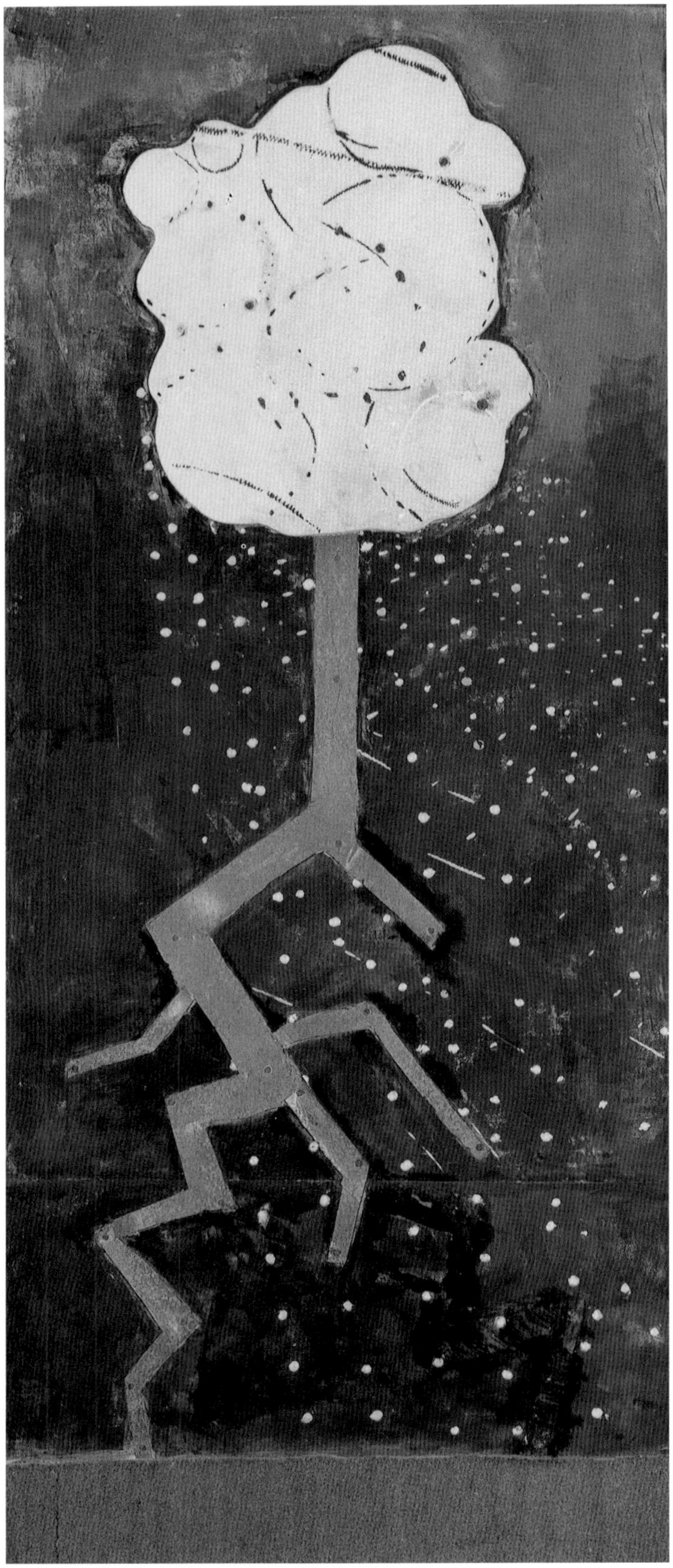

WHAT LIGHTNING WAS LIKE IN THE 1970S

Virtuosity, unless it move the heart, goes at the head of the whole parade to dust.
—Eudora Welty

Something in us loves those works of art that have within their body or paint or words a sense that they have only just survived their making. Nothing is more powerful to us.

Nearly all of Paterson Ewen's work has this quality—from those early, almost inarticulate, attempts at drawing the human body to his wondrous leap in the 1970s with his portraits of phenomena. These great metaphors of the heavens, made with simple utensils from hardware stores, feel like cargo cult objects put together by a man who has walked back into the darkened cave after staring at the sun.

Hailstorms, a thousand versions of rain, so many moons, fog, star traces, are the familiar and vast subject of his art. But how do you evoke a moon in rain except with tin, plywood, steel bolts, galvanized iron? How do you narrate a comet or the northern lights without hammers, wire brushes, electric routers that turn at 25 thousand revolutions a minute? Ewen recreates the natural world around him in the language of a blacksmith. "Cocoa matting is the stuff at the bottom of *Storm over the Prairies* . . . I wander around hardware stores. I saw that matting and I said well I have to have some of that . . . That cloud up there is a piece of plywood and over the piece of plywood is glued a piece of battleship linoleum and into that I grooved the marks. This cloud is bolted onto the base plywood . . . The lightning is galvanized iron." There is a Blakean visionary here, a profound and innocent soul that can say "a length of wire becomes rain, a piece of link fence becomes fog." First principles of art.

But the works are also, as he says, "inner phenomena." And so alongside the tough, grounded, iron-bound feeling in the sculptural works or the routered, large permanence of the big paintings, is

Facing page:
STORM OVER THE PRAIRIES 1971
Metal, acrylic on plywood
244.0 x 101.0
Private Collection

Page 5:
HALLEY'S COMET AS SEEN BY GIOTTO 1979
Acrylic and fluorescent paint on galvanized steel and gouged plywood
229.0 x 244.0
Art Gallery of Ontario

an indelible sense of precariousness, of a mutable world. We have a broken tree, a bandaged man, a thin sliver of tin surrounded by vast and dark swirls of weather to suggest one frail white cloud over water.

And viewer and painter are too far into the storm for comfort. You look at a work like *Eclipse of the Moon*, and your focus and position are no longer certain. You wonder is it moon or biological detail, outer or inner phenomena?

There is also the great emotional range in Paterson Ewen's work. We can move from the primal conceits of *Thunder Chain* and *Rocks Moving in the Current of a Stream* to the ravishing *Halley's Comet as Seen by Giotto*—a great work, fully lyrical, lyrical even close up in the crimson gouges and in the brutal power of the imagined comet's journey.

It is this remarkable recreation of power in Ewen's work that grounds them and gives them permanence. We have in these works a vision of nature beyond the human ego: on one hand huge in scope, on the other hand humble in its point of view and its sense of equalness. The irony of a phenomenal wonder being named after Halley and seen in the context of Giotto partly mocks our human desire for naming. But it is, from another angle, a tender celebration of these two men. And the brilliant colour of it has enough of an echo of Giotto . . . almost as if a detail from one of his frescoes has been blown up, dangerous and glorious. In one of Robert Hass's books of poetry, he writes about a seventeenth-century encounter with a sea creature: "We asked the Captain what course of action he proposed to take towards a beast so large, terrifying, and unpredictable. He hesitated to answer, and then said judiciously: 'I think I shall praise it.' "

There is a profound peace when you come into a gallery and see a work like *Portrait of Vincent* or *Rain Over Water* or *Halley's Comet as Seen by Giotto* after a gap of years. I'm not sure why this happens to me only with Paterson Ewen's work. Perhaps there is a balance and security in these precarious works because of the very fact that they seem to have been torn out of the heart and earth, that they were made with great difficulty as something to hold on to. These are the only safe things. They often are the only things we can have faith in.

Michael Ondaatje
Toronto, 1996

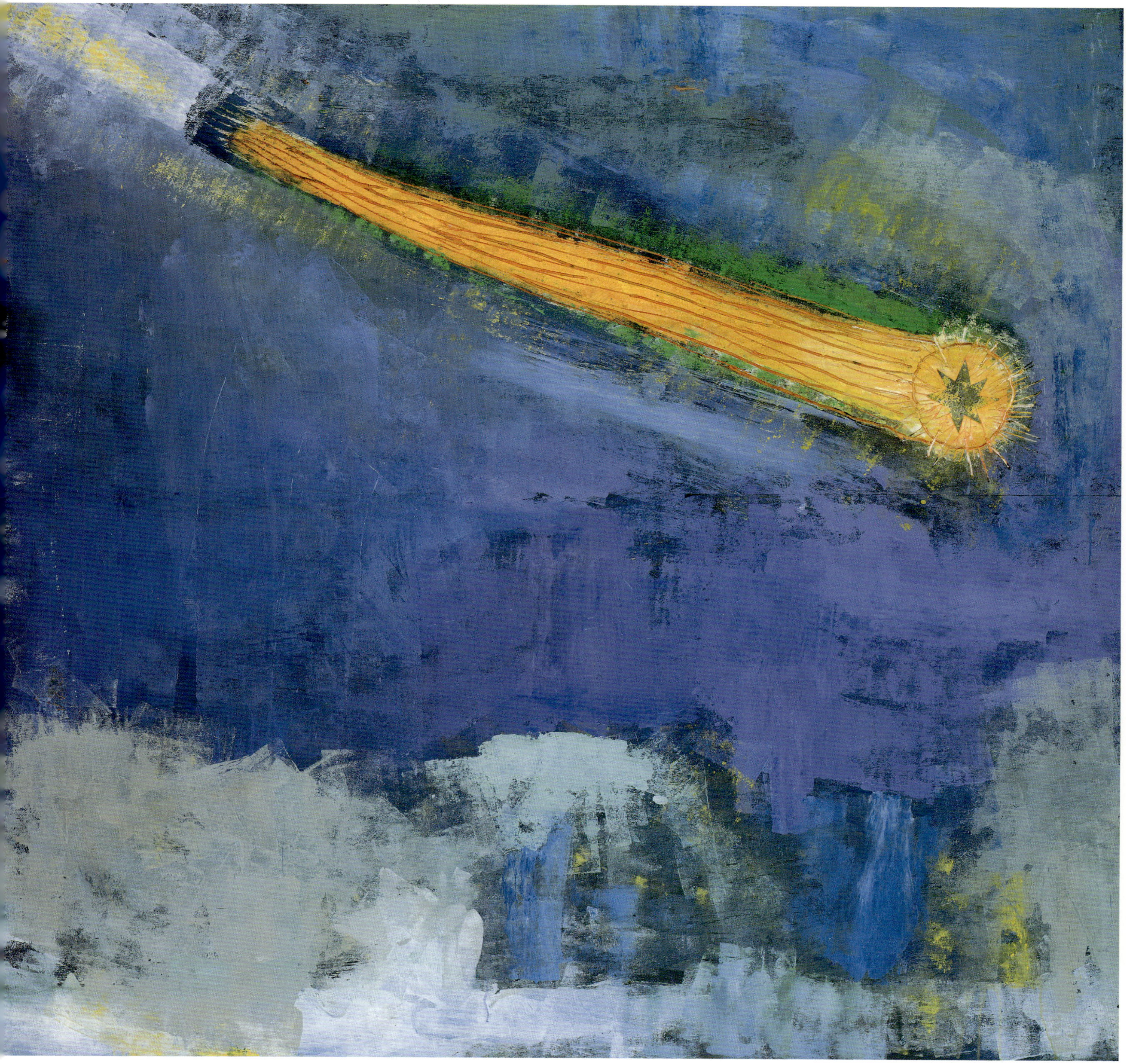

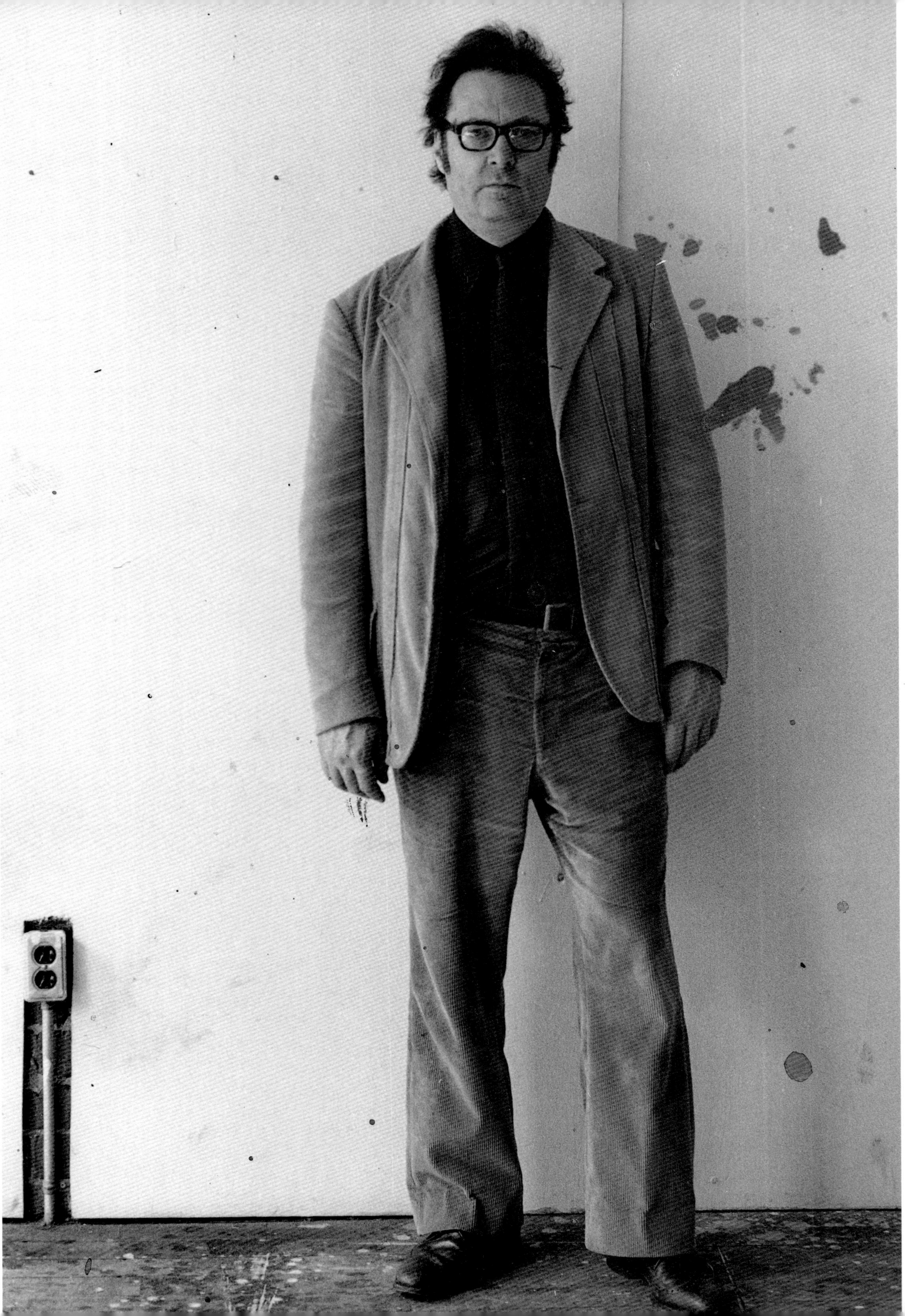

TWENTY-FOUR SKETCHES FOR A PORTRAIT OF PATERSON EWEN

by Ron Graham

ONE

There is a squalid district of London, Ontario, east along Dundas Street from the city core, a down-and-out strip of discount stores, cheap cafés, beer hotels, pawnshops, and boarded-up crack houses. Here, among the welfare mothers and rummy pensioners, Paterson Ewen has worked—and periodically lived—since 1986, though almost invisibly. He deliberately avoids eye contact as he walks from the bus stop to his studio, so as not to attract any notice or trouble, and there is nothing on the outside of the dilapidated two-storey cinder-block factory to call attention to the presence on its ground floor of such a major Canadian artist.

Nor is there much in Paterson's own look and manner to distinguish him by background or genius from all the other septuagenarian war vets in the area bearing the weight, in their faces as well as their bodies, of ceaseless battles with depression and drink. Though he has prevailed over both, he can still appear more like a victim than a victor, with his soft face, heavy movement, and passive amiability, reliant on glasses and two hearing aids, his hands sore with arthritis. No one could detect, within that vulnerable hulk, the handsome athlete Paterson Ewen once was or the powerful creator he still is.

Like the blank façade of his studio, his stoic fortitude conceals complexities, surprises, contradictions, emotions, even incidents of delirium. Behind the sensitive, considerate persona who finds it hard to say no lurks an angry child with a fierce competitiveness, an exaggerated reputation as a streetfighter, and an unassailable regard for his own self. "Even in occupational therapy, you have to be the best, don't you?" a psychiatrist once chided when Paterson Ewen insisted on making the most beautiful bracelet of them all.

Paterson Ewen, photograph for *Self-Portrait* (1986), c. 1978

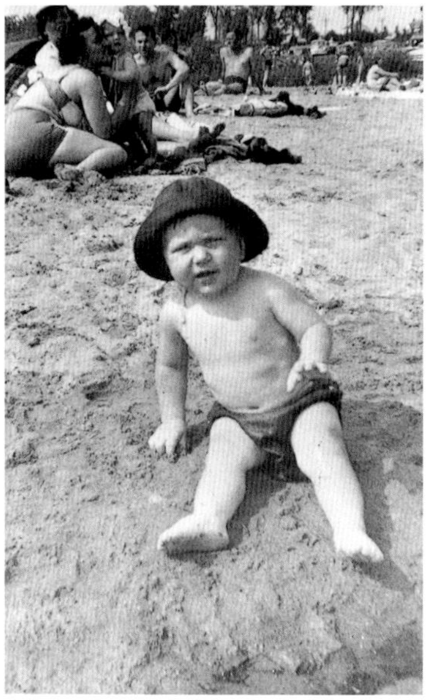

Paterson Ewen, c. 1927

William (Bill) Ewen, c. 1915

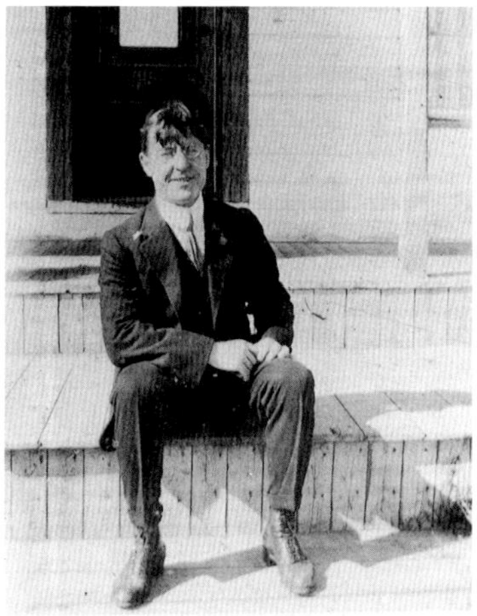

TWO

Every summer, when Paterson was a boy growing up in Montreal, his parents would drive him and his sister Marjorie to a two-week holiday at the Vermont Hotel in Old Orchard Beach, Maine. He remembers those vacations with delight, except for the time, aged five or six, when he came across a Punch and Judy puppet show under a red and white striped canopy. When Punch hit his wife over the head with a stick, Paterson began to scream hysterically, and for days afterwards the mere sight of the canopy was enough to set him screaming all over again.

He was a strangely sensitive child. He couldn't bear the bang of fireworks; violent movies sent him running from the theatre in fright; he would become upset whenever Amos started yelling at Andy on the radio. He hated circus clowns, Halloween masks, grotesque caricatures: "Anything that looked human," is how he describes what terrorized him, "but wasn't."

His behaviour seemed inexplicable at the time. Later, he didn't think it odd at all: he saw in the clowns, the masks, and Punch's fury unsettling reflections of his father's alcoholic rages.

THREE

William Ewen—Will or Willy within the family, Bill to others—could be an intimidating man even without drink. He was a short, dark, taciturn Scot, with a weathered face and the remnants of a brogue, who had been born in a brutal district of Aberdeen in 1888. When he was still a lad, his mother, née Mary Ann Paterson, died after thirteen pregnancies, leaving her six surviving children to the care of their father, George Ewen. He was a poor cobbler who specialized in making shoes for deformed feet, sported a red tie on behalf of his socialist principles, and kept the peace in a neighbourhood the police feared to enter.

Bill was able to lift himself out of this Dickensian underworld because he did well in school up to grade six, he was ruthlessly honest, and he was as tough as his old man. His chance came when recruiters from the Hudson's Bay Company offered him adventure and freedom as a fur trader in northern Canada, just as his father's father had once been before returning to Scotland with a bride from Trois-Rivières. At the age of seventeen Bill crossed the Atlantic and headed north. He was indentured there for the next eleven years.

"Though he educated himself up north by reading all of Dickens and so forth," Paterson says, "civilization became difficult for him in some ways. After so many years of wearing moccasins, he couldn't stand wearing shoes. He'd take them off and walk around holding them. And when he married my mother, he wasn't used to sleeping in a bed, so he slept on the floor. Her family feared a scandal that she had married an Indian."

FOUR

While working for the Hudson's Bay Company in the northern Manitoba post of York Factory, Bill Ewen met a schoolteacher named Edith Griffis. Though she was not interested in marriage herself, she apparently thought him a decent prospect for her younger sister Elora or her friend Mary Bell (according to varying accounts), both of whom were living in Winnipeg at the time with another of Edith's sisters, Edna. Edna had also taught for a while, in a one-room schoolhouse in northern Ontario, but the strain of disciplining rambunctious frontier boys almost her own age and size triggered a nervous breakdown, for which she was prescribed laudanum and the constant recitation of the multiplication tables. However unsuited to teaching, Edna was intelligent and highly capable, and she subsequently landed an office job with the Winnipeg School Board.

With Edith's introduction in his pocket, Bill Ewen journeyed three hundred miles by dogsled, then south by train to Winnipeg, and showed up unannounced at the door. When Edna answered, fresh from having just washed her long curls, a single glance caused Bill to forget about anyone else. Two years of letters followed before they finally married in July 1917—Bill was twenty-nine, Edna thirty-one—but not until she had extracted a futile promise of no alcohol and no sex.

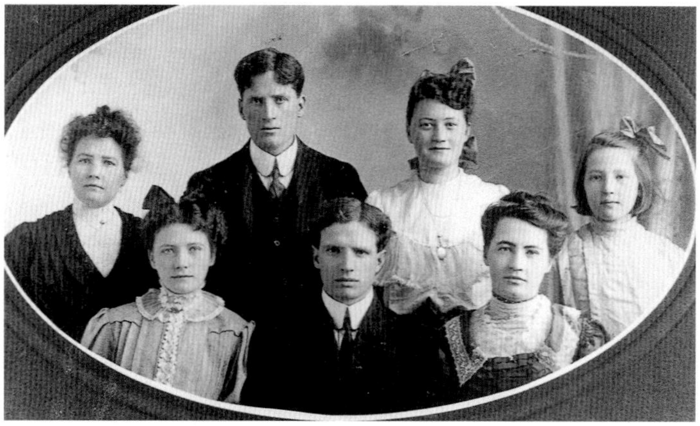

Edna Griffis (*front row, left*) with her siblings

Edna may have been smart and by general consensus the most beautiful of the five Griffis sisters, but she was also the least demonstrative. "All the girls had a tremendous sense of humour," says her niece Doris McNab. "They were great laughers and great criers. But Paterson's mother seemed more inhibited and rigid in her personality than the others. And she had this really big hangup about booze. It must have been something that stemmed from her father."

Silas Israel Griffis, born in 1849 of a Welsh father and Dutch mother near St. Catharines in Upper Canada, was both a charming rogue and a hard drinker. One of Edna's earliest memories was of him sadistically pretending to carve her kitten instead of the roast. At fourteen he had bade farewell to his widowed mother and run off to join the United States Army—in order to get himself a horse, reputedly, on which he then rode away to Illinois. There he met Seth and Doris Ingoldsby, who had migrated from New York State in 1858 to a farm near Chicago, and in 1870 he accompanied them west by covered wagon to Kansas. A year later Silas married their daughter Emma, three years his junior.

In 1885, after failing at homesteading and serving as county sheriff, Silas took Emma and their growing family back east to the province of Ontario, first to St. Catharines on the Niagara Peninsula and then to Rat Portage (later renamed Kenora) on Lake of the Woods, where he wheeled and dealed in property speculation, mining claims, and wooden ties for the new railroad. When he was flush, he and his family lived high off the hog. When he was bust, he headed to Montana to drink and play cards with a bunch of rough diamonds he knew: he'd peddle stocks in some worthless gold mines, then return home a few months later with trunkloads of new clothes for his wife and seven children.

In contrast to Silas's roustabout ways, Emma appears to have been a devotional and guilt-ridden Victorian romantic who sought to raise her daughters—Edith M., Emma M., Edna M., Elora M., and Enid M.—as proper young ladies until her death from cancer in 1897, when she was only forty-five years old. All but one grew up to be either a nurse or a teacher. Enid, the exception, had an interesting career as a magazine writer and professor's secretary in New York City, offset by several mental breakdowns. The two boys fared less well. The older, Raymond, was a reclusive Bible-reader who went to work in the coal mines of Drumheller, Alberta, and died there from cancer. The younger, Silas junior, achieved some renown as "Big Moose" Griffis, a hockey star with the Vancouver Millionaires and Kenora Thistles, but he slid into alcohol, divorce, depression, and finally evangelical Christianity while working in the advertising business in Vancouver.

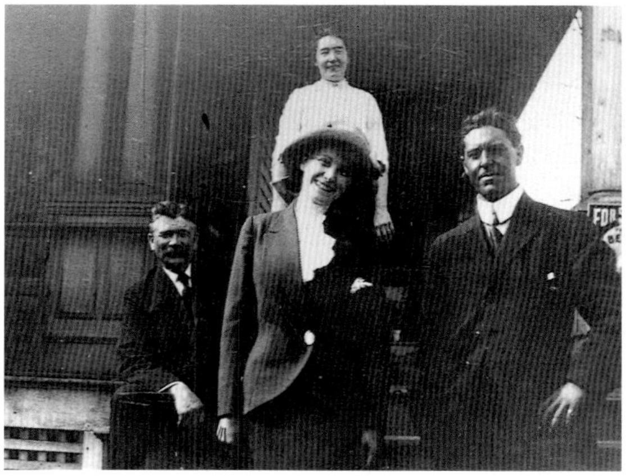

Edna and Bill Ewen on their wedding day, 1917

There had been an eighth child, another daughter whom everyone adored. She died when she was seven, a year after Silas and Emma's arrival in St. Catharines. According to family lore, Emma was in her sixth pregnancy at the time of the death, but the provincial records show she had already delivered her sixth child five months before. Out of grief and somewhat morbidly, the new baby girl—born February 12, 1886—was given the deceased girl's name, Edna, though the family always referred to Paterson's mother as "Teen."

After her marriage to Bill Ewen, Edna dedicated herself to cooking fine meals, sewing nice clothes, and managing the household finances for her husband and children, but she seemed marked by her mother's premature death, the depression that crippled at least three of her siblings, and perhaps the burden of her dead sister's name. And, like all the Griffis children, she had become alienated from her father after his marriage to a much younger French-Canadian woman—which ended when he shot himself to death, at the age of sixty-two, in 1912.

"My mother was a very caring person who'd do anything for my sister and me," Paterson recalls, "so long as it didn't involve showing affection. Once, when I was a teenager and she was going on about something, I told her to shut up. She was so mad, she went to slap my face, but she stopped herself at the very last moment so her hand just slid down my cheek. That was the only caress I ever got from her."

FIVE

Unable to bear the constant wind and social isolation at Bersimis, a tiny community on the barren north shore of the St. Lawrence River where Bill had been sent as the Hudson's Bay factor, Edna persuaded him to quit the Company of Adventurers for a more mundane existence sorting mink pelts for Holt Renfrew back in Winnipeg. He moved on almost immediately for a better-paying management job with Canadian Fur Auction Sales in Montreal, where he and Edna settled in the midst of the downtown Jewish district—first on Fairmount Avenue, then on Esplanade at Bernard, in both cases in top-storey flats because Edna couldn't stand the idea of having people over her head.

"I don't think my father knew enough French Canadians to feel one way or another about them," Paterson says, "although he had an 'official' prejudice against Roman Catholics as a very active Mason. The only personal advice he ever gave me was not to get mixed up with some Catholic girl—he thought it would kill my mother—so that's exactly what I did, of course. But he had a lot of Jewish friends in the fur business. He found them interesting and they respected his fairness."

The Ewens' first child, Marjorie, was born in September 1920, and after four miscarriages, Paterson followed on April 7, 1925. Soon afterwards, the family started to trek toward Edna's ultimate dream of having a house in one of the leafy—and very Protestant—suburbs springing up far to the west of the city centre. They took a nicer, bigger apartment on Sherbrooke Street West near Westmore Avenue, then a duplex only slightly to the north on Westmore across from the apple orchards and farmland beyond Somerled Boulevard, then a detached house with a birch tree on the front lawn and a large backyard at 317 Ballantyne Avenue North in the town of Montreal West, which they rented between 1932 and 1939 from a man who had been hit by the hard times.

"We were middle-class on the verge of upper-middle-class," Paterson says, "because my father was earning the grand sum of $6,000 a year during the Depression. He eventually became assistant general manager of the company, but was still paid extra for working overtime and weekends. Even though his drinking became heavier and heavier—he had bottles hidden all over the office—it never affected his job."

It did affect his family, however. Most evenings, Bill Ewen drove all the way home from downtown Montreal tipsy, and the first thing he did was head for the little bit of sherry Edna permitted in the house. There were nights, especially around the weeks of the fur auctions, when Paterson would wait up with his mother for the sound of the Buick pulling into the drive. They heard the car door slam—then nothing. His father had collapsed in a stupor on the lawn, his glasses broken, and had to be carried to bed. And then came the fights, which Paterson recalled as "violent and loud and frequent," and his mother's sobs. He watched helplessly as she sought refuge in a room of her own, Sunday services at the United Church, golf, and tracts from the British Israelites and various other crackpot cults.

SIX

Every Christmas, the Ewens threw a big open-house party for neighbours, business associates, and the relatives Bill had brought over from Scotland: his father George, his sister Annie, and his ne'er-do-well brother Innes. It was an occasion on which joy was mixed with trepidation, because no one knew when Bill would show the effects of one drink too many. He wasn't responsible for the most dramatic brawl, however. It began when his father accused him of not doing enough for his indigent brother, despite all the clothes and toys Edna had placed under the tree for Innes's five children. Innes, drunk and perhaps feeling beholden, flew up in a rage and punched the old man. Amid the falling of ferns, Bill struggled to subdue them, Annie fainted, Edna summoned the police, and the children were hustled upstairs in fear.

Grandfather Ewen lived with his daughter Annie and her common-law husband Cecil not far from Innes's shack in a semirural slum across the river from Montreal, but theirs was a solid, two-storey house from which she operated a general store and her father repaired shoes. A tall, lean, white-bearded figure, he often sat alone in Annie's garden, staring for hours into space, and though he adored Marjorie and always gave Paterson a nickel as a present, he was generally grumpy and incommunicative. Part of the problem was his thick Aberdeen accent. "He didn't have too much time for me," Paterson says. "He was just another entity I couldn't reach as a boy."

Long after his grandfather's fatal stroke, Paterson learned of George Ewen's talent and reputation as a sculptor in Aberdeen. They were enough to earn him regular commissions to do clay busts of the mayor and other city officials, which were then cast into bronze by local Italian artisans. Two doctors from London once happened to see one of the busts and recognized its quality. They sought out George and offered him a post as medical artist at the University of London. He would have gone if his wife hadn't refused to leave Scotland.

Paterson later wondered if that lost opportunity, that frustrated creativity, wasn't the root of his grandfather's sadness in the garden. Or the source of his own mysterious artistic longings.

Clockwise from top: Grandfather George, Edna, Marjorie, Annie and Cecil, c. 1923

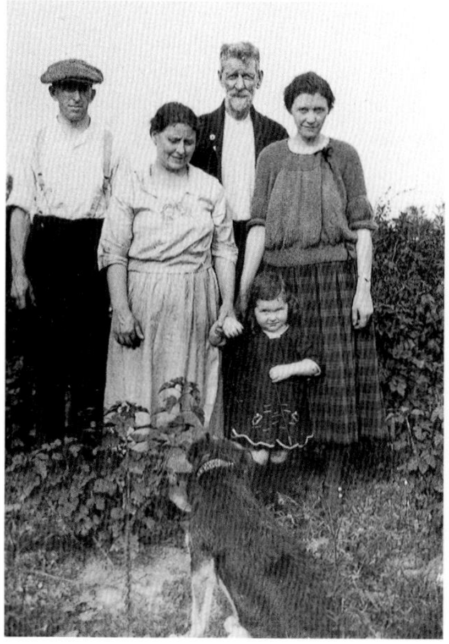

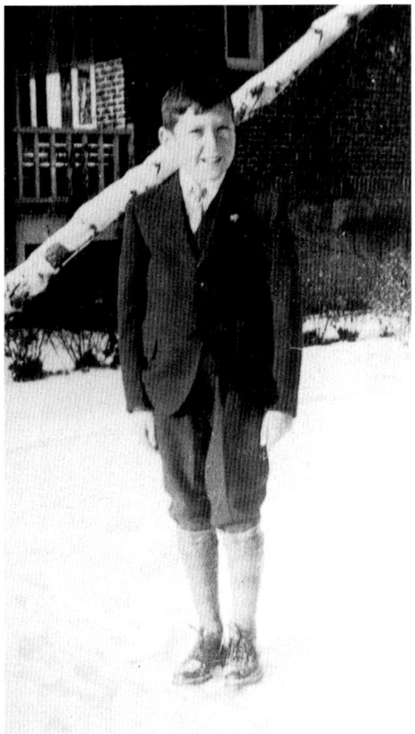

Paterson Ewen, c. 1932

SEVEN

In addition to his hysteria over clowns and violence, Paterson's nervousness manifested itself as physical agitation and chronic ailments. Every spring, he was bedridden for three weeks with bronchitis. "My sister thought I used to take advantage of it," he says, "by getting my mother to apply cold compresses to my head. That was the closest she came to touching."

One March, while still a toddler, he unexpectedly asked his mother if she would give him some wax. Paterson chewed the slabs of wax into a malleable ball. He then passed the days working the wax with his hands into small figures and a very beautiful tree. Years later, in his mid-teens, inspired by one of his grandfather's busts he had seen, Paterson attempted a clay model of Marjorie's face. "It came out looking more like me, but with more delicate features," he says. "It should have been called *Paterson Ewen as a Sixteen-Year-Old Girl*."

Neither parent showed any interest in art. The walls and hardwood floors were all but bare, with only a framed cover from a newsprint colour section of a woman wearing pearls, a mediocre watercolour of a field done by Aunt Elora, a tiny European scene by some minor artist named Chatillon, a wicker basket with some ferns, and a few ornamental brass plates in the dining room. "Teen was a perfectionist housekeeper," Doris McNab recalls from visiting her aunt's family on Ballantyne Avenue as a child, "and she used to say she never wanted to own anything that she'd be upset if it broke—which is kind of sad, don't you think? There was certainly nothing to inspire an artist."

Indeed, Paterson found most of his early inspiration on his visits to Doris's family in Ottawa. Her mother was Edna's sister Emma; her father was deputy minister of Indian Affairs; and they lived in an apartment across Argyle Street from the National Museum of Man. Paterson spent hours in the museum, either with the rock samples and dinosaur bones in the science section or the Group of Seven landscapes in the art gallery. Through the McNabs, he also became friendly with a Japanese diplomat's family who, on a visit to the Ewens in Montreal, presented him with a book of Hiroshige prints. He treasured it for decades.

When Paterson was around thirteen, he became bothered by the lack of any decent art in the house. He asked his mother if she would get him something for his room besides the old photo of Uncle Si winning the Stanley Cup with the Kenora Thistles. She came home with reproductions of Gainsborough's *Blue Boy*, Millet's *Gleaners*, and Greuze's *Boy with a Rabbit*.

"I came to art on my own," he says. "I had only periodic art classes in grade school—you know, how to make rainbows—and even my high-school classes never got much beyond caricature. None of my friends had any connection with art. Other than my grandfather, I had no role model as an artist. I liked drawing and trying to make something out of wood or plasticine, but I was always discouraged that my cows never looked like cows. I thought you needed a special gift from heaven to be an artist, and I didn't have it."

EIGHT

One afternoon, when Paterson was eleven, he and some friends came across an iron bar lying in a field. The other boys could hardly lift it, but Paterson found—to his astonishment—that he could hoist it easily above his head. He took up gymnastics and weightlifting; he proved a champion at both the 50-yard dash and the broad jump; and though he couldn't play hockey because of his poor eyesight, he became a football star at Montreal West High School.

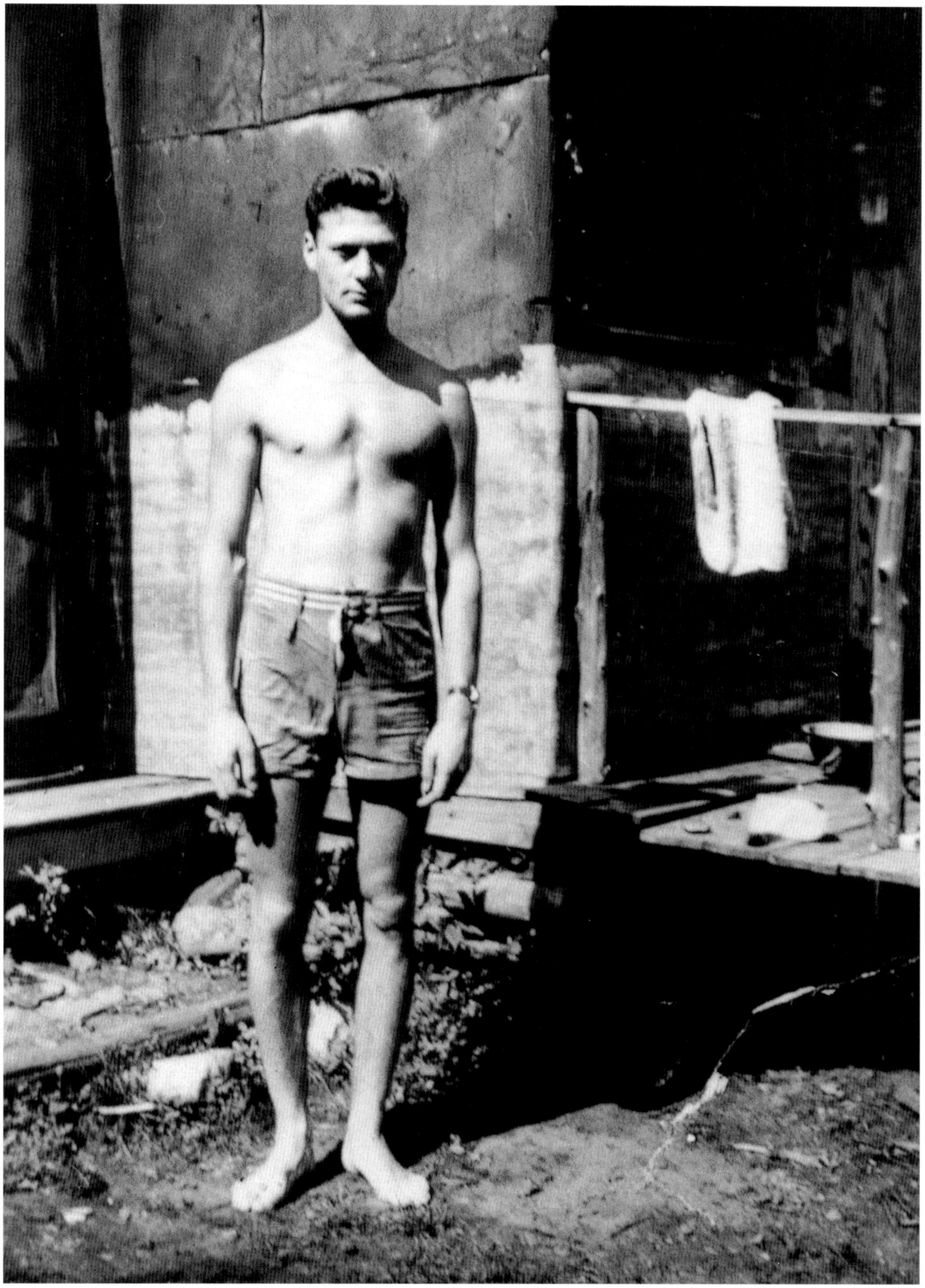

Paterson Ewen, c. 1943

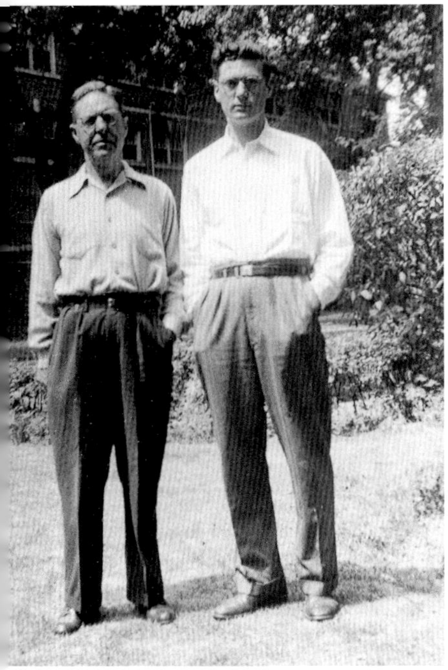

Paterson and Bill Ewen, c. 1946

Doing well at sports was more important to him than doing well in class. Usually he sat through the lessons doodling Spitfires in a kind of daydream, made worse by his not getting glasses to overcome his shortsightedness until he was fourteen. His only ambition upon graduating by the skin of his teeth in 1943 was to get into the war as quickly as possible. "The best thing would have been to get not too big a wound and come back a hero," was his attitude. "The next best thing would have been to get killed."

In fact, he didn't get overseas until December 1944. Placed with a reconnaissance regiment, the Princess Louise Dragoon Guard, he was given a dangerous job: to set off with a machine gun, a wireless set, and a driver in an armoured car in advance of the Allied troops to scout what soldiers, tanks, or landmines the Germans might have had "off the map" to the north of the Dutch front. But, except for almost killing several of his own men when his submachine gun went off accidentally one night, Paterson saw no action at all. For at dawn on May 8, 1945, as the regiment was nervously awaiting the code word "Rainbow" to signal the launch of a major assault on Amersfoort, the ceasefire was declared.

"The war was called off just before I probably would have been killed," he says. "I was almost disappointed."

NINE

Paterson found it hard to be back as an adult in the upper-storey, three-bedroom duplex he and his parents had occupied at 8025 Western Avenue since 1939, with his father again storming into his room in the middle of the night and shaking him awake to rant drunkenly, "I *made* the Canadian ranch mink business! Don't go to sleep, I'm telling you something!"

He enrolled for a B.A. at McGill University with a vague notion of becoming a geologist, though he also considered making a permanent career in the army as a way to avoid the "real" world. Just for fun, during a summer programme with the Canadian Officers Training Corps at Val-Cartier near Quebec City, he began teaching himself how to draw by copying the illustrated covers of adventure magazines. Then, feeling ready to attempt something more ambitious, he bought a professional pad and pencils and sat down to render a fairly complex scene involving the Citadel, a moat, the river, some factories, and a convent. While he was working on it, a woman approached from behind and asked, "Are you an artist?"

"No," he answered, without turning around. "This is my first drawing. I still have to learn."

"Nonsense," she said. "You *are* an artist. That's very well drawn. Just go, buy a box of paints, and paint." Then she vanished, sight unseen.

It took him three months to complete that first painting. Though it was a naive work in what he later dismissed as the style of Grandma Moses, it determined his vocation. "I decided to become an artist," he says. "I prepared myself for the worst—and it came."

TEN

When Paterson returned for his second year at McGill, he shifted into a drawing course given by John Lyman, the noted Montreal painter whose Post-Impressionist portraits and still lifes had been marked by his apprenticeship in France with Henri Matisse and James Wilson Morrice. But Paterson didn't think much of either Lyman or Lyman's work, and he felt deliberately ignored as the one male student among sixty-four young women. "Lyman was a nasty person," he says, "and I think he may have been jealous of me as the only other man in the room."

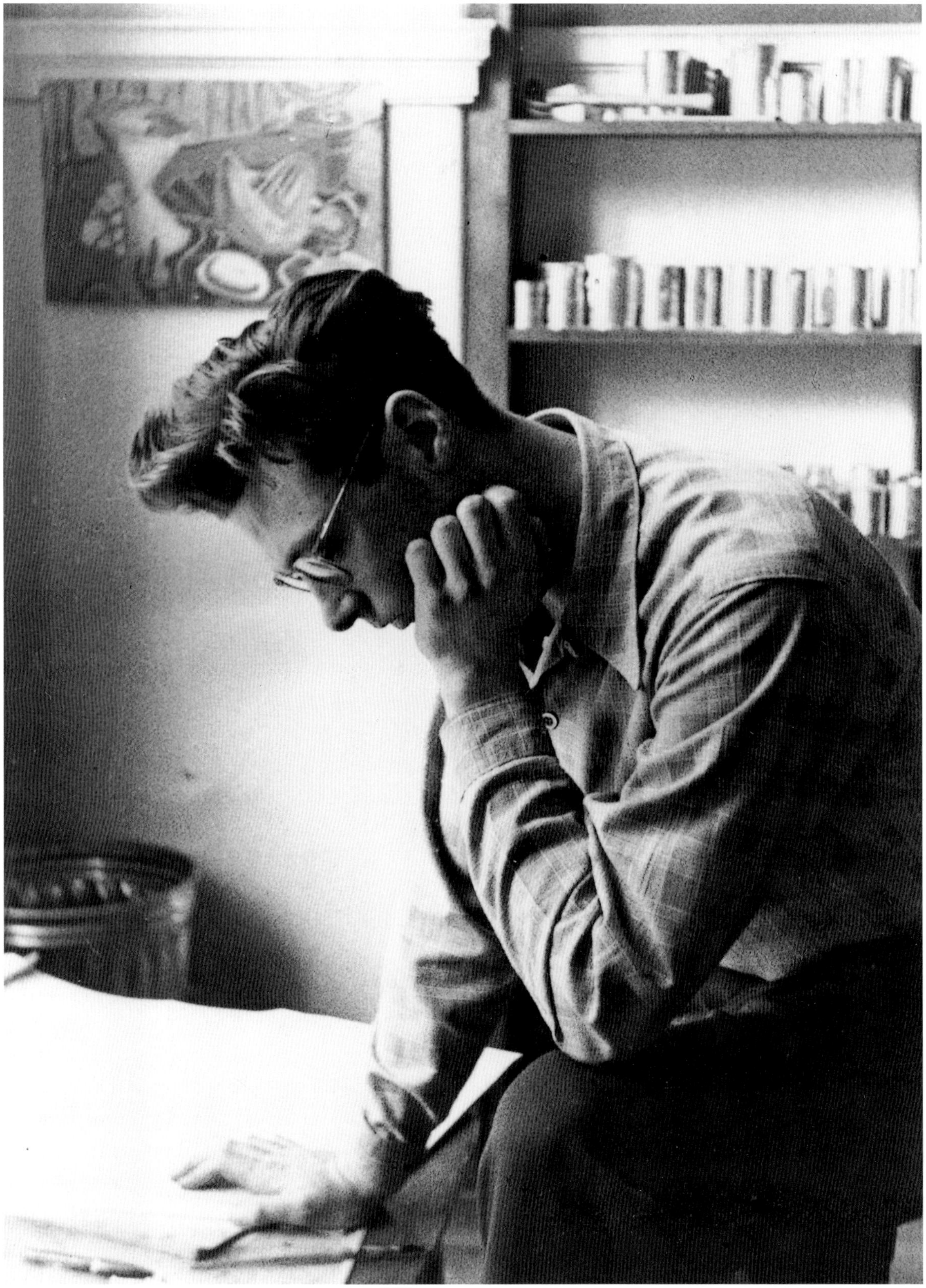

Paterson Ewen, 1948

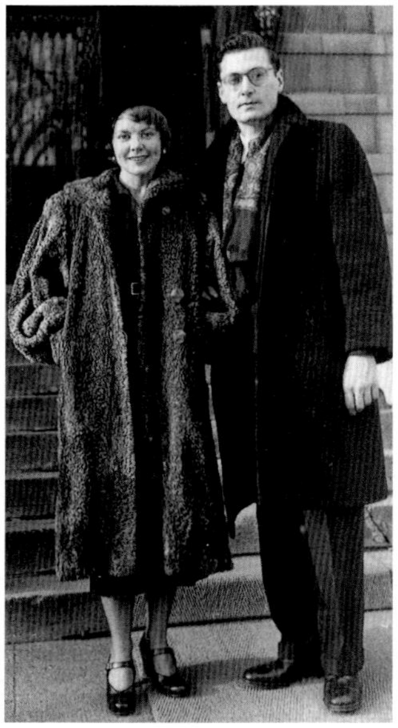

Paterson Ewen and Françoise Sullivan on their wedding day, December 1949

In February 1948, he took a wise dean's advice to transfer from McGill to the School of Art and Design at the Montreal Museum of Fine Arts. Under the direction of Arthur Lismer, the Group of Seven painter, it offered Paterson a feast of first-year courses in drawing, painting, sculpture, fresco, illustration, design, and printmaking within a congenial atmosphere of sympathetic teachers. He was especially impressed by Goodridge Roberts, the Canadian artist he most admired in those days, to the point of imitating the elegant intonation of his voice and his languid way of reaching for things.

Roberts, then in his mid-forties, came from a distinguished family of writers and poets. He was a tall, lean, good-looking man whose landscapes and standing figures were influenced by Matisse and Cézanne via Morrice. Despite his humour and charm as a raconteur and the romantic panache with which he strode along Sherbrooke Street in his long grey RCAF coat, he always seemed to carry a black cloud over his head and, indeed, was under psychiatric counselling for depression.

"My landscapes didn't look that much like Goodridge's," Paterson says, "but the *idea* of sitting out in a field, doing a painting, came from him." Like Roberts, too, Paterson found in painting both an emotional expression and therapeutic release for his psychological agitation.

ELEVEN

One evening in the spring of 1949, at the start of Paterson's second year at the museum school, he and his girlfriend attended a lecture given by Claude Gauvreau at a leftist cultural club. Gauvreau was a brilliant French-Canadian poet and thinker who had become one of the earliest and most ardent champions of the group of avant-garde Quebec artists known as the Automatistes. As resoundingly proclaimed in their 1948 manifesto, *Refus global*, whose main text was written by Paul-Émile Borduas and signed by such notable figures as Jean-Paul Riopelle, Fernand Leduc, Jean-Paul Mousseau, and Claude Gauvreau's brother Pierre, they were interested not only in freeing the subconscious through abstraction and Surrealism but also in freeing Quebec society from political and religious oppression.

Though Paterson was far from being either an artistic or social rebel, he was intrigued enough to attend the second lecture in the series. It was given by a beautiful, free-spirited artist and dancer named Françoise Sullivan, whom he had run into a couple of times with Brian Macdonald, a friend of his from McGill and a student of hers. The only daughter of John Sullivan, a French-speaking lawyer and former Conservative MP, she had taken dance lessons at the age of nine, then studied painting at Montreal's École des Beaux-Arts when she was only sixteen years old. She showed a precocious talent, placing at the top of her class with her childhood friend Pierre Gauvreau, even though they ran afoul of their instructors by falling under the influence of Paul-Émile Borduas. Then Françoise shifted her interest to dance. She studied in New York for a couple of seasons and returned to author an essay in *Refus global*, celebrating the primitive and instinctive in modern dance.

The essay formed the basis of her lecture, and while she talked about dance as "a spontaneous expression of intensely felt emotions," her gaze seemed fixed on Paterson. "Our relationship wasn't founded on a lot of affection so much as on a physical attraction," he remembers. "And we had the same ideas and aims, though we each had our own vocations."

Within weeks of their first date, Paterson joined Françoise when she went back to New York City to take a dance class from Martha Graham in the summer of 1949. And upon his return to Montreal, he was increasingly drawn into her world—the French-speaking world of Surrealist poets and Automatiste painters—though his French never became more than proficient. Françoise took him to visit Borduas at his home in Saint-Hilaire across the St. Lawrence River. "He was in his mid-forties then," Paterson recalls, "very short, bald, strongly built, with a bad set of false teeth—not at all like Roberts!"

Paterson did not instantly fall under the great man's sway. He didn't consider this Borduas's best period and thought it ironic that Borduas was still inspired by forms he found in rivers and landscapes for what were supposed to be "automatic" paintings. Borduas, on the other hand, was supportive and complimentary about the landscapes and still lifes that Paterson was doing under the strong influence of Roberts, Cézanne, and Bonnard. "I was enjoying the best of both worlds," Paterson says.

His unusual position became apparent in March 1950. Two of his early pieces were accepted for the Montreal Museum of Fine Arts' *67th Annual Spring Exhibiton*, which had raised the ire of the Automatistes by rejecting all but one work by Borduas. They counterattacked with an exhibition of their own, *L'Exposition des Rebelles*, and in order to show their own openmindedness, they included two of Paterson's landscapes. That—and a press report referring to Paterson, who was teaching some young people's classes and assisting Goodridge Roberts, as a *professeur*—got Arthur Lismer's goat.

"Halfway through my second term," Paterson says, "I met Lismer in the hall and he said I didn't have to stay around any longer—it was obvious I had decided to be a painter—and he handed me my diploma in high standing."

If Lismer had intended his action as a compliment, it hit Paterson like a disaster. He had just married Françoise in December 1949; she was pregnant; and now they would lose the monthly cheque for $120 he was getting as a war vet with a family as long as he remained in school. Now he would have to get a "real" job, fast.

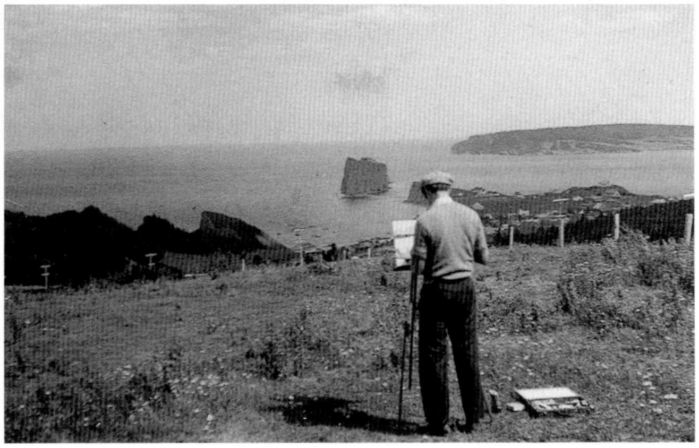

Paterson Ewen, c. 1950

TWELVE

Responding to an ad in the newspaper, Paterson was hired by the My Lady hat factory near St. Lawrence and St. Catherine. For $40 a week, regular hours, he put hats into boxes. He quit after a few months in order to sell rugs at Ogilvy's, a downtown department store. "I liked that," he says. "I had been a little depressed at the hat factory, but here I got $60 a week, plus commissions, and there wasn't any strain. It turned out I was a good salesman. I had a polite manner, I was helpful and honest, and people used to come back if they needed a carpet for another room."

At the same time, late into the night and on Sundays, he painted in a tiny room in the small apartment he and Françoise had rented on Fort Street, beside the Montreal Forum, while she rehearsed for her many television appearances dancing to the music of Ravel, Debussy, and Rameau. It was a tiring routine, but Paterson felt little emotional stress or personal frustration, not least because his work was being relatively well-received. In May 1950, he rented a storefront space at 1445 Crescent Street and mounted his first solo exhibition. A crowd of friends turned out for the opening; his father, no less, supplied the liquor for the party and bought a large still life for $90; and Paterson managed to sell most of the show and gain some good reviews in the *Herald* and *Le Devoir*.

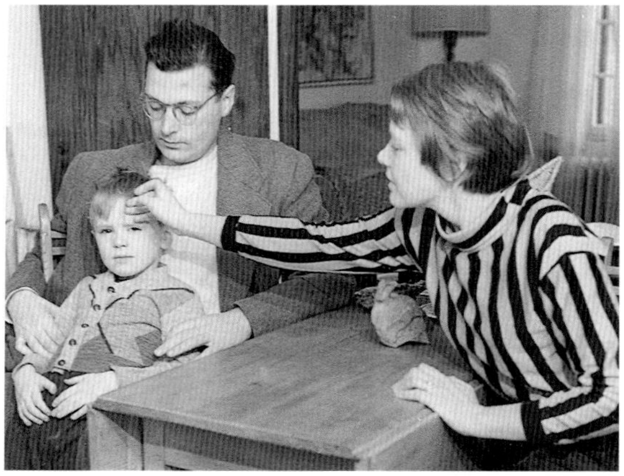

Paterson Ewen with Vincent and Françoise Sullivan, c. 1954

On June 15, in the wake of that success, Françoise gave birth to Vincent, named in honour of van Gogh, who was later discovered to be an exceptional child. Though he couldn't talk till the age of four or master many normal childhood activities, he wrote prodigious poetry between the ages of six and nine, and by the time he was fourteen could recite the Latin names of flowers and trees, compare the merits of Arnold Toynbee with those of other historians, and state how high Mondrian wanted his paintings to be from the floor.

The next year, Paterson's mother died of cancer at the age of sixty-five. Subsequently, until his own death in an Ottawa nursing home in 1960, Bill Ewen came to live with Paterson and Françoise, doing little but sipping a 40-ounce bottle of whisky a day—until his blood pressure, the cost, and a brief stay in a Chicago clinic made him quit cold turkey. "He became quite a sad figure," Paterson says. "Everything stopped after he retired and my mother died. He didn't go to the Masonic lodge any more, he didn't play golf any more, he didn't have close friends. When he stopped drinking, he became almost silent. I now realize he must have been very depressed."

THIRTEEN

In the hope of salvaging more time for his art, Paterson allowed himself to be lured away from Ogilvy's by an offer to become caretaker of a compound of cottages in the Laurentians near Saint-Adèle. "I was getting a pittance to do things I wasn't good at and didn't enjoy," he remembers. He, Françoise, and Vincent didn't last the winter. When they got back to the city, they moved into an apartment at 5590 Victoria Avenue along with his father, and Paterson went off to a training course on how to sell insurance. But the very prospect of peddling to strangers and friends sent him to bed with the shakes for a couple of weeks.

His father-in-law, meanwhile, was feeling the pinch of his small federal pension and had phoned his old friend Maurice Duplessis, the premier and patronage boss of Quebec, to plead for a government job. "Why don't you get Pat one while you're at it?" one of his sons suggested, with a bit of an edge. And so Paterson Ewen was appointed assistant secretary to the chief administrator—that is, John Sullivan—of the rent control board for Verdun and Montreal West at $3,000 a year. Except for a few busy days of hearings in the moving month of May, he had little to do but hand out information and improve his spoken French. In fact, he took a couple of night jobs, too, sorting mail at the post office from seven to nine, and clerking at a motel.

"At all my jobs," he says, "I used to feel like an eight-cylinder car working on four cylinders. They were so easy compared to painting."

Feeling he had reached the limits of landscapes and still lifes, he became increasingly interested in the nonfigurative elements of composition and colour and started to crave the freedom of abstraction. "I didn't give up my figurative work because it wasn't selling," he says, "but it did have a lot to do with the fact that everybody around me was doing abstract work."

Near the end of 1954, he did his first abstract, using landscape colours but placing the forms more or less arbitrarily. A year later, five of Paterson's new abstracts were included in an important show of contemporary work, *Espace 55*, organized by Claude Gauvreau at the Montreal Museum of Fine Arts. "But I could never be an Automatiste or an abstract expressionist," he says, "because it wasn't in my temperament to do anything quite that unstructured." Nor was he yet attracted to doing hard-edge geometric pieces like Guido Molinari and the other Plasticien painters who wanted to replace the unconscious spontaneity of the Automatistes with "perfect forms in a perfect order."

By the mid-fifties, most of the Automatistes had scattered abroad or hit some sort of personal and artistic crisis. Molinari's group came, as Paterson puts it, to "rule the roost." In June 1955 Molinari opened the most important venue for contemporary art in Montreal, Galerie L'Actuelle, where Paterson exhibited each year until it closed in 1957. And, in February 1956, Molinari was a key figure in launching the Non-Figurative Artists' Association of Montreal, of which Paterson was a founding member. "The truth is," he says, "I always wanted to succeed, both in doing the best work and in a worldly way. I sometimes imagined myself as a great undiscovered artist, but I took every chance to be discovered."

In 1955, for example, Paterson loaded seven of his paintings into his secondhand Vanguard, drove to New York City, checked into the YMCA, and pounded the pavement to get himself a New York dealer. Eventually, he stumbled upon Harold Rubin and Robert Keyser at the Parma Gallery. They gave him two one-man shows, as well as a group show with Molinari, Leduc, and other Montreal artists, but one day he showed up to find the gallery gone—and twelve of his paintings with it.

FOURTEEN

Following the birth of their second child, Geoffrey, and a move to a duplex at 5421 Monkland Avenue in Notre-Dame-de-Grâce, Paterson decided to seek a job with better pay and regular hours for the sake of his family and his art. With his working knowledge of French, he had little trouble landing a position as employment supervisor at Bathurst Containers' box factory in East End Montreal, a neglected and negligent plant with an appalling rate of lost-time

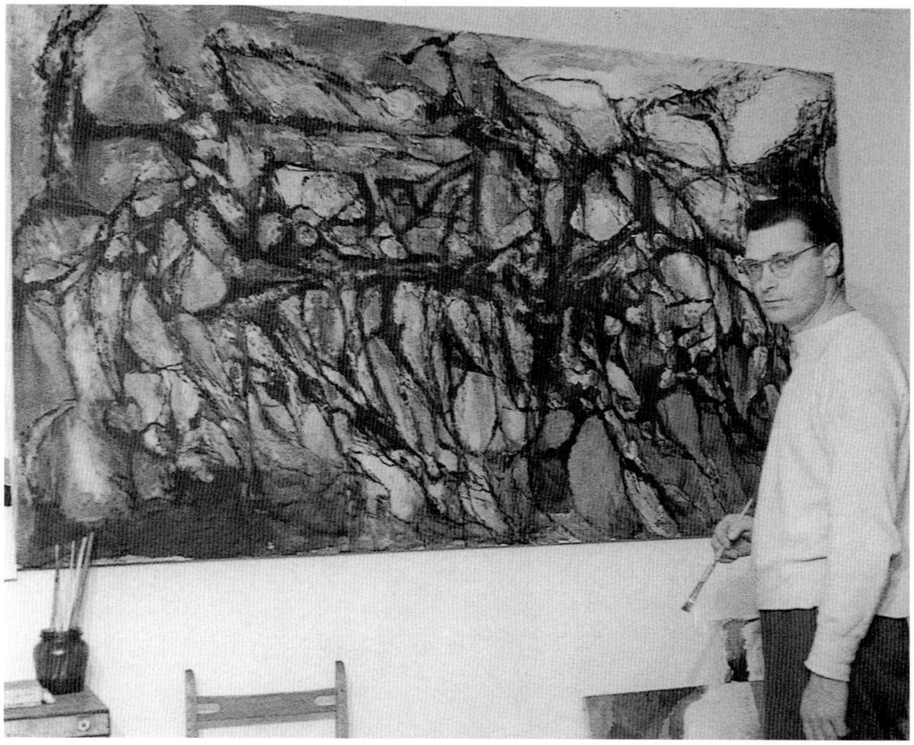

Paterson Ewen, c. 1956

accidents, including an amputated finger, an amputated thumb, and a fractured skull. "The management couldn't care less," Paterson recalls.

So, in addition to his day-to-day responsibilities for the hundred or so hourly employees, he started a one-man campaign to protect their health and welfare. He read a host of safety manuals; he arranged for regular inspections by the provincial authorities and a full-time nurse; he convinced his superiors that they could increase profits and productivity by reducing the compensation costs and lost time; and he designed a chart with a rocket that soared toward Saturn and Jupiter (and a $50 draw) with every accident-free week.

Though he continued to paint steadily, won an important Quebec prize in 1957, and showed at the Galerie Denyse Delrue every year but one from 1958 to 1963—as well as in New York, Toronto, and the Non-Figurative Artists' Association exhibitions—he still had not found a form that satisfied his ambition, as he put it at the time, "to create a

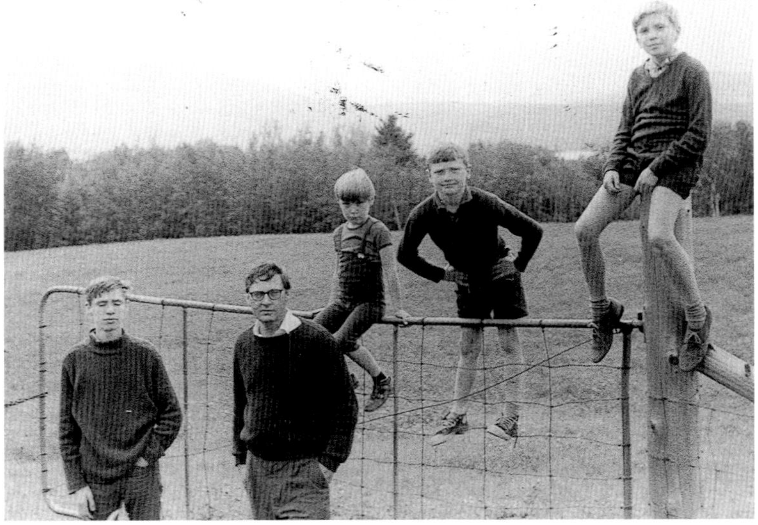

Paterson Ewen with his sons, c. 1963

painting as original—as personal—as possible."

"Brilliantly demoniac," the *Montreal Gazette*'s critic raved about his work in 1961, "a younger Canadian painter to be reckoned with." But Paterson was nearly thirty-five years old, he had been painting for almost fifteen years, and the review had spelled his name incorrectly.

FIFTEEN

After several years of accomplishment at Bathurst's East End plant, Paterson was promoted to training co-ordinator for all the company's factories, based downtown in the Sun Life Building. Gone were the three hours of reading time he had enjoyed riding back and forth on the bus each day from 2349 Grand Avenue, where he and Françoise had moved to accommodate two more sons, Jean-Christophe and Francis. Gone were the regular hours and working-class camaraderie. Instead, he found himself sent away on business trips and lost among all the suits in head office—with less time for his painting.

In 1965, told he would have to wait for an overdue raise, he walked out of Bathurst and into two jobs he found in the same building, first as junior partner in a small executive placements firm, then as personnel manager at Associated Textiles. The pay was better, but he found he had absolutely nothing to do. So he jumped again to become training manager for Miracle Mart, the Steinbergs' new supermarket chain, where he was actually told not to interfere with the training of the stores' employees. Worse, his immediate boss expected Paterson to go drinking with him every day. "I couldn't stand it," he says. "It was such a mess, I just wanted out."

Nor was that the only mess he wanted out of.

Age and the children had taken their toll on Françoise's dancing career. Though she would later revisit the field as a choreographer and teacher, she took a welding course and transferred her formidable energy and talent to sculpture. By 1963, working out of the unheated garage at the back of the house she and Paterson had bought at 4127 Wilson Avenue, she exhibited in a joint show with Jack Bush at the Montreal Museum of Fine Arts and won an important provincial prize. "We weren't supposed to be competing," Paterson says, "but I guess we really were." And, considering how much of his own art he had had to sacrifice to allow Françoise to pursue hers, he couldn't help but feel some resentment that her reputation was greater than his.

Soon after their move to Wilson Avenue, he discovered that she had been having a love affair with one of their good friends. His immediate reaction was to drink more and seek out an affair of his own. "It was a crazy world for a while," he says, "and there came a point where I didn't like it. I decided rather belatedly that I had loved Françoise."

Late in 1965, Paterson asked her to stop seeing her lover—or else he would leave. "Maybe I wanted out myself," he says, "but I thought she would go along with it because of the four children and because I had always worked as the breadwinner while she was free to do whatever she wanted. But she said she couldn't give him up. So I walked out the front door."

Facing page: Paterson Ewen, 1962

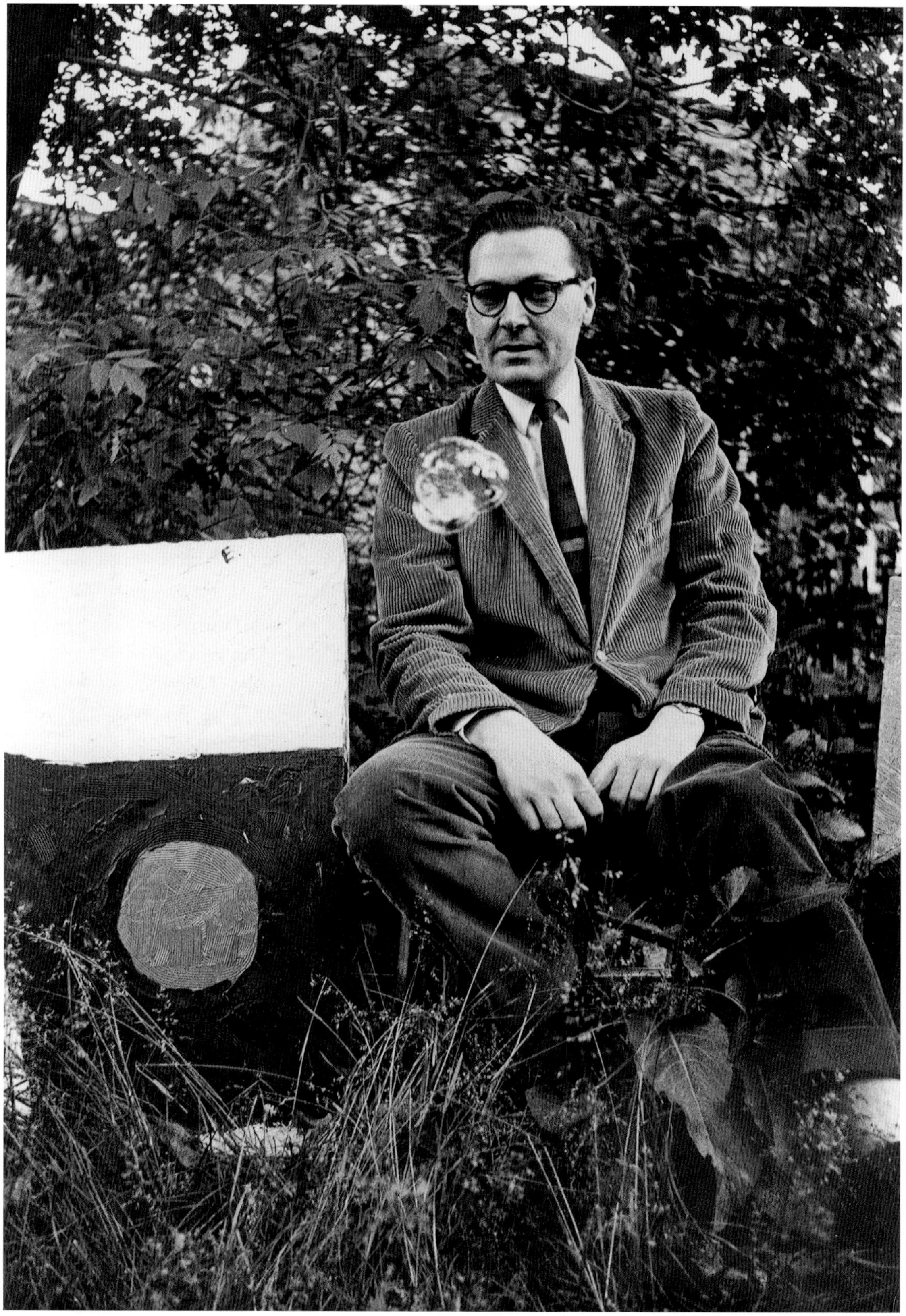

Facing page:
Paterson Ewen with a student's work, 1970

SIXTEEN

Between jobs and his marriage over, Paterson was unhappy and drinking too much. He painted in a studio he shared on Rue Saint-Christophe with Guido Molinari and Claude Tousignant, then moved into Molinari's studio on Visitation Street, an old boxing arena that previously had been used as a secret training centre for militant separatists. Paterson set up a cot in the shower stalls and painted near the ring. "That's when I got to know Molinari well," he says, "not just socially. I still wasn't influenced by his hard-edged geometry, but he did teach me how to achieve a perfectly straight line, which I later put to use in my minimal pieces."

In late 1966, Paterson rented a small house in the working-class district of Saint-Henri and took yet another personnel job. RCA Victor was at the start of a major recruiting drive for its new space programme, and it sent him across Canada to interview engineering graduates. But he soon got caught up in the party atmosphere of Expo 67 and the hippie phenomenon sweeping North America during that Summer of Love. He tried marijuana and had two LSD trips—one absolutely terrifying, one visually interesting, but neither particularly cosmic nor spiritual.

His bohemian life quickly caught up with his corporate life when he made a number of significant errors in listing RCA's salary offers to its job applicants. As soon as that was discovered, his manager showed up at Paterson's house and fired him. "I couldn't have cared less," he says. "And I got lucky, which seems to be a habit of mine. Just at that time Ben and Yael Dunkelman walked in, bought five large paintings, and set a date for a show at their gallery in Toronto."

The Dunkelmans gave him two shows—a group exhibition in September 1967 and a solo exhibition the following March—but losing his wife, his job, and his home made Paterson confused, agitated, and depressed. Following his spring show at the Dunkelman Gallery, he returned to Montreal in a somewhat hysterical state and entered the Queen Mary Veterans Hospital for treatment, including insulin injections that put him in a kind of semicoma for several hours. "It worked," he says. "I became calm, except for a few panic attacks. But the treatment has since been abandoned as too dangerous: apparently some patients went into the coma and never came out."

Upon his release, directionless and destitute, he was invited to live for a while with his sister Marjorie and her husband in a well-to-do neighbourhood of Kitchener, Ontario. They bought him paints and an easel and improvised a studio for him in the basement. Within a few weeks, however, feeling alone and trapped in an alien suburb, he started to descend into depression and eventually stopped talking altogether. Marjorie, herself a victim of depression, sent him to her psychiatrist—who urged him to admit himself at once, as a war vet, to the Westminster Veterans Hospital in London, Ontario.

There, in the late summer of 1968, Paterson submitted to electroconvulsive therapy, the most popular and effective treatment for depression at the time. Shock therapy doesn't always work quickly; sometimes it doesn't work at all; but in Paterson's case the results were immediate and profound. When he phoned Marjorie after the first session, she was amazed to hear his normal voice again. When he seemed well enough to leave, he even thought about returning to his family in Montreal.

"Oh, no, you're not," his doctor said. He was so sure, in fact, that Paterson would have another breakdown if he went back that he immediately wrote Françoise a letter informing her of his medical decision. "As it turned out, I needn't have worried," Paterson reflects. "Once I got out of her way, she did very well. We both did better, in fact."

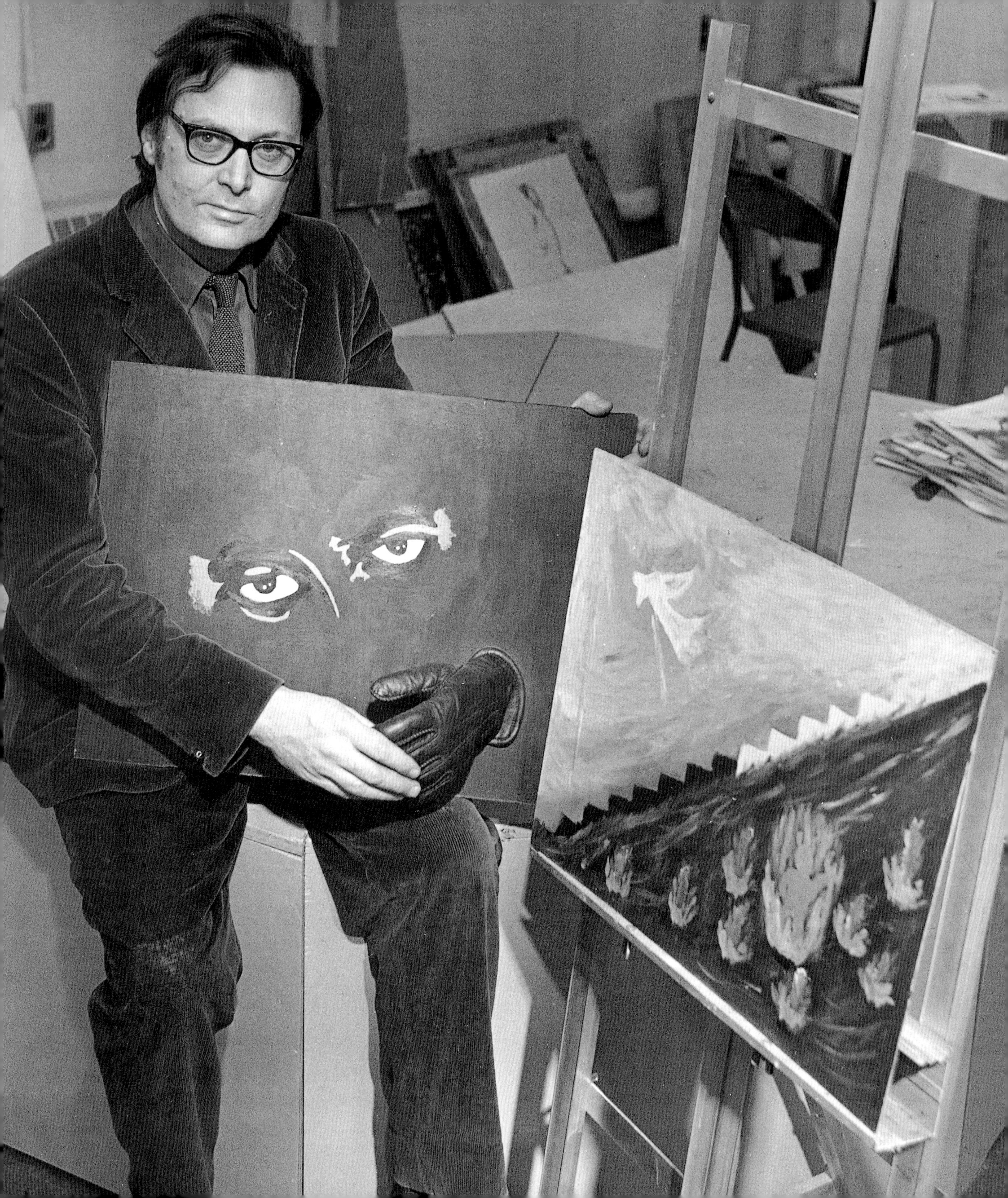

Paterson Ewen, 1971

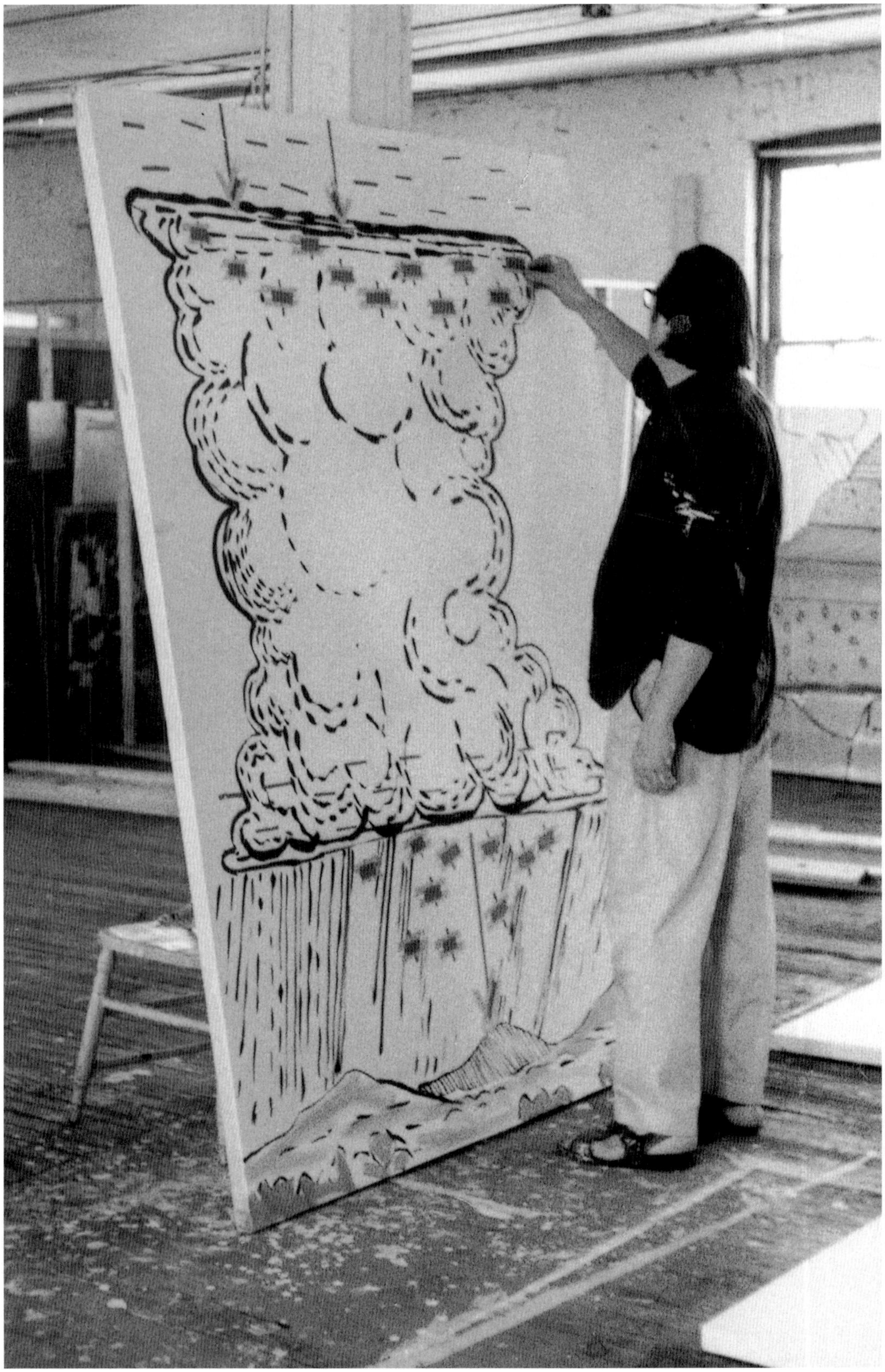

SEVENTEEN

Paterson Ewen was discharged from Westminster Veterans Hospital near the end of 1968 with no family, no home, and no job. Far from being concerned, he felt confident: he was finally free to be a full-time artist. Indeed, when the employment office sent him a notice four months later to report to the Jolly Green Giant factory, he just threw it away. And since chance had brought him to London, London was where he stayed.

After a few weeks at the York Hotel, a seedy place whose beer room was the favourite hangout for London artists, he rented a rat-infested studio at 521 Richmond Street. By day he painted, continuing the hard-edge minimal work he had begun in Montreal, but giving it a more energetic expression. Instead of applying methodical bands of colour to a solid background colour, for instance, he would charge across the studio as though across a football field, with a length of masking tape outstretched in his hands, leap up and zip it across the canvas in a wild gesture, then paint a line of colour along whatever course the tape had made.

By night he got to know the scene. Through Marjorie, he had met Doreen Curry, a kindhearted librarian of his own vintage who had taken him on a leave from the hospital to see the *Heart of London* exhibition at the London Public Library and Art Museum. It was a showcase for the exciting group of local artists that included Greg Curnoe, Jack Chambers, Ron Martin, Murray Favro, Tony Urquhart, and David and Royden Rabinowitch. Curnoe, the undisputed leader of the pack, knowing of Paterson's reputation in Montreal, had already visited him at Westminster, and he introduced Paterson to the rest of the group at the York, where they all gathered to drink and hear Curnoe play with his bebop Nihilist Spasm Band on Tuesday nights.

"London had a lot of good artists and patrons," Paterson says, "and I gained a lot of confidence that first year because I was able to make a living, painting for the local market." Indeed, in September 1969, he had a three-man show with the Rabinowitches' minimalist sculptures at the London Public Library and Art Museum. That was followed in January 1970 by a one-man retrospective at the 20/20 Gallery. By contrast, he had always resented that he was the only significant artist from his Montreal set not to have been given a solo exhibition at the Musée d'art contemporain.

"I hear you're now one of Greg's boys," an old friend said. But, even though Paterson was *on* the London scene, he never became *of* it. "Greg and I never really felt like rivals," he says. He hadn't arrived in time to be considered for the *Heart of London* show; his background excluded him from identifying with Curnoe's fervent anti-American and regionalist politics; he was a generation older than most of the crowd; and, thanks to the efforts of the artist David Bolduc, he began showing at the Carmen Lamanna Gallery in Toronto in October 1969.

Despite the purchases of loyal friends, Paterson had to scrape by on very little money until he got a job teaching art at H. B. Beal Secondary School. Soon after starting there in the fall of 1969, he bade farewell to the rats of Richmond Street and moved into a cleaner studio in an old cigar factory at 19 King Street, where a number of younger artists such as Dave Gordon and Jamelie Hassan lived and worked. Paterson, meanwhile, was growing bored with the restrictions of minimal abstraction, indeed of the whole art business. He was even in the throes of threatening to sue Carmen Lamanna for dropping him from a European show of Canadian artists.

"I was in my 'Fuck You' period where I didn't care if anyone bought or even showed what I was doing," he says. "I was only going to do things because I felt like doing them."

EIGHTEEN

One day on a visit to Toronto, where Paterson and several other London painters were trying to arrange their *Pie in the Sky* exhibition in an empty space loaned by a Cadillac dealer on Avenue Road, he happened to wander into an old-fashioned fabric store and came out with a piece of felt for 35 cents. He had it cut into various shapes, then used them instead of a brush to paint a broken line of black dots across an off-white canvas. Stepping back, he saw that this "anti-art" gesture evoked the path of something moving through space. "I was surprised, it seemed so far out," he remembers. "It was clear I was on to something."

Traces through Space, as he called it, inspired Paterson to concentrate on natural and astronomical phenomena in his art. Sometimes he simply had to look out his window: London is noted for the frequency and violence of its electrical storms. Once he became so intrigued watching the approach of a tornado that he almost neglected to rush into the house. More often, he took his images from diagrams and explanations about hailstorms, solar prominences, northern lights, rainfall, icebergs, and galaxies that he found in out-of-date textbooks, encyclopedias, and navigation manuals. "I deliberately used old texts," he says, "so that no scientist could fuss that this isn't the way things really work."

After doing a small number of related paintings, he decided he was actually tired of canvas itself. He turned to sheets of galvanized iron, to which he attached lengths of chain, pieces of plywood and linoleum, and hundreds of nuts and bolts to depict the feel of thunder, rocks moving in a stream, or a scientific account of lightning. Then he had the bizarre idea of producing a series of gigantic woodblock prints by digging deep cuts with a hand gouge into four-by-eight, good one side, ¾-inch plywood.

"But then as I was doing this and as I was painting in the gouges and as I was rolling it over with a printer's roller," he told an interviewer in 1975, "I realized that that *was* the work."

In June 1971 he received a senior Canada Council grant of $7,500. Though it meant a cut in his salary, he took a leave of absence from his teaching job at Beal in order to spend a year working and making contacts in Toronto, where he found a basement studio on Front Street next door to the old St. Lawrence Market. Paterson himself is not sure whether he had already begun the plywood pieces by then or made that breakthrough here.

Paterson knew only a handful of people in the city. One of them, Don Norman, a young artist with a long double-pointed beard who liked to bicycle around town wearing a vest he had made completely out of zippers and a thick plastic rod through his ear, offered to lend him an electric router in place of the hand gouge. The small machine, which Paterson soon bought from Norman for $50, had the impact of a creative revelation.

What would have taken a month with the hand gouge now took a week, with a lot more freedom of movement, and Paterson was able to choose the width and depth of the cuts by changing the router's bit. "And I enjoyed the physicality of it," he says, "particularly after the meticulousness of hard-edge painting. It was like a kind of therapy. I may not have felt the tension and anger pouring out of me when I did it, but I felt awfully good afterwards."

But when he first showed the plywood pieces at Carmen Lamanna's in January 1972, they were more a critical than a commercial success. "Paterson got great satisfaction personally," Lamanna recalled years later. "I got a lot of satisfaction. But selling? We couldn't sell a thing."

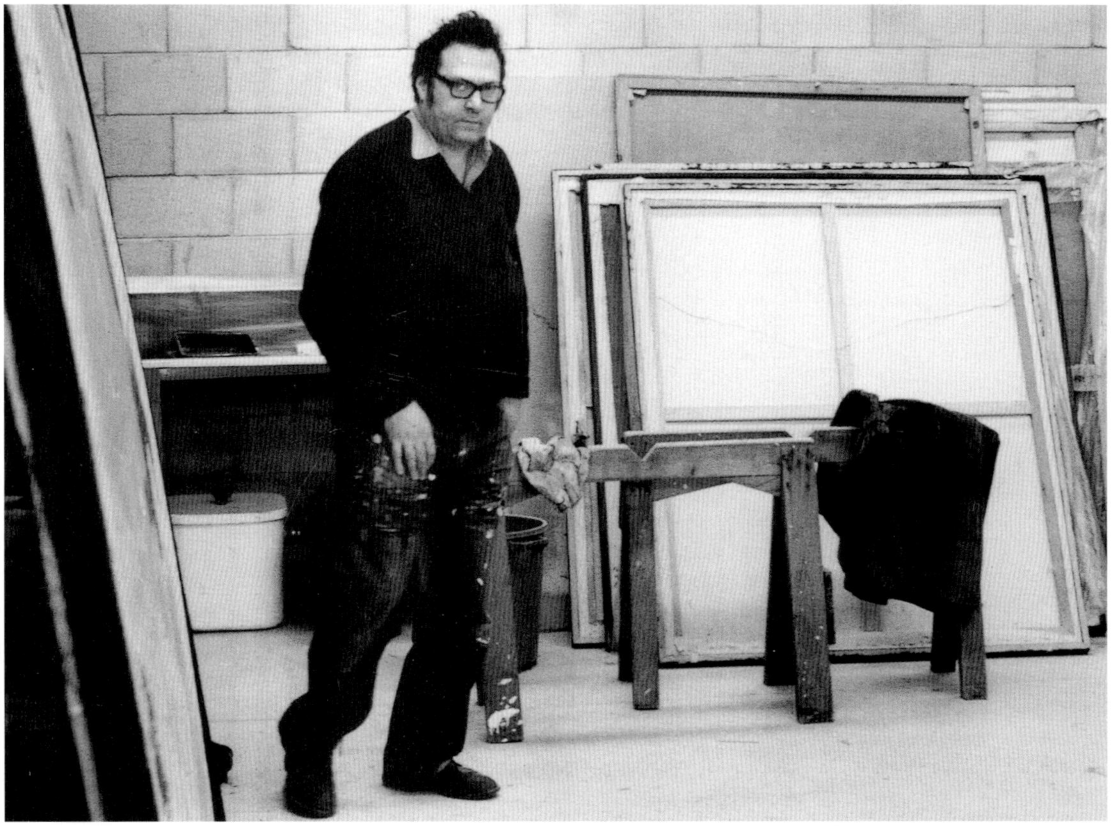

Paterson Ewen, 1980

NINETEEN

In the spring of 1972, as Paterson was preparing to return to London, he heard that his teaching job at Beal had been given away. He sent out fifteen applications to various other institutions around the country and received fifteen polite rejections—until luck again came to his rescue. The University of Western Ontario needed a painting teacher and they found Paterson's letter on file. So he returned to London, first as a lecturer, eventually becoming an associate professor with tenure, a studio of his own, and all the time he needed for his painting.

Those were relatively happy and prosperous years. Alcohol, Valium, and lithium suppressed his black depression and chronic anxiety. He enjoyed teaching and was generally considered a good teacher by his students and colleagues. He became an inspiration and support to a host of up-and-coming London artists, including Ron Benner, Bryan Maycock, Ron Martin, and Lynn Donoghue, generously swapping his work for theirs. And, from 1973 on, his regular shows at the Carmen Lamanna Gallery were financial as well as critical successes.

"Sometime in 1973," he remembers, "shortly after a visit that Pierre Théberge had made to London to visit artists' studios, I called the National Gallery, furious that he hadn't come to see me. I don't remember whether I got through to him. Probably not. Shortly afterwards, Pierre did come, this time with Brydon Smith, and they purchased three paintings through Carmen Lamanna, my first big sale to a major institution."

TWENTY

Although Paterson does not remember it, Mary Handford was once in his University of Western

Paterson Ewen, 1987

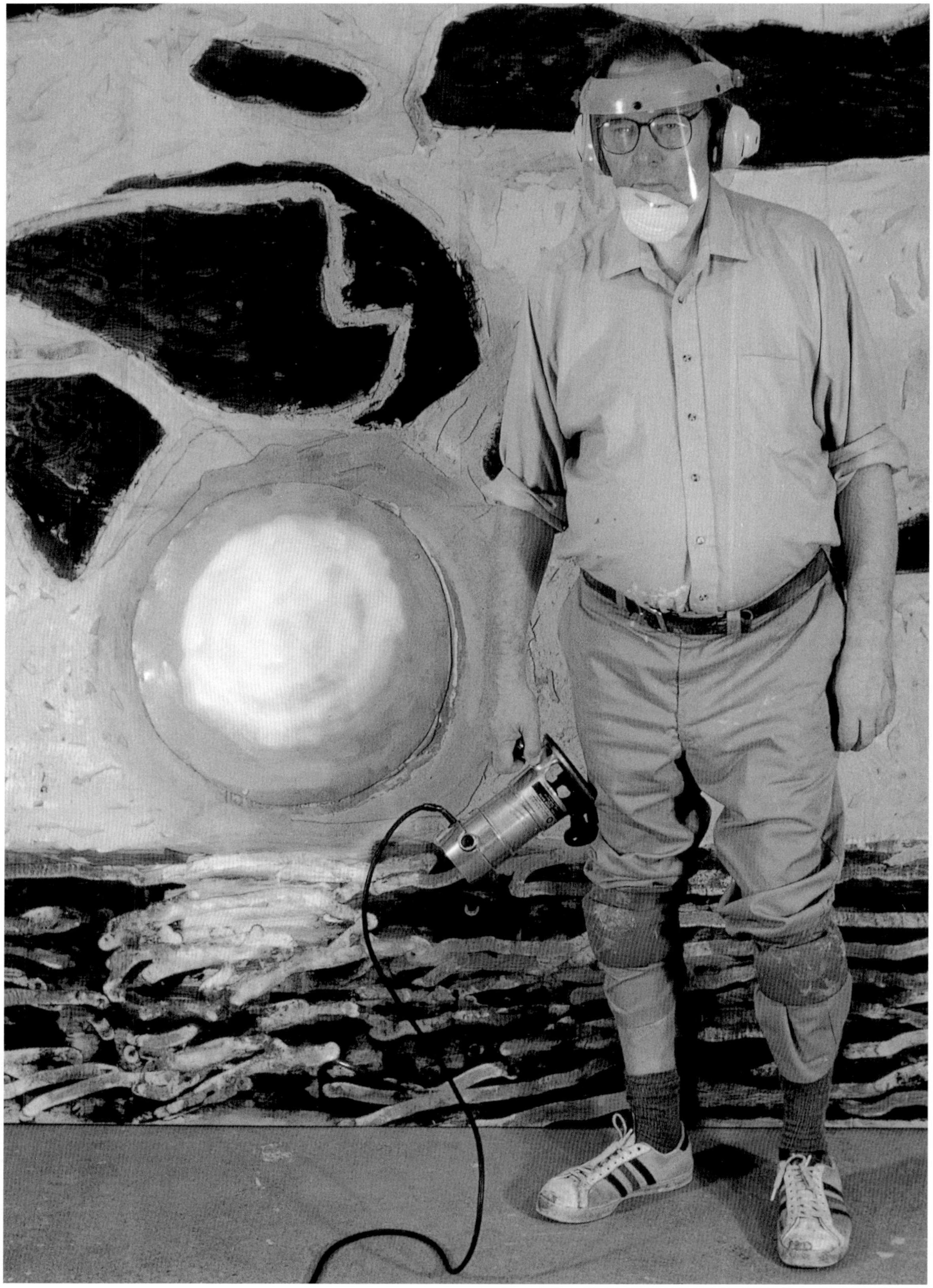

Ontario painting class, where he gave her the only B in her string of straight As. But the bright and attractive student from Owen Sound quickly established a strong place in his life. In the spring of 1979, he invited her to a party at the Victorian brick home he had bought on Maitland Street, and he visited her that summer in Owen Sound. In July 1980, after she won the gold medal upon graduation, they flew to Paris and travelled south to Barcelona. On their return, Mary took up residence with him on Maitland.

In 1982, however, the year Paterson was chosen as Canada's representative at the Venice Biennale, Mary began studying for a degree in architecture at the University of Waterloo, travelling back to London only for weekends. As she grew busier and he grew lonelier, tensions mounted between them; and though he was never a nasty drunk, she was also becoming fed up with his alcoholic rants.

Finally, in July 1986, when it looked as though Mary had left him forever, Paterson sold the house and moved into a large industrial space he had found on Dundas Street East. Almost all of it was for his work, except for a twelve-by-twelve cubicle for his bed, a kitchen area, and a cosy living room with burlap curtains, assorted furniture from Maitland Street, a few works by his friends, a small bookcase crammed with illustrated guides to solar physics and the weather, an old radio, and his rock collection. He had more than $500,000 cash sitting in his bank account at the time.

TWENTY-ONE

Alone, he began drinking even more heavily, until one day he blacked out on the street. In late December 1986, on his doctor's advice, he was admitted to Homewood, an alcohol treatment clinic in Guelph. He felt better at first, as though relieved of an unbearable burden, but he had not only been pulled off drink: they took him off the Valium and lithium to which he was heavily addicted. Within days, he started slipping down into severe withdrawal symptoms, including acute depression and, for the first time, paranoid delusion. He imagined that water had flooded the room up to the height of his bed, for example, or that he was carrying a highly infectious disease capable of killing whoever touched him. Then, in the midst of that, he suffered an umbilical hernia and had to be rushed for an emergency operation at the Guelph Hospital. While recovering, he became almost suicidal at the sight of the sick and dying patients in the hallways.

"I got the notion there was a crowd gathering outside the hospital to torture me to death, it was so frightening," he remembers. "I heard someone cry, 'The nun is dead!' and I thought I was next. I saw a city bus and I thought it was full of people being brought in to make a circus of my torture. These terrors seemed so real. That went on for a few days, then stopped."

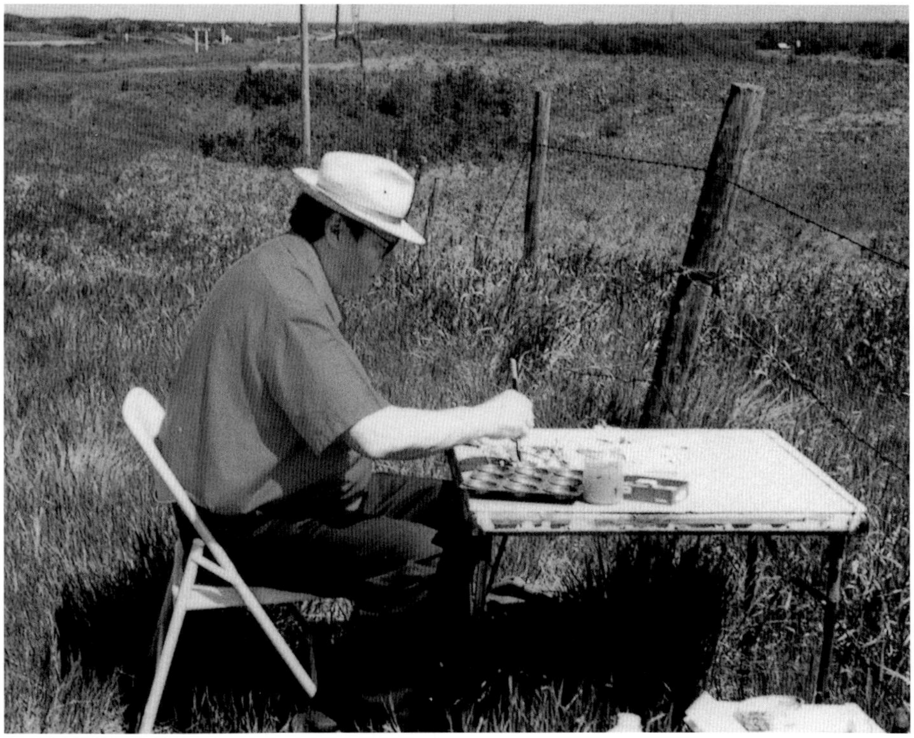

Paterson Ewen, 1987

By June, he seemed well enough to be discharged. He didn't even need to finish the treatment at Homewood: the mere sight of three men who had been there with him, drunk once more on the street, scared him into giving up alcohol altogether. In the meantime, by mutual agreement, the university had arranged for him to take early retirement. So Paterson went to live and work somewhat reclusively in his studio, with weekend visits by his son Geoffrey, who was doing graduate work at Glendon College in Toronto, to do his laundry and make sure he ate a proper meal. Geoffrey was amazed by the energy and creativity with which his father transformed the big boards into wonderful paintings from one visit to the next.

"It's mostly being alone I don't like," Paterson told a *Canadian Art* writer at the time. "I don't know what's happened. I just hope I can get into the next period from here. When you're turning large, major pieces, it's heaven. But in between, it's kind of grim."

He was out only until September before another setback sent him into St. Joseph's Hospital for the remainder of 1987. While he was there, reduced to painting a portrait of Santa Claus as a Christmas decoration for the ward, his reputation was on the verge of soaring higher than ever before. In November, the Mendel Art Gallery in Saskatoon opened *Paterson Ewen: The Montreal Years*, a comprehensive survey of his figurative and abstract paintings that subsequently travelled to London, Windsor, Montreal, and Halifax. The Art Gallery of Ontario followed in January 1988 with *Phenomena*, a selection of forty-one works done after 1971, which also travelled to London, Vancouver, Halifax, Ottawa, and Calgary.

What should have been his moment of triumph felt more like a trial. In the wake of the AGO opening, partly as a consequence of becoming confused and agitated by all the attention, Paterson had to enter St. Joseph's again in March for further shock treatments. He stayed there, under the care of Dr. Ashok Malla, until the summer.

TWENTY-TWO

Shortly after he got back to his studio in June 1988, Mary Handford phoned to say hello, and Paterson invited her to visit. They had been in touch occasionally, but Geoffrey had warned her away, and Mary herself had been preoccupied with her architectural courses and professional training in Waterloo, Toronto, and Rome. Now they started seeing each other regularly, travelling between London and Barrie during the fall of 1988 and spending Thanksgiving weekend together at her family's cottage at Tobermory. They grabbed a few visits together during the first half of 1989 while she raced to finish her thesis and get her degree in Waterloo. That done, she returned to London in August, and two months later she and Paterson bought a handsome house near the university at the north end of Wellington Street.

Paterson was still rather fragile. He had set out for two weeks in July as artist-in-residence at Emma Lake, Saskatchewan, but had left after a week because of the heat, the mosquitoes, and an attack of claustrophobia. Still, he and Mary began to enjoy another stable period. Most days he went down to the "salt mines" in East London to transmute more plywood into paintings. They travelled to Europe in the spring of 1990 to see the two huge exhibitions of van Gogh's paintings and drawings in Holland and visit the Turners and Constables in England. Back home, they bought two black American cocker spaniels, Basil and Java, to complete the scene of domesticity.

Their peace was shattered in January 1992, when Paterson was rushed into emergency at St. Joseph's with a severe pain in his lower abdomen. It turned out to be a twisted bowel. To repair it, the doctors had to cut him open, and while they were about it, they removed his gall bladder and appendix. The operation itself went without a hitch, but as a consequence of being taken off his regular medications, Paterson's mind again started to sink. In March he was transferred to the psychiatric ward at Victoria Hospital, where his condition continued to deteriorate.

None of the old combinations of drugs took hold any more, nor did the series of shock treatments that Paterson very reluctantly accepted as a last resort. He stopped eating and his weight fell to 160 pounds; his speech became incoherent monosyllables; he couldn't sleep even after an experiment in sleep deprivation. There were worries he might have suffered brain damage and there was talk of shipping him to Parkwood, a long-term care hospital for geriatric and chronic cases. Instead, thanks to Mary's persistence, Paterson was returned to the care of Dr. Malla, by then Victoria Hospital's Chief of Psychiatry. Malla referred him to the London Psychiatric Hospital for further tests and a second opinion. Before that could happen, however, Paterson had to pass a truly dreadful interlude at home from mid-August to mid-October. His anxiety was heightened by his certainty that he would never be able to paint again.

"I wasn't psychotic," he says, "but I was still extremely agitated. I had to sleep on the couch, and I could hardly sit down for about three months. All day, every day that autumn, I just walked around and around the block, but only clockwise, and when the cold weather came, I paced around and around inside the garage. It was really strange."

Eventually Dr. Malla was able to hit upon the right combination of the tranquillizer Clonazepam and the antidepressant Desipramine. Paterson began to feel normal within a week.

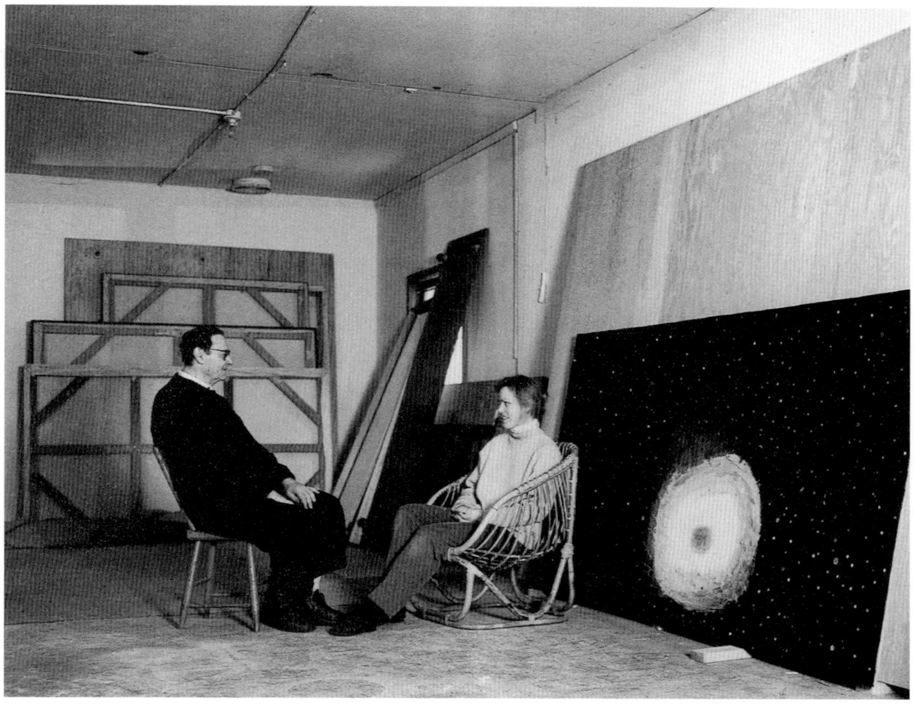

Paterson Ewen and Mary Handford in the studio, 1992

"Though Mary didn't exactly save my life, she did save me from Parkwood," he says. "I used to be known as a streetfighter, but I'm not like that any more—and not only because I'd lose. I'm more thoughtful, I think things over, and I've learned to rely on others, especially on Mary. I don't know what would have happened to me without her."

In August 1995, at the age of seventy, he married Mary Handford in a quiet ceremony at a nearby United Church. Paterson hadn't been in a church for years, and the sight of a Mason's ring on the minister's finger—just like the one his father had worn—reminded him why.

TWENTY-THREE

Paterson is no longer a strong ox. He moves heavily and carefully. Sometimes, when Mary can't drive him, the bus trip from the house to Dundas Street East leaves him too tired to work. He is regularly beset by arthritis in his hands and bursitis in his arms. Most days he needs to nap before dinner,

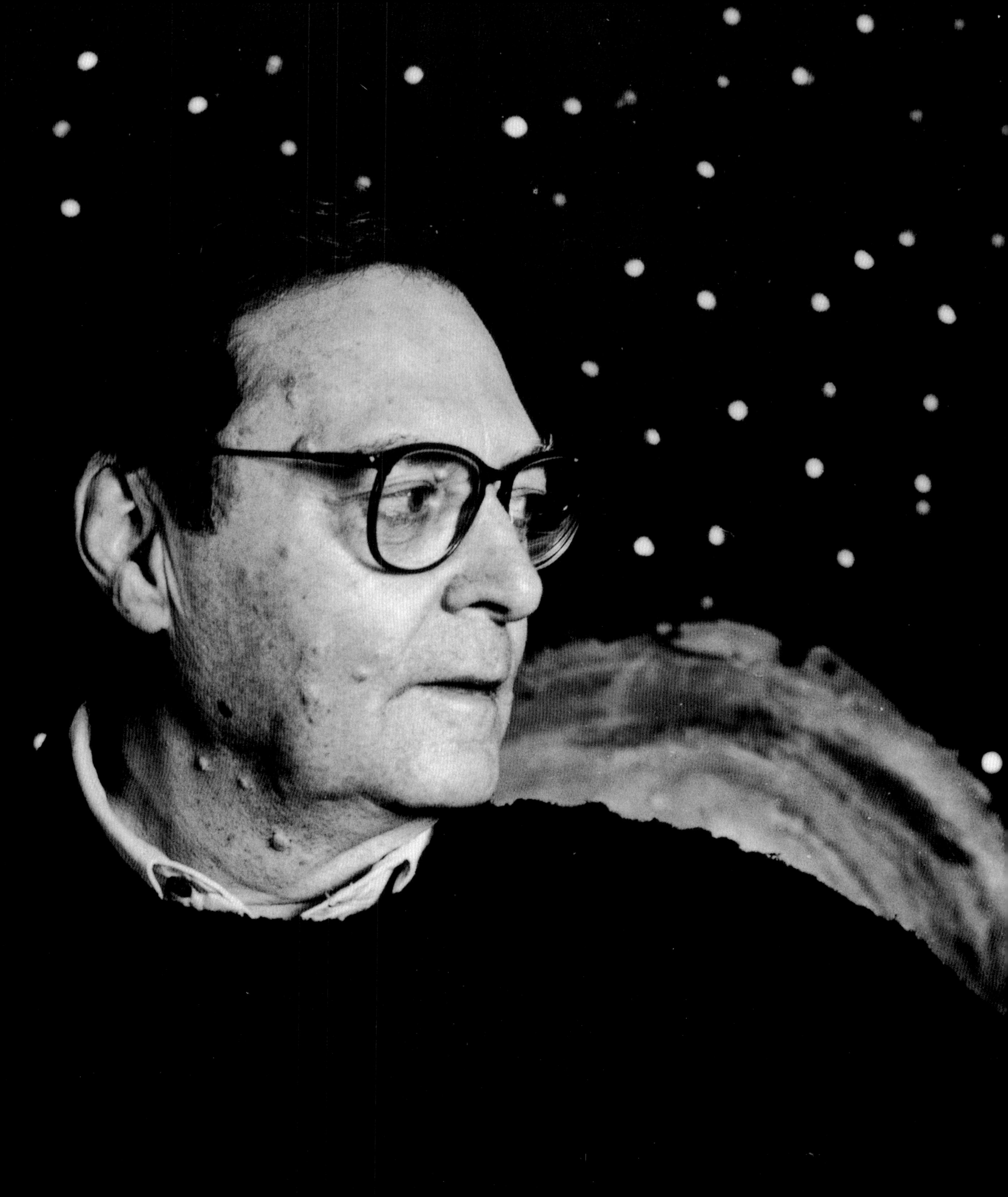

often because he's been awake during the night, reading an art catalogue or a book of fiction in the living room. And while he has come to rely on Mary at home, he has come to rely in the studio on his part-time assistant, Iain Turner, who hoists the plywood sheets as though they weigh nothing, has a reckless familiarity with the power tools, and never tries to push his own creative ideas.

At first Turner just performed the arduous task of taking off the top layer of the boards with a planer, something Paterson had begun doing in order to paint on the softer texture underneath. Then, in the fall of 1995, to Mary's amazement, Turner was occasionally allowed to wield the router. "I draw an outline of the image, just like I usually have," Paterson says, "then I tell Iain exactly where I want the router to go, at what depth, at what angle, with or against the grain. He works so fast, with such a disregard for the safety rules, that I'm able to get more done during a Saturday with him than a week by myself."

Paterson's physical and psychological frailty has not diminished his imaginative force. One day, when the router accidentally pierced all the way through the board, he saw it as an aesthetic breakthrough: he cut out round pieces and pasted the discs on the board or affixed sheets of galvanized iron behind the holes they left. Another time, inspired by a work of Seurat in which the painting had spilled onto the frame, he roughly cut small frames from plywood, backed them with squares of painted steel of the same size, then gouged, painted and etched cosmic scenes and falling trees on both the wood and metal.

"I'm not much of an existentialist any more," he says. "Though I don't go to church, I pray a lot to God, whom I'm not sure is there but who represents in my mind all things that are good. I guess I'm a kind of pantheist: I believe God is in nature. Sometimes when a painting becomes extremely difficult, I start to pray, not because I think that the Almighty is concerned with this particular work, but because everything starts to fit in, as though it's been taken out of my hands. I may be doing the gestures, but when I'm working totally by instinct, I feel guided. It can be rationalized, I suppose, as the subconscious at work, but that doesn't take anything away from the sense of spiritual power."

Paterson Ewen, 1992

TWENTY-FOUR

"It's not that difficult to become one of the best painters in Canada and be recognized for it," Goodridge Roberts told Paterson Ewen, and Paterson Ewen told his students, "because everybody else quits."

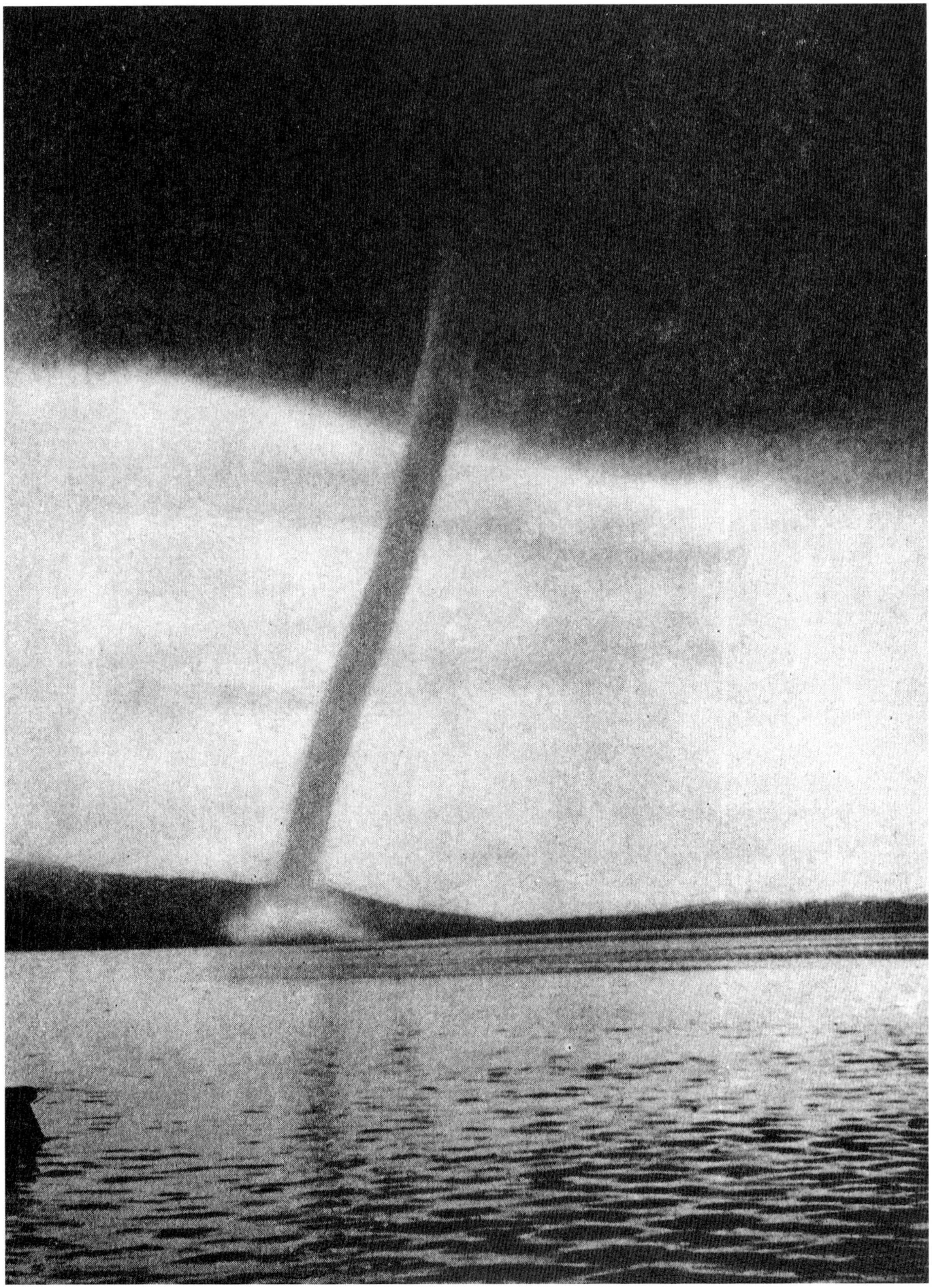

"Waterspout"
Figure 31
from Ivan Ray Tannehill,
Weather Around the World,
(Princeton: Princeton
University Press, 1943)

PATERSON EWEN: COMETS AND OTHER UNKNOWABLE THINGS

by Matthew Teitelbaum

In the early 1970s Paterson Ewen gave up on much that was familiar to him as an artist, or perhaps convention gave up on him. Gone were the traditional tools on which his trade had long flourished: the wooden stretcher and canvas pulled taut. In their place were large sheets of plywood, on which an electric router disrupted and ravaged the surface with fury. Wire, metal sheets, nails, screws, bolts and chainlink fence were soon added as representations of those terrestrial and heavenly phenomena that compelled and moved him. Conjuring landscape as a mere framing device, Ewen has explored the phenomena of natural events and scientific principles for more than twenty-five years since. While the visual effects of specific scientific phenomena are the imagery of his art, manifestation of such images on a grand scale and in rigorous and unusual methods has become his subject. For Paterson Ewen, subject lies in the connection of his images to the power of their realization, and the force of the image, knowable and unknowable, is continually equalled by the force of its creation.

For those who had followed Ewen's often hesitant development as an artist through the 1950s and 1960s, there was a recognition in the early 1970s that the plywood works represented a continuum of interest in imagery linked to the natural world. After all, many of the earliest paintings resemble subsequent work on plywood, and a range of comparisons provoke a snap of visual recognition. *Blackout* (1961) and *Constellation Piece* (1977), *Lifestream* (1959) and *Rocks Moving in the Current of a Stream* (1971), *Untitled* (1962) and *Full Moon* (1984): each pairing suggests a similarity of visual interests. Yet few among those who knew Ewen's development would have expected the radical turn in 1971 towards the new and ultimately liberating materials through which the images were realized. Where earlier work suggested a deep and abiding connection to the visual lyricism of natural forms, the plywood work seemed, and still does, to explode the lyrical into the epic. Where the earlier canvas paintings seemed a modest expression of transcribed lived experience, the plywood paintings suggest a

BLACKOUT 1961

Oil on canvas

21.0 x 27.9

Private Collection

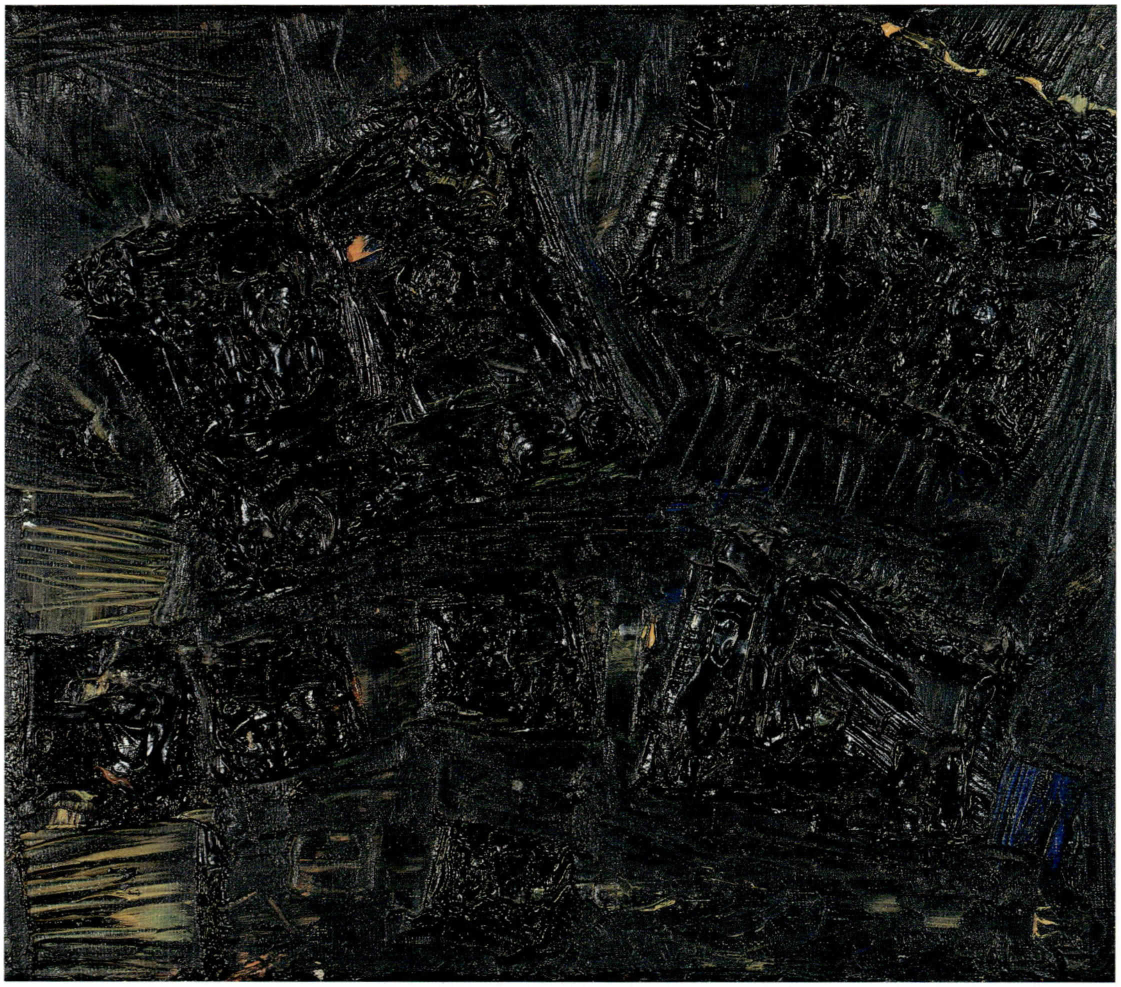

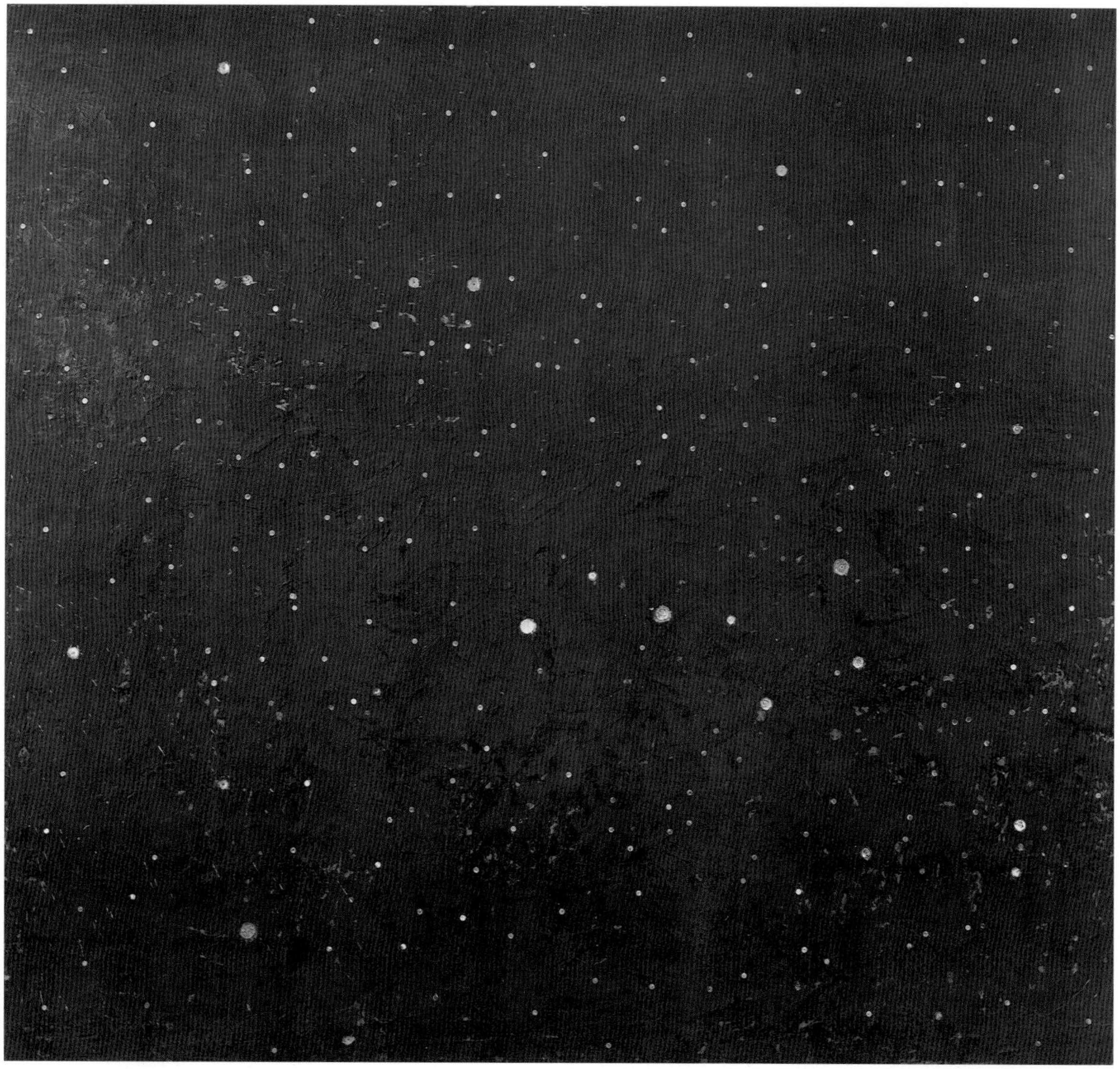

CONSTELLATION PIECE 1977
Acrylic, metal and tar on gouged plywood
228.6 x 243.8
The Art Gallery of Peterborough

Page 38:
LIFESTREAM 1958
Oil on canvas
46.0 x 152.5
Private Collection

Page 39:
ROCKS MOVING IN THE CURRENT OF A STREAM 1971
Steel screws and bolts and nuts, rubber, linoleum, plywood, acrylic paint, galvanized steel
153.3 x 245.3
Art Gallery of Ontario

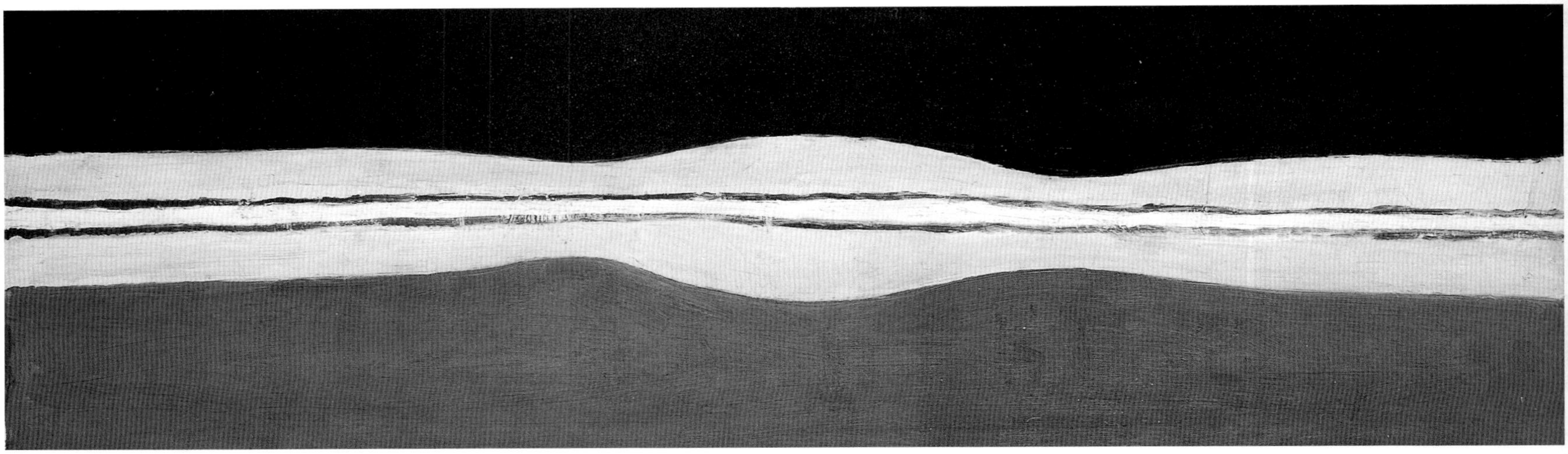

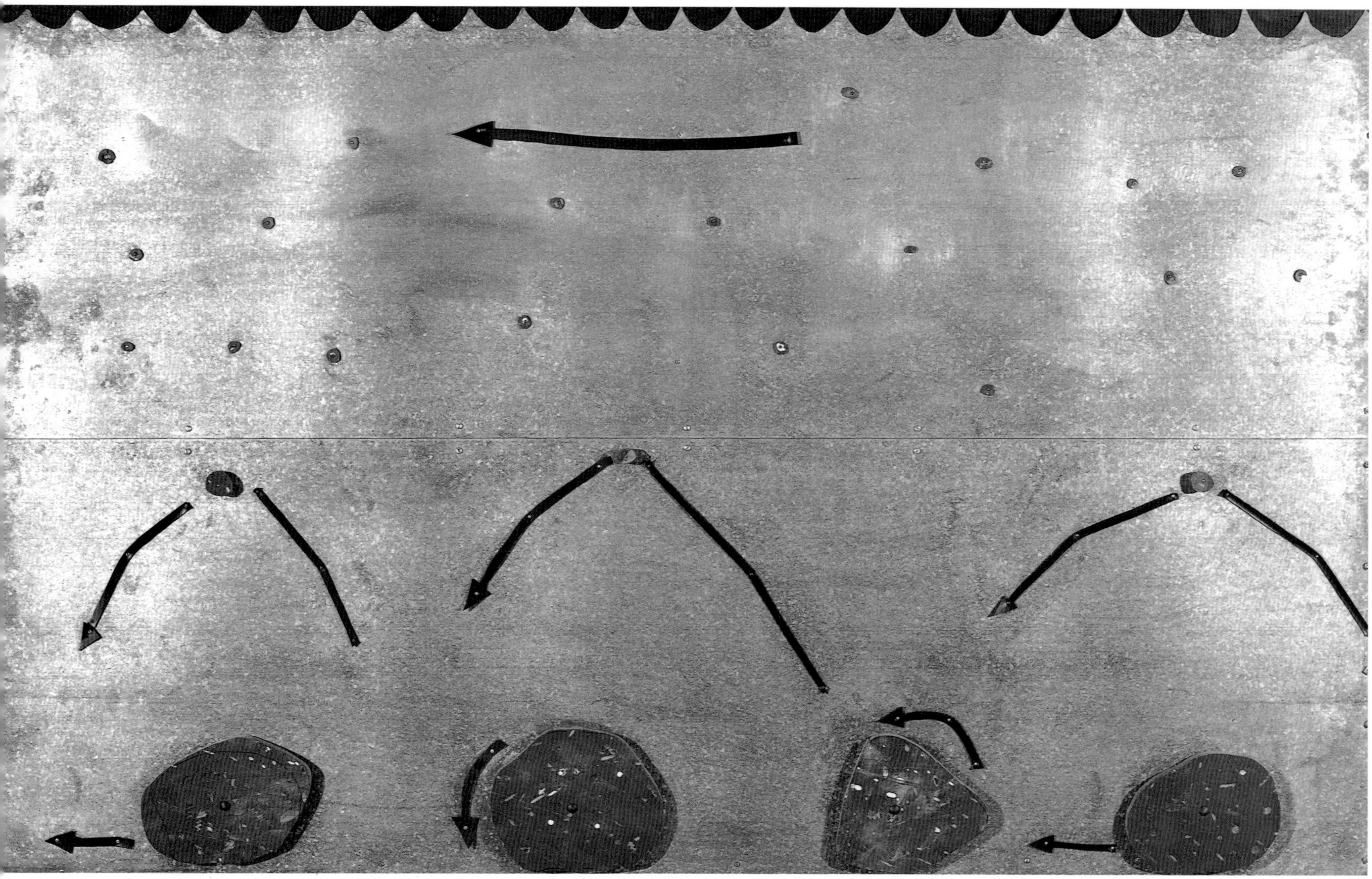

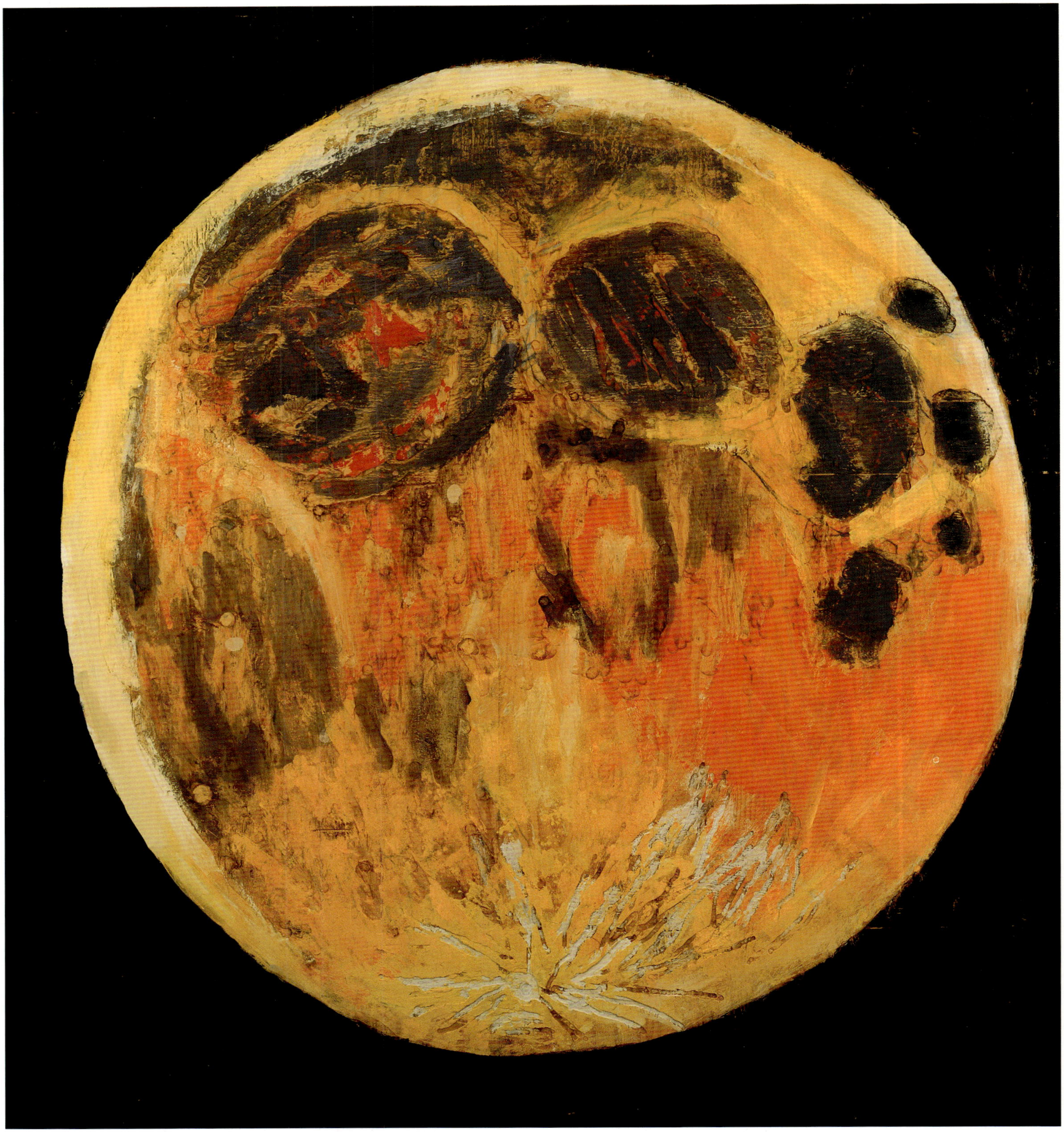

40 PATERSON EWEN

grand, almost operatic, declaration of connection to the natural world. For Ewen, it is the realization of imagery through process that articulates power, inevitability and wonder on a grand scale.

Subject, then, has its roots in the beginnings of Ewen's career; that is, in his long-standing interest in fields of imagery. His subject is transformed through scale and process, encouraged through the discovery of a revitalized engagement with materials. In scale, often eight feet square, Ewen's phenomena-scapes seem to reach around the viewer; in material, they are tough, declarative and never-ending. They are routed, chipped, and gouged, nailed into and stapled onto, scarred by attacks on the wooden surface. In visual effect, they seem very much alive, radiating a virtual force-field of energy that spills into each viewer's space, unconfined by the finite edge of the support. They are, in a very real sense, monumental, and in their sustained power, they extend the experience and traditions of landscape painting in Canada.

There is a moment in the development of all artists when subject matter inherent in all work is expressed with a clarity that makes it seem new. This text explores "newness" in Ewen's work by tracing the development of imagery and the consequential discovery of subject. Inherently questioning Ewen's own self-proclaimed myth of immediate breakthrough, the image of the prospector who suddenly discovers gold with one tap of the hammer is replaced by the image of the prospector whose sifting of sand uncovers small nuggets that lead to larger discoveries. There is a connectedness in Ewen's interests that must be charted in order to establish the development of compelling subject. Not subject in the sense of a thing to draw or paint, but a subject to represent experience through a method and material practice fully resonant with the means and personality of the artist. For subject matter connects image to process, and suggests a certain subjectivity of experience when the force of the image is continually equalled by the communicated forces of its realization. Ewen's landscapes seem to say to us that to see a landscape is to be within it.

1954–55

When Paterson Ewen married the Automatiste dancer Françoise Sullivan in December of 1949, he had been painting for just over two years. Then a twenty-four-year-old student at the school of the Montreal Museum of Fine Arts, Ewen was studying with Arthur Lismer, Goodridge Roberts, Marian Scott, Eldon Grier, and William Armstrong among others, and teaching children's art classes on the weekends. Engaged with the three traditional subjects of the artists—the figure, the landscape, and the still life, each in equal measure—Ewen studied carefully the principles of Post-Impressionist painting. The ordering of architectonic form, the carefully woven relations of tonal fields, the fracture of surface that allows light to emphasize geometric structure—these were the lessons he learned from Paul Cézanne, Vincent van Gogh, and finally Pierre Bonnard.

The vitality of Ewen's paintings of the early 1950s reflected his commitment to the visible world, a commitment encouraged by the example of his most important teacher, Goodridge Roberts. For Paterson and his friends at the museum school, Roberts's resolute engagement with the problems of painting was inspirational. Roberts believed that study from "a connection to surroundings"[1] was crucial for an artist's understanding of his subject. For him, the problem of painting was not to discover symbolic value for images in the manner of Victorian painters (and perhaps the Group of Seven) but rather to explore visual equivalents for the experienced world. Those problems, articulated in Roberts's painting of the time, had been formulated in a range of texts inspired by the writings of Roger Fry.

Facing page:

FULL MOON 1984
Acrylic on gouged plywood
243.8 x 228.6
Collection Garth H. Drabinsky

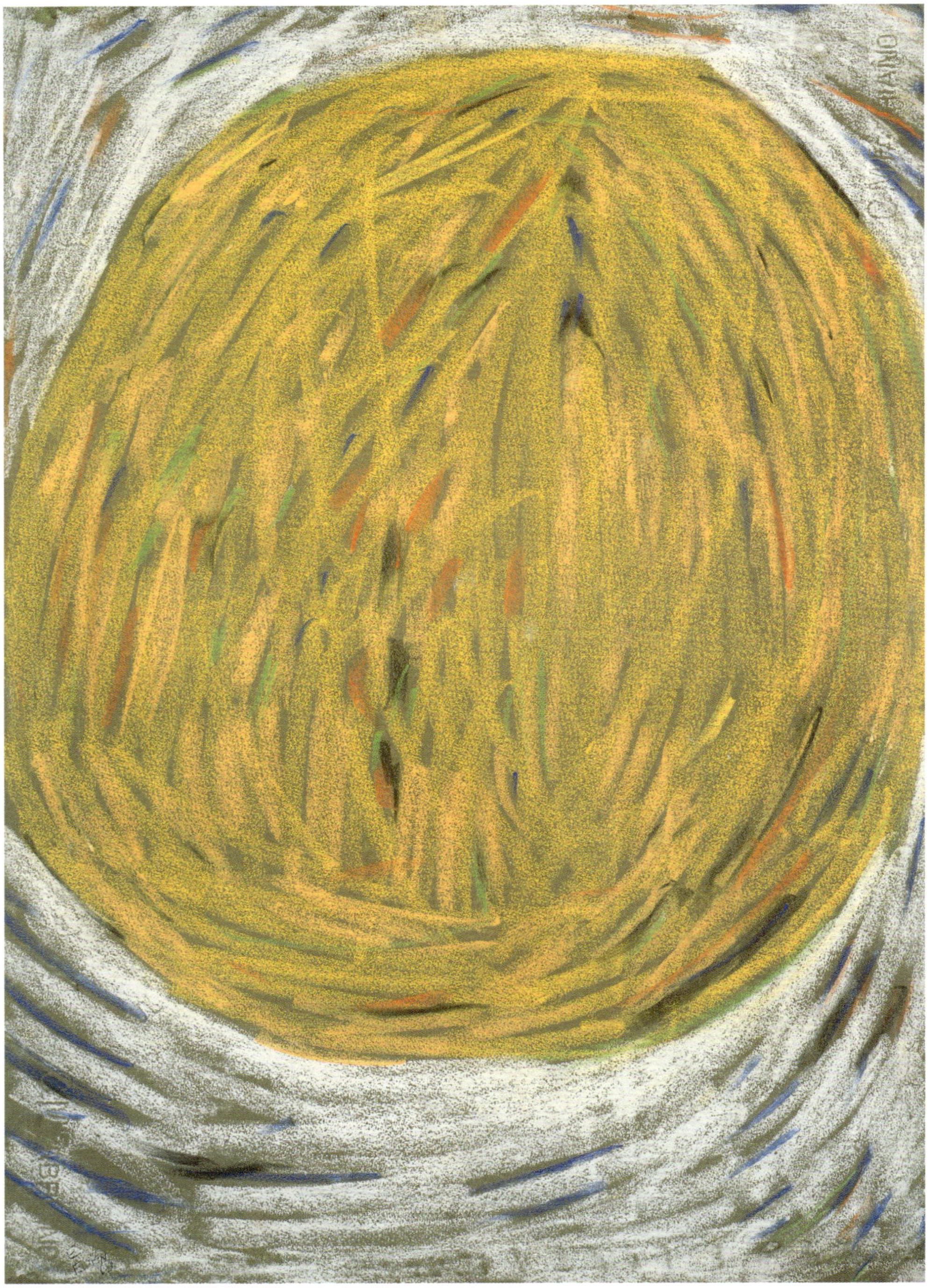

UNTITLED 1962
Pastel on brown
Fabriano paper
64.8 x 47.6
Private Collection

Paterson knew these books by Fry, Clive Bell, and John Cowper Powys, but he absorbed most intensely the ideas of Arthur Howell, a British critic and aesthetician whose major work *The Meaning and Purpose of Art* Ewen first read in 1948.[2] Howell argued, much as Fry and others had before him, that art was a way of being in the world and not merely a way of apprehending visual signs. The making of art was a lifestance, an openness to experience that forged a unity between a loosely spiritual world and that of material things. In a book filled with encouragement and fervour, Howell wrote of conscious acts of creation, and of a painting and sculptural practice fuelled by an urge to unify creative instincts. When he pantheistically declared that "emotion is proverbially the motive of a work of art,"[3] he aligned himself with those who saw aesthetic experience as the root of such emotion. The artist translated what was seen into conceptual form, and his achievement was tied to an acceptance that "to construct is to design, which is to put into order."[4] Such values of coherence and unity were articulated in the work of Roberts and the painters he admired. With colleagues John Fox, Don Barrett, and Matthew Babinski, Ewen cherished the permanent installation of sketches by James Wilson Morrice at the Montreal Museum of Fine Arts. Much like Fox, Ewen gravitated towards the intimacy of Morrice's scale, and the sensitivity to a light at once crystalline and transitory.

The Montreal art community of the early 1950s was fractious. By the late 1940s, the Contemporary Arts Society, the most adventurous and important of the exhibiting organizations, had disbanded, and by 1950 many of the Automatistes had ceased to regard themselves as a cohesive unit. By the time of the exhibition *L'Exposition des Rebelles*, mounted in specific and bold opposition to the Montreal Museum of Fine Arts's annual spring show, the museum seemed hardly a place to reflect on the most advanced painting of the time. Francophone and anglophone artists had few "spaces" in which to interact, and fewer opportunities to have their work shown together. Linguistic fissures existed, to be sure, and so did gaps of purpose, intention, and acknowledged lineage. Just as Social Realists had been dismissed in the United States by many of the leading Abstract Expressionists then working, so too were the documentary styles of Montreal painters such as Stanley Cosgrove, Philip Surrey and Louis Muhlstock rejected by the forward-looking Automatistes.[5]

Ewen was introduced to Automatisme through Françoise Sullivan's writings, the recounting of her experiences studying with the legendary dancer and teacher Franziska Boas in New York, and her continuing friendships with Automatiste painters Jean-Paul Mousseau and Pierre Gauvreau. His own connection to Automatiste values was nourished through his sustaining friendships with the poets Rémi-Paul Forgues and, most centrally, Claude Gauvreau.[6] Importantly, Ewen's introduction to "the French side of Montreal," following his courtship of Françoise in the spring of 1949, came at a moment when the Automatistes were not only disbanding physically—two leading members, Jean-Paul Riopelle and Fernand Leduc, had moved to France—but divisions in Automatiste intellectual positions were beginning to be felt. They occurred largely around arguments over Surrealism's reliance on intention and known fact,[7] effectively ensuring that group manifestations and exhibitions after 1949 would always be qualified by the involvement of some and the exclusion or refusal of others. It certainly meant that the role of Surrealism in the painting ethos of the time remained far from universally influential.

It was in this environment, at the beginning of the 1950s, that Ewen started to exhibit his work publicly. Paintings such as *Still Life with Hat* (1951), *Interior, Fort Street, Montreal* (1951), and *Portrait of Poet (Rémi-Paul Forgues)* (1950) had a

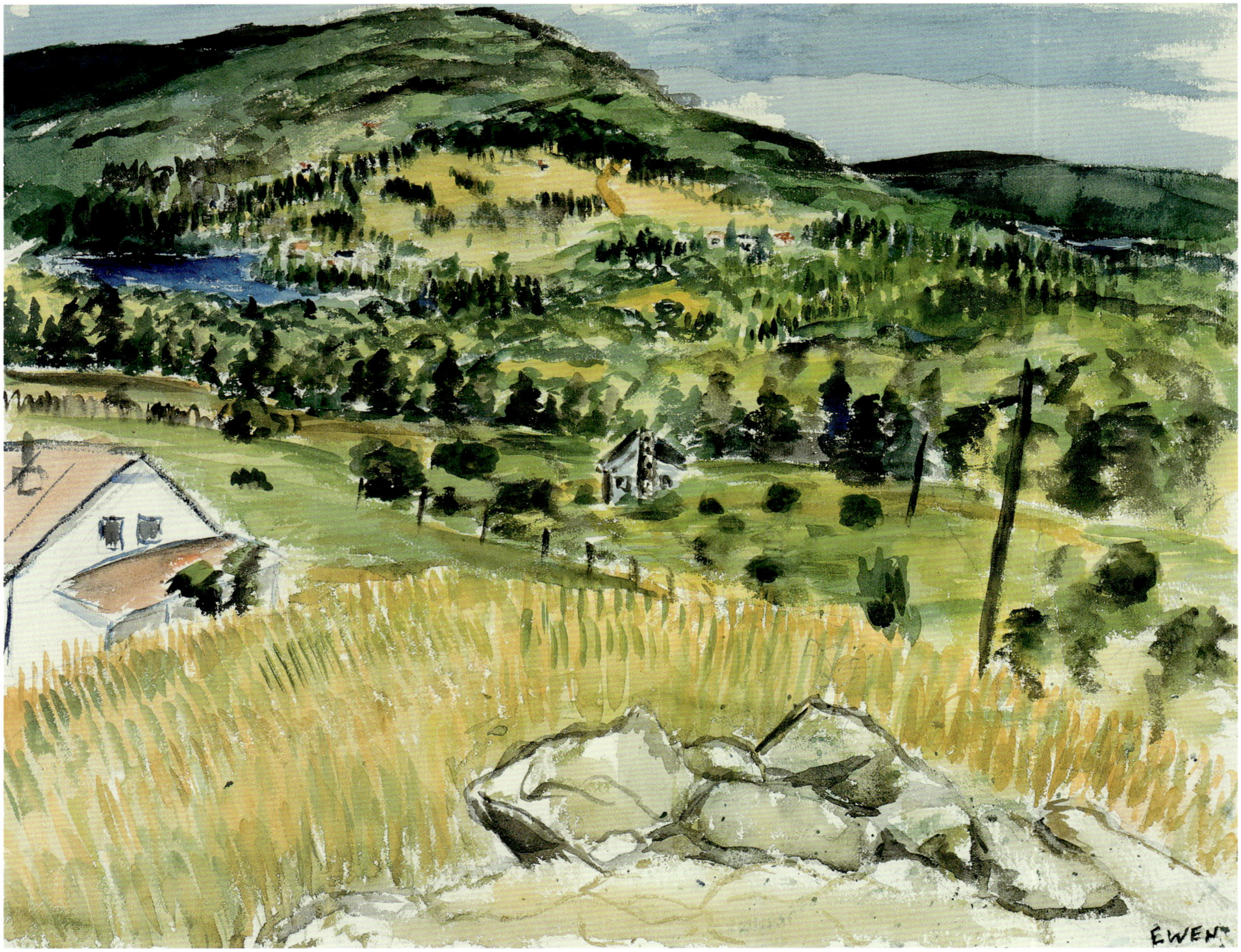
EWEN

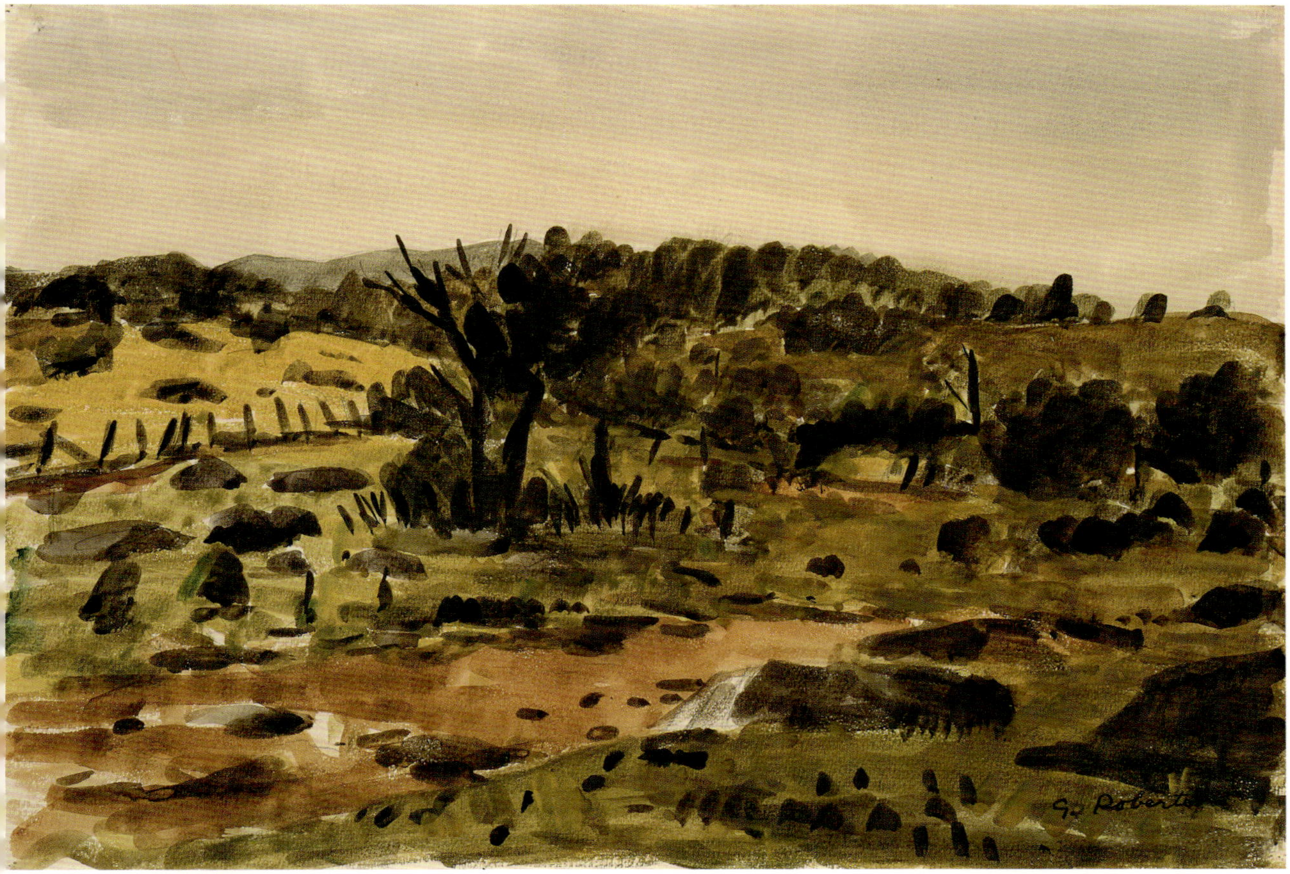

Goodridge Roberts

FOURTEEN ISLAND LAKE 1949

Watercolour on paper

40.6 x 50.8

Private Collection

Facing page:

UNTITLED (FOURTEEN ISLAND LAKE) 1949

Watercolour on paper

50.2 x 65.5

Collection Marjorie M. Margesson

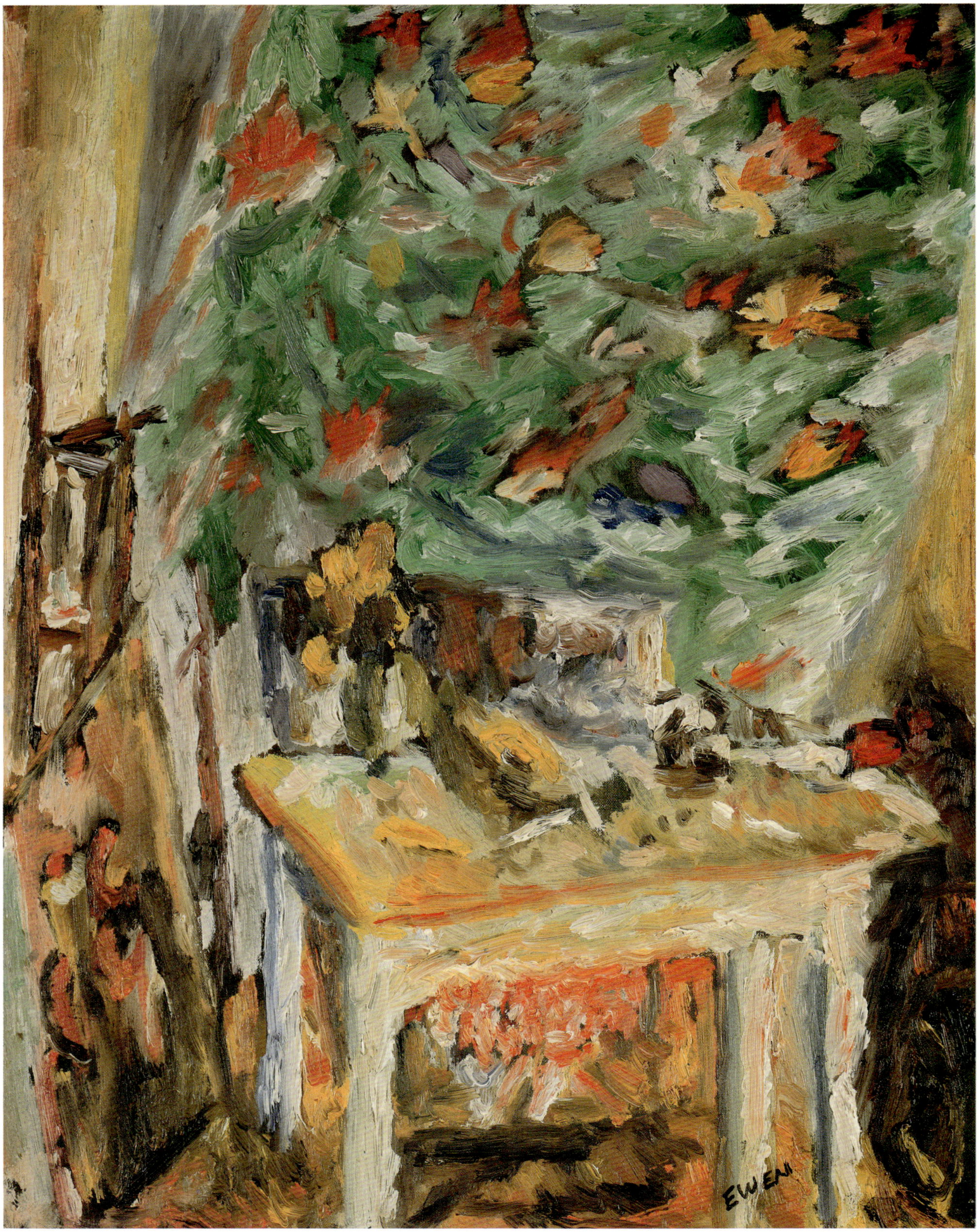
EWEN

small but appreciative following. Presented only in a handful of exhibitions, including his first (self-promoted) one-man show in May of 1950, the works were regarded by one critic as indicative of a "powerful temperament [that] questions everything."[8] The painters in the Automatiste group familiar to him through Françoise had embraced Ewen not so much as a fellow spirit but as an artist of commitment and integrity. Individually, they encouraged him. While Jean-Paul Mousseau respected the forceful way in which Ewen's paintings of the early 1950s worked through the inspiration of "optics and impressionism,"[9] Paul-Émile Borduas acknowledged the "generosity"[10] of his landscapes. Pierre Gauvreau, whose paintings were the first Automatiste works Ewen had seen, heralded Ewen as an artist "with no sense of censorship in himself"[11] and openly admired "the brutal way he painted [without] theory, and against almost everything, including good taste." Pierre's brother, Claude Gauvreau, acknowledged by many as the heart and soul of the group following publication of *Refus global*, was particularly close, casually assisting in the hanging of Ewen's one-man exhibition and purposefully if didactically arguing for inclusion of Ewen's work in two important group exhibitions: *L'Exposition des Rebelles* in March of 1950 and *Les Étapes du vivant* in May of 1951. Defending Ewen against the criticism of a colleague who questioned his inclusion in *L'Exposition des Rebelles*, Gauvreau wrote of Ewen's "authentic" contribution.[12]

In March of 1950, while still a student at the Montreal Museum of Fine Arts School of Art and Design, Ewen showed at the museum's *67th Annual Spring Exhibiton* and, simultaneously, in the *Rebelles* exhibition organized by Jean-Paul Mousseau to protest the "counterfeit juries" of the museum who had discouraged recognition of Automatiste work in their selection.[13] Mousseau's invitation to Ewen was meant to reinforce the Automatiste search for engagement and freedom—after all, they were opening categories and recognizing work by artists of varied sensibility at the very moment that the *Spring Exhibition* jury seemed narrow and limited in its recognition of new art forms. Ewen's paintings, and those by other representational painters such as Matthew Babinski, suggested Automatiste openness and thus ironically provided a purposeful contrast with the closed categories of pictorial realism the museum jury had applied to its selections. Yet the Automatistes self-consciously and purposefully opened themselves to the work of a "representational" anglophone artist for another reason as well. For the Automatistes, Ewen's dark-toned images, knitted together through their scumbled, textured surfaces, captured a sense of objects at the very moment prior to their disintegration and seemed to represent that final instant before opening into abstraction. In a declarative desire to iterate the development of abstraction in Montreal, Ewen's paintings had an aesthetic and didactic function in the Automatistes' world.[14]

Yet, while Ewen's wide ranging intellectual interests and personal affinities allowed him access to the Automatiste community, his work, and the temperament it revealed, determined that he would remain far from its real centre. Though intellectually engaged with the freedom of gesture and the unconscious proposed in Automatiste painting—the idea of the attack—Ewen's representational work was not created in the same spirit. The Automatiste painters rejected imagery, believing that abstraction offered the truest release from the constraints of order.

Displaced from the English community by his questioning of the conventions of traditional pictorialism, yet distanced from the Automatistes by reference to subject matter, Ewen was an artist with neither a definable public nor a sustainable direction. In January of 1955, he spoke of the consequential

Facing page:
INTERIOR, FORT STREET, MONTREAL
[#1] 1951
Oil on canvas board
50.5 x 40.5
Art Gallery of Ontario

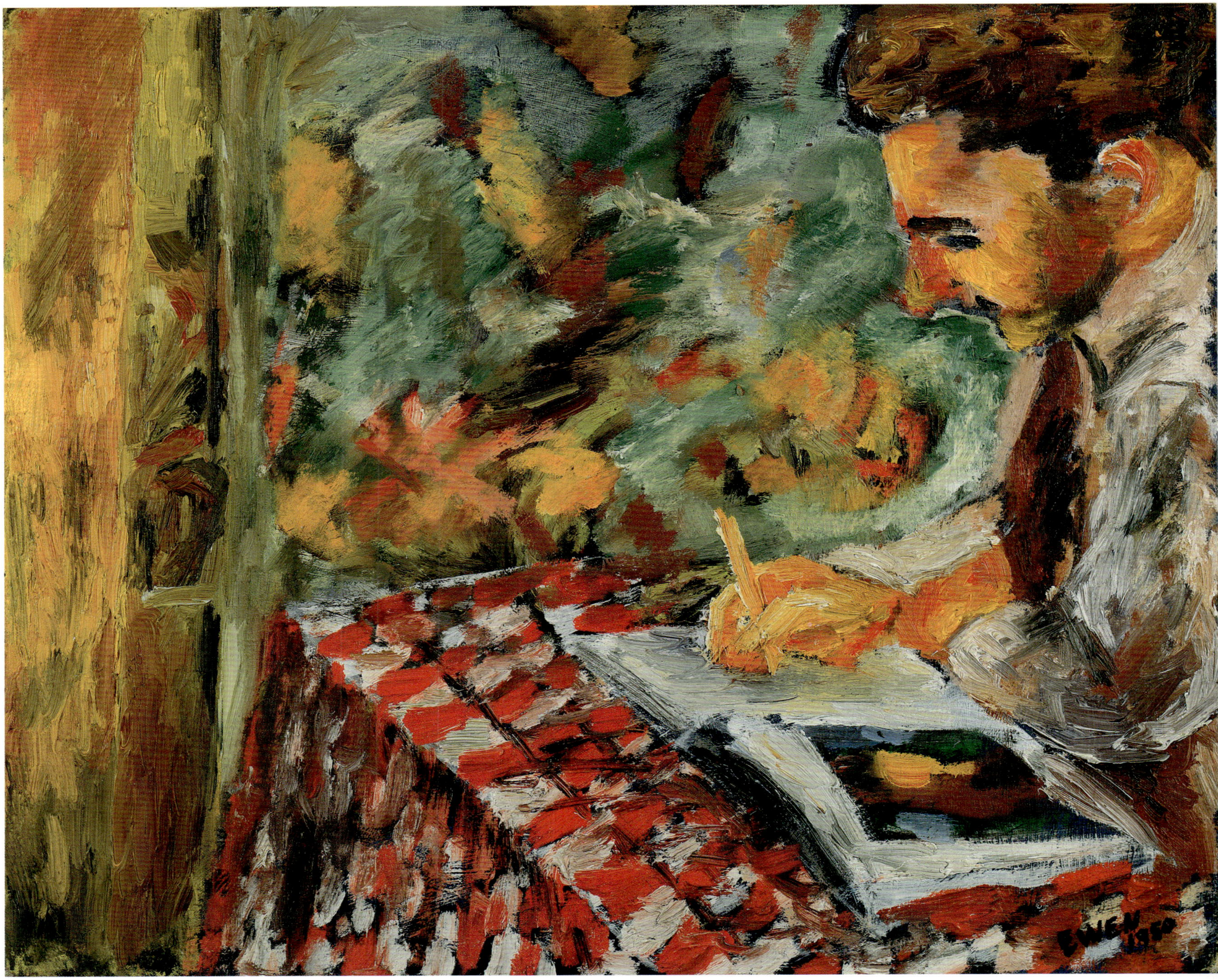
EWEN 1950

uncertainty of his work of 1953/54[15] by noting: "I was trying to find a justification in an always tighter composition but then, the realism of the scene was lost."[16] In 1969, speaking retrospectively of that time, Ewen recalled: "I intellectually accepted the idea that all painting was abstract and that there were too many sentimentalities attached to my figurative work . . . for me, naturalism just wore out."[17]

Portrait of Poet (Rémi-Paul Forgues) **(1951). In this, one of two known portraits of the Automatiste poet Rémi-Paul Forgues, all of Ewen's openness to the sensibility of Bonnard is expressed. In the manner of Intimist painting, the poet is seen in private activity within a domestically scaled interior, an homage that extends to the red and white checkered tablecloth—a staple of late nineteenth-century dining tables captured in Bonnard's feathery interiors. It is a moment of solitude suggesting the intimacy of the task at hand; the subject's concentration on his own activity, and his humility, suggest deep feeling. Colours release themselves into one another, and the edges of objects open into other forms. There is reflected light everywhere. Indeed, there are many lessons learned from Bonnard: the creation of a single, flattened painted surface, the disappearance of focus which reflects the temperamental disordering of reality and, perhaps most importantly, the compositional tendency to bury incidents of colour and form on the edge of the canvas as a means of emphasizing their transitory presence in nature. Using a compositional structure learned from the study of photographs, the subject careens off the edge of the canvasboard, his positioning in the frame a wistful recollection of the family snapshot. The poet's quiet task is here valued as subject matter just as the domestic chore was valued by Bonnard, and imbued with a sense of the exalted.** ***Portrait of Poet (Rémi-Paul Forgues),*** **like other paintings of the time, reflects a desire for intimacy and sensuousness within a system of ordered reality.**

Paterson Ewen exhibited his first abstract paintings in Montreal in one of the centrally important exhibitions of the decade, *Espace 55*. Organized by the artist Gilles Corbeil for the Montreal Museum of Fine Arts, *Espace 55* was developed to explore links between the Automatistes and the inheritance of Surrealism. It suggested that new currents in abstraction challenged the loose, accidental nonstructures of the Automatistes. Corbeil sought to reveal "a new order . . . a spatial reality,"[18] by profiling two dominant tendencies in abstract painting of the time—the free gestural work of Noël Lajoie, Robert Dupras, and Louis Émond, and the flattened, overlapping planar constructions of Jean-Paul Mousseau and Fernand Leduc. The tendencies were, in many ways, incompatible with, indeed hostile to, one another; a latter-day automatism suggested the legitimacy and sustainability of gesture as liberation, while geometrically determined space—an approach that migrated quickly to what was to become known as Plasticien painting—anticipated a return to classical order. At issue, purposefully for Corbeil and provocatively for the community, was the psychic space of Automatisme, and the battleground was the creation of such space in nonrepresentational painting through painterly means. When Leduc and Mousseau exhibited paintings which juxtaposed flattened colour fields to suggest an almost illusionistic depth, it seemed a virtual call to arms.

Ewen was a spectator to the debate, in no way a participant. His work of the time was constructed around a dominant, gridlike calligraphy that was opened, centralized, and organized by concentric thrust. Where the Automatistes encouraged blended colour harmonies induced equally by the palette knife and the dripping of paint, Ewen maintained discreet colour; where the soon-to-be-called Plasticiens flattened composition by working the surface evenly and filling the corners with incidents of colour, Ewen held on to the centralized image. His interest in

Facing page:
PORTRAIT OF POET (RÉMI-PAUL FORGUES)
1950
Oil on canvas board
40.6 x 50.8
Art Gallery of Ontario

UNTITLED 1954
Oil on canvas
78.6 x 97.2
Collection Mr. and Mrs. H. Arnold Steinberg

Facing page, top:
Paul-Émile Borduas
À LA FALAISE DE LA VOIE LACTÉE 1950
Coloured inks on paper
21.0 x 27.3
Art Gallery of Ontario

Facing page, bottom:
UNTITLED 1956
Gouache on paper
45.8 x 60.8
Collection Guido Molinari

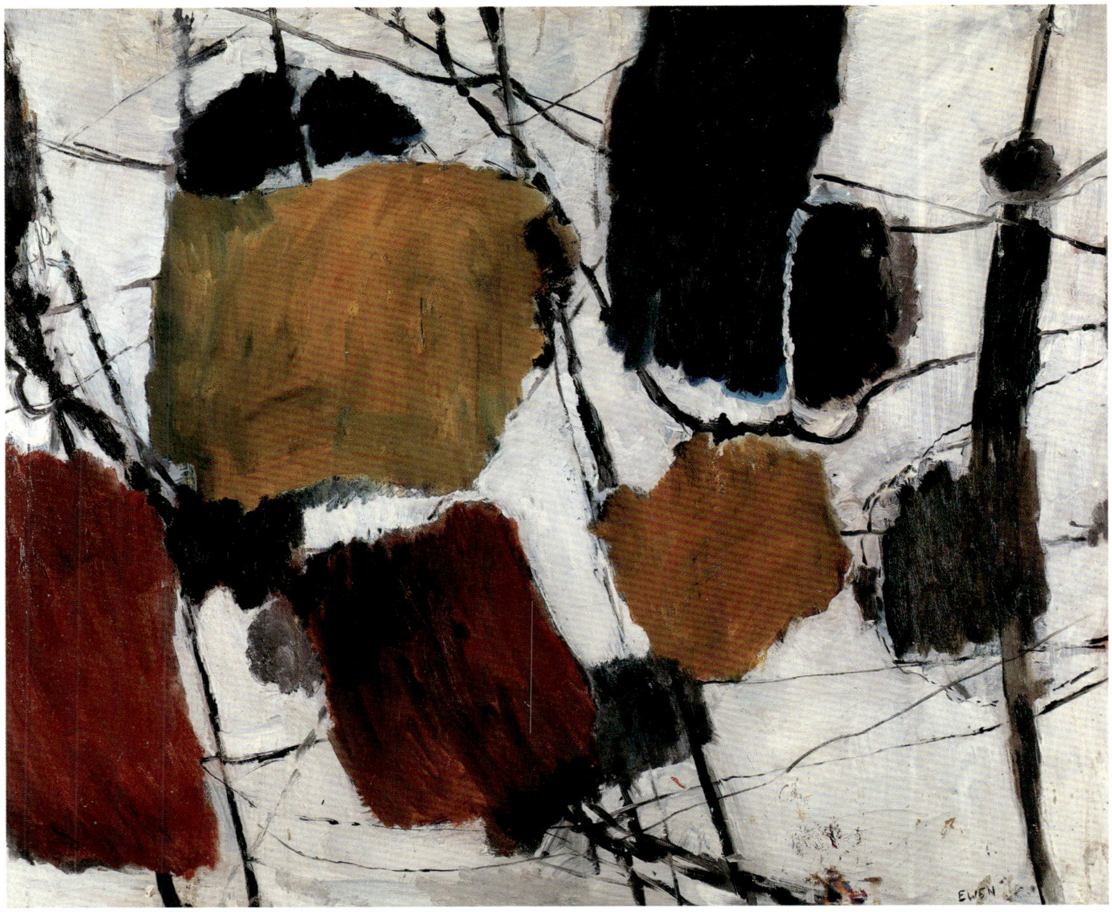

Leduc's work, which he saw as the most important in *Espace 55*, did not discourage his own continuing exploration of freer abstract expressionist gestures proposed not only by Borduas but by a generation of American painters then exhibiting in New York. Emblematically, Ewen found himself positioned in *Espace 55* exactly where he would be for much of the following decade: simply put, *between* positions of ideological authority that were exuberant in their rhetoric and unshakable in their aesthetic sensitivities.

It was Ewen's circumstance in the abstract painting circles of late 1950s Montreal to find himself not so much late (as in behind), but rather between (as in unaffiliated), not so much a follower as an explorer. When his colleagues referred to him as "the prospector," it was surely because, unlike artists who encapsulate energy in a community, he seemed always to be seeking, trying to take hold of and possess a way of finding that secret subject inside. His successive abstract explorations—many of which provided quiet levels of recognition within the specific context of Quebec painting and modest acclaim elsewhere—were often based on series which had loose landscape affiliations varied in format, colour, and surface texture. Each series had coherence and a sustained thrust, though no one idea carried him for very long. These series shared a denial of the gesturalism of automatic painting and the scale of the Plasticien aesthetic; they spoke for the lyrical over the epic.[19]

In each series, a process suggested itself. It was, simply put, the reduction of visual phenomena to a system of signs, marks on the canvas that had apparent and real relation to the idea of a graph or a diagram. The predominant aesthetic was a loosely based abstract lyricism rooted in the observation of natural phenomena. The process of reduction which any diagram or schema implies—of grand form to miniaturized form, from the three dimensionality of an object in space to a flattened atonal sphere—was a tendency Ewen had long believed in.

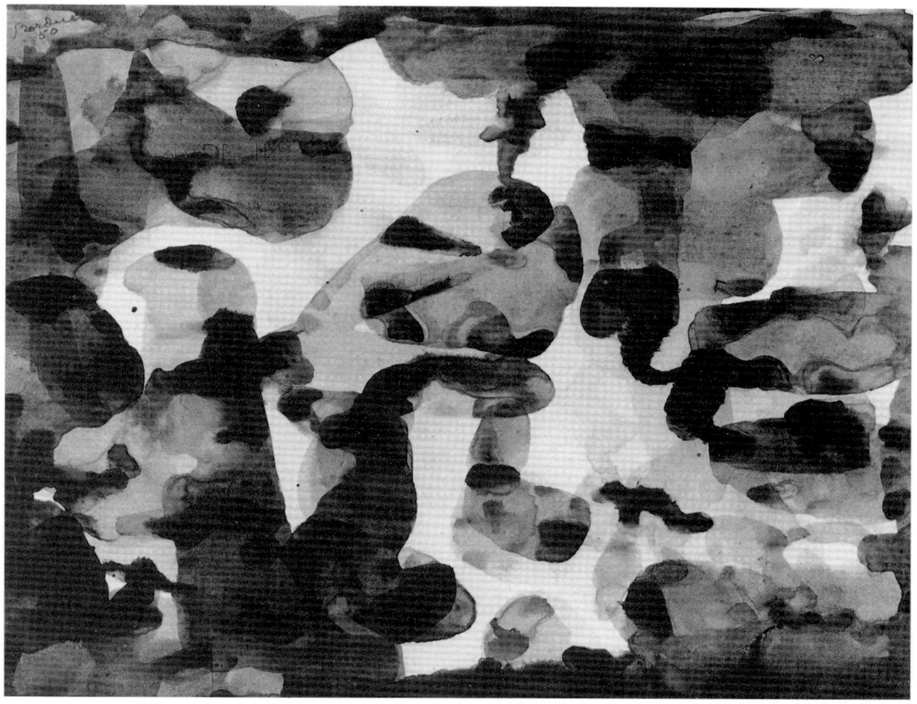

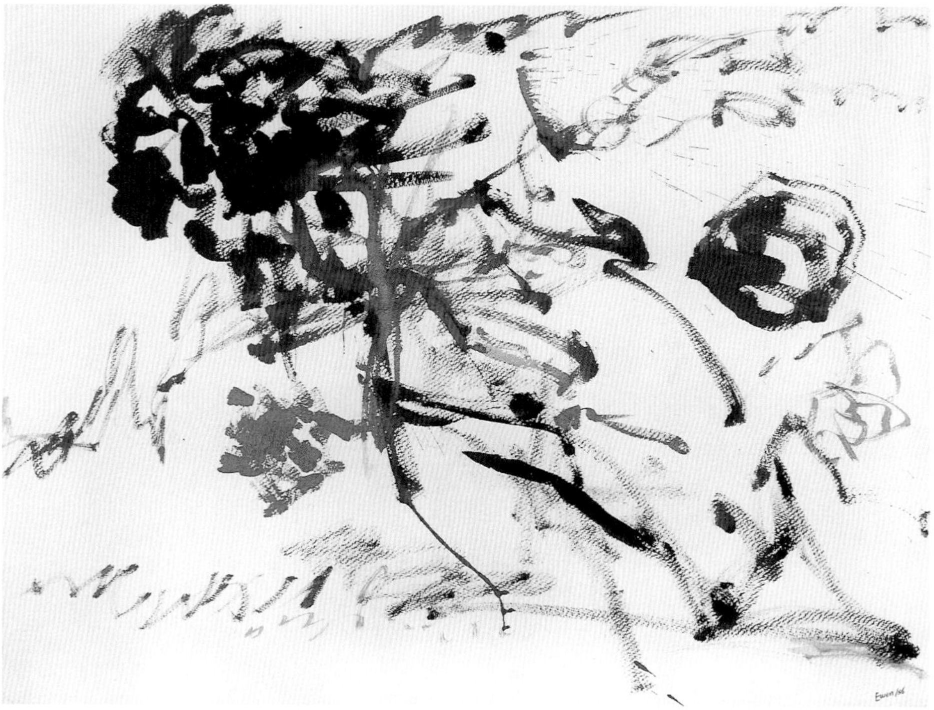

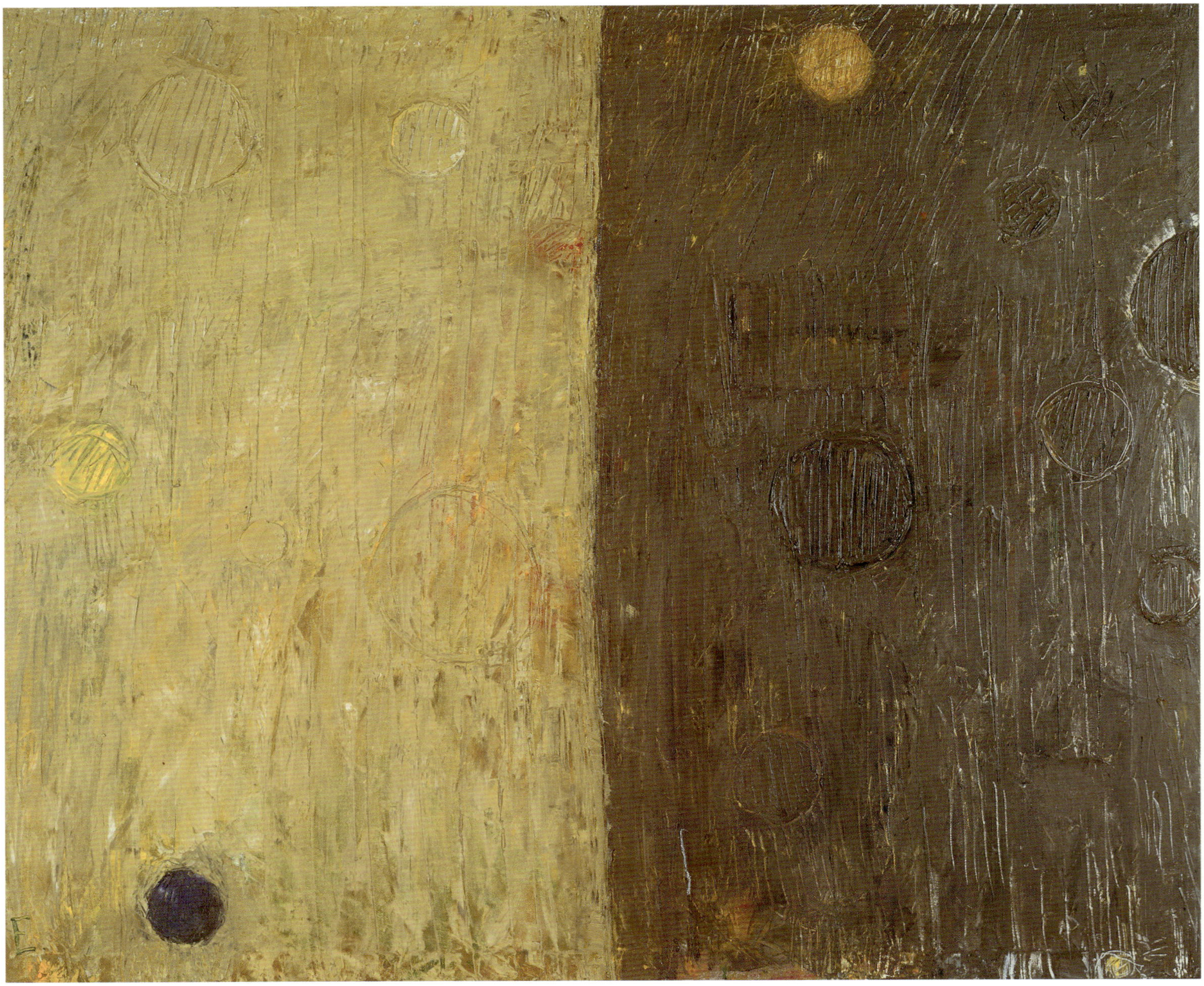

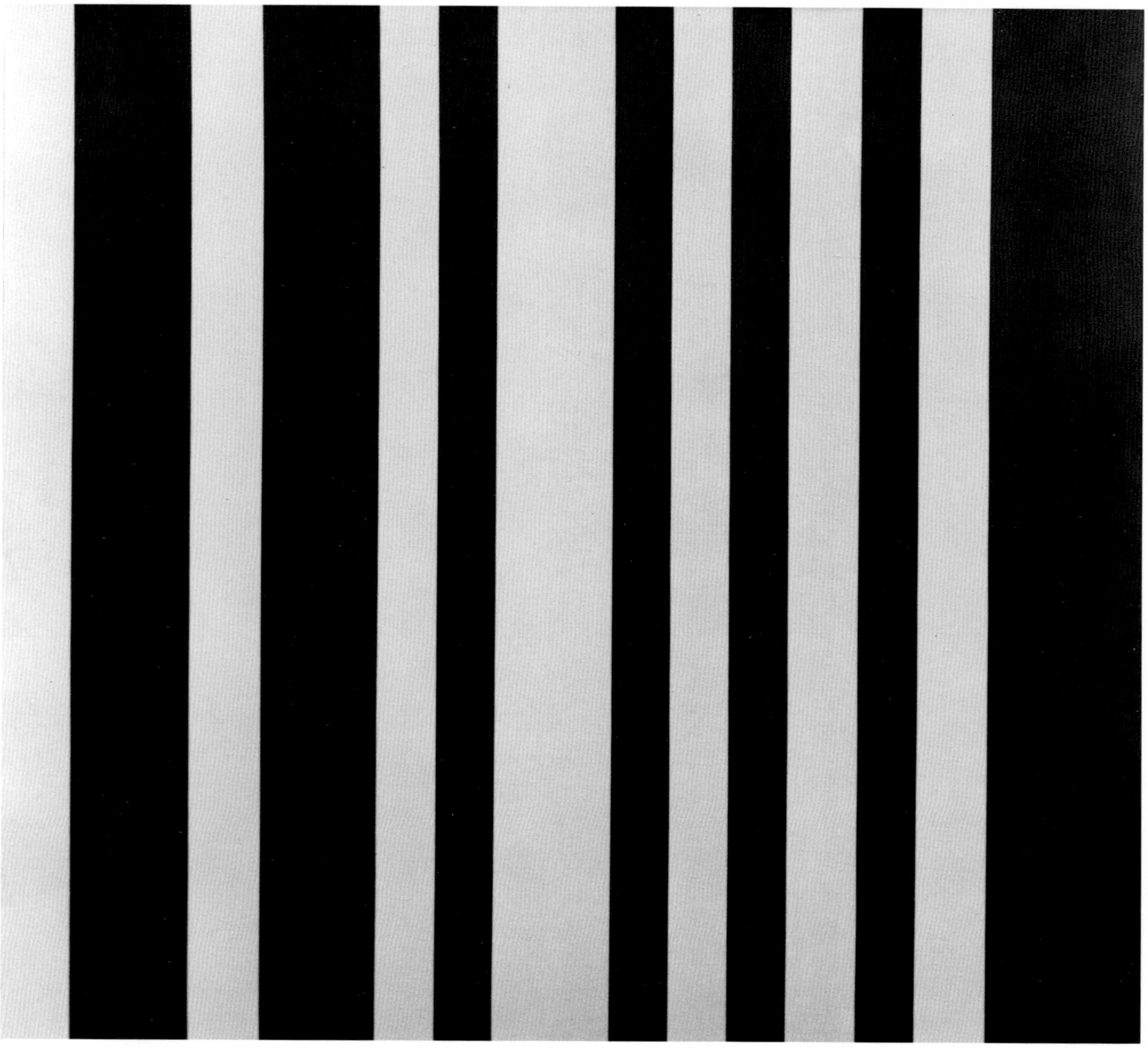

Guido Molinari

MULTINOIR 1962

Acrylic on canvas

114.3 x 124.5

Art Gallery of Ontario

Facing page:

UNTITLED 1962

Oil on canvas

122.5 x 152.5

Private Collection

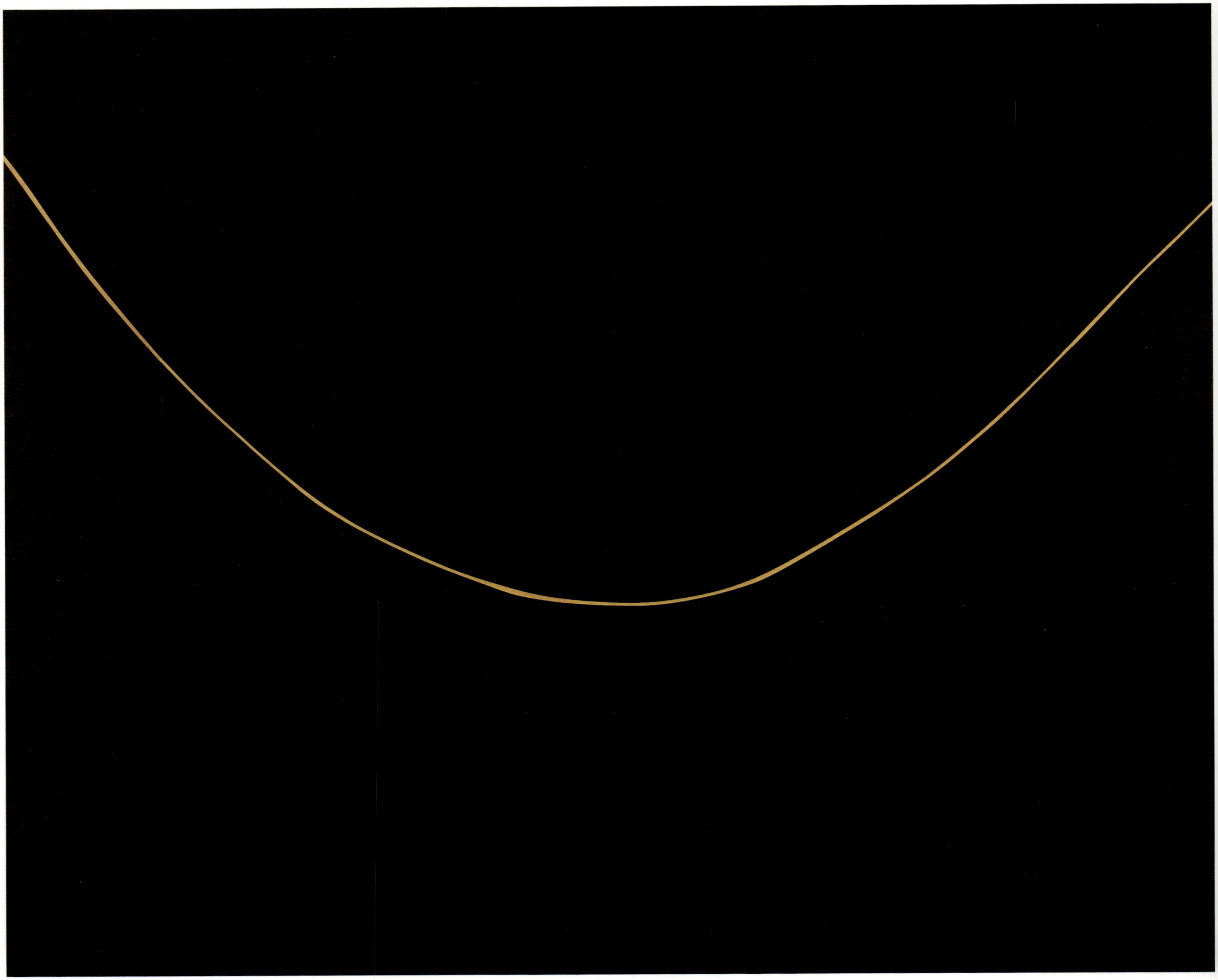

The concept of abstracting—taking from the visible world and reducing observed phenomena to constituent elements—was eschewed by both the Automatistes and the Plasticiens, who saw deep space and tonal gradation as Old-World values: images based on, rather than in, an experience of the world.

Where the Plasticiens criticized the illusion of lyricism and gestural liberation in Automatisme, their own development consistently denied any engagement with deep space in both phases of Plasticien development: the first, which utilized texture and cubist structure to pull images towards the surface, and the second, where the energy of highly keyed colour exploded across brutally frontal planar fields. But not so among other artists with whom Ewen felt affinity—Ulysse Comtois, Rita Letendre, and Marcelle Maltais among the Montreal painters; Adolph Gotlieb, Bradley Walker Tomlin, and John Ferren among those artists whose work he admired in New York.

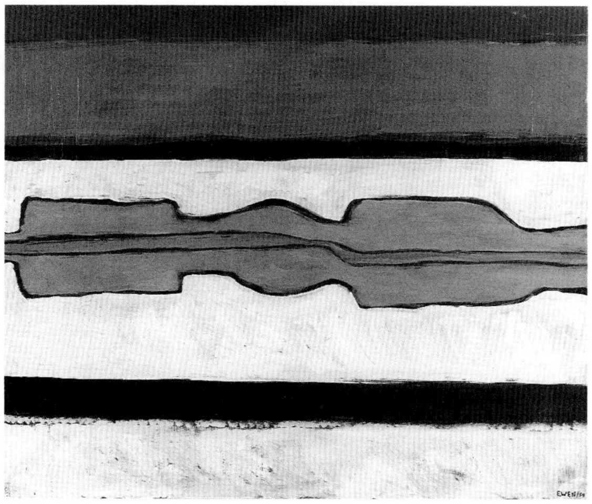

LIFESTREAM 1959
Oil on canvas
76.3 x 91.4
Collection Ross and Marion Woodman

Facing page:
UNTITLED #1 1969
Acrylic on canvas
241.5 x 305.0
Art Gallery of Ontario

Page 56:
UNTITLED #2 1969
Acrylic on canvas
241.5 x 305.0
Art Gallery of Ontario

Page 57:
UNTITLED #3 1969
Acrylic on canvas
241.5 x 305.0
Art Gallery of Ontario

1970–71

In the 1950s and 1960s, Ewen saw painting tied to the referential fact of the observable world. His engagement was with phenomena transcribed from nature, beginning with the simple declaration that traditional art forms were outworn repetitions of known facts, and evolving into a conviction that abstraction distilled and thus intensified experience by making tangible the essence of things. Philip Guston, an American artist of consequential interest for Ewen by 1960,[20] wrote of just such an ethics of sight: "I doubt if this ethic would be real enough without the pull of the known image for its own 'light,' its sense of place."[21] So too for Ewen, who saw in this process of reduction for visual effect a relationship to work by artists he continued to admire—Cézanne and Bonnard particularly. Much of that visual richness Ewen observed in Bonnard he sought to transcribe into abstract painting,[22] namely, that oscillation around objects that keyed colour and opened brushstrokes can give, and the suggestion of transitory or fleeting sensations aroused by intense light. Ewen rooted his paintings in observable phenomena, and turned the idea of observation back upon the viewer in ways that Bonnard had many years before, by capturing those memories of effects or sensations which disappear when we sustain attention on objects in the world.

Lifestream **(1959): The series of** ***Lifestream*** **paintings, first shown in 1958, explores movement through space in a landscape format. Masses that suggest living form push and pull against one another, conjuring elemental forces through an almost graphlike schema. The** ***Lifestream*** **works are resolutely horizontal and organized around loosely brushed though discrete bands of colour. The bands float on top of fluid grounds which consistently break to the edge of the canvas, balancing and combining the depiction of discrete form with an interest in using the canvas as a total ground for action. Adopting only that idea of allovERness from the Plasticiens, Ewen equalized all of the painting surfaces by pulling incidents away from the corners. Colours are consistently related by tone and tend towards what Ewen calls "earthy browns." Black outlines are conventionally used to contain**

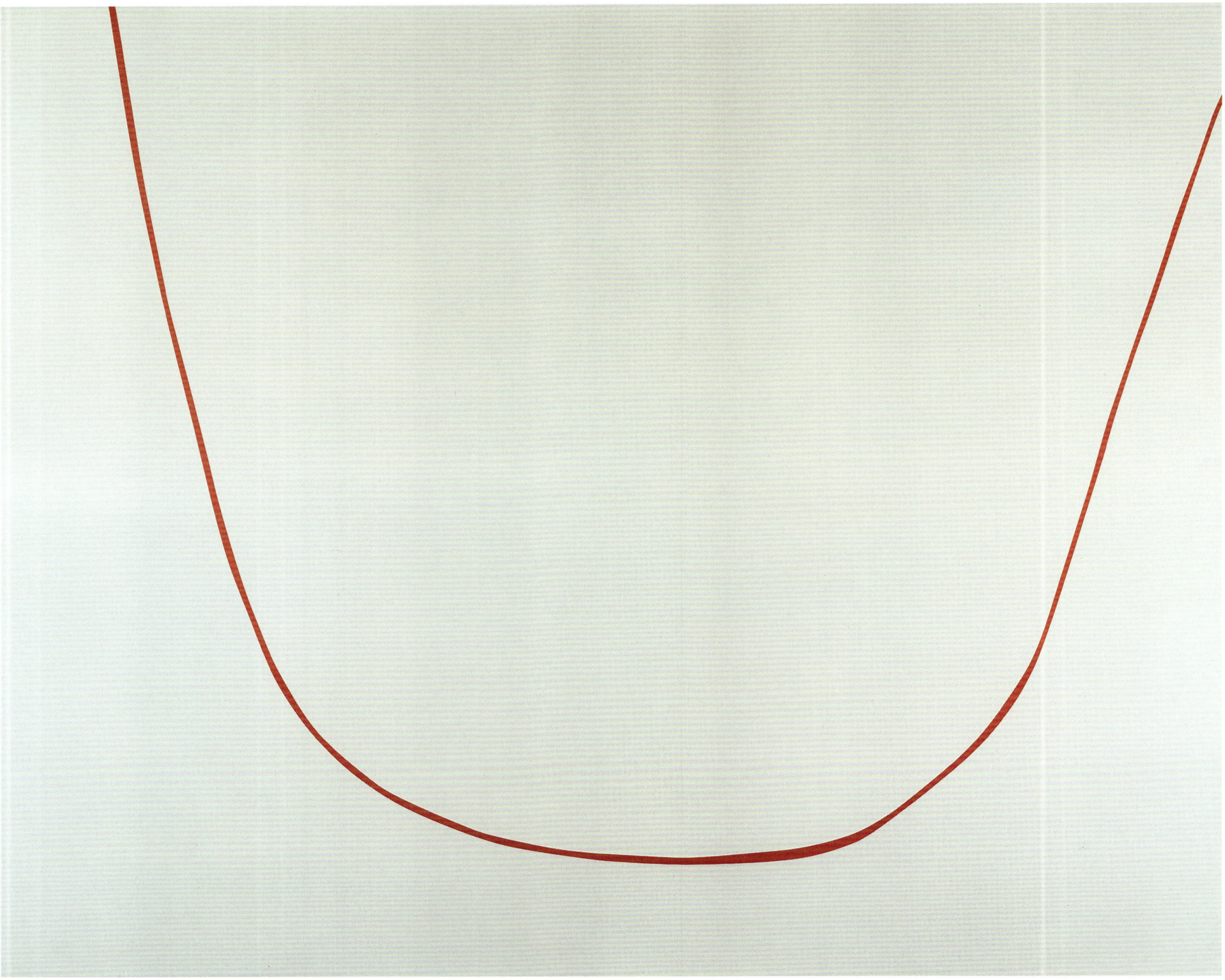

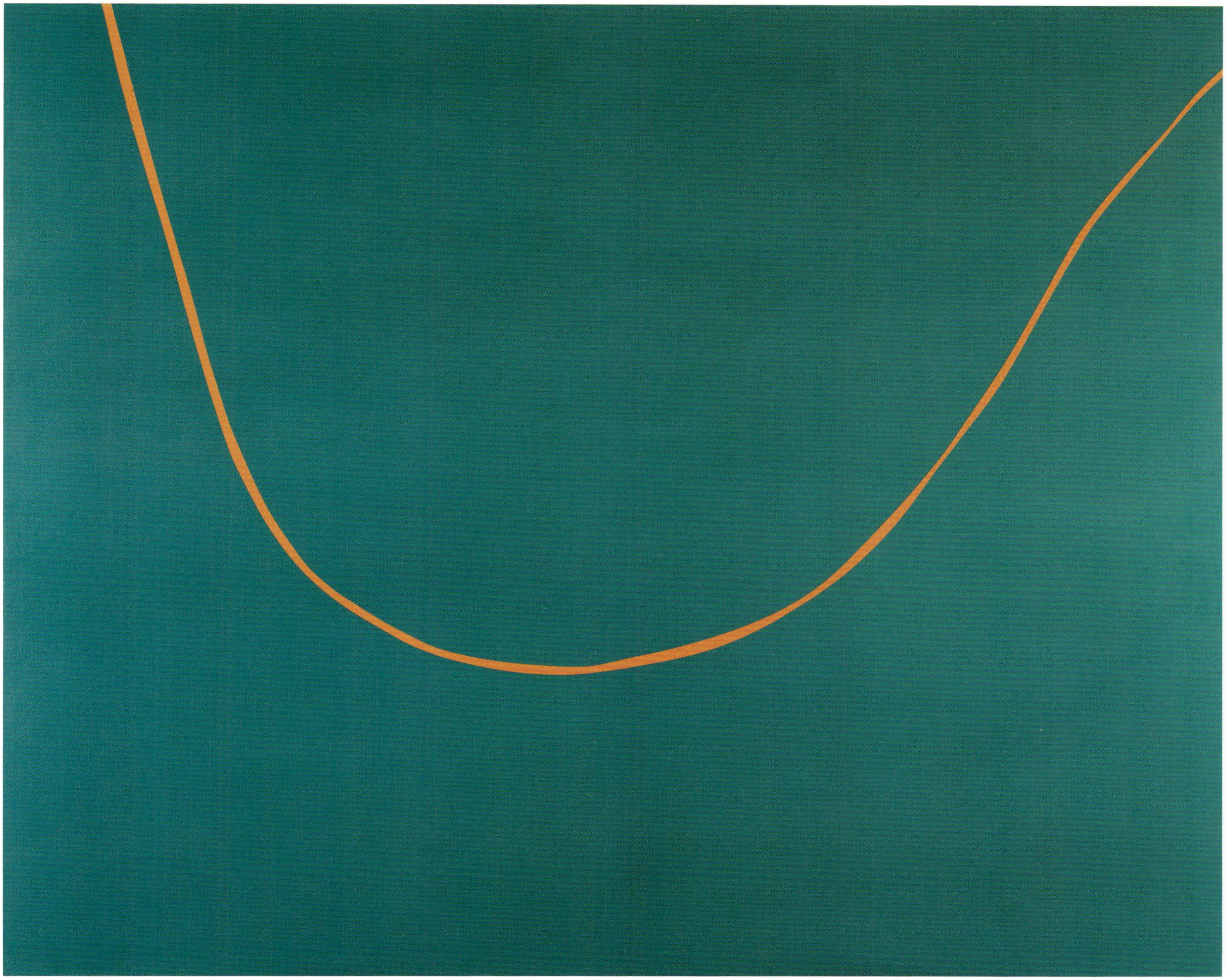

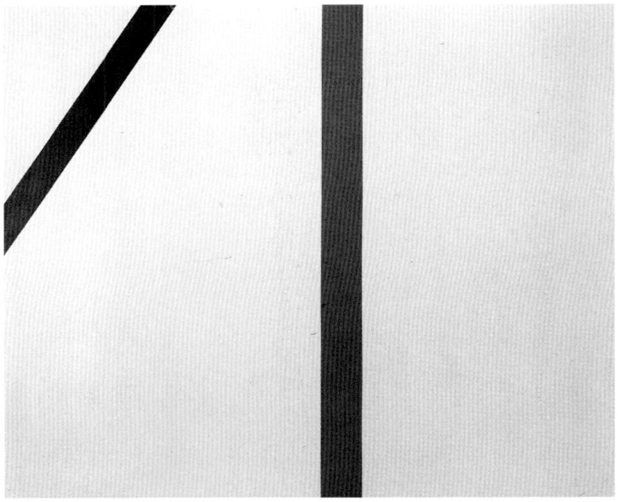

CLOSE UP #2 1967
Acrylic on canvas
170.5 x 213.7
Rose Art Museum, Brandeis University

forms and hold them in place, while simultaneously suggesting continuity. In the *Lifestream* paintings, black often unifies through outline, recalling Cézanne's impulse to reduce objects to essential form. In format, they evoke contemporary painting, recalling both the fluid calligraphy of Bradley Walker Tomlin's earlier work and Adolph Gotlieb's carefully arranged landscape symbols, while referring, in organizational structure, to the interlocking "wired" paintings of the then-contemporary, now oft-forgotten Italian abstractionist Giuseppe Capogrossi, whom Ewen regarded, for one brief moment, as a key influence on his work.[23]

In a community where disagreements regarding the surface texture of a painting in relation to hue and tone could cause barroom brawls, Ewen seemed continually restless, regarded by many as too willing to begin a new exploration and set himself a new pictorial problem. His interest in lyrical abstraction was not widely shared[24]—though John Fox shared his enthusiasm for the Italian artist Giuseppe Capogrossi, and Molinari shared his admiration for Ellsworth Kelly. Whatever Ewen's ambition, his achievement was regarded by peers and critics alike as accomplished if not, finally, fully authoritative. Molinari, a friend and admirer since the mid 1950s, recalls that in part because of his interests, "Paterson was not in the dialectic"[25] of Montreal painting.

Ewen moved to London, Ontario, in November of 1968, six months following the release of Stanley Kubrick's film *2001: A Space Odyssey*, just eight months before Neil Armstrong's walk on the moon, and barely half a year after Pierre Elliott Trudeau's prime ministerial promise of a just society. In a time of societal change, permissiveness, and deep cynicism about the prevailing political orthodoxies, Ewen moved to a city of just over 180,000 people, into an art scene that was gaining wide national attention for its liveliness, daring, and youthfulness. Its vitality was captured in the national press and celebrated in local artistic circles as well. By 1966, London had *20 Cents Magazine*, an irreverent and challenging publication on culture in and around London, and 20/20 Gallery, long regarded as the first publicly funded parallel centre in Canada, dedicated both as a "showcase for the exuberant and growing comments of artists in London"[26] and as a gallery which would "bring to London the work of major Canadian artists and exhibits from farther afield." (And succeed it did, with exhibitions by Bruce Nauman, Michael Snow, and Joyce Wieland, among others.)

"What are the signs of life?" a writer asked in the first issue of *20 Cents Magazine*, and the answer came:

> In painting, during the past year, four major Canadian painters have been working in London: Chambers, Curnoe, Trottier and Urquhart—and they are not alone; there are other established artists working here, and several younger artists who show signs of gaining recognition. Movies have been made in London that have gained recognition in major festivals in the U.S. People write poetry and plays here: James Reaney, Colleen Thiboudeau, Ronald Bates, Rae Davis, and others. They gain recognition outside of London, and

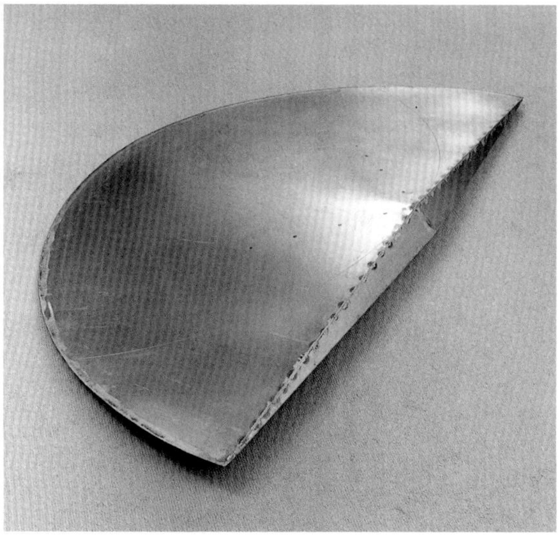 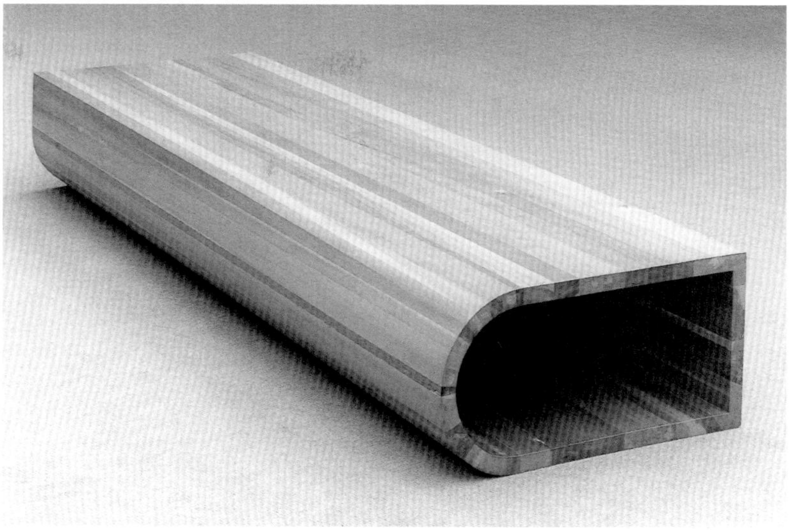

local performers play them alongside work from outside this city: Campus Players, Theatre Group, Second Theatre. London has enjoyed productions of contemporary theatre that would do credit to much larger centres. And there is an audience for this sort of thing; you can't get tickets for Second Theatre. We also have a private press and publish little magazines. In music there are organizations that exist, not on municipal or foundation support, but on the mere assumption that decent work can be done here, and that there is an audience for it. George Black's London Singers sell out year after year. Gordon Jeffrey has the nerve to put on Mozart operas and other good things in Aeolian Hall. And, in all these cases, the aim is not a church-hall amateurism, but an intellectually and artistically committed, youthful, often experimental, professionalism in the arts.[27]

Chroniclers of London's scene stressed its key qualities: namely, multidisciplinary and intergenerational conversation, and experimentation and risk. They obliquely referred to an overriding and admirable feature of the arts community, namely, its collective ambition.

Shortly before moving to London for good, it turned out, Ewen visited the London Public Library and Art Museum to see the National Gallery of Canada's presentation, the *Heart of London*, a celebration of the work of eleven London and area artists. Here the work of Greg Curnoe, Royden Rabinowitch, Bev Kelly, and Ron Martin, among others, was presented together, indicating not so much a similarity of style or intent but a collective ambition to achieve work of evident quality, responsive to the discussion and dialectic of the community. Here, Curnoe's impassioned belief about the importance of region, Jack Chambers's exquisite visual sensitivity, and David Rabinowitch's elegant and expansive sheets of rolled metal stood together not so much as a testimony to a single way of thinking, but as a commitment to the rigour of ideas formulated, refined, and rearticulated through the activity and experience of living in London.

In a matter of weeks after arriving in London, Ewen began a new series of paintings surprisingly different in meaning and subject from his previous work. Regardless of the apparent visual similarities to earlier work of flat colour and taped edges (the *Close Up* paintings, which used a bisected structure

Left:
Royden Rabinowitch
FACETED TURNOVER
1967
Welded mild sheet steel
Approx. 51.6 x 25.9 x 11.4
Art Gallery of Ontario

Right:
David Rabinowitch
OPEN PINE PIECE
1967–68
Glued laminated pine wood
304.8 x 92.1 x 45.7
Art Gallery of Ontario

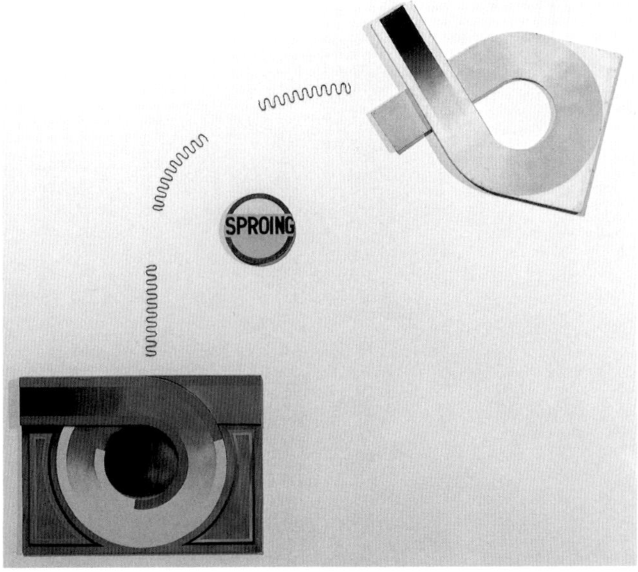

Murray Favro
SPROING 1965
Oil and automative paint on hardboard, three steel springs
77.0 x 105.5 x 4.5 (left panel), 31.0 x 2.2 (centre panel), 108.5 x 70.7 x 4.5 (right panel)
Art Gallery of Ontario

to suggest an object in both deep and immediate space), the new paintings had bold references to natural phenomena on a large scale. For nearly eighteen months, Ewen worked on three series of *Lifestream* paintings.

In each series, the *Lifestream* paintings were distilled to two colours, and the subject was their relationship—lines of one colour, whether broken or continuous, floated on a field of another colour. Rejecting the carefully placed masking tape and the fetishized paint application of his Montreal contemporaries, Ewen chose to "attack" the canvas physically: he ran at the primed canvas from a distance of five or six feet and applied masking tape in the arc of the arm's gesture or a flick of the wrist. Parallel lines were then applied with tape, and the apparently quivering, folding, and twisting line which revealed itself was painted a different colour from the ground. Lines were left to seemingly float through the ground of the painting. This was an attempt to "marry gesture and hard-edge"[28] painting and to revitalize his own interest in the creation of images.

As long as Ewen was developing imagery based on the grid and the divided canvas, as he was for almost four years, his work was roughly aligned with that of the Plasticiens. Following in their footsteps, but telescoping his own development considerably, Ewen eliminated perspective both by dividing the square and the rectangle and having each fold in upon itself, and by reducing the use of value contrasts. The effects were retinal, and colour and form played upon the responsive eye.

With the *Lifestream* paintings, Ewen's subject, for the first time, was defined within a form and a scale commensurate with its image. In relatively large canvases, Ewen suggested an interest not so much in retinal effect but rather in translating objects observed in space into a phenomenon of appearance: cognitive references and reduced signs for landscape, space, form, and calligraphy which suggested shadows, jet streams, and magnetic currents painted on the surface of the canvas. Certainly, this is how the *Lifestream* paintings were received by artists in the community. In a review of Ewen's 1970 retrospective at the 20/20 Gallery, London artist Steve Parzybok wrote of scientific principles captured in the *Lifestream* paintings, viewing them as electromagnetic wavelengths depicting colour and movement in space.[29] In a journal entry published in *20 Cents Magazine* in April of 1969, London artist Murray Favro implicitly acknowledged the context in which such paintings would be viewed, writing of Robert Fones's interest in the theory of infinity, and his own focus on issues of gravity and the discovery of space.[30] Their flat, monochromatic fields of colour notwithstanding and their Plasticien inheritance acknowledged, the *Lifestream* works very much responded to, or were a part of, the locale of their making—of Royden Rabinowitch's interest in the graphs of the audible cosmorama, of Murray Favro's depictions of objects bound by gravity (paintings such as *Sproing* and *Clunk*), and of Chris Dewdney's writings about objects moving through outer space.

In 1969, Clare Bice, the curator of the public gallery, identified at least formal similarities in highlighting Ewen's *Lifestream* paintings alongside the sculptural work of David and Royden Rabinowitch.

When Ewen moved away from Montreal in the late 1960s, he left a rigorous painting community respectful of the purity of the artistic project. London was much less committed to the orthodoxies of artmaking and far more tolerant of the speculative and the provisional in the production of art works. Where the advanced Montreal painting community of the 1960s seems, in retrospect, to have been directly tied to the Minimalist values of simplicity of gesture, severe reduction in means, and an interest in the continuum of aesthetic experience, the London art scene saw a convergence of artistic disciplines, an openness to the use of varied materials, and a notable responsiveness to the exploding values of conceptual art practices. Artmaking was, in the spirit of conceptual art, episodic not serial, bound by a spirit of living and not merely expressive of an aesthetic unity. Categories seemed to overlap, and no identity was singular and pure: Chambers was a painter and a filmmaker; Robert Fones was a maker of objects and a poet; Greg Curnoe, John Boyle, Murray Favro, and the Rabinowitch brothers were artists and musicians.

Ewen, and other artists working in London at the close of the 1960s, gained from conceptual art's expressed desire for a new articulation of "community" and a set of social relations not governed by the traditional art world orthodoxies. They rejected, as the conceptual artists did, what the critic Lucy Lippard has called the "frame and pedestal syndrome."[31] And, while Ewen's own pleasure in the sensuality of materials suggests a distance from conceptual art in any pure and theoretical sense, the dramatic break within the material conventions of his own artmaking practice[32] was unthinkable without the example of artists "making use of non-art forms and systems drawn from the everyday conventions of life, and of diverse disciplines such as anthropology, philosophy and literature."[33] Risks with materials were encouraged in the London community: Ron Benner used plywood, Dorene Inglis incorporated sheet metal in her paintings, and Dave Gordon applied self-adhesive stars to the surface of his drawings. Fascination with conceptual art practices pointedly removed from the traditional objects of art was shared by a range of London artists. Certainly, artists in London were responsive to the ideals of conceptual art in their work, even if the applications were oddball and the work markedly different in appearance from the work of contemporaries such as Hanne Darboven, Sol Lewitt, Robert Smithson, Victor Burgin, or Gilbert and George. Steve Parzybok and Murray Favro created machines which played with the optics of sight and the layering of visual fields, and Greg Curnoe had long held dear a central tenet of conceptual art, namely to deny any split between art and life.[34] Conceptual art's dominance at the time—at least in a scholarly and critical milieu—determined that traditional painting practices were looked at anew. Ewen was not alone in questioning his past practice: in 1969 Murray Favro destroyed much of his previous work when, as he wrote, "I could not accept any of my work as being any good."[35]

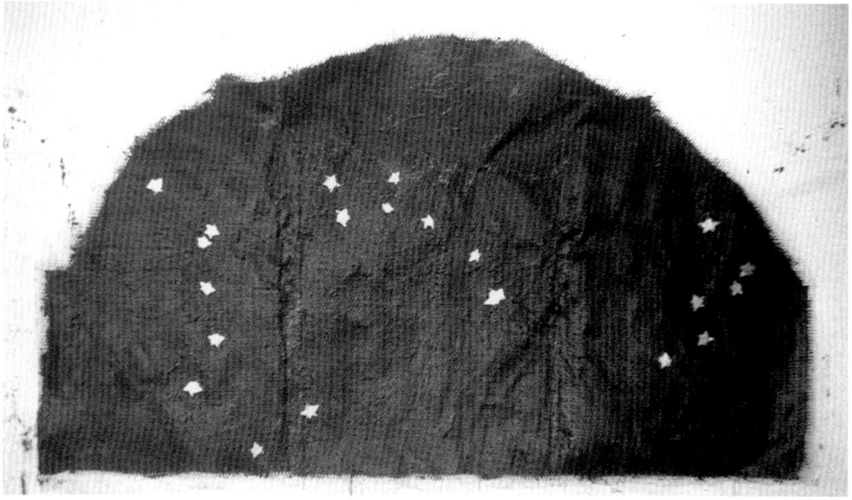

Dave Gordon
THREE CONSTELLATIONS 1971
Chicken wire, cheese-cloth, acrylic, latex, metal
152.4 x 304.8
Collection of the artist

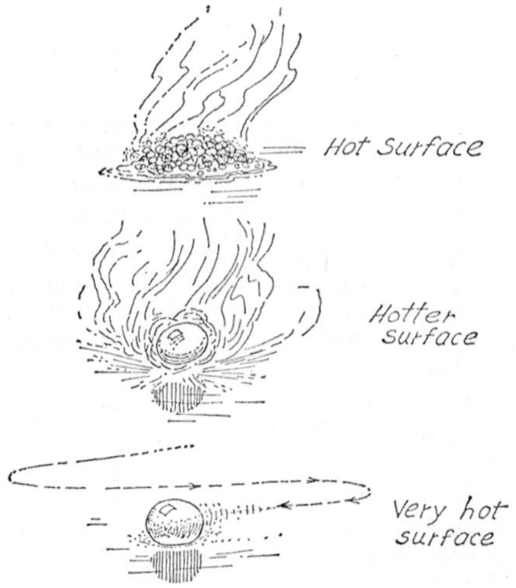

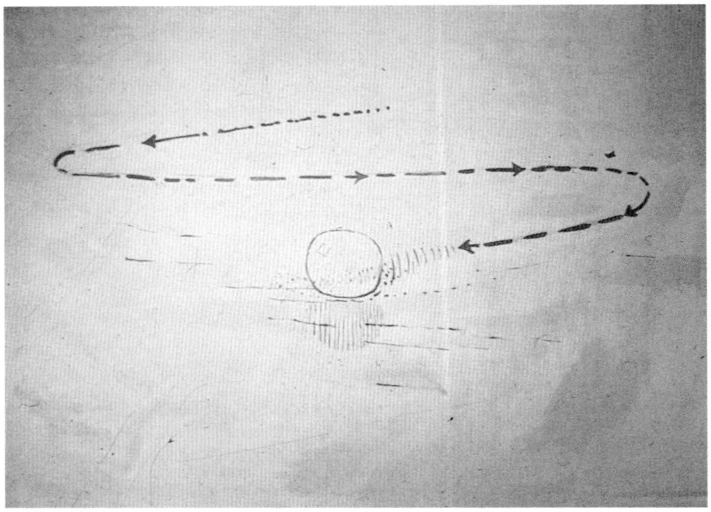

Left:
"Drop of water in a hot frying pan"
Figure 37 from D.C. Blanchard, *From Raindrops to Volcanoes* (New York: Doubleday, 1967)

Right:
DROP OF WATER ON A HOT SURFACE 1970
Acrylic on canvas
304.8 x 365.8
(Destroyed)

Facing page:
HOW LIGHTNING WORKED IN 1925 1971
Metal, rubber and wood on plywood
3 units ea. 121.9 x 242.5
Carmen Lamanna Gallery

Ewen was certainly encouraged by the climate of experimentation in the London art community. No doubt challenged by some to break with past practice—David Rabinowitch apparently criticized his overtly formalist tendencies[36]—Ewen was a part of the community and open to the impulses that came from late-night conversations. Phenomena, after all, was a concept very much in the discourse of the London community in 1969. The Rabinowitch brothers often talked of mass and volume in relation to the phenomenon of objects moving in space, and both Dave Gordon's constellation pieces and Murray Favro's "dreams of mechanical Op Art—lots of little moving moons"[37]—were part of the London scene. (Favro had realized his *Flapping Machine* in 1967, literalizing a desire to explore space.) The idea of the fantastic was very much present, as was the heralding of highly personalized cosmologies. In this small group of artists, there was much talk and enthusiasm for the new work of the American painter Philip Guston. As Dave Gordon recalled: "Guston's crazy cartoon-like paintings with the hob-nail boots and sinister Ku Klux Klansmen in hoods were showing up in the magazines in '69 and '70 and I think they had a big effect. We saw Guston's new work as a huge breakthrough by a respected, gilt-edge Abstract Expressionist that sanctioned humour, pathos, and the personal as content."[38]

Ewen saw in Guston's example a willingness to accept representational imagery again and a related conviction that old themes of art could be imbued with meaning resonant with contemporary values. He responded to Guston's creation of a personal world, realized on a grand scale. No doubt he also saw in Guston's depictions of a solitary figure struggling with constraints of history and convention a parallel to his own battle with the history of painting practices, and the often overwhelming problematic question: how do I find my place and my escape at the same time?

Ewen did something different with this impulse and graphic subject matter from what his fellow artists in London did: he took it out of the everyday and cloaked it with the heroic. Following *Traces Through Space* (1970), Ewen realized a number of large-scale paintings on canvas that made explicit, in greater degree, his interest in phenomena. Collectively, these works are joined by an articulation of the diagrammatic. They represent natural phenomena not through pictorial means but through schema, namely translations into a system of making marks. Various symbols—positive and negative signs, arrows, circles as droplets of rain—are used to

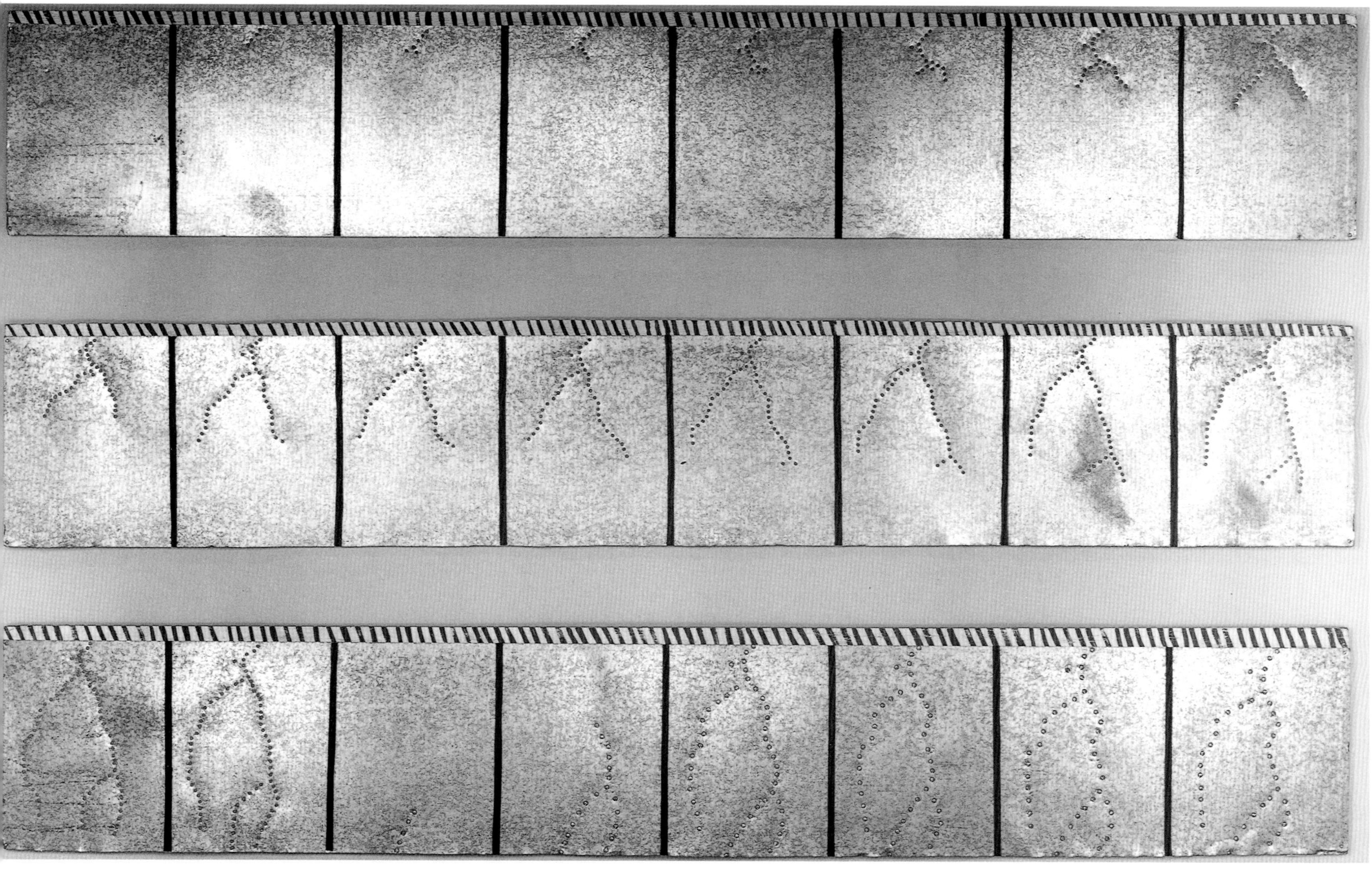

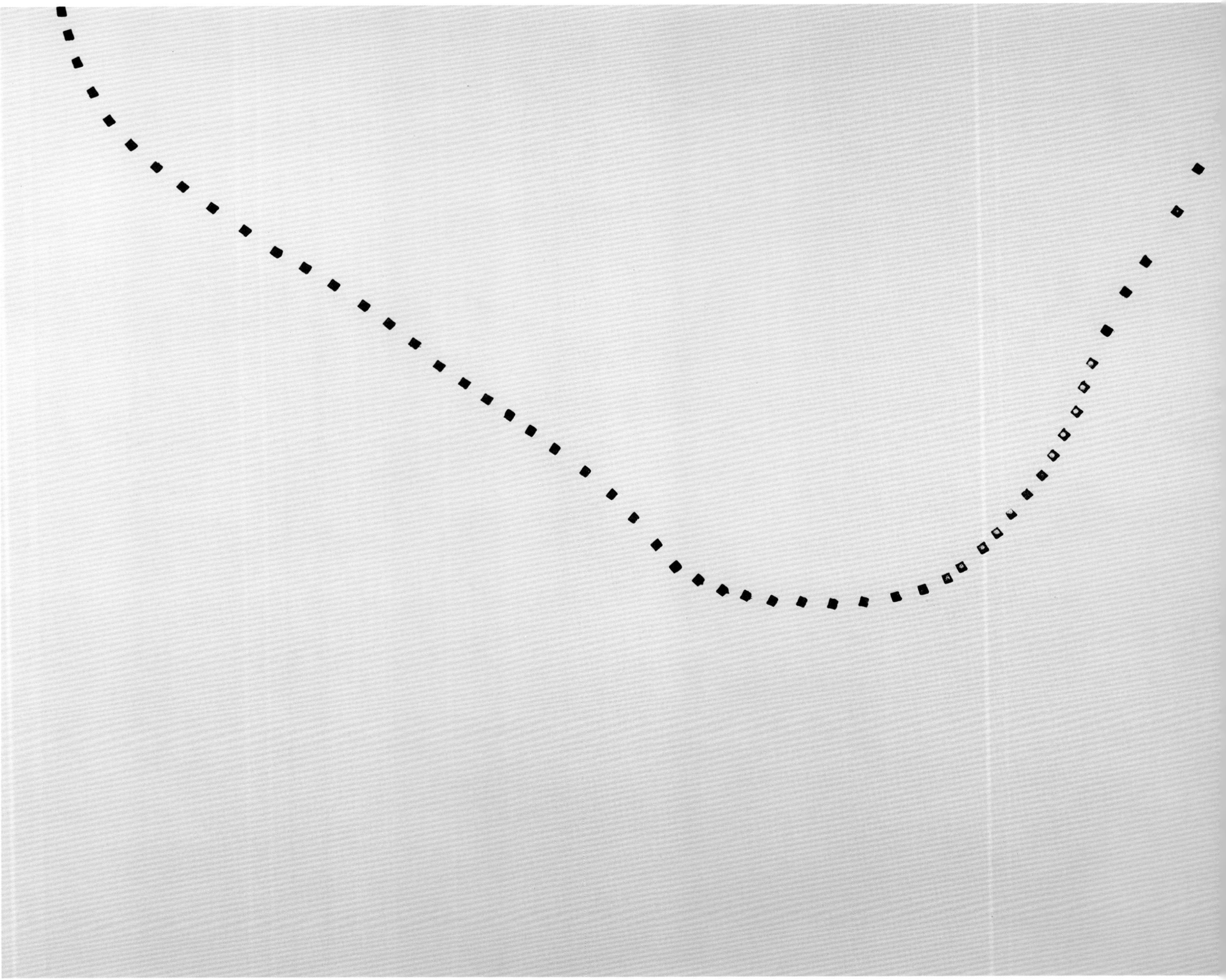

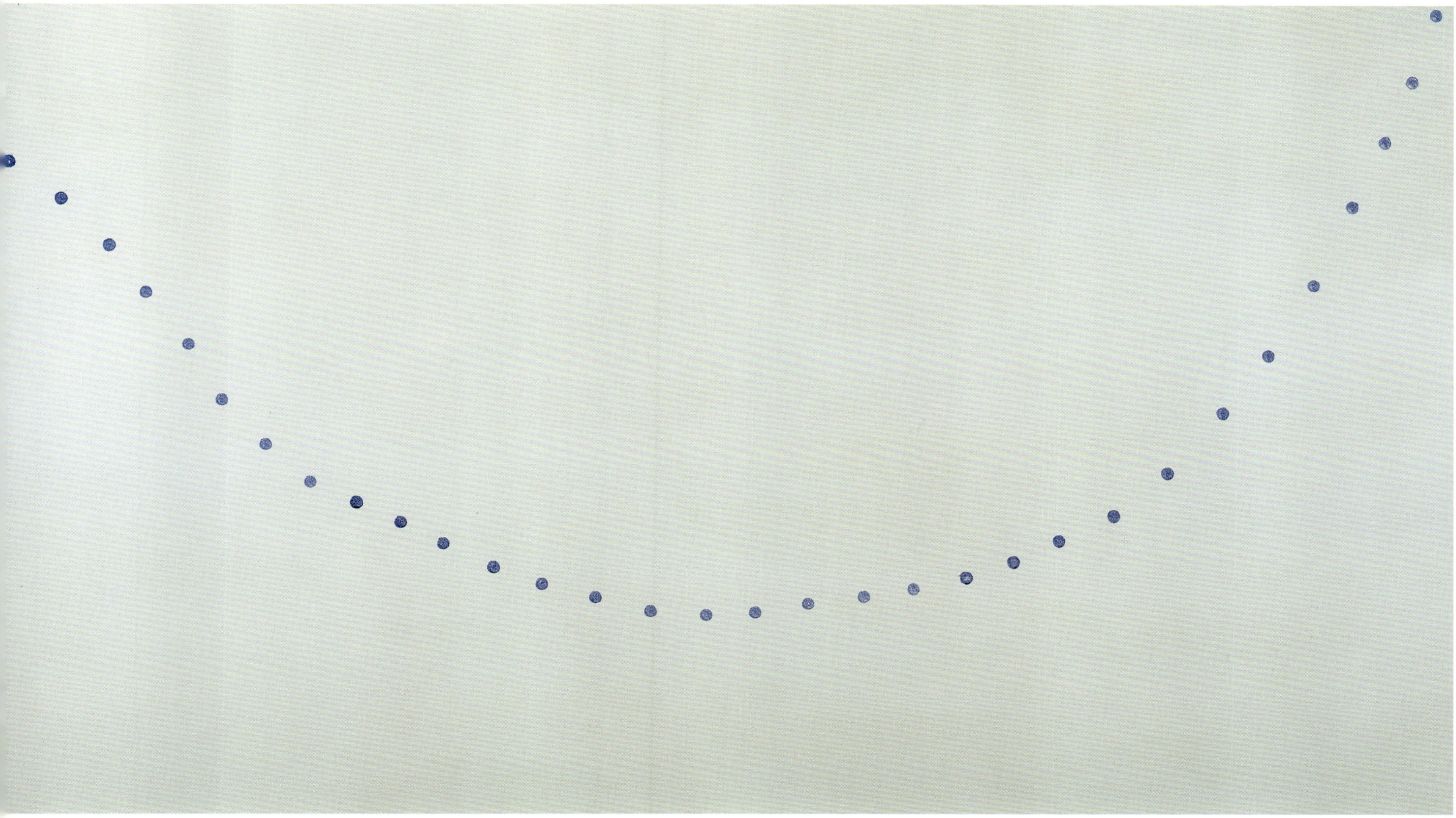

FORKED LIGHTNING

1971

Mixed media on plywood

244.0 x 122.0

Private Collection

Page 64:

TRACES THROUGH SPACE 1970

Acrylic on canvas

172.7 x 213.4

Art Gallery of Ontario

Page 65:

BLUE DOTS 1971

Acrylic on canvas

136.5 x 243.7

Art Gallery of Ontario

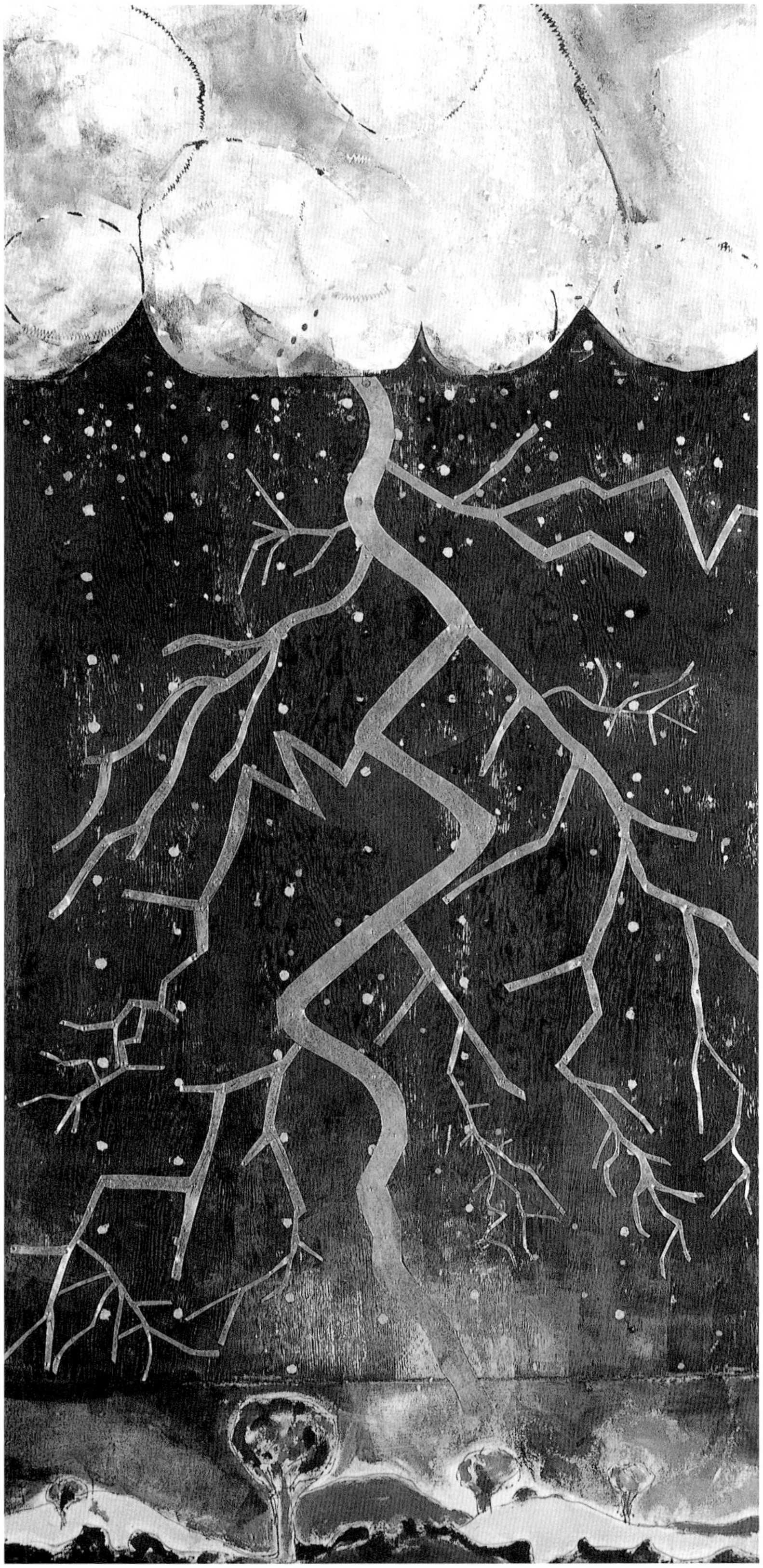

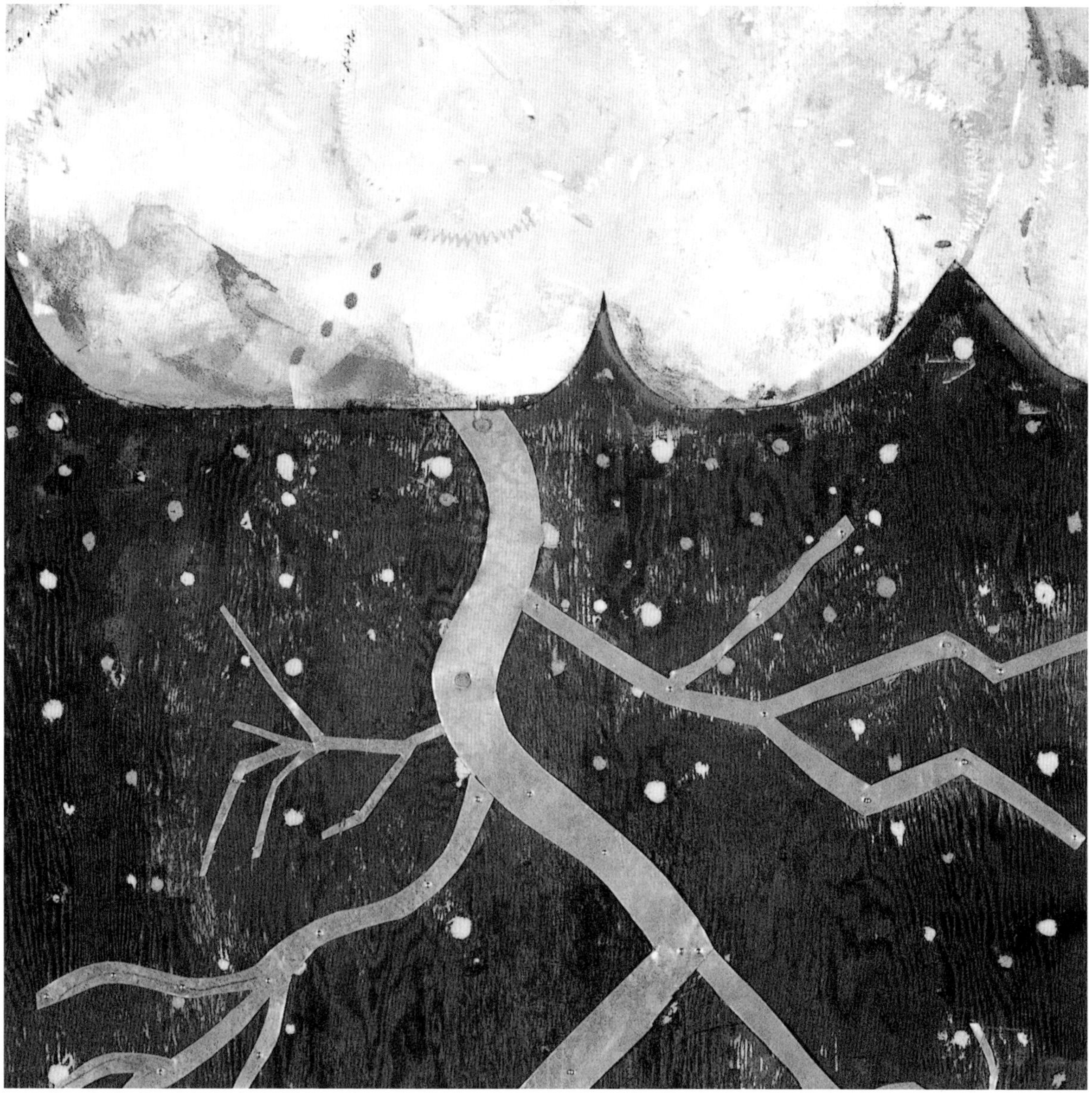

FORKED LIGHTNING

(detail) 1971

Mixed media on plywood

244.0 x 122.0

Private Collection

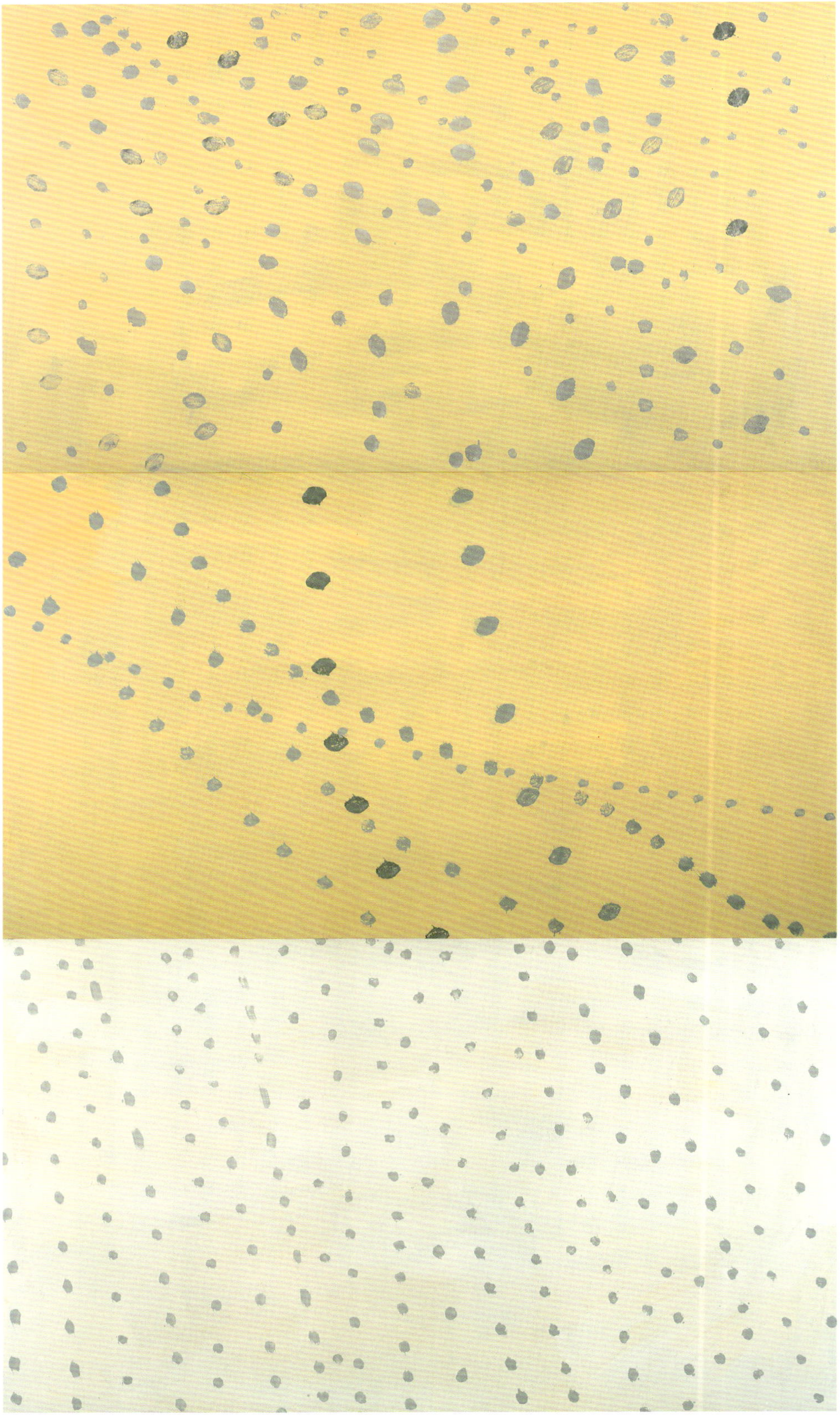

RAIN TRIPTYCH 1970
Acrylic on canvas
136.0 x 243.5 (each panel)
Art Gallery of Ontario

Facing page:
SOLAR ECLIPSE 1971
Acrylic on engraved plywood
121.9 x 243.8
Vancouver Art Gallery

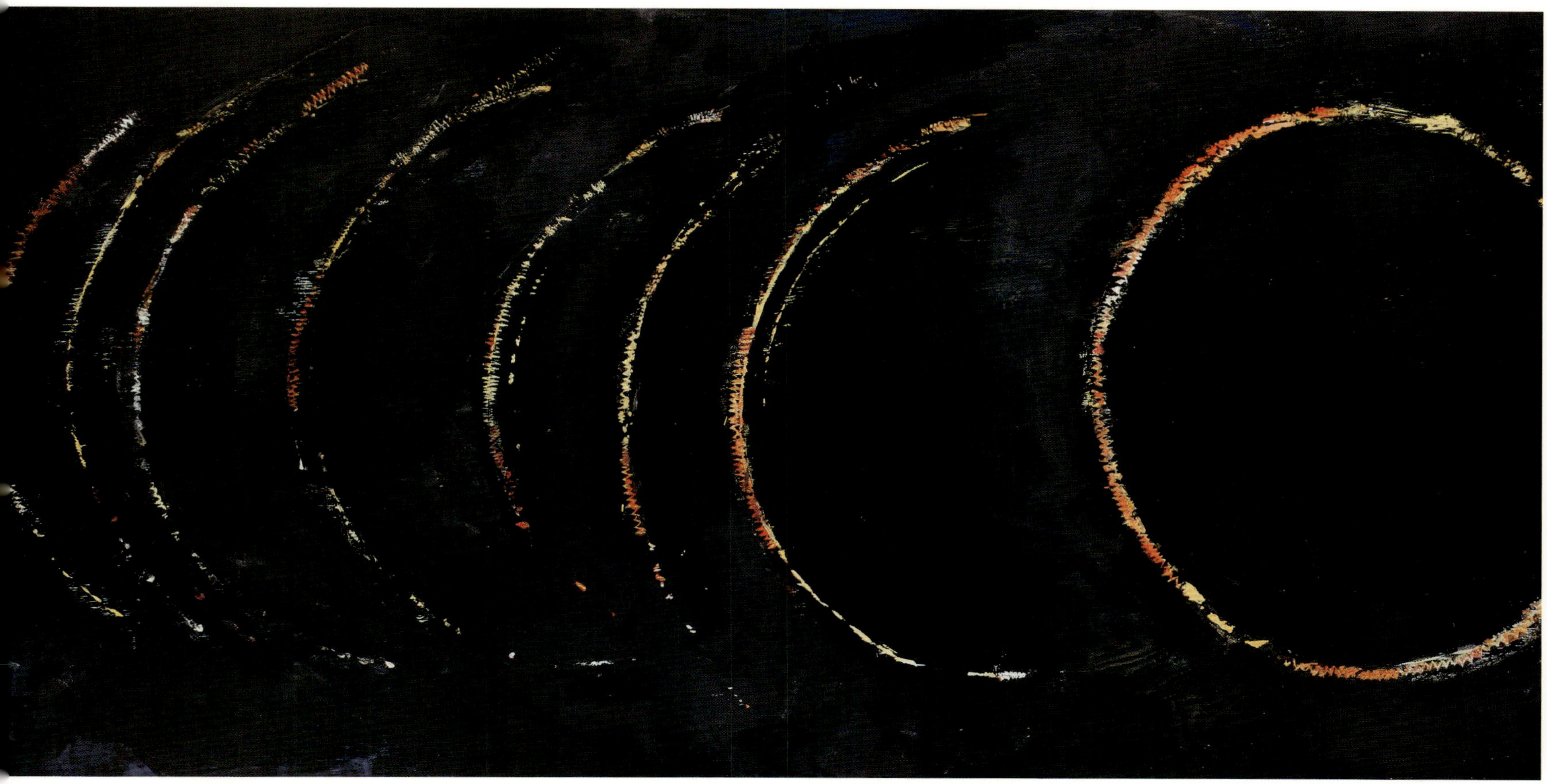

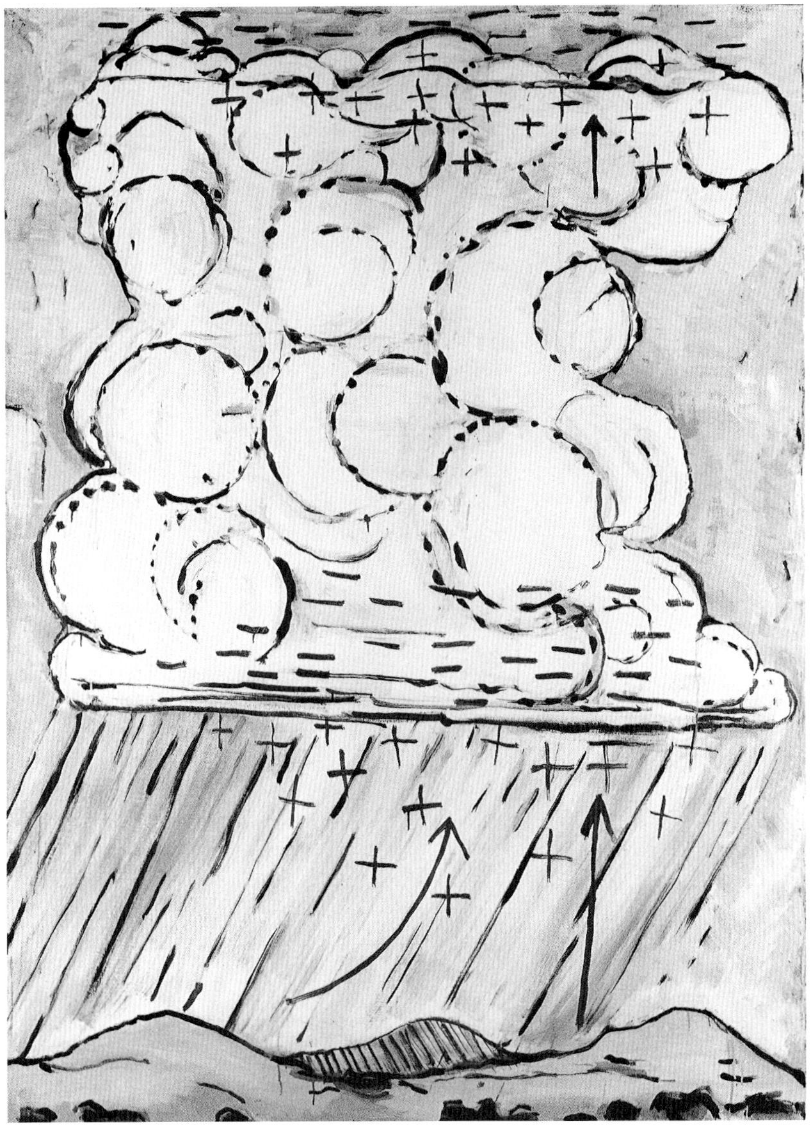

THUNDER CLOUD AS GENERATOR #1 1971
Acrylic on canvas
213.4 x 152.4
London Regional Art Gallery

Facing page:
THUNDER CLOUD AS GENERATOR #2 1971
Acrylic on canvas
244.5 x 183.0
Art Gallery of Ontario

explain the observed world and thus articulate the reasons why certain phenomena occur. These were: first *Drop of Water on a Hot Surface* (1970), *Rain Triptych* (1970), then *Blue Dots* (1971), *Flag Effect* (1971), *Artesian Well* (1971) and later, two versions of *Thunder Cloud as Generator*.[39] At the same time, he completed a short series of works on paper, titled simply *Rain*.

Thunder Cloud as Generator #2 (1971): With its pendant, Thunder Cloud as Generator #1 (1971), this work is a crucial expression of an articulate interest in the power of natural phenomena. Where Traces Through Space (1970) and other works articulate an interest in the way things work, Thunder Cloud as Generator #2 conjures up directly the consequential power and inevitability of the cycles of nature, literally a depiction of a relation of natural elements which creates energy as a generator does. Here, power and movement are suggested as a diagram of the literal energy force that natural elements create: a dance of positive and negative fields, air masses that twist and explode when confronted with one another.

Ewen's interest in the schematic was rooted in a childhood fascination with amateur science (and an early sense that art and science were somehow linked as fields of exploration). Thunder Cloud as Generator #2 is thus linked to the concerns of the Lifestream paintings. "I got interested in air currents," Ewen later remarked, "and well, there are scientific diagrams [where] you can't really see an air current, so they're always described diagrammatically in science books, and those dotted lines and dashes and things fascinated me, it reminds me of Leonardo da Vinci's drawing, you know he tends to draw in dots and dashes."[40] Indeed, in those celestial maps of the sixteenth and seventeenth centuries realized in da Vinci's time, a clear cartographic language is apparent. Cartographers of the heavens utilized the technique of projection, co-ordinates, and symbols in order to translate information and concepts into graphic form, and Ewen translated these into principles of a modernist painting practice.

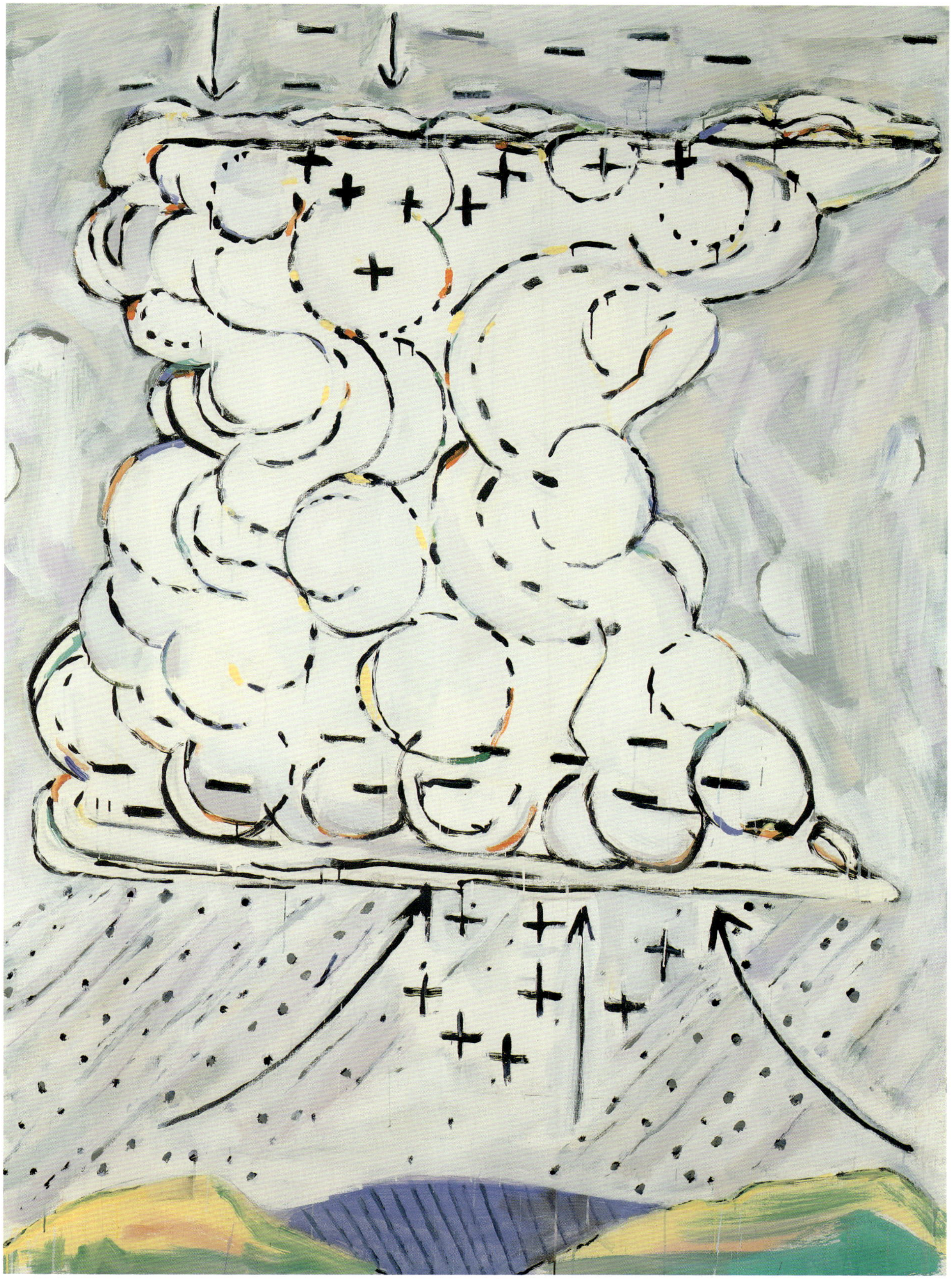

MOON OVER WATER

1977

Acrylic on galvanized steel and gouged plywood

228.6 x 243.8

Art Gallery of Ontario

Three paintings on wood supports followed in the spring of 1971: *Rocks Moving in the Current of a Stream*, *How Lightning Worked in 1925*, and *Thunderchain*. Each shared the incorporation of varied materials including plywood, sheet metal, and aluminum screws. Each was diagrammatic, as were the previous paintings, though each was characterized both by a use of sculptural material and by addressing isolated rather than continuous elements of natural phenomena. In *How Lightning Worked in 1925*, still images of forked lightning were placed one beside another, in the manner of film frames, to suggest the movement of a thunderbolt; in *Thunderchain*, small incidents of nature—suspended wooden blocks—stood as "pieces" of rain and earth, and the sound of the thunderclap (always a potential thunderclap) was represented through the long, heavy chain. Nature was represented as possessed of a forceful inevitability, and the painting's capacity to signify this power was reinforced through the use of sturdy, substantial materials. Whatever ability schema had to make the natural world understandable—controllable by placing an ordering system over the seemingly unexplainable—it gained greater expressive power from the elemental feel of the materials, their unconventionality and link to everyday experience.

In the late summer of 1971, Ewen moved to Toronto (for a year). He took with him the unfinished *Thunder Cloud as Generator #1* (which he finished days after settling into his studio) and quickly realized its companion, *Thunder Cloud as Generator #2*. These were his last paintings on canvas.

And then, in a story often told, he decided to abandon painting altogether in any traditional sense: he decided to make a large Japanese woodblock print, pulled from a gouged plywood relief. He began, and it took him more than a week: the gouge pulling the surface of the plywood apart, one short pull after the other, the density of the plywood stopping or impeding the exorable push of the gouge. Paint was applied with printer's rollers "very thin so it [sank] into the unprepared wood."[41] And then: "As I was doing this and as I was painting in the gouges and as I was rolling it over with a printer's roller I realized that that was the work, and that's how it happened."[42] *Solar Eclipse* was the first work, followed quickly by *Solar Eruption*, notable for its addition of cut sheet metal to mark the edge of the sun, and soon after by three more works: *Storm over the Prairies*, *Forked Lightning*, and *City Storm with Chain Lightning*, which incorporated variously linoleum, coco-matting and chainlink on a painted and routed plywood ground. Each was large in scale, with the phenomenon of lightning represented as literally overwhelming the miniaturized and purposefully benign terrestrial ground of wheat field, countryside, and cityscape respectively.

1990–91

It was not until 1974, with paintings such as *Coastal Trip* and *Rain over Coastline*, that Ewen began in any traditional sense to incorporate the landscape into his work, and at that it became not so much corporeal presence as a framing device, a place where something happened. Since then, in concentrated series of work, Ewen's interest has predominantly been the sky by day and night, the sky in wondrous uncertainty, the sky known and unknowable.

***Moon Over Water* (1977): The broken surfaces of *Moon Over Water* evoke Ewen's lifelong interest in British painting, particularly works by Constable and Turner: more particularly, from Constable, the closely related tones brought alive in a dramatized sky, and from Turner, the ethereal light reflected off the water's surface. The incandescent moon is reflected on the surface of the water through a wisplike dusting of a thin coat of paint. It is a startling contrast to the deep, forceful gouging of the plywood sheet which leaves surfaces torn to the bare wood, and to the**

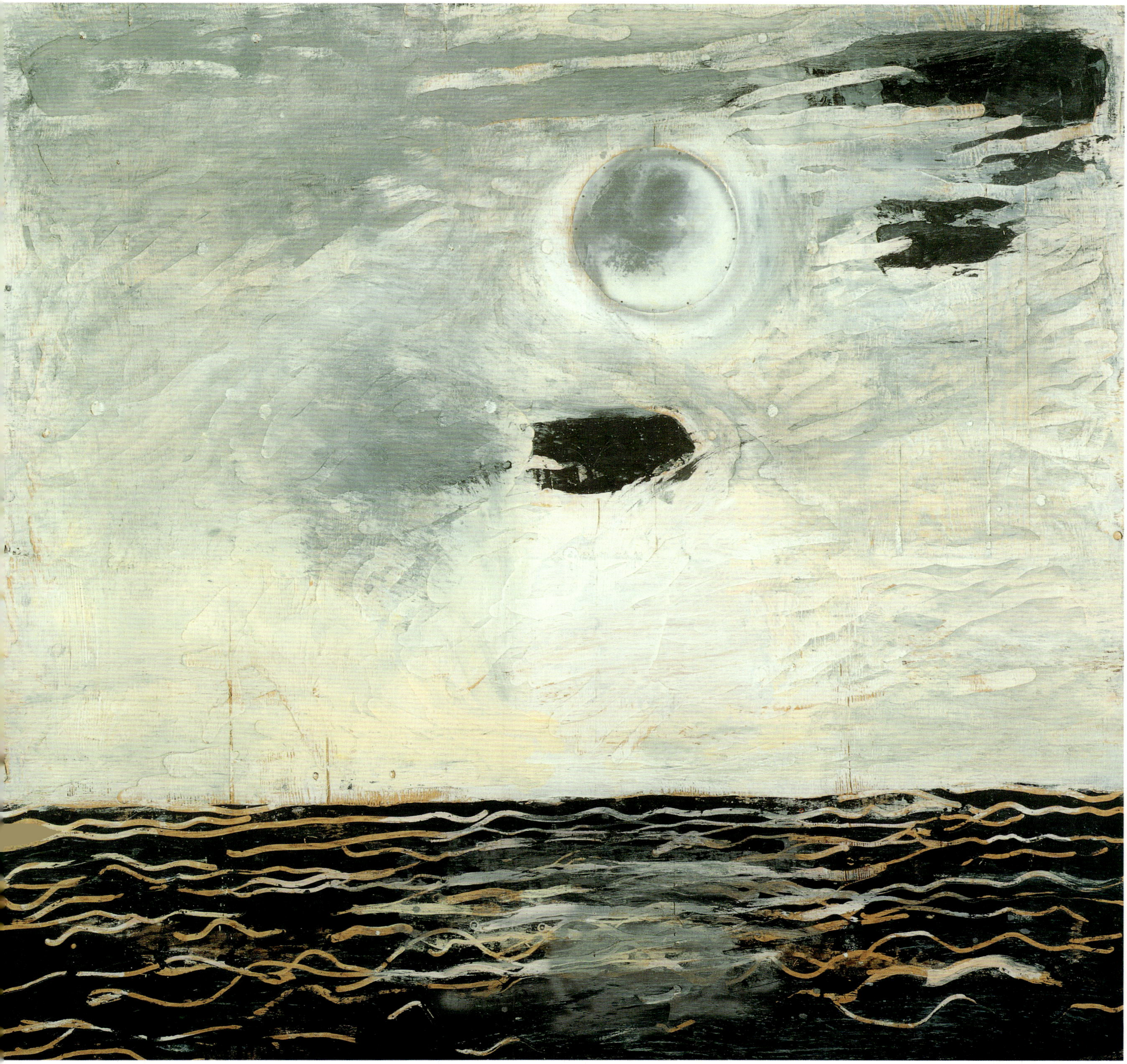

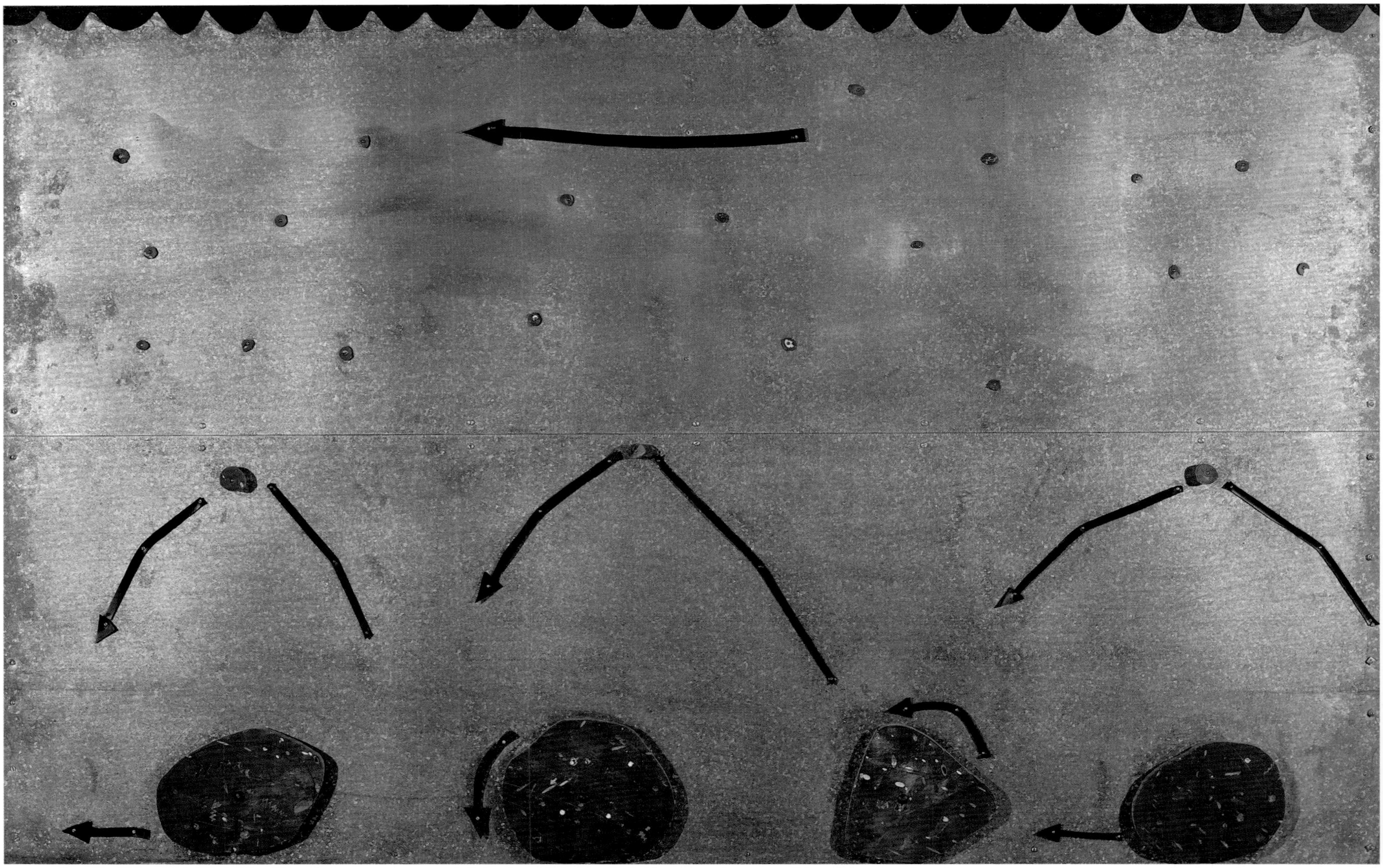

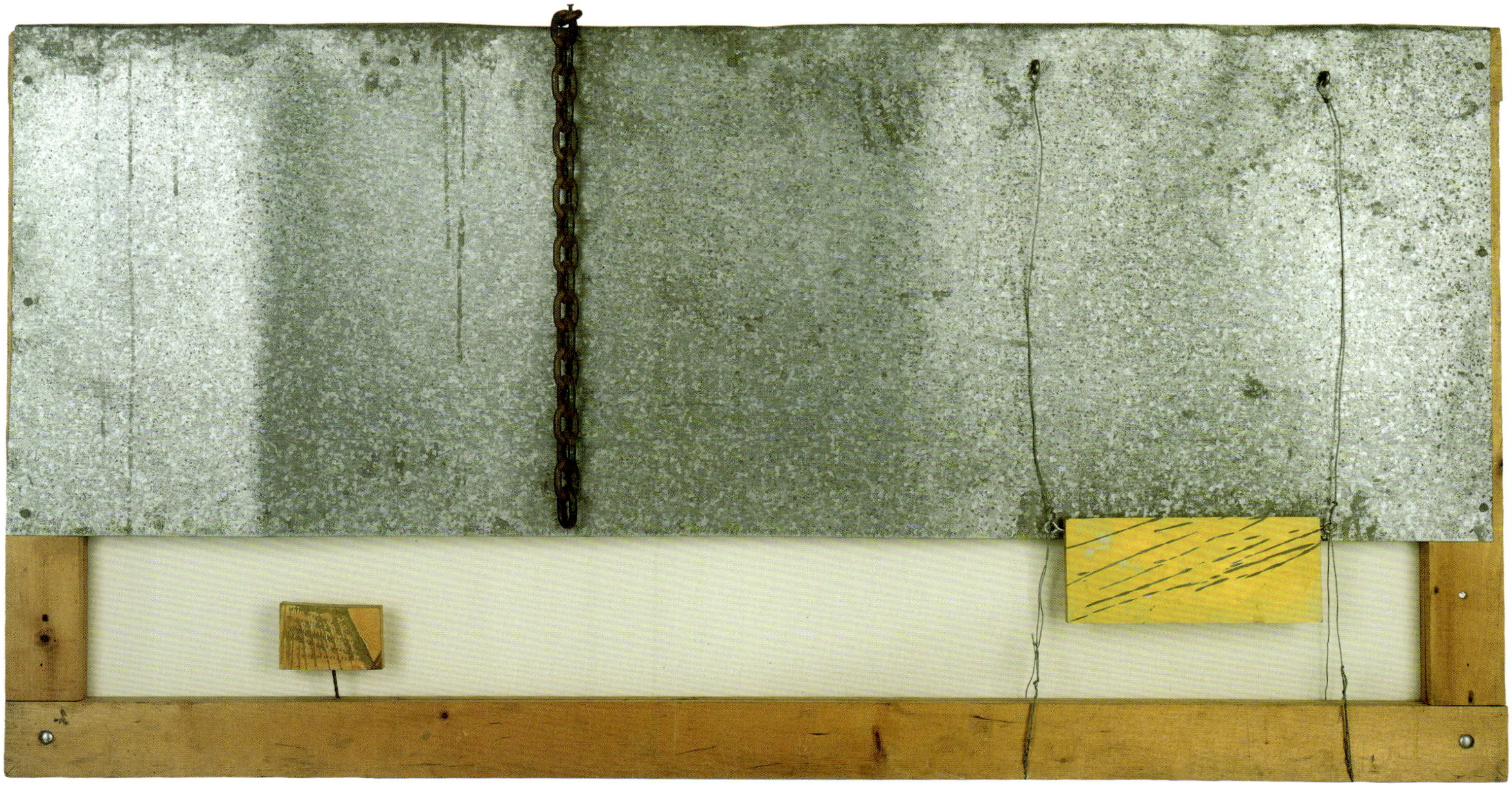

metallic insistence of the aluminum moon, riveted to the wood with scarcely hidden nails. The contrast is startling enough to seem whimsical, the painter's deft touch mimicking the softness of reflected light. It is a painting of transcribed connectedness, recalling both the beauty and pathos of nature. It is a painting so much about sensibility as to leave the word invention behind. "I don't have anything in common with Picasso emotionally as I do, let's say, with Turner," Ewen once remarked.[43]

CLOUD OVER WATER
1979
Acrylic on galvanized steel and gouged plywood
244.0 x 335.0
Art Gallery of Ontario

Page 74:
ROCKS MOVING IN THE CURRENT OF A STREAM
1971
Steel screws and bolts and nuts, rubber, linoleum, plywood, acrylic paint, galvanized steel
153.3 x 245.3
Art Gallery of Ontario

Page 75:
THUNDERCHAIN
1971
Steel bolts, wire and chain, galvanized steel, engraved linoleum, wood
94.0 x 183.0
Art Gallery of Ontario

Much has been written in recent years about the contestation of ownership and use of the land and its bounty. The landscape is, for many, no longer a neutral ground on which aspiration, fantasy, and desire are projected. It is, rather, a place possessed, and the artist's conscious decision to choose one place as subject over the other has become a key determinant of its meaning. While landscape is always layered with our obsessions, the sky is our secret place of projection—unverifiable, speculative, a place to dream. It is a place of wonder. Ewen paints things we cannot know empirically, and it is the power of the work that the hand-gouged, body-present routing that so scars the face of the wood seems to make it almost real. However much Ewen breaks through the surface of the large scarred plywood sheets and makes the personal into an epic statement, he never loses the apparent direct relation to the image. The plywood reveals struggle, hard work, engagement, connectedness. The work continually unveils process and wrests, through material, some transposed power from the depicted image. It is a strength of the work that the image feels like something, as much as it looks like a phenomenon observed.

In Ewen's work, the urge is to represent and capture the rigorous language of making something. This capturing of process exists in equal part with the desire to create an experienced

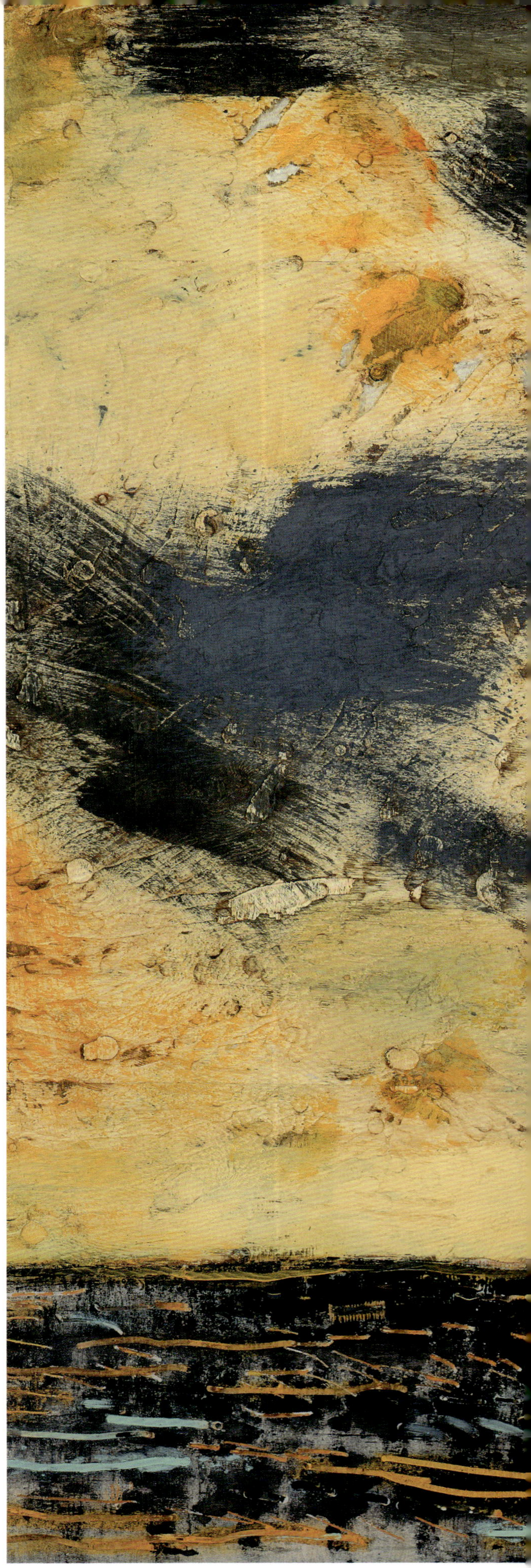

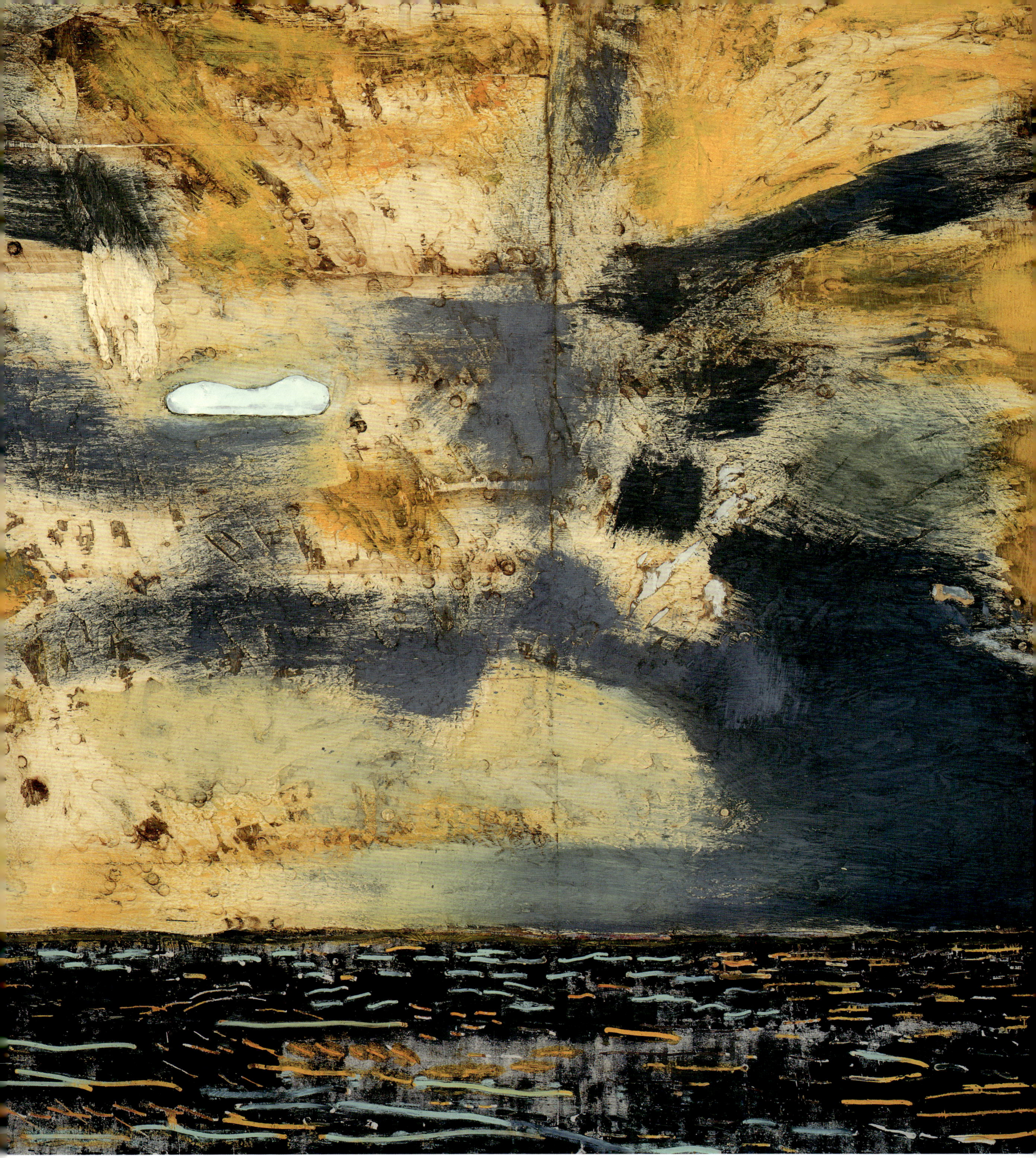

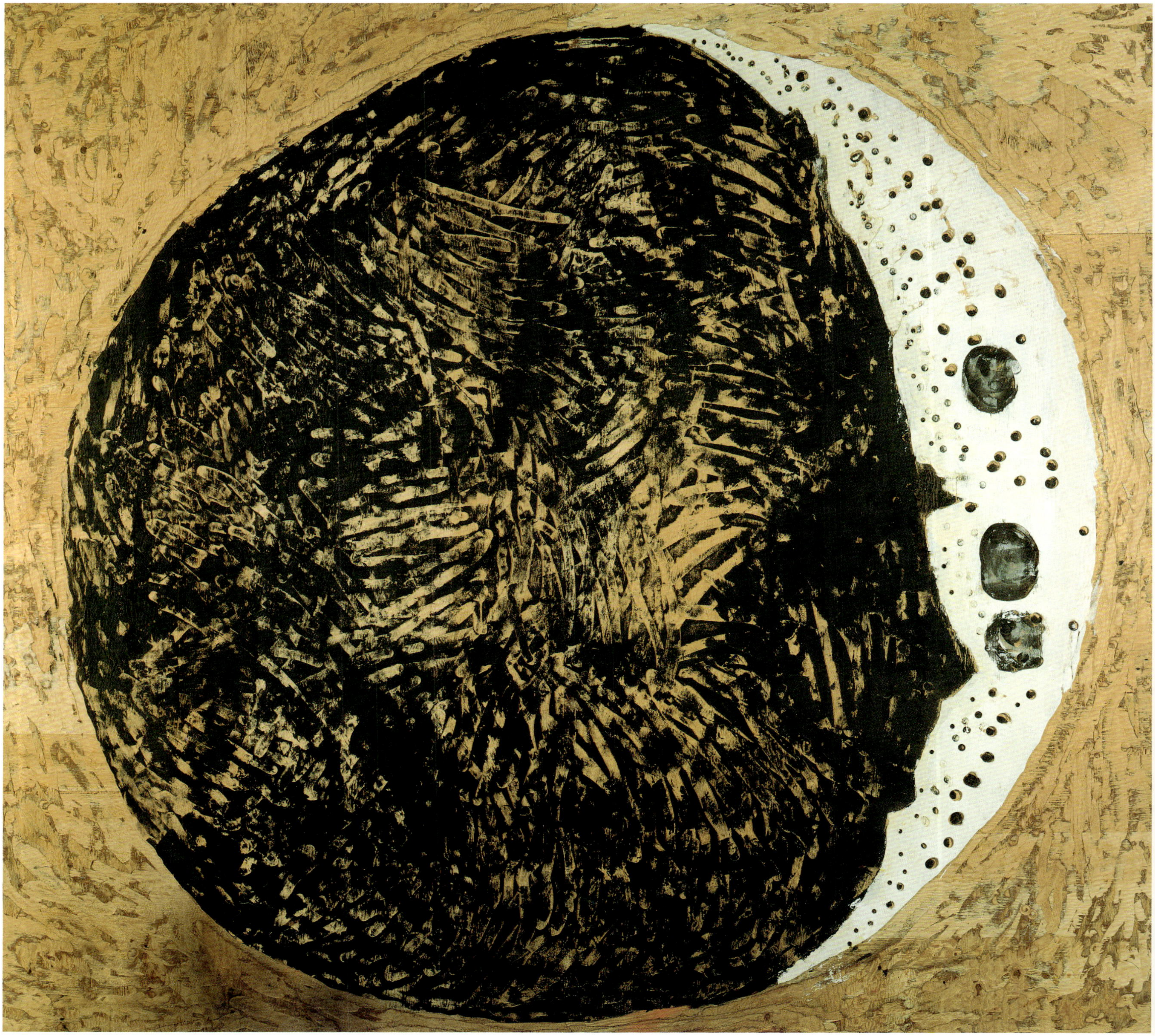

reality—a force of nature itself. Nature is mirrored in the creative act: "I observe, contemplate and then attack."[44] Movement, force, risk, these are all the qualities of creation that Ewen stresses and believes are transferred to the experience of looking. "You have to remember that up on two saw horses about four feet high it is a platform . . . I [got] up on all fours in the middle of this platform and went to work. All over the whole thing I grooved into the wood with the electrical router, changing the bit as I felt the grooves should be larger or smaller. And keeping in mind at this point now what it is that I want in terms of direction and velocity and proportion, I have to put myself in the centre of the whole thing that's going on and hold it together."[45] Ewen, in the centre of "the whole thing," encourages an empathetic relationship with the viewer who, through scale alone, is placed within the centre of the image, the landscape, the depicted deep space. By 1974, with few exceptions, Ewen began to create images with a radiant centre—moon, sun, single tree—whose energy flies unconstrained beyond the plywood edge. Here the force of nature is seen and felt as a part of the viewer's space.

The viewer is surrounded, thus thrust into space—"the centre of the whole thing that's going on"—at the moment the elegiac image is brought forward to us. We are, seemingly, given access to an image otherwise unknowable and impalpable. Through a sensibility informed in part by the Romantic tradition, we are invited to engage with something outside of ordinary experience which nevertheless completes experience. The unknowable is made real, or seemingly real, in the manner of astronomy itself. The history of astronomy is, in fact, a search for humanity's place in the centre of observable phenomena. The inexorable push is to replace popular belief, tall tales, and fanciful projections with a verifiable knowledge which can give order to the mystery of the sky. To watch and interpret the skies has been, after all, for many centuries a fundamental activity. Civilizations were developed in darkness, and ancient civilizations often knew more about the sky than about the earth. It was certainly so in matters of culture and learning. "The movements of the stars were, so to speak, the diagram of the universe as a created order," Northrop Frye has written, "and astronomy was the one science that a learned medieval poet such as Dante or Chaucer, would naturally be assumed to know. Dante's Paradiso is symbolized by the heavenly bodies, and the starry spheres, with their unheard harmonies, form the central image of nature as God had originally designed it, before the lower part 'fell' with man into unsymmetrical chaos."[46] Older cultures used and shared this knowledge (everyone could see the sky) in their search for order and common codes: in other words, their search for ordered space. To search in the sky is to establish what is real, to make empirical what seems ephemeral, and to root us more securely to where we stand. The sky we dream into is the sky that leads us to the act of measuring, of creating calendars, and of establishing fixity in the structure of time.

***Eclipse of the Moon* (1990): The moon is not a human creation, but our pictures of it are. We know the moon through television, the map, the photograph, the diagram. It is real to us by virtue of the images that we make of it. Since 1971, the moon has been Ewen's most favoured subject, a virtual field in which great and varied states are recorded: a day moon, a night moon, a gibbous moon, a half moon. *Eclipse of the Moon* represents the dark emptiness cast by the moving moon as it passes the sun. The deeply routed surface evokes the meeting of two energy forces directly tied to both the earth's rotation, and changes in the cycles of days and months.**

ECLIPSE OF THE MOON

1990

Acrylic on gouged plywood

266.8 x 297.6

Art Gallery of Ontario

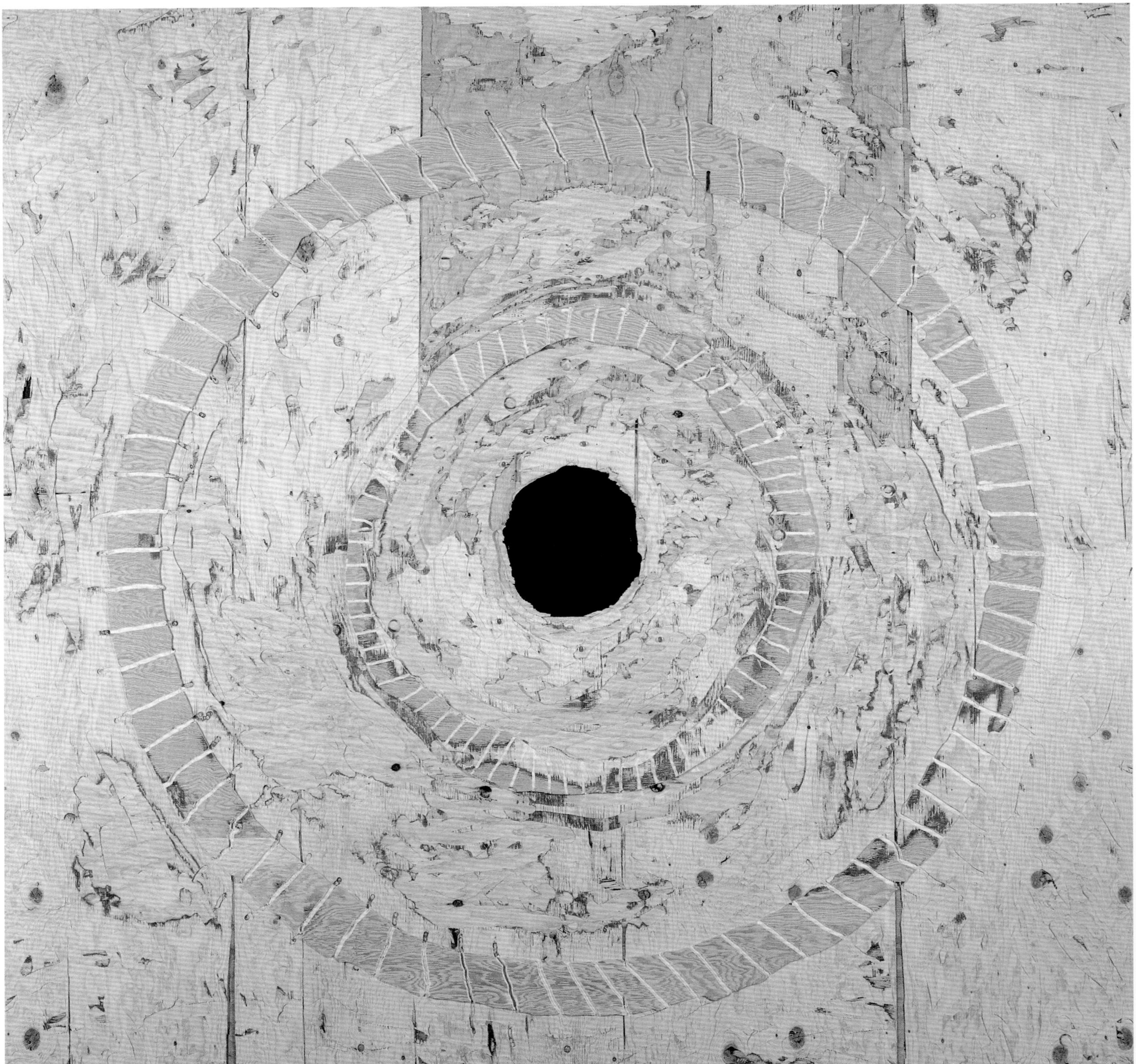

For Ewen, process is directly linked to scale. To an evident degree, the scale of the plywood work serves to place us within the phenomenon we see, and the surface activity of the worked plywood reaches out to us. The act of gouging, routing, chiselling, of taking away from the surface of the wood, is a form of restoration. That the energy of the distressed surface becomes the energy of the wood itself is nowhere more apparent than in a number of works notably pared down in colour, completed between 1989 and 1991. More dependent than ever before on the inherent life of the plywood itself (and less on the surface drama that colour provides), the accent is on one embedded gesture or another. In images routed from the bare plywood, the subject is present as ghosts might be. It is precisely the power of the paintings that they bring us close without unlocking the mystery of the image. Power again: these works inevitably lead us through the amateur scientist's quest to the impulse to see nature as operatic and individualistic. Ewen—an artist who has never depicted a figure in a landscape nor created an image of two figures interacting—believes as the Romantics did in a "kind of creative and healing alienation to be gained from solitary contact with the order of nature outside of society."[47]

Satan's Pit **(1991): With paint applied only in reflected light of the moon,** ***Satan's Pit*** **is surprising for its minimal means. It relies on stark contrast: the dark void of the moon itself—here realized as a sheet of darkened steel affixed to the plywood from behind—set against the bare wood (a seemingly infinite field).** ***Satan's Pit*** **was made, the fifth in a series, by routing through the plywood rather than simply on its surface. Its subject is image and process; its image mimics its making. The energy of the painting collapses completely inward, towards the centre, and then outward again, as if on the rebound. The black hole, which is the scarred centre of the work itself, absorbs and reflects, bringing the viewer in and pushing out at the same time.**

Where do these paintings come from? What are their sources, their inspiration, and what is the experience of the artist that leads to the creation of imagery and bonds this imagery to subject matter? Simply put: the struggle for comprehension.

In a career now spanning six decades, the desire to link the apprehended natural world with an affective transcription of the power of its phenomena has led Ewen through various phases of development and insight. Such a desire, with its related struggle, has been a constant in all that he has done. For Ewen, the natural world, constituted from separate parts, is made whole in the act of making a painting; comprehension is that level of understanding that allows the parts to coalesce into one. From his first explorations with the reduction of form nearly fifty years ago, through the schematic illustration of process at the close of the 1960s, to a new continuing mimetic recreation of nature's grandeur, Ewen's search has been, almost without exception, to make the observed world tangible and real. The breakthrough for Ewen came at that moment when he found his own way to articulate and represent not the look of the natural world, but the principles of how it could function. Although the seeds of achievement and attainment were there long before, his breakthrough was realized through his own engagement with process, a renewed commitment to materials and a release into epic scale. His work of the last twenty-five years has stood as testimony to the cycles of nature, its terror, and its beauty. He has created images to believe in, and he has done so through a subject rooted in the image's making. Ewen leads us into the dramatic action; he never withdraws us from it. We are on the edge, between what we know and what is unknowable, and it rains.

SATAN'S PIT 1991
Coloured steel, bolts and acrylic paint on gouged plywood
229.0 x 244.0
Art Gallery of Ontario

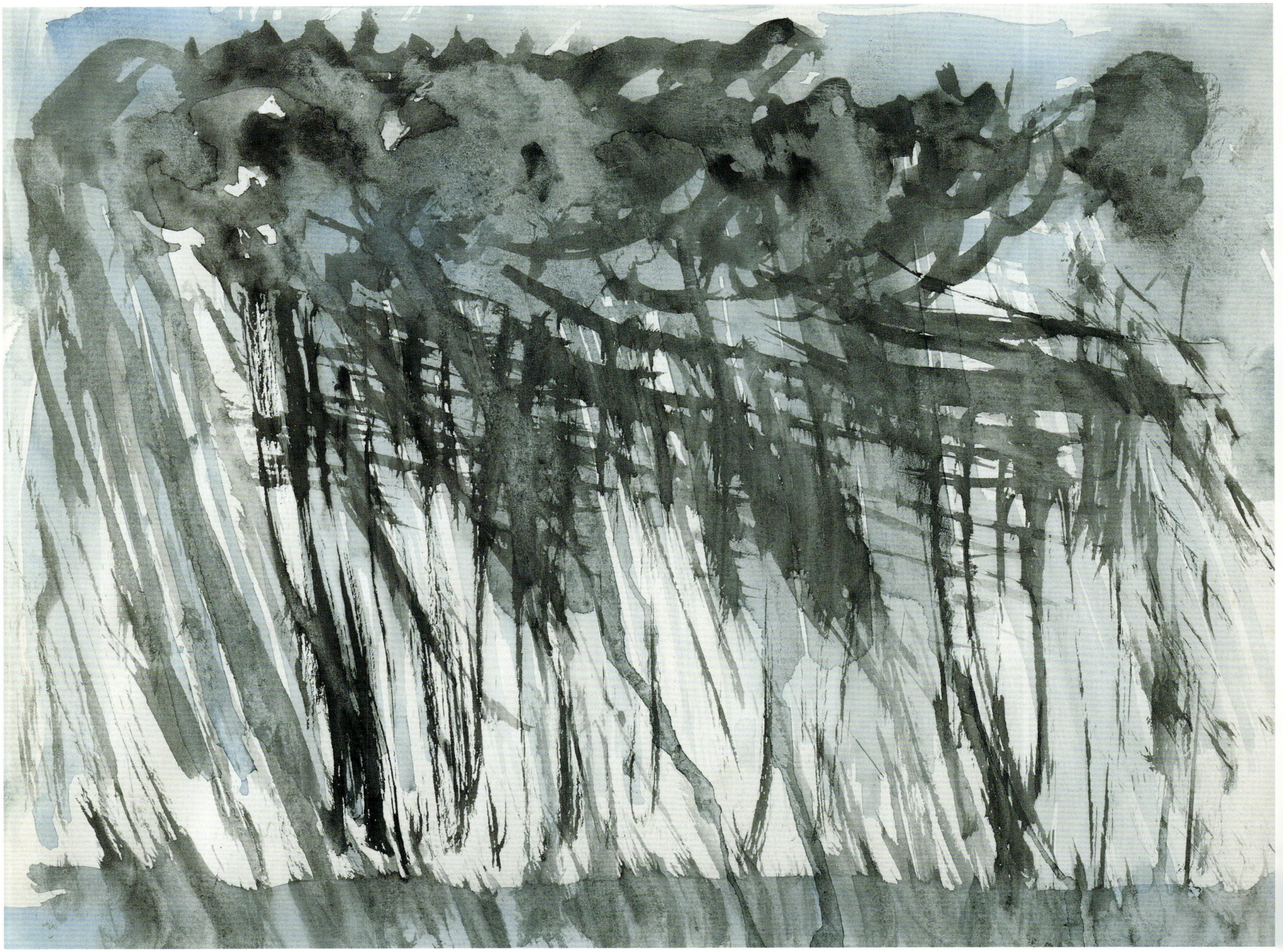

ENDNOTES

1. Goodridge Roberts, "From This Point I Looked Out," *Queen's Quarterly*, Autumn 1953.
2. Ewen read *The Meaning and Purpose of Art* in 1948, on the recommendation of Tony Wand, his closest friend in the Canadian Army, with whom he shared considerable reading interests during the war and afterwards.
3. Arthur Howell, *The Meaning and Purpose of Art* (The Ditchling Press: Ditchling, Sussex, 1945), p. xv.
4. Howell, p. 57.
5. The Automatistes committed themselves to an art freed from history, from intention, and from the constraints of convention and expectation. Magic, spontaneity, surrationality, and automatisme: these words are used again and again in various writings by group members to suggest an art born of free will itself. They were directly and purposefully opposed to all expressions of intention. For Borduas, as for others, intention was "the two-edged, perilous sword of REASON." Reason implied control and hierarchy, values resonant with much that was considered negative in a religious orthodoxy that was all-pervasive. (Indeed, so rigid was the orthodoxy that, in 1950, two seminary students were expelled from study simply for viewing an exhibition by Jean-Paul Mousseau and Marcelle Ferron.) Intention implied all those plastic values that Automatisme rejected, namely illusionistic perspective, tonal modelling, and sequential arrangement of form.

   For the Automatistes, freedom was expressed through paintings, dance, and texts which celebrated chance as an opening to the unknown. Chance, or accident, was heralded as a sign of true release into unpremeditated space, a pathway to the unconscious. In "Dance and Hope," her text for the Automatiste manifesto, *Refus global*, Françoise Sullivan reflected a generally shared enthusiasm for the Surrealist exploration of the unconscious and wrote of her belief that the "true and profound treasure to be found in the unconscious is energy." The result was an art that discovered and opened new worlds for artist and audience alike. Sullivan wrote: "The spectator witnesses an efflorescence

STORM WITH WIND

1987

Watercolour on paper

22.8 x 30.4

Art Gallery of Ontario

of life taking shape before his eyes. He can be moved by the pathos, or transported by ecstasy. The spectacle must act upon him, change something in him. That is the source of its usefulness, of its magic."

6. It is not surprising that of the Automatistes closest to Ewen—his wife Françoise and Claude Gauvreau—neither was a painter. Each, as a dancer and playwright respectively, realized their work through actual representations of the body, the corporeal being in real space, no matter how abstracted the vehicles of shadow, light, movement, and gesture became. Above all, and in distinction to those painters with whom they were connected, Sullivan and Gauvreau depicted a corporeal livingness through figures embodying feeling and life experience.
7. For an excellent account of these fissures, see Ray Ellenwood, *Egregore* (Toronto: Exile, 1992), pp. 243-53.
8. Jean Dénéchaud, "Paterson Ewen," *La Presse*, Montreal, May 10, 1950.
9. Jean-Paul Mousseau in conversation with the author, Montreal, November 10, 1986.
10. To date, no recorded comments by Borduas on Ewen's work have been verified. The word "generosity" was recalled by Ewen in a conversation with Doris Shadbolt. See Doris Shadbolt, *Paterson Ewen: Recent Works* (Vancouver Art Gallery: Vancouver, 1977), unpaginated. In his files, Borduas kept a note, likely written by the poet Rémi-Paul Forgues on the invitation card for *Les Étapes du vivant*, which states: "une espèce de Soutine via Bonnard."
11. Pierre Gauvreau in conversation with the author, by telephone from St. Armand Ouest, Quebec, February 8, 1987.
12. The full quote reads: "You are judging Pat Ewen too harshly. Appearances can be deceiving! Granted Ewen's current work contributed nothing to knowledge, nor does it yet have the visual brilliance of other artists, but at least what he did exhibit was authentic. Pat's work will develop." Gauvreau to Jean-Claude Dussault in Claude Gauvreau, *Correspondance, 1949–1950* (Montreal: l'Hexagone, 1993). I am grateful to Ray Ellenwood for bringing this letter to my attention.
13. Jean-Paul Mousseau and Marcelle Ferron had been rejected by the jury, and Paul-Émile Borduas alone among the Automatistes had been accepted. Among the twelve artists in *L'Exposition des Rebelles*, three had shown in the spring exhibition that year—Borduas, Matthew Babinski and Ewen.
14. The expressed theme of *Les Étapes du vivant* was to "illustrate how the visual arts evolved from nature to the representational to automatisme."
15. Ewen's paintings placed him outside the Montreal Museum of Fine Arts' exhibition *The Borduas Group* in January of 1952; he chose not to put forward any work for *Place des artistes*, an exhibition organized by Fernand Leduc, Marcelle Ferron, and Robert Roussil in May of 1953; nor was he included in *La matière chante*, an exhibition staged in April of 1954, organized by Claude Gauvreau and selected by Borduas, which highlighted the role of accident in Montreal painting.
16. Ewen, quoted in Rodolphe de Repentigny, "Comment la peinture de Pat Ewen passa du paysage lyrique à l'abstraction," *La Presse* [Montreal], January 27, 1955.
17. Ewen, in a taped conversation with Greg Curnoe, London, Ontario, March 18, 1969.
18. Gilles Corbeil, *Espace 55* (Montreal: Montreal Museum of Fine Arts, 1955) unpaginated.
19. To simplify for emphasis: the *Lifestream* paintings of the late 1950s were followed by the *Blackout*s, then the *Alert*s, then untitled geometric works inspired by Malevich's floating square. One series was followed by another, none lasted for more than eighteen months, and each was tightly focused: each idea was worn out, played through in almost (apparently) breathless activity. The process was

rigorous and the images largely worked in a manner that suggested intense bodily engagement, a painterly fulsomeness, no matter how modest the domestic scale of the works.

20. In 1960, the year of its publication, Ewen had acquired the first monograph on Guston, Dore Ashton's *Philip Guston* (Grove Press; New York, 1960). Other books on American artists in Ewen's library by 1966 included John Baur's *Bradley Walker Tomlin* and Lloyd Goodrich's *Albert Pinkham Ryder*.
21. Philip Guston quoted in "Nature in Abstraction" *Arts* (February 1958), p. 32.
22. Ulysse Comtois recalled in a conversation with the author, Montreal, June 13, 1987, that in the mid-fifties, Ewen vehemently insisted that a work by Bonnard had as much "sensibility, spontaneity and truth" as works by Jackson Pollock.
23. The *Lifestream* paintings followed Ewen's visit in the spring of 1958 to Toronto, where he went to the Royal Ontario Museum. There, his viewing of decorations on native canoes and the two great Haida totem poles in the central stairwells had great visual effect. Certainly, it built upon a sympathy for indigenous art encouraged by his wife Françoise. Sullivan's own deep interest in the concept of "the primitive" reinforced Ewen's own somewhat romantic ideal of indigenous life suggested by his father's frequent travels to the North in the 1920s. Of his father's tales of the North, Ewen has remarked, "I heard his stories of Northern Canadian Indians and Eskimos and I guess I always had this almost romantic attitude to the space up there." (Nick Johnson, "Paterson Ewen: Rain," *artscanada* 32:1, 196/197 [March 1975], p. 42.)

    Ewen developed and sustained his own amateur interest in the art of First Nations peoples, and manifested this influence through the simplification of formal outline and the repetition of sign (or form), namely the objects which systematically break the movement of the lifestream.

    It is worth noting that, virtually alone amongst the Automatistes—perhaps Mousseau would be the exception—Sullivan explored and utilized an interest in "the primitive" as a means to "get away from taboos, and establish a raw truth." Her dance study with Franziska Boas in 1945/46 stressed corporeality as it was rooted in ritual and the practices of older cultures. Boas, the daughter of the seminal anthropologist Franz Boas, used Pacific Northwest Kwakiutl Indian initiation dances in her classes to suggest not only new ways to think of tone relations and melody but as a means to stress the centrality of expressiveness to the feeling and history of a culture. Choreographed shifts of balance, sequential arm movement, contrasts between fluid and static limbs were all cherished in the Kwakiutl dance and in Boas's teaching, linking dance with what she called "a renewal of life, a stimulus of creative action and certainly a better understanding of the intricacies of human nature." Values of older cultures were used by Boas to reinforce the idea of freedom, the very values that Sullivan upheld in her writing and her work, and shared with Ewen. Françoise Sullivan in conversation with the author, Montreal, November 9, 1986; Boas's statement is from her book, *The Function of Dance in Human Society* (Brooklyn, New York: Dance Horizons, 1972), preface.
24. In January of 1960, Ewen and three other painters similarly distanced from the centres of discussion—Ray Mead, Henriette Fauteux-Massé, and Virginia de Vera—exhibited in the Stable Gallery at the Montreal Museum of Fine Arts as the newly constituted Formal Lyricists. Their short association (they disbanded after the exhibition) was marked by what Ray Mead called a "protest against rigid geometric painting," but a concurrent realization that each was positioned outside the dominant critical debates of the time. Their explicit aim as painters was to find a balance between "lyricism and formalism."

ECLIPSE OF THE MOON

(detail) 1990

Acrylic on gouged plywood

266.8 x 294.6

Art Gallery of Ontario

25. Guido Molinari in conversation with the author, Montreal, November 10, 1986.
26. Robert C. Mackenzie, "20/20 Gallery Closes," *20 Cents Magazine*, vol. iv, no. 7 (September 1970) unpaginated.
27. A.R. "Twenty-Twenty: The New Gallery," *20 Cents Magazine*, vol. 1, no. 1 (September 1966), unpaginated.
28. Paterson Ewen in conversation with the author, Saskatoon, June 10, 1986.
29. Steve Parzybok, "Ron Martin's New Work and Paterson's Retrospective Show," *20 Cents Magazine*, vol. iv, no. 3 (March 1970), unpaginated. Parzybok wrote, in part: "About Paterson Ewen's new paintings in his retrospective show at 20/20 Gallery. Colour: objects absorb all colours except the colour they appear, which they reflect; black absorbs all colours . . . the term 'light' refers to the radiation of electromagnetic force at wavelengths that are compatible with the receptivity of the human eye . . . Inherent in the modern theory of quantum mechanics is Heisenberg's Uncertainty Principle which states the position and momentum of a particle can never be accurately determined simultaneously."
30. "Murray Favro's Journal," *20 Cents Magazine*, vol. 3. nos. 1-2 (April 1969), unpaginated.
31. Lucy Lippard, "Escape Attempts," in Anne Goldstein and Anne Rorimer (eds.) *Reconsidering the Object of Art: 1965–1975* (Museum of Contemporary Art: Los Angeles, 1996), p. 18.
32. Of this break, Ewen is quoted as saying: "About five years ago I became bored with art in the formal sense. This doesn't mean that I became bored with the work of other artists, but I became bored with my own work. There are only two things to do at that point: either stop making art or change the rules of the game. My change was to go from canvas and abstract painting to wood and imagery." Geoffrey James, *Contemporary Canadian Painters* (Ottawa: Department of External Affairs and Canada Council Art Bank, 1978), unpaginated.
33. Anne Goldstein and Anne Rorimer, "Introduction," *Reconsidering the Object of Art: 1965–1975* (Museum of Contemporary Art: Los Angeles, 1996), p. 13.
34. Conceptual art was a topic of some conversation in London circles, in part indirectly through a shared enthusiasm for the work of Marcel Duchamp. It is interesting to note that Greg Curnoe was one of only six Canadian artists included in Lucy Lippard's ground-breaking exhibition *955,000*, presented at the Vancouver Art Gallery in 1970.
35. Favro quoted in Marie Fleming, *Murray Favro* (Art Gallery of Ontario: Toronto, 1983), p. 41.
36. See Greg Curnoe, "Monk's Dream," *Parachute* (July/August/September, 1989) p. 62.
37. "Murray Favro's Journal," *20 Cents Magazine* vol. 3. nos. 1-2 (April 1969) unpaginated.
38. David Gordon in a letter to the author, Kingston, July 26, 1986.
39. The image of *Thunder Cloud as Generator* is one that Ewen has returned to often in smaller works on paper. In 1976, given the opportunity to create a lithograph at the Nova Scotia College of Art and Design where he was a guest instructor, Ewen used the image once again.
40. Ewen quoted in Shadbolt, unpaginated.
41. Ewen quoted in Shadbolt, unpaginated.
42. Ewen quoted in Nick Johnson, "Paterson Ewen: Rain," *artscanada* 32:1, 196/197 (March 1975) p. 41.
43. Ewen in conversation with the author, Saskatoon, 1992.
44. Ewen quoted in *Chinook* 1:3 (Spring 1979).
45. Ewen quoted in Johnson, p. 41.
46. Northrop Frye, *A Study of English Romanticism* (New York: Random House, 1968), p. 7.
47. Frye, p. 47.

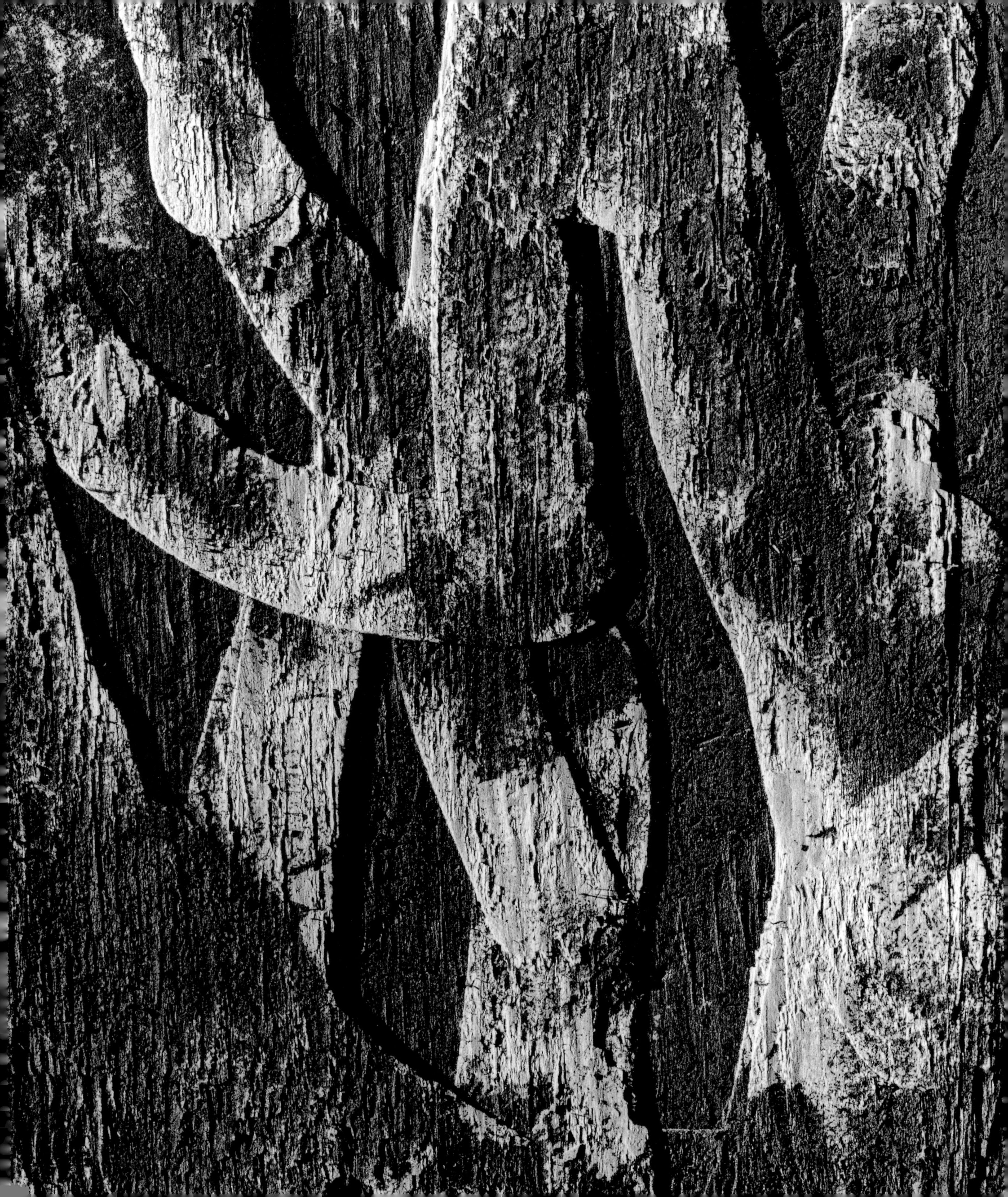

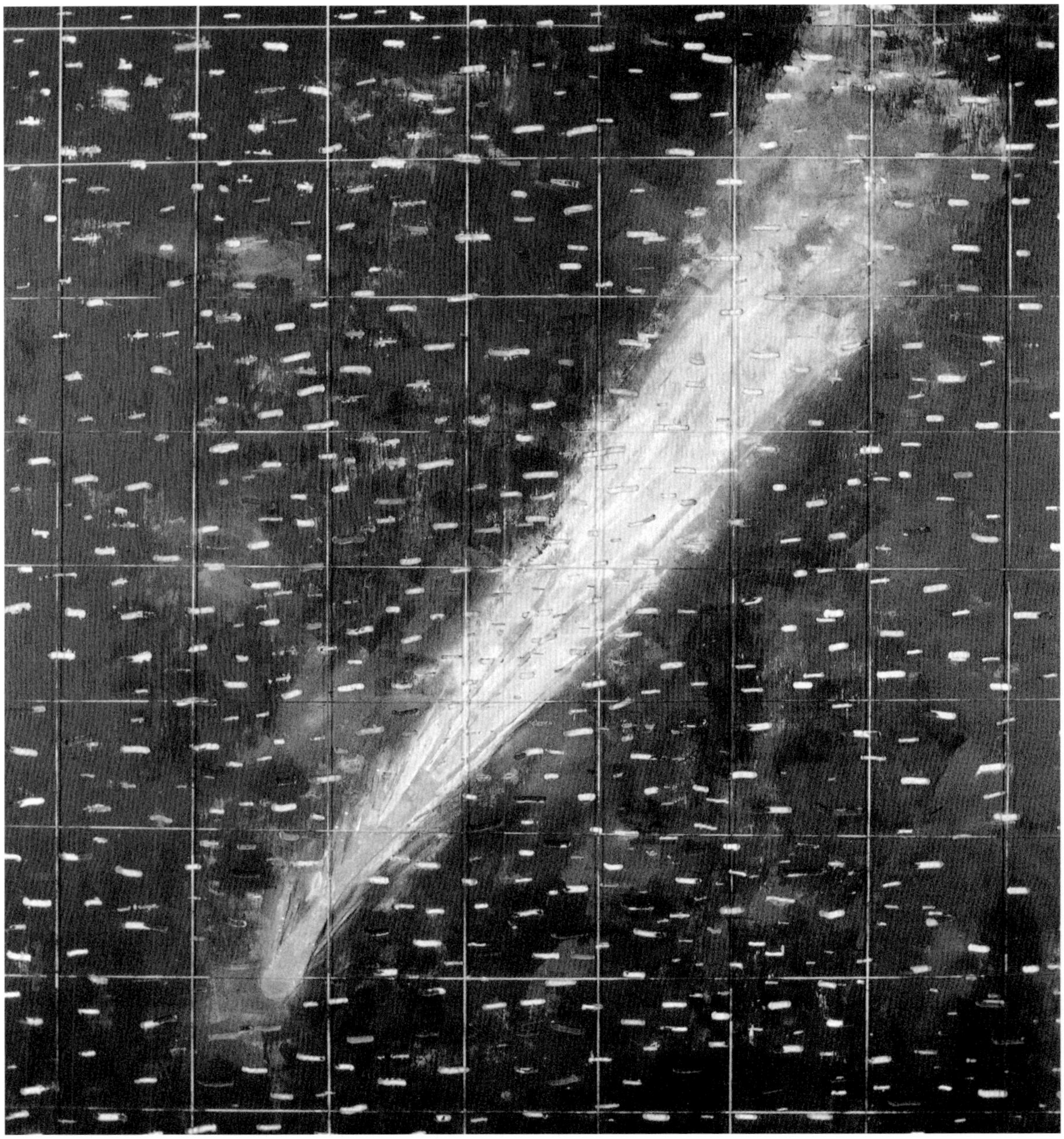

AFTERWORD

The first time I met Paterson was in March of 1976, when he came to the Nova Scotia College of Art and Design to give a lecture. He must have brought about five carousels of slides, and two hours into the talk he was only up to 1959. It was one of the most rambling, anecdotal talks I'd ever heard, and wonderful to listen to. It was all about Montreal in the 1950s, the characters that he met up with, and filled with heartwrenching stories like losing all his Christmas gifts when he went into a bar on the way home from shopping. The talk went on forever.

I had invited him to the school, where I taught, after his work caught my eye in 1975, when we were both included in *The Canadian Canvas* exhibition. Paterson not only had a strong influence on the students but also on me. He gave permission to explore imagery and processes other than the more rigorous formalist and conceptual stuff that dominated the art world. I was going through a transition in my painting at the time, which was moving towards figurative work, and I used him to reinforce my position.

Shortly after *The Canadian Canvas,* where I showed the last two formal abstract paintings that I did, I dramatically reduced the scale in my work and began to work with architectonic forms. I cut the corners off an oil on plywood painting I was working on, and it reminded me of a house. I began to play around with it. Abstraction began to take on names and nouns like bridge, tunnel, boat, house, houseboat, boathouse. The forms were very associative and held within them a kind of psychological metaphor. By 1976, when I met Paterson, the abstraction had given way to narrative and the architecture had become secondary to the people that inhabited it.

The thing I responded to in Paterson was that, in part, he too had made the transition from abstraction to some kind of imagistic painting. He also had—and still has—that wonderful sense of nontraditional material. I really liked the apparent innocence of what he did. Clearly, you could see in his paintings an intelligence that was smarter than the images themselves. The New York painter

MOORE HOUSE COMET

1974

Acrylic and metal on gouged plywood

228.6 x 243.8

Private Collection

ECLIPSE OF THE MOON

(detail) 1990
Acrylic on gouged plywood
266.8 x 297.6
Art Gallery of Ontario

Steve Gianakos once wrote: "Smart from dumb, good; smart from smart, not good." Paterson was that: smart from dumb. In his paintings, there is an intelligence—both a painterly and a historical intelligence at the same time. I found Paterson's sincerity towards his subject very uplifting—this flat-footed presentation, this dumb, literal use of material, where shiny materials are lightning and rain. It also had, as humour often does, a way of liberating you, in a more radical way, from the constraints of previous work. I think of him along with Jonathan Borofsky in this way—each has worked to get away from the hegemony of minimalism and conceptual art and back into a kind of fresh painting and image making.

For painters, at the end of the 1970s, scale was absolutely an issue. Paterson was doing something on the grand scale when other people working with new imagery—Borofsky, Schapiro, and others—were working on a more modest scale. They used intimate scale as a way of getting away from the sense of the heroic, while pursuing the idea of the sincere self. Paterson was doing this, but on a grand scale, and I found this very compelling. Curiously, it was similar to the appeal that Julian Schnabel had among artists and the public, the kind of grandiosity of gesture that was tied to an intimate, personal iconography.

In many ways Paterson's paintings were a natural extension of what is, I think, a profound Canadian experience: namely, nature and the painting of the landscape. Here was someone who, in the 1970s, found a way of reinvigorating that tradition in an authentic way by recalling the power of nature. Paterson wasn't the romantic traveller, trekking up to the North Pole to paint icebergs, but at the same time he was able to rekindle the wonder of them.

For me, Paterson is inspirational—by example. We have different sensibilities, and though I didn't have to go through his work to get to where I wanted to go, I have found a kind of poetry to his work, and this has meant a lot to me.

Eric Fischl
New York, February 1996

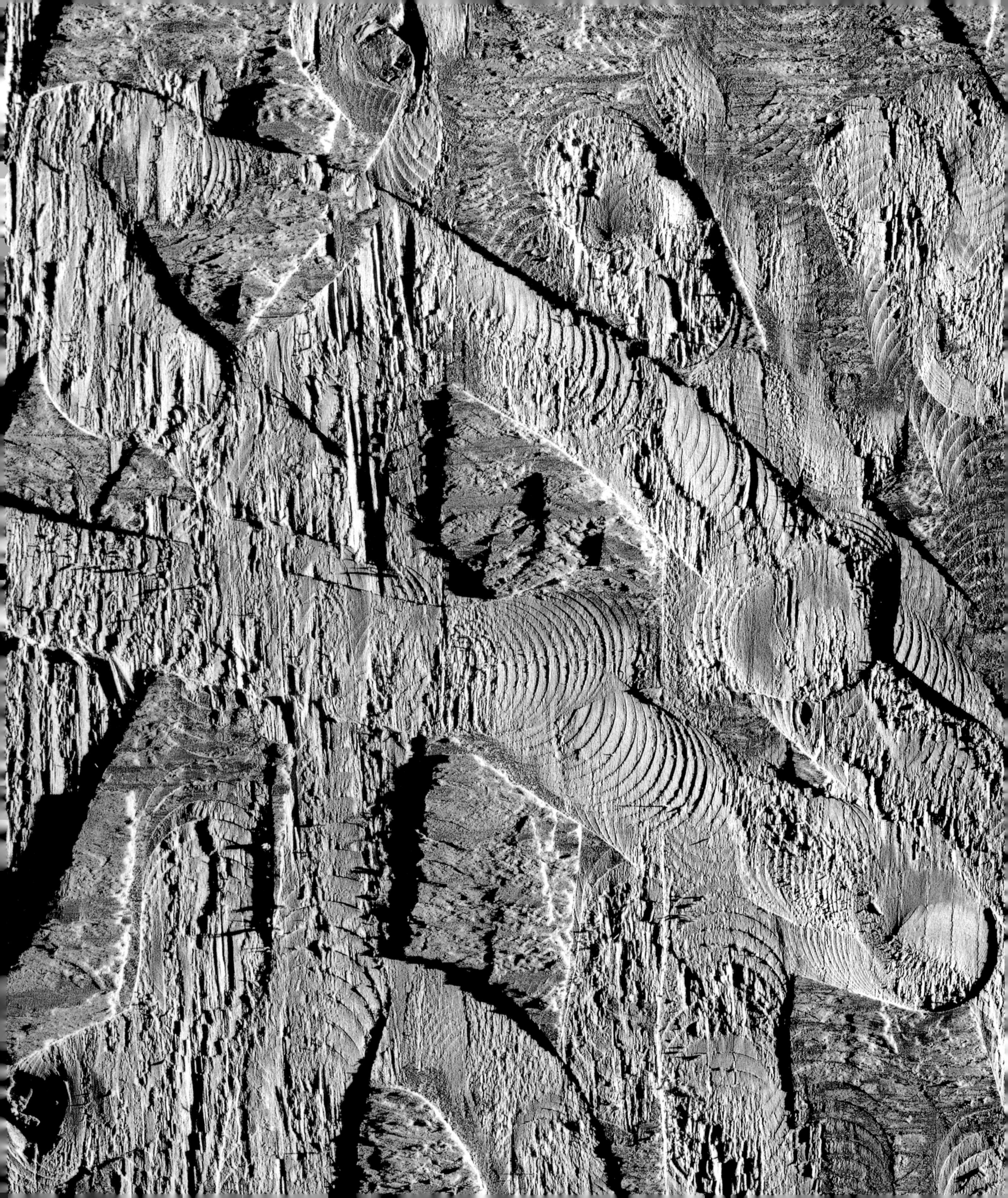

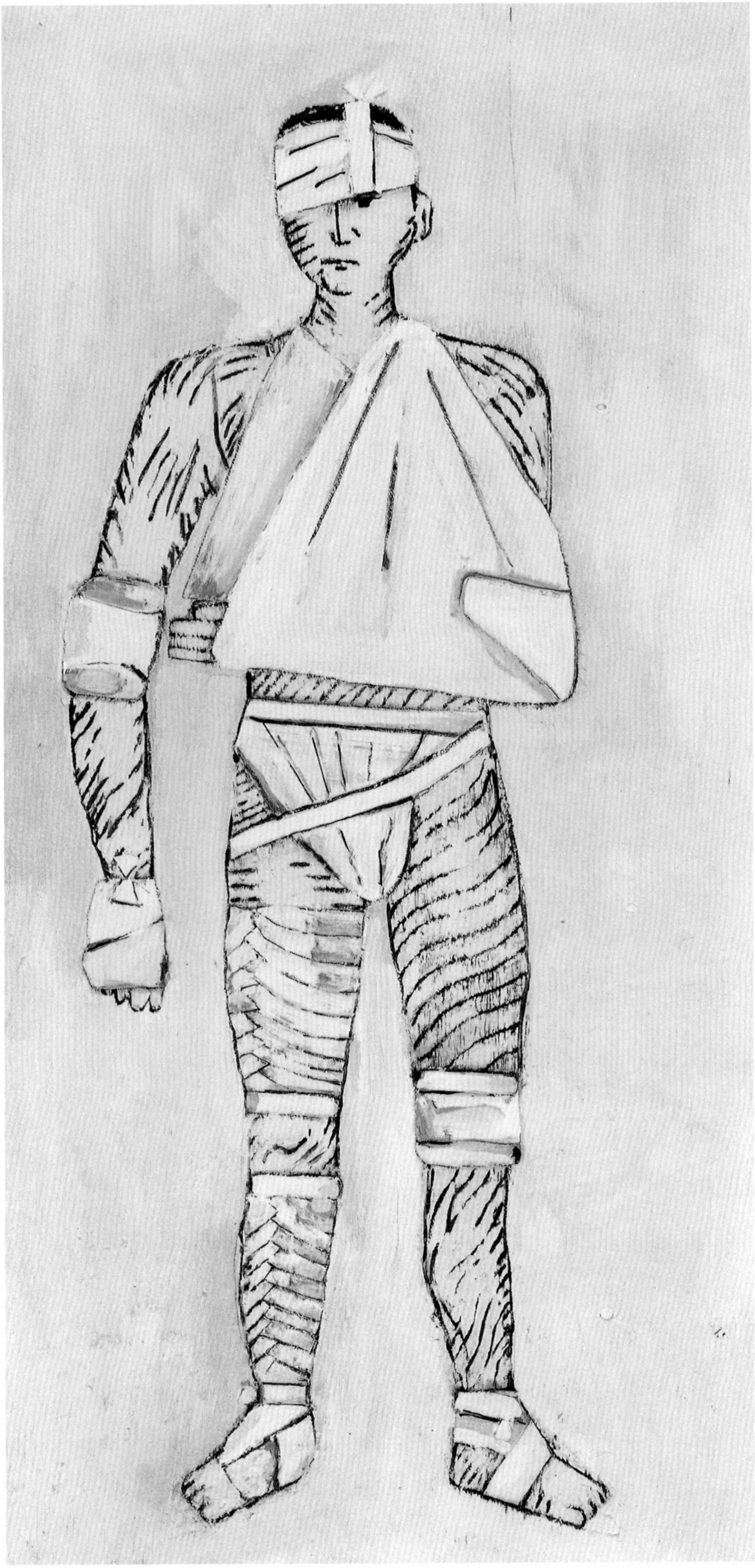

CHRONOLOGY

BANDAGED MAN 1973
Acrylic and cloth on plywood
243.8 x 121.9
National Gallery of Canada

Note: This chronology includes the following:

- *taped interviews with Paterson Ewen and other writings and comments by the artist* (in regular type)
- *critical commentary from published sources such as reviews in newspapers and magazines, exhibition catalogues and personal reminiscences (in italic type)*
- *events and significant developments in Paterson Ewen's life and his career as an artist* (**in bold type**)
- *a chronological listing of exhibitions (one-person exhibitions are noted with an asterisk**)

Full citations for the sources (published and unpublished) from which the quotations below have been taken are in the bibliography.

1925 to 1945

PATERSON EWEN IS BORN ON APRIL 7, 1925, IN MONTREAL, QUEBEC.

I was brought up in the west end of Montreal. It was not only English-speaking, but it was . . . absolutely Protestant. [We lived in] the west end of Montreal—literally. Past where we lived, in a nice self-contained brick house, was a creek, in fact two creeks. Both creeks were within 45 minutes walking distance from the house. I know it sounds like I'm making it up but there was a watering hole there too. My grandfather, my father's father in Aberdeen, was a shoemaker who made shoes for crippled people. He was also a famous local character. They used to send policemen down into that district of Aberdeen . . . but the sport was to beat them up when they got down there, so they just didn't bother. It was sort of like the Charlie Chaplin film *East Street*. They had their own local law. My grandfather was a large man for those days . . . so when someone would go mad and race across the rooftops screaming, they'd send for George Ewen. He was an amateur sculptor. He was offered a job to go to the University of London and be a medical artist, but his wife wouldn't leave Scotland for a foreign country. He was my mythological hero, I guess. I saw some of his work as a child, and I think that was a big influence. (III. Presentation by Ewen, 1976)

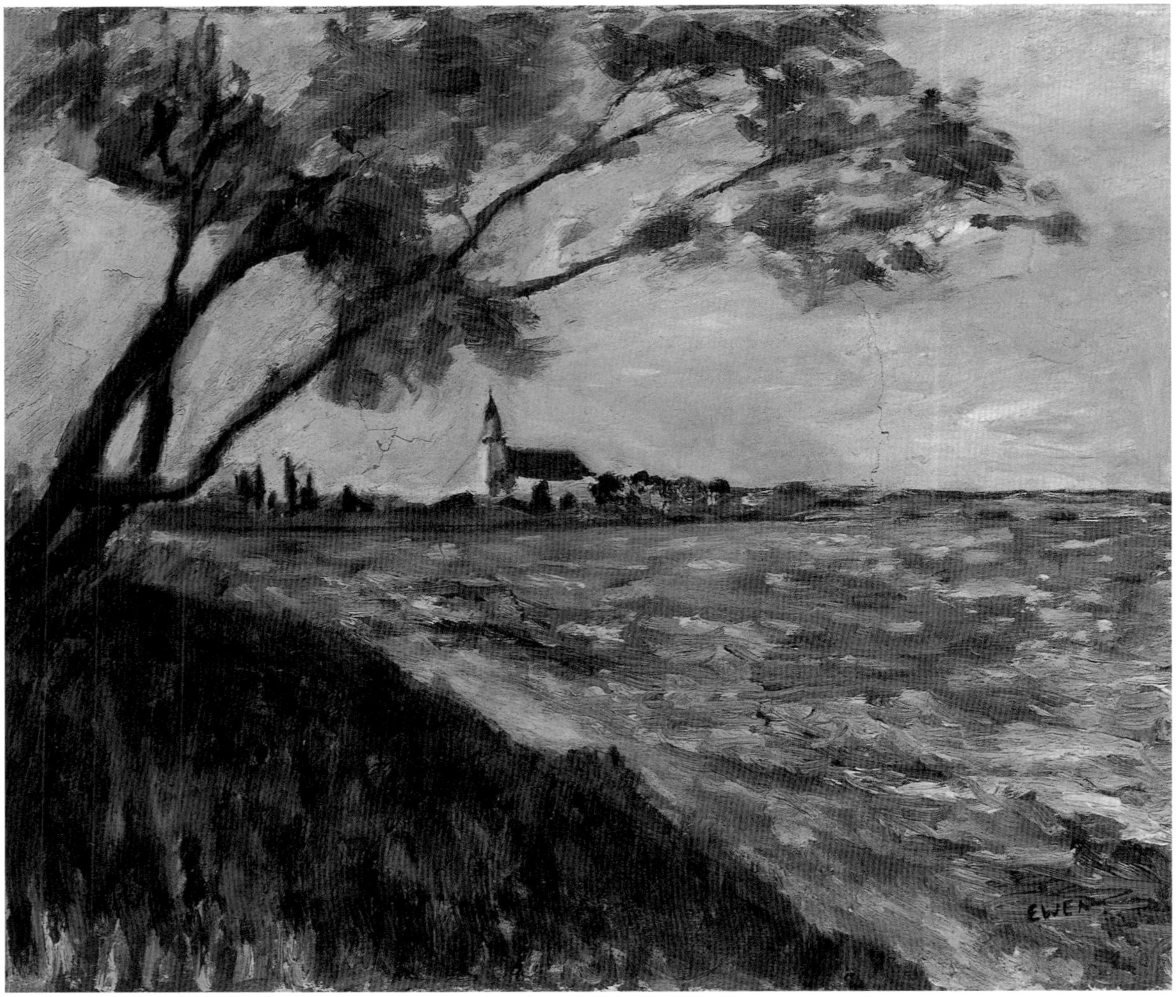

GONOR, MANITOBA

1947
Oil on canvas
46.2 x 56.2
Art Gallery of Ontario

As many artists do, I recall from childhood visual delight—birds, snow, the colour of Sunday comics. I can't remember not trying to be an artist. This meant looking at animals, trees, studying their movements, and then trying to draw them. [I thought these attempts were] unsuccessful because they were not "realistic" enough. (11. Ewen, 1989)

I was fourteen when the war started and could only think of getting into the war. I knew I could never be a pilot or a paratrooper because of my myopia so [when I was 18] I volunteered for active service in a reconnaissance regiment where I was a machine gunner in a light scout car. The happiest day of my life was when I boarded the troopship—I was free of my puritanical Anglo-Saxon environment. I was nineteen and looking for adventure and experience. My war record was totally undistinguished. I managed to set fire to myself by mistaking gasoline for water. I sent a burst of machine gun fire into a group of sleeping comrades (miraculously no one was hit). As we began to close with the enemy, I became more nervous and developed a variety of symptoms such as vomiting. Since I was clearly expendable I was kept in the lead car as we reconnoitred around the Zeider Zee. Just as we were to launch an attack on the town of Amersfoort where the enemy had dug in, they called the war off. I was embarrassed to return home unscathed and undecorated. (11. Biographical statement, Dunkelman Gallery papers, 1968).

1946

June: Ewen returns from military service in Europe.

At that age—18—you have no real concept of death. You don't think it's ever going to be you. Also, you have a death wish and I certainly did. The best thing would have been to get a not-too-big wound and then come back a hero. (III. Teitelbaum interview, 1986)

September: Ewen enrols in the Bachelor of Arts program at McGill University in Montreal. First-year studies, with science major, includes mathematics and geology.

The Earth and The Solar System. Its composition by minerals and rocks. Erosive forces (weather, wind, rivers, waves, etc.) modifying its surface and deformative factors (temperature, compression, etc.) affecting its subsurface structure are thoroughly treated. The origin and historical development of the earth and of living things are briefly considered. (Geology year one, McGill University Calendar, 1946)

As a boy, I wanted to be a geologist. I thought geology had to do with shapes and color. (III. Teitelbaum interview, 1986)

Thereafter the world consisted of trying to see how things worked and how I could represent them. (II. Ewen, 1989)

1947

Summer: Ewen spends the summer in Quebec City enrolled in the Canadian Officers Training Corps. He paints his first two works: *Citadel, Quebec* and *Landscape with Monastery.*

September: Ewen transfers to the Bachelor of Fine Arts program at McGill University; he studies figure drawing with John Lyman in a course titled *Art 1.* Later in the fall, he paints *Gonor, Manitoba* based on a photograph from a magazine.

Art 1 *consists of 24, 3 hr. periods in drawing, painting, modelling and experiments in the forms and techniques of historic style.* Art 1 *also includes a chronological survey of the changes in painting and sculpture from prehistoric times to present day. 24 lectures of one hour. Illustrated notes are required.* (McGill University Calendar, 1947/48)

Lyman had a stamp that said "Fine Arts 1" . . . and he'd stamp that down on the page of newsprint you were drawing on if he thought it was especially good. He hardly ever looked at what I was doing. [It was] very unpleasant . . . One day he made a mistake. I was way over at the other end of the large room during drawing class. All of a sudden he said, "Who did this, who did this?!" Several of the girls said, "Oh, that's Pat." Of course his face fell. He took out his stamp, and walked on. (III. Teitelbaum interview, 1986)

1948

February: Ewen transfers to the School of Art and Design at the Montreal Museum of Fine Arts, where he studies with Goodridge Roberts, Arthur Lismer, Marian Scott, Jacques de Tonnancour, Eldon Grier and William Armstrong.

Those were the happiest days of my life. The first year we took drawing, painting, print-making, illustration, commercial art, fresco and sculpture. You had to take them all—it was full-time days. Saturday morning you helped Lismer in his program of teaching child art. After my second year [1950] he graduated me in the hall by just handing me my scroll. It was both good and bad, but there wasn't any reason for me to be there by then. I was exhibiting with the Automatistes. (III. Teitelbaum interview, 1986)

I saw [Goodridge Roberts's work] at Stern's. I'd go in probably once a week. Part of my self-education program. I got to know junk from good work. Spotted a Roberts there before I met him. (III. Teitelbaum interview, 1986)

Summer: Ewen visits New York and sees the retrospective exhibition *Pierre Bonnard* at the Museum of Modern Art, of nearly 150 oil paintings, watercolours, drawings, prints and illustrated books. While in New York, he visits the Metropolitan Museum and private galleries to see paintings by Albert Pinkham Ryder. *Moonlight Marine* (c. 1890) and *Toilers of the Sea* (c. 1884) were on display at the Metropolitan.

1949

Spring: Ewen attends meetings of a left-wing cultural group and hears presentations by Claude Gauvreau and Françoise Sullivan. Views the work of Pierre Gauvreau, Claude's brother and a childhood friend of Françoise. These are the first Automatiste paintings he sees.

May: With fellow fraternity member, dance student Brian Macdonald, Ewen sees Françoise Sullivan's *La Danse* at the Théâtre des Compagnons. Of particular importance is *Black and Tan,* in which Sullivan dances wearing a costume designed by Jean-Paul Mousseau.

Françoise sort of took me in hand and that way I got to meet, well, everybody in the [Automatiste] group, [including] Mousseau, Barbeau, Leduc, their wives, who often did things on their own. I integrated into the French side without completely losing the English side. (III. Teitelbaum interview, 1986)

Summer: Ewen travels to New York with Sullivan; spends three weeks at Fourteen Mile Lake in the Laurentians with John Fox and Don Barrett, fellow students at the Museum of Fine Arts school. Joined for one week by Goodridge Roberts.

December: Ewen and Françoise Sullivan are married.

I chose to integrate into the 80 per cent French-Canadian side of Montreal. Consequently, I met Paul-Émile Borduas and Riopelle and Marcel Barbeau and Jean-Paul Mousseau. It was difficult. I don't have a flair for languages so I would sit without taking part in the conversation all that much, but of course it was enriching. I had the best of both worlds. I had Arthur Lismer as the head of the art school I was going to, and at this point I made contact with . . . the painters known as the Automatistes. (III. Presentation by Ewen, 1976)

Marian Scott was my teacher for thirty minutes at the Montreal Museum in 1949. (I. Ewen, 1969)

1950

March: Ewen shows at the *67th Annual Spring Exhibition* at the Montreal Museum of Fine Arts and at *L'Exposition des Rebelles*, organized by Jean-Paul Mousseau as a protest against the *Spring Exhibition.* Matthew Babinski, Borduas and Ewen are the only artists to be included in both shows. These are Ewen's first exhibitions of work in Montreal.

April: Ewen graduates from the School of Art and Design, Montreal Museum of Fine Arts. Works in the My Lady hat factory; later, he sells rugs at Ogilvy's department store in Montreal.

You have to remember there isn't only a question of cerebral direction. You have to remember that while I was doing some of this work, I was working in a hat factory for $40.00 a week and had to be there at 8:00, [and the day] ended at 6:00. Then I got home to have supper and start painting. So the output is not that great. Most of these were done in one go. I would start to work about 8:30 and work until 1:00 or 2:00 and be done and go to bed and get up early to go to the job. (III. Teitelbaum interview, 1986)

May: Ewen organizes an exhibition of his work at a rented storefront space at 1445 Crescent Street, Montreal. Claude Gauvreau, Matthew Babinski and Françoise Sullivan help with the organization and installation.

June: Birth of his first son, Vincent, who is named after Vincent van Gogh. Three more sons are subsequently born: Geoffrey (June 1955), Jean-Christophe (September 1957) and Francis (August 1958).

[Of his painting *Portrait of Vincent* realized in 1974]: This painting took me the longest to do of any of these works, and it was the trickiest because if you do a portrait of your son there is the danger of sentimentality. Then I took it from a 35mm. slide that I took at his grandmother's funeral . . . and he is standing beside a bush that has pink flowers on it so I was faced with having to deal with pink which is a dangerous colour in my opinion and can turn out sweet. . . I took a number of photos and this one happened to be the last frame on the roll and consequently it cut him off at about the knees and it cut off a bit of the top of his head. The fact is that he is an emotionally disturbed young man and so is somewhat handicapped . . . his disturbance is quite severe. I thought this was a true portrait of him and I had to tread a line somewhere between being cruel or sentimental, and that's why it took me so long. I used real cloth for jacket and trousers, and part of the creases in the trousers are actually the cloth folded over, others are painted on very roughly. The buttons are pieces of galvanized iron sprayed on with gold spray paint and a few squiggles of black to suggest the indentations. It took me six weeks and it came off . . . I think it is one of my better pieces. I think I succeeded in showing that he had and has a handicap without it being cruel and I think it avoided sentimentality. In reality he was holding a lady's umbrella for her and you could only see the red handle in his hand and I transposed that and made it a flower to represent his sensibility, . . . a flower like those on the bush he is standing beside. And at the same time that he may be somewhat handicapped (and I thought this cutting off in the photograph expressed that) he has something in its place, some kind of justice, if you like. He was a kind of prodigy . . . he wrote poetry . . . he didn't talk until he was five years old and then he wrote a series of thirty poems between the ages of 6 and 9, a number of which were published in an adult poetry review. . . . It was Louis Dudek and Frank Scott, Canadian poets, who decided to publish the poems . . . and I thought I would put one of the poems in that blank space. (V. Shadbolt and Johnson, 1977)

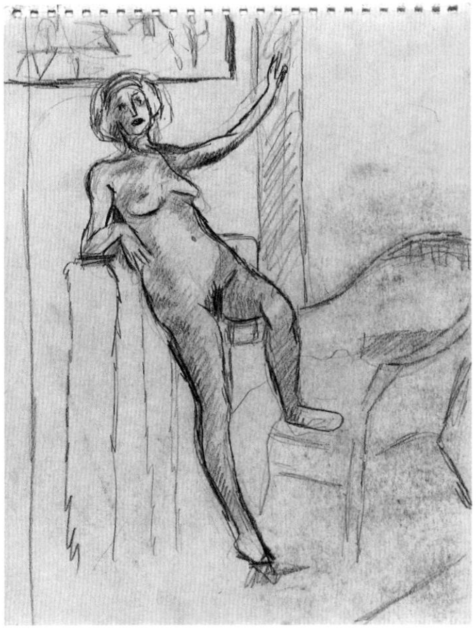 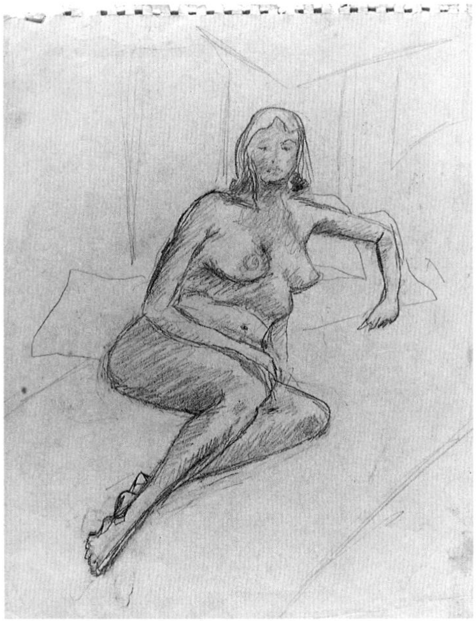 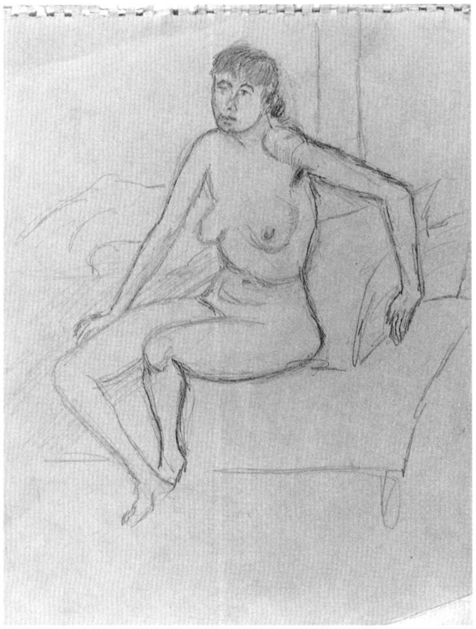

Left to right:
NUDE #4 1950
Graphite on
sketchbook page
30.4 x 23.0
Art Gallery of Ontario

NUDE #10 1950
Graphite on
sketchbook page
30.4 x 23.0
Art Gallery of Ontario

NUDE #11 1950
Graphite on
sketchbook page
30.4 x 23.0
Art Gallery of Ontario

Summer 1950 through 1953: The Ewen family occasionally spends time in Saint-Hilaire at the family homes of Madeleine and Carl Dubuc, and of Pierre Gauvreau.

Autumn 1950 through 1955: Works part-time at the rent control board for Verdun and Montreal West and trains to sell insurance.

To go and visit Borduas and meet that group was the only stimulus you could find at that time. (III. Curnoe interview, 1969)

"Still life with Bottles" looks dirty but it has quality. (VIII. Ayre, 1950)

Paterson Ewen belongs to no school. He has had the courage to question everything he was doing, to shed preconceived opinions and to start anew. He wants to impose his very own impression of the world . . . His last watercolors prove that he has broken away from the influence of Goodridge Roberts which seemed obvious in some of his early paintings. (VIII. Dénéchaud, 1950)

March 14–April 9: *67th Annual Spring Exhibition*, Montreal Museum of Fine Arts, Montreal, Quebec.

March 18–25: *L'Exposition des Rebelles*, 2035 Mansfield Street, Montreal, Quebec, organized by Marcelle Ferron, Jean-Paul Mousseau and Claude Gauvreau.

May: *Studio exhibition*, 1445 Crescent Street, Montreal, Quebec.*

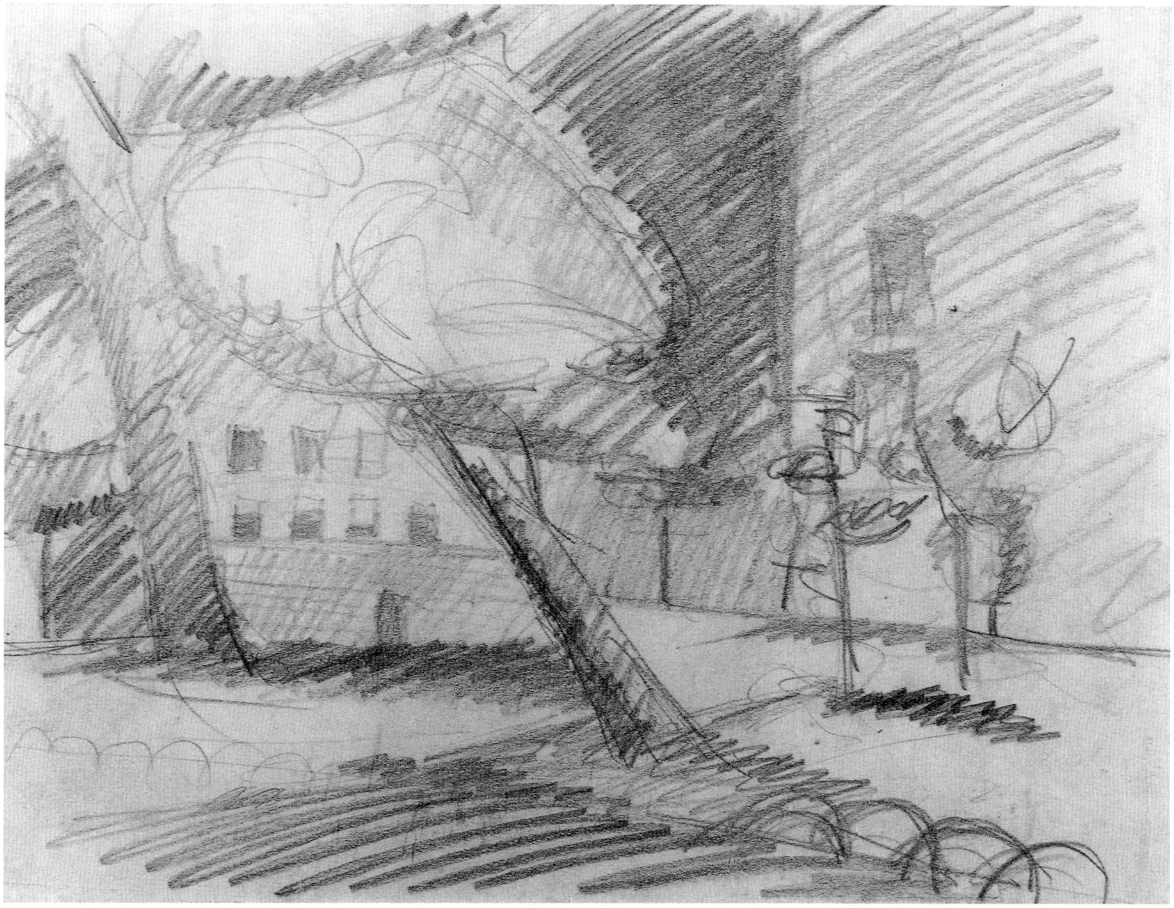

WASHINGTON SQUARE, NEW YORK #3 1950
Graphite on paper
22.5 x 29.8
Art Gallery of Ontario

1951

May 16–31: *Les Étapes du vivant,* Ontario Street, Montreal, Quebec (Barbeau, Blair, Champeau, Depairon, Eckers, Emond, Ewen, Ferron, Gauvreau, LeFebuse, Mongeau, Morin, Mousseau, Phenix and Riopelle).

1953

I started on the English side and I was a landscape painter. I also did interiors and still lives. I was a pretty straight forward figurative painter influenced by the Post-Impressionists for the first eight years of my work. (III. Curnoe interview, 1969)

1955

February: Ewen shows abstract work, for the first time, in *Espace 55,* an exhibition organized by Gilles Corbeil for the Montreal Museum of Fine Arts.

May: Exhibits with Paul Andrew in a two-person show at the Montreal Museum of Fine Arts. Ewen chooses to exhibit 9 paintings, 7 of which are landscapes and domestic interiors done as early as 1950. These include landscapes from Saint-Hilaire and his two portraits of the Automatiste poet Rémi-Paul Forgues.

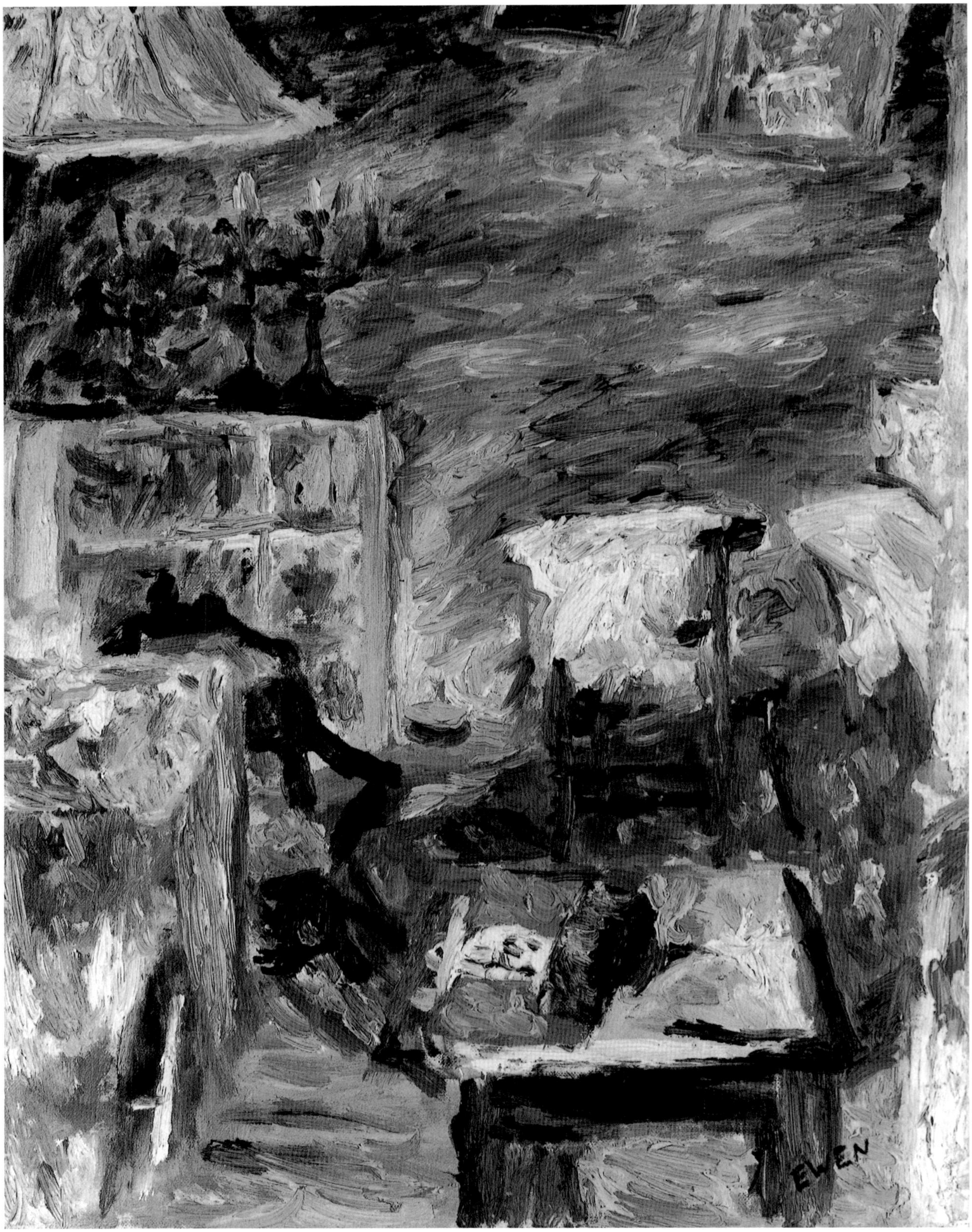
EWEN

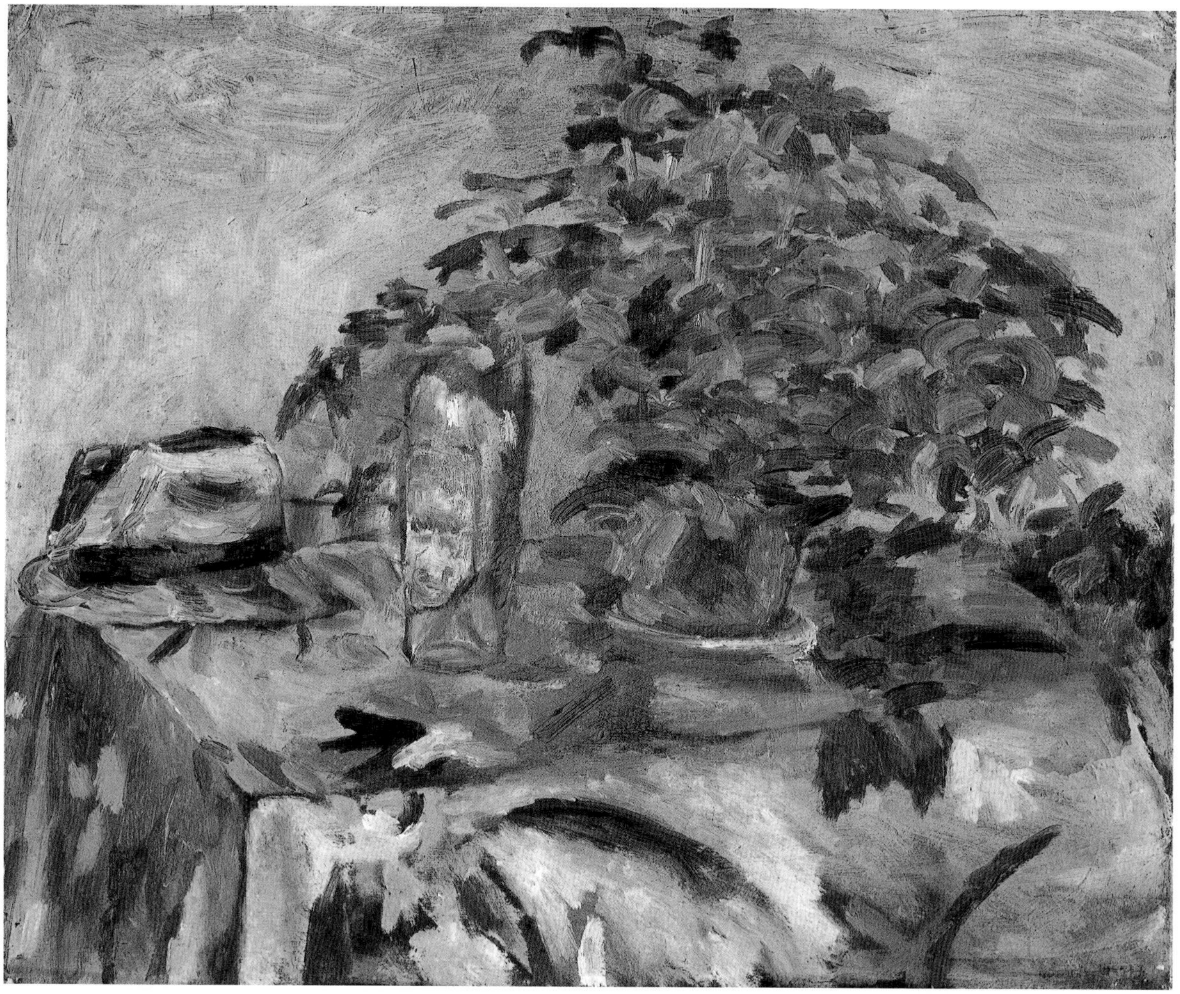

STILL LIFE WITH HAT

1951

Oil on canvas board

50.6 x 60.0

Art Gallery of Ontario

Facing page:

INTERIOR, FORT STREET, MONTREAL [#2] 1951

Oil on canvas board

50.5 x 40.5

Art Gallery of Ontario

July: Ewen travels to New York with Guido Molinari and Fernande Saint-Martin; shows work to a number of galleries including Parma Gallery. Visits Paul-Émile Borduas in his New York studio.

I went from gallery to gallery, not with slides but with paintings under my arm. I didn't do badly. One gallery director of a cooperative gallery bought a work for himself and said I could join that cooperative if I wanted to. I showed work to Borduas's dealer. Another gallery, Parma Gallery, offered me a one-man show, and I accepted their offer. (III. presentation by Ewen, 1976)

February 11–28: *Espace 55,* Montreal Museum of Fine Arts, Montreal, Quebec (Comtois, Dupras, Émond, Ewen, Gauvreau, Lajoie, Leduc, Letendre, McEwen, Molinari and Mousseau).

May 6–22: *Paterson Ewen and Paul Andrew,* Galleries XII and XIII, Montreal Museum of Fine Arts, Montreal, Quebec.

May 28–June 18: *Inaugural Exhibition,* Galerie l'Actuelle, Montreal, Quebec (Belzile, Blair, Borduas, Bourassa, Comtois, Dupras, Émond, Ewen, Gauvreau, Goguen, Jauran, Jérôme, Leduc, Letendre, McEwen, Molinari, Mousseau, Riopelle, Lajoie, Toupin and Tousignant).

August 27–September 18: *Summer Salon,* Galerie l'Actuelle, Montreal, Quebec (Beaudin, Blair, Colemar, Comtois, Dupras, Ewen, Lajoie, Letendre and Mousseau).

November: *Group Exhibition at the Graduate School of Commerce,* 540 de La Gauchetière Street East, Montreal, Quebec, organized by the Students Association of the Graduate School of Commerce, University of Montreal.

December: *Group Exhibition,* in the hall of the University of Montreal, Montreal, Quebec (Barbeau, Blair, Borduas, Comtois, Corbeil, Ewen, Gauvreau, Goguen, Leduc, Letendre and McEwen).

1956

Winter: Ewen begins work as an employment supervisor at Bathurst Containers, where he remains for 10 years.

February: Travels to New York for the opening of his first one-man exhibition outside Montreal, at Parma Gallery, a co-operative gallery run by Harold Rubin and the American artist Robert Keyser.

I moved from painting with an emphasis on landscape to something that might resemble Abstract Expressionism as it was going on in New York at the time. It didn't represent the kind of Automatisme that Borduas was pushing because I didn't believe in the palette knife and the palette knife scraping look, so mine were a little more formally organized and they had a landscape quality. That's when, and also probably why, I managed to get a show in New York. (III. Curnoe interview, 1969)

February/April: Although not a signatory to the founding manifesto of The Non-Figurative Artists' Association of Montreal (NFAAM), shows in the first exhibition and at each of the subsequent exhibitions through 1960. The Non-Figurative Artists' Association of Montreal was formed to promote the exhibiting interests of a range of abstract painters then working in Montreal. They organized and promoted their own exhibitions, and pushed (successfully) for recognition both by the Museum of Fine Arts in Montreal and the National Gallery of Canada. As Fernand Leduc noted: *It was a way for us to unite artists who would impose on society a form of art that it rejected, who would oblige the museums to open their doors, who would force public officials to recognize the group.* (x. Leduc, 1971)

September: Travels to New York for the opening of a group exhibition, *Modern Canadian Painters*, at Parma Gallery, organized as an exchange with Galerie l'Actuelle in Montreal.

[From 1955 to 1958] I saw a lot, and I liked a lot . . . I saw some Ad Reinhardt, and thought that was terrific. Looked like a black painting. After a while [it] turned out to be a very strong and sensitive piece of work . . . Ellsworth Kelly and Clyfford Still. I was seeing Motherwell, Kline, Still. (iii. Teitelbaum interview, 1986)

Paterson Ewen, young Montreal painter, has his first exhibition here of oils and watercolors falling loosely into three categories: Cézanne-like abstractions based on rock and tree views, Non-Objective arrangements of blots and lines on a single plane, and horizontal abstractions with compressed, low-lying images suggesting mountains or reclining figures. The first group is the most successful and strong, and within it one particular study very close to Cézanne—a view through a wooded ravine where from a cleared area a dark horizontal crosses and unites a series of folded spaces falling deep into the background . . . All together, a promising debut if one not entirely pointing direction. (viii. Munro, 1956)

Paterson Ewen: The earlier, more solidly constructed paintings appear all the more substantial in comparison with the later, thin Kandinsky-like abstractions. (viii. Mellow, March 1956)

Pat Ewen's painting with its black grid is a network of fascinating variations, highlighted by unexpected colour effects which brighten it like so many light bulbs; it illustrates a link between Montrealers' individualism and the collective ingenuity of Western painters. (x. R. de Repentigny, 1956)

Paterson Ewen, whose work, shown here last spring, seemed to suffer from a transitional looseness, clinches his new style with a tighter structure and a richer complexity in his areas of color. (viii. Mellow, September 1956)

January–February 5: Galerie l'Actuelle, Montreal, Quebec (Borduas, Corbeil, Ewen, Sam Francis, McEwen, Mousseau and Riopelle).

February: Parma Gallery, New York, New York.*

February 27–April 3: *The Non-Figurative Artists' Association of Montreal,* at the restaurant Ste-Hélène de Champlain, L'île Ste-Hélène, Montreal, Quebec (Barbeau, Beaudin, Bellefleur, Belzile, Blair, Borremans, Bourassa, Delrue, Ewen, Goguen, Gauvreau, Giguère, Guilbault, Jasmin, Jauran (Rodolphe de Repentigny), Jérôme, Landsley, Leduc, Letendre, McEwen, Millet, Molinari, Morin, Mousseau, Raymond, Simard, Tousignant, Toupin, Tremblay, Truchon and Webber).

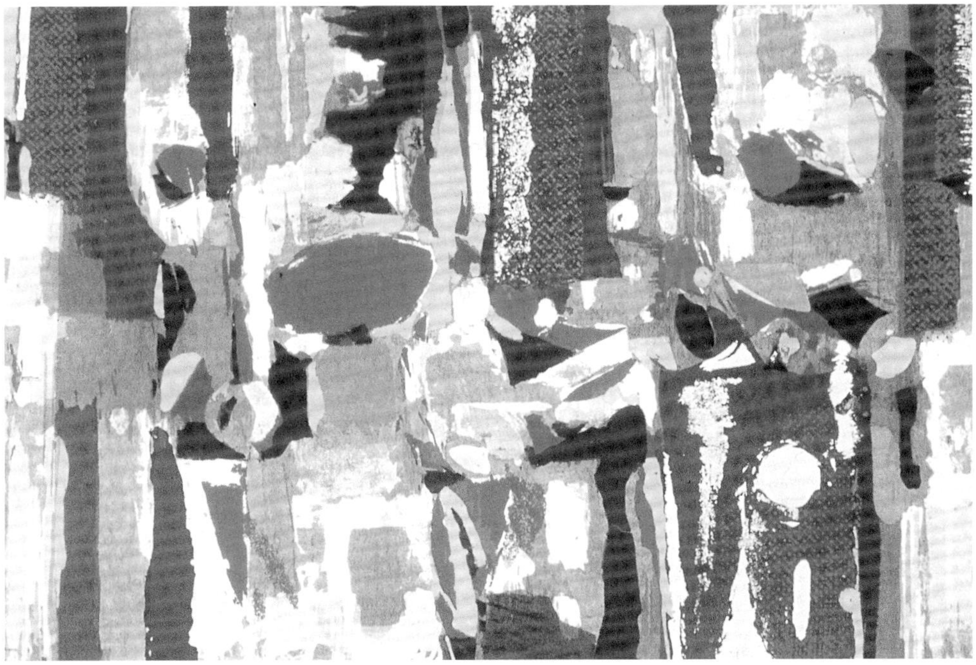

BLAST 1957
Serigraph on paper, 14/50
50.9 x 66.3
Musée d'art contemporain de Montréal

May 23–June 7: *Group Exhibition at L'Actuelle,* Montreal, Quebec (Belleville, Ewen, Leduc, Letendre, McEwen, Mousseau and Toupin).

June–July 3: *Canadian Abstract Painting,* National Gallery of Canada, Ottawa, Ontario, curated by Jean-René Ostiguy. The exhibition went on to the Western Canadian Art Circuit and travelled to ten public galleries and museums of the western provinces (Alleyn, Bellefleur, Borduas, Bowles, Cahen, Corbeil, Dumouchel, Ewen, Filion, Harris, Hodgson, Jérôme, Leduc, Letendre, Mead, Mousseau, Nakamura, Riopelle, Ronald, Smith, Tanabe, Town and Wilson).

August 7–31: *Arts au Québec,* Montreal Museum of Fine Arts, Montreal, Quebec, organized by Les Festivals de Montréal (14 non-figurative painters from the NFAAM showed paintings, sculpture and ceramics).

September: *Modern Canadian Painters,* Parma Gallery, New York, New York (Blair, Comtois, Corbeil, Ewen, Lajoie, Leduc, Molinari, Toupin and Tousignant).

October 9–21: *The Non-Figurative Artists' Association of Montreal,* Norman MacKenzie Art Gallery, Regina, Saskatchewan, organized by Rodolphe de Repentigny (Bellefleur, Belzile, Borduas, Dumouchel, Ewen, Giguère, Gauvreau, Jérôme, Jones, Landsley, Leduc, Letendre, McEwen, Molinari, Mousseau, Raymond, Tremblay and Toupin).

November: *Paintings and Sculptures,* Université de Sherbrooke, Sherbrooke, Quebec.

1957

August: Ewen awarded the Prix des Laurentides in a provincewide painting competition.

September: Ewen is one of 21 artists to exhibit at the opening of Galerie Denyse Delrue on September 18, 1957, one of only two galleries in Montreal devoted to nonrepresentational art. Exhibits in December 1957 in a group show of serigraphy; *Blast* is Ewen's contribution to a project originated by Jean-Pierre Beaudin, who asked nine artists to execute an "original serigraph" under his direction.

January 19–February 3: *35 Painters Today*, Montreal Museum of Fine Arts, Montreal, Quebec, organized by the University of Montreal and McGill University.

February 22–March 17: *The Non-Figurative Artists' Association of Montreal: Second Annual Show*, Montreal Museum of Fine Arts, Montreal, Quebec (also exhibited at Cowansville Art Centre and Salle Morrice, Musée du Québec).

May–June: *Group Exhibition at L'Actuelle*, Montreal, Quebec.

Summer: *Group Exhibition of Members from the NFAAM*, at the restaurant Ste-Hélène de Champlain, L'île Ste-Hélène, Montreal, Quebec.

July 1–August 1: *Paintings on Exhibition* (The Non-Figurative Artists' Association of Montreal), YMCA, Montreal, Quebec.

August: *Arts of Quebec*, Montreal Museum of Fine Arts, Montreal, Quebec.

September 18: *Inaugural Exhibition*, Galerie Denyse Delrue, 1520 rue Crescent, Montreal, Quebec (Beaulieu, Bellefleur, Borduas, Dallaire, Daudelin, de Tonnancour, Dumouchel, Emond, Ewen, Filion, Giguère, Jackson, Jasmin, Juneau, Kahane, Leduc, McEwen, Mousseau, Pellan, Riopelle and Tremblay).

December 7–15: *Group Exhibition*, Galerie Denyse Delrue, Montreal, Quebec, organized by Jean-Pierre Beaudin, who also directed the production of serigraphs by Giguère, Ewen, Mousseau, Beaudin, Bellefleur, Dumouchel, Raymond and Jasmin.

1958

Summer: Ewen's first visit as an adult to Toronto. At the Royal Ontario Museum, the display of Northwest Coast Indian objects is of particular interest.

It's the canoe that particularly sticks in my mind. It had all around its edge a very formalized design. I did a series really influenced more by the Haida Indian motif than anything else. (III. McKaskell interview, 1976)

Paterson Ewen, young Montreal painter, is having his second New York show. The earlier pictures in this group are composed of grey rectangular shapes like flagstones; later ones almost bury the geometrical division under loose "New York" brushwork. Été Ardent *is both freer and more controlled than the earlier pictures, and solves the hitherto puzzling problem of what to do with the center of the canvas.* (VIII. Ashberry, 1958)

Pat Ewen's exhibition at Galerie Delrue offers works in many hues and tones, although the basic composition is always similar: this composition is basically an approximate straight line—vertical or horizontal depending on the shape of the painting—crisscrossed by perpendicular lines; in the areas thus formed, the painter groups colour masses . . . Most of the paintings illustrate a dynamic sense of balance, which might explain the exacerbation of colours: the painter wants to destroy the form to which he freely submitted himself. (x. R. de Repentigny, 1958)

January: Parma Gallery, New York, New York.*

February 10-22: Galerie Denyse Delrue, Montreal, Quebec.*

June–July: *36 Canadian Painters*, at the restaurant Ste-Hélène de Champlain, L'île Ste-Hélène, Montreal, Quebec.

August 1–23: *The Non-Figurative Artists' Association of Montreal: Third Annual Show*, Montreal Museum of Fine Arts, Montreal, Quebec.

September: *Recent Work* [Gallery Artists], Galerie Denyse Delrue, Montreal, Quebec.

October 31–November 15: *Painters Eleven and Ten Quebec Artists*, Park Gallery, 17 Avenue Road, Toronto, Ontario (Bush, Cahen, Gordon, Hodgson, Luke, MacDonald, Mead, Nakamura, Ronald, Town and Yarwood; Bellefleur, Borduas, Dumouchel, Ewen, McEwen, Pellan, Picher, Riopelle, de Tonnancour and Mousseau).

November: *Group Exhibition of Members from the NFAAM*, Galerie Denyse Delrue, Montreal, Quebec.

1959

December: Ewen joins Ray Mead, Henriette Fauteux-Massé and Virginia de Vera as the Formal Lyricists and exhibits *Lifestream* paintings with them at the Stable Gallery of the Montreal Museum of Fine Arts in January 1960. The Formal Lyricists were consciously formed to present an alternative to both the Automatistes and Plasticien painters by suggesting lyrical and hand-worked concerns in abstract painting.

[The *Stream of Life*] is a landscape, but it is stylized to the point of being almost symbolic. When you put it altogether it flows. It's about life in the most basic sense—mountains, rivers, boulders . . . I wasn't too conscious of it at the time except that I suspected . . . that the Haida Indians took their motif from the basic things in nature. (III. Teitelbaum interview, 1986)

I was just thunderstruck by the designs along the sides of the canoes and . . . it seemed like insignia or stylization of the Haida Indians. [I] went back and did a few paintings at least somewhat influenced by them. (III. Teitelbaum interview, 1986)

January–February: *Group Exhibition and Auction*, Théâtre-Club, rue St-Luc, Montreal, Quebec (40 artists participated; the auction was in support of the strike at Radio-Canada).

January 28–February 5: *Annual Exhibition and Sale of Paintings*, Montreal Museum of Fine Arts, Montreal, Quebec, organized by the Ladies Committee of the museum.

February 23–March 16: *Exposition d'art* (The Non-Figurative Artists' Association), Collège Saint-Laurent, Montreal, Quebec.

April 16–May 21: *20th Biennial International Watercolor Exhibition*, Brooklyn Museum, New York, New York (included artists from the U.S.A., Mexico and Canada).

Autumn: *The Non-Figurative Artists' Association*, L'île Ste-Hélène, Montreal, Quebec, organized by the Service of Parks of Montreal.

October/November: *Painters Eleven Invitational*, Park Gallery, Toronto, Ontario.

October/November: *Twenty Artists from Montreal*, Here and Now Gallery, Toronto, Ontario.

November 10–21: *Paterson Ewen and Armand Vaillancourt*, Galerie Denyse Delrue, Montreal, Quebec.

December: *Aspects of Canadian Painting*, Canada House, New York, New York.

1960

Early Summer: Ewen travels to New York with his ten-year-old son, Vincent.

Pat had a regular job. At the time I remember it was as a personnel manager at an east-end Montreal box factory working for Bathurst Containers. And so he would work an eight hour day and then he would come home and he would work often another full day painting in the basement where he had a small, almost cramped studio. (x. Geoffrey Ewen in Rochon, 1988)

January 8–February 7: *Formal Lyricists*, Stable Gallery, Montreal Museum of Fine Arts, Montreal, Quebec (Ewen, Henriette Fauteux-Massé, Ray Mead and Virginia de Vera).

January 14–30: *Exposition* (The Non-Figurative Artists' Association of Montreal), École des Beaux-Arts de Montréal, Montreal, Quebec.

June–July 1: *Artists of the Gallery*, Galerie Denyse Delrue, Montreal, Quebec.

December 1960–January 1961: *The Non-Figurative Artists' Association of Montreal*, National Gallery of Canada, Ottawa, Ontario, a touring exhibition curated by Claude Picher and the president of the NFAAM, Jean McEwen (Bellefleur, Bruneau, Ewen, Fauteux-Massé, Ferron, Gendron, Goguen, Jérôme, Juneau, Leduc, Letendre, McEwen, Major, Maltais, Mead, Meloche, Molinari, Raymond, Rivard, Steinhouse, Toupin and Tousignant). This exhibition travelled to Brandon Allied Arts Centre, New Westminster Public Library, Norman MacKenzie Art Gallery, Banff School of Fine Arts, Edmonton Art Gallery and University of Alberta, Calgary.

1961

Spring: Ewen's *Nuit d'Été* (1958) is awarded a purchase prize at the *68th Annual Spring Exhibition*, Montreal Museum of Fine Arts.

Summer: Spends the summer weekends in the country outside of Montreal where, following family outings to observe the night sky, he begins a series of paintings based on constellations. These are subsequently called *Blackout*s and are shown alongside a concurrent series realized in the studio titled *Alerts*.

UNTITLED 1962
Pastel on brown Fabriano paper
65.0 x 47.0
Art Gallery of Ontario

[The *Blackout* paintings were . . .] done in bright sunlight out in the country. Denyse [Delrue] came out and saw a group of these and I didn't know what the hell they were. They were supposed to be abstract paintings, but I'll tell you what I realized after—what they really were. [It] won't come as too much of a surprise. That was the night sky that we would see out in the country . . . but I wasn't that conscious of it . . . I was very interested in the stars at that time. I can't say astrology because I don't know that much about it. I was very interested in some of the large patterns like the Milky Way. Vincent and I used to go every evening with the binoculars and look up into the sky. Then in the daytime I'd paint what I felt was an abstract painting. But the [*Blackout*] painting is quite clearly the night sky. A sort of rectangle and geometry that different cultures make different things of. I just formalized it into those rectangles. (III. Teitelbaum interview, 1986)

[The *Blackouts* and the *Alerts*] were painted in an unusual way. I bought one of those pistol-handled saws in Kresge's or Woolworth's that had five blades that would attach to a butterfly screw. I just threw away the handle and used the blades to lay the paint on. (III. Teitelbaum interview, 1986)

Blackout . . . *is definitely [a] step forward in the development of the painter. Here he is not given to facility. To work in black is not always a sinecure. In this study of textures, on which . . . colours flicker there is an attempt at negative modelling of light, a brush full of obscurity which takes on resounding dimensions.* (VIII. Sarrazin, 1961)

Paterson Ewen paints with a number of extremely interesting fixations. First of all, his surfaces are lined, streaked, scraped with parallel, very deep lines; surfaces on which the light plays as it did on the first Impressionist pictures. But in this case, the artist is not trying to represent the light; he simply gives it a way to manifest itself. The second characteristic is the overwhelming presence of blacks which brings the artist as well as the viewer into a mystery, itself very intricate, of shadows and highlights. Also the few strokes of bright colours which one can see on all of Ewen's works. They spread, scatter the emotion, and the work is organized around these vibrant constellations while the eye brushes over it all and never stops working. Finally, the extreme acidity of certain colours, the exacerbated range of violets, stagnant greens, damp earth, which wraps the whole work in sadness, but also in a calmness from the depth. (VIII. Folch, 1961–62)

April/May: *78th Annual Spring Exhibition*, Montreal Museum of Fine Arts, Montreal, Quebec.

Summer: *Group Exhibition*, Galerie Denyse Delrue, Montreal, Quebec (this show closed *The NFAAM*, National Gallery of Canada touring exhibition of 1960–61).

November 13–December 2: Galerie Denyse Delrue, Montreal, Quebec.*

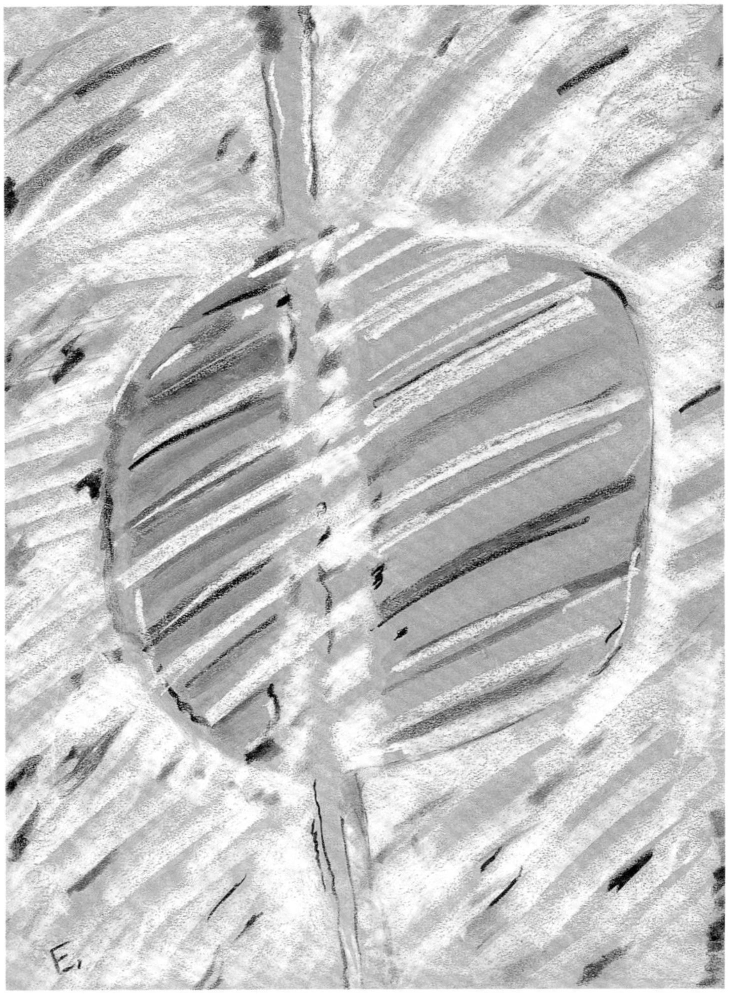

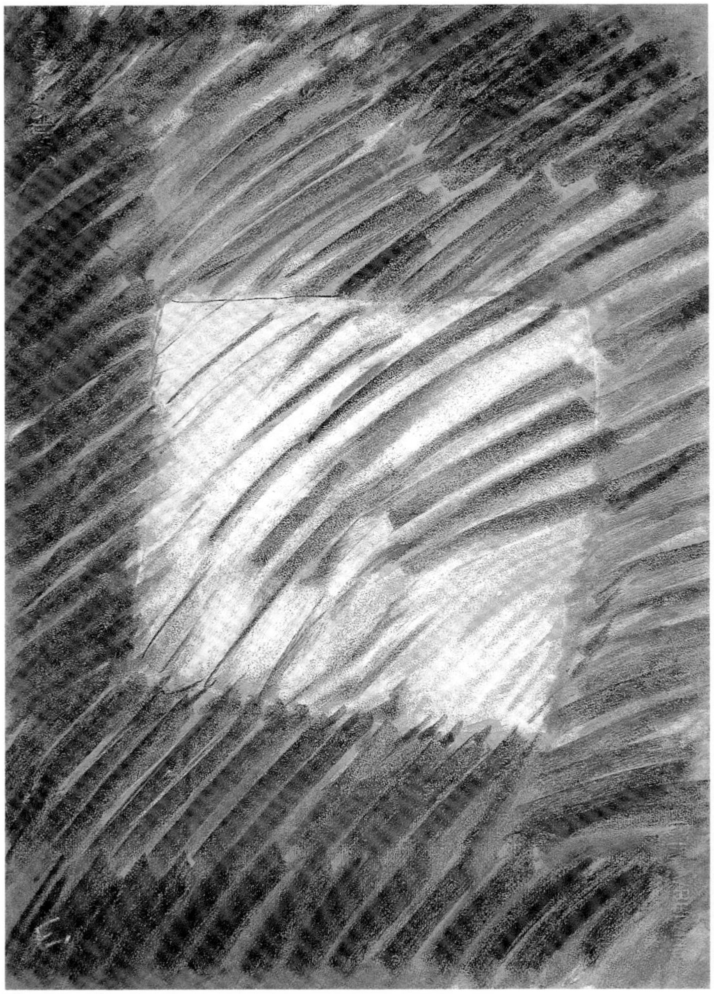

Left:
UNTITLED 1962
Pastel on paper
64.8 x 47.6
Musée d'art contemporain de Montréal

Right:
UNTITLED 1962
Pastel on paper
64.8 x 47.6
Private Collection

1962

June: Ewen shows in *La Peinture Canadienne Moderne,* a large exhibition of contemporary French-Canadian painting organized by Charles Delloye in conjunction with Michel Lortie and presented in Spoleto, Italy.

Autumn: Begins a series of monochrome paintings and a series of paper works realized in pastel. The monochromes reflect a newly defined respect for Borduas's late work that Ewen had seen for the first time in January 1962 at the retrospective mounted at the Montreal Museum of Fine Arts. The pastels on paper followed his reading of Camilla Gray's *The Great Russian Experiment.* Interest in Russian constructivism ran high in the Montreal community in the early sixties, and Gray's book was an important source for many artists.

[Of Borduas's work in the late 1940s:] I didn't like that particular period. In fact, I was quite upset. I began to understand the notion of not having a clear distinction between figure and ground. [I remember . . .] he told me himself [that] he was supposed to be an automatic painter, but . . . he got a lot of his forms from looking down in the Richelieu River . . . These forms sit against a background. For me that wasn't exciting at all. [Yet] I respected Borduas and [went to] visit him in New York . . . he [saw] . . . even in his fifties, that work very similar to his, called Abstract Expressionism, was being done five times the size . . . he had the guts to learn, and when I visited him in New York, he had got rid of the figure-ground [distinction]. He was doing white paintings, with black . . . and they were great . . . Later he was doing monochromes and they are works of genius. (III. Teitelbaum interview, 1986)

Although the influence of automatism has been strong, it has not reached easily all those who, later on, were to find inspiration in it, or make similar findings. Protected by a cool, forbidding exterior, Paterson Ewen expected from Impressionism the intimate well-being he was lacking. This aptitude to concentrate on a microscopic world expressed a personal confusion as well as a way of looking at reality to expose its fundamental truths. Paterson Ewen, shy and puritan, expressed through the flowered rainbows of his paintings a sensitivity which was his only way of capturing the softness he needed. Paterson Ewen has had a hard time coming out of his shell: his hesitation was understandable. The quality of his paintings, rustling of leaves, Renoir-like sensuous luminescence, shattered light à la Monet, were testimonies of how elegantly he had assimilated the classic heritage. Classic is not vain or derogative: on the contrary, in this disciple of French masters was a sensibility, capable of extravagances. (VI. Delloye, 1962)

Paterson Ewen is one of the most talented and serious painters from Montreal's school of young artists. Extremely rigorous in his research, Ewen has never painted to conform to the fashions or the clichés of the moment. On the contrary, he goes his own way with integrity and courage. For the 10 years that I've followed Ewen's career, I have found that his production never ceases to grow in quality. I unreservedly support his grant request. (II. Guy Viau, referee, Canada Council application, 1962)

February: *Collection of Charles Delloye*, Galerie Denyse Delrue, Montreal, Quebec.

March–April: *79th Annual Spring Exhibition*, Montreal Museum of Fine Arts, Montreal, Quebec.

April 26–May 6: *Group Exhibition*, Centre d'Art d'Argenteuil, Lachute, Quebec (Arsenault, Barbeau, Bellefleur, Borduas, Ewen, Fiore, Gagnon, Gauvreau, Germain, Haworth, Hurtubise, Leroux, Maltais, Morin, Racine and Steinhouse).

June 11–July 11: *Françoise Sullivan Ewen and Paterson Ewen*, The Montreal Society of Architects, Montreal, Quebec.

June 26–August 23: *La Peinture Canadienne Moderne*, Fifth Festival dei du Mondi, Spoleto, Italy.

1963

February: Ewen exhibits monochrome paintings at Galerie Denyse Delrue.

November: A later series of Ewen's monochromes, including pastel works on paper, is shown at the Montreal Museum of Fine Arts.

Ewen's more subdued . . . color pastels nervously rubbed on paper in a manner of personal artistic penmanship, while vaguely disturbing and antagonistic, nevertheless are works of considerable interest. The wooly textural effects and the rounded or rectangular forms achieved by this method of approach prove both harmonious and unusually even. They also may appear to some merely as strenuous finger exercises in form and color. (VIII. Pfeiffer, 1963)

February 18–March: Galerie Denyse Delrue, Montreal, Quebec.*

March–April: *80th Annual Spring Exhibition*, Montreal Museum of Fine Arts, Montreal, Quebec.

June/August: *Painters of the Gallery*, Galerie du Siècle, Montreal, Quebec.

November 1–17: *Paterson Ewen and Yves Trudeau*, Galerie XII, Montreal Museum of Fine Arts, Montreal, Quebec.

1964

February: Ewen is awarded a Canada Council fellowship on the basis of recent monochrome paintings and Constructivist-influenced works. He begins a series of flat-coloured works highlighting carefully ordered irregular geometric shapes.

This applicant paints most seriously notwithstanding the rather difficult circumstances encountered over the past seventeen years. I think that if I could show the kind of perseverance and patience over this period which is needed to create serious work, then I have what we call a vocation. My programme is very simply this—to continue to paint. (II. Canada Council application, 1964)

October: Ewen travels to New York.

Paterson Ewen allows himself texture and the freedom of the blurred edge, with the sensitiveness of a Rothko, in laying out his orange, grape and yellow bands on a black ground. (VIII. Ayre, 1964)

At first sight, Paterson Ewen's paintings look childish and derivative, as though they're simply made up of clichés handed down from abstract expressionism. But there's more to them than that: there's a free-wheeling nonchalance in the way in which their motifs relate to their squarish formats that I find stays in the memory. And, working in thick, impastoed paint for some years now, Ewen has advantageously built into his system the cubist urge to create rather than accept a flat (and in his case, a non-overlapping) surface. (X. Hudson, 1964)

March 28–April: *Dynamisme 64*, Galerie du Siècle, Montreal, Quebec (Barbeau, Bellefleur, Ewen, Gervais, Goulet, Goguen, Hurtubise, Juneau, Mead, Molinari, Renaud, Soucey, Sullivan, Taylor and Tousignant).

Autumn: *Quebec Artists*, International Congress of the Junior Chamber of Commerce, Oklahoma City, Oklahoma, organized by the Galerie du Siècle (Barbeau, Bellefleur, Ewen, Gaucher, Gervais, Goguen, Goulet, Hurtubise, Mead, Molinari, Renaud, Sullivan, Soucy and Tousignant).

1965

Winter: Ewen uses the Saint-Christophe Street studio space of Guido Molinari and Claude Tousignant in the evenings.

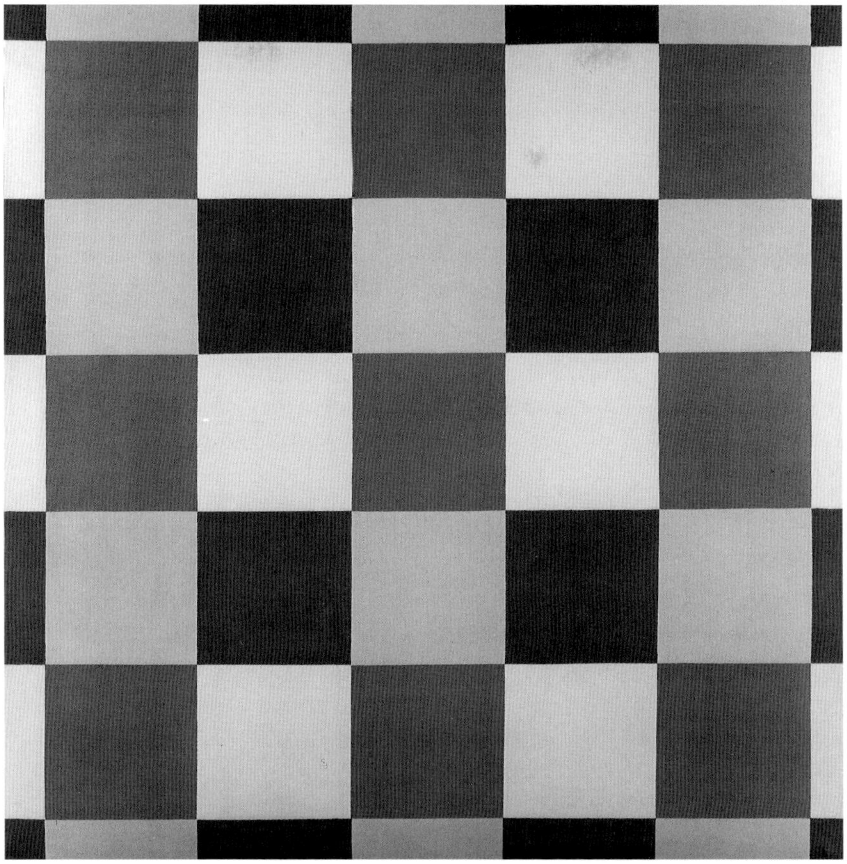

UNTITLED 1965
Acrylic on canvas
169.5 x 166.0
Art Gallery of Ontario

Tousignant was doing targets and Molinari was doing vertical stripes and I was doing neither of those things. But . . . [in] sharing a studio with both of them, and then later sharing another studio with Molinari, I picked up the technique . . . of how to lay on paint and how to get a perfect line. Molinari was fanatic about that. By then . . . I knew how to do hard edge. Not as precise as theirs, but precise enough for me. (III. Teitelbaum interview, 1986)

Autumn: Ewen and Sullivan organize a basement exhibition of small drawings by their nine-year-old son, Geoffrey. Among the artists who come to the modest opening are Henry Saxe, Armand Vaillancourt, Charles Gagnon and Claude Tousignant. The Automatistes encouraged children's explorations as a sign of freedom of inspiration. Borduas, for example, had given children's art classes in his home and presented exhibitions of their work. In 1953, Sullivan became involved with folk culture of the Gaspé in preparation for the choreography of a dance. The interest in the "naive" was shared by Ewen and Sullivan.

1966

Early Autumn: After separating from his family, Ewen lives in an abandoned boxing arena on Visitation Street that Molinari uses as a studio. He sleeps on a cot in the locker room. He paints and works full-time. Continues a series of paintings, *Diagram of a Multiple Personality* and begins *Zig Zag* works.

November: Ewen formally separates from Françoise Sullivan.

Late Autumn through Early Winter 1967: Gets a personnel job at RCA Victor.

One of the earliest paintings in the show, Diagram of a Multiple Personality, *consists of a blue frame with 12 yellow panes over which wandering orange lines offer a contrast with the rigidity. A smaller version is much more closed and concentrated, with an orange frame and black panes cut by diagonal yellow stripes. For the spectator, not as involved as the painter in working out geometrical relationships, some of Mr. Ewen's handsome schemes, uncluttered by associations, come out as merely decorative. Others, especially the big ones, have more to offer for contemplation.* (x. Ayre, 1966)

His career as a painter is presented in stages characterized by the production of short series of works that are based on ideological concerns and where the difficulty to paint and to express oneself is always conveyed in some way. Therefore, it is painting that is deeply tragic . . . More and more, having completely eliminated all texture from his pictures, he evolves with very limited means, which nevertheless convey symbols that are constantly charged with dynamism and significance. (x. Saint-Martin, 1966)

May 16–June 6: Galerie du Siècle, Montreal, Quebec.*

1967

Early August: Ewen is visited by Yael and Ben Dunkelman, who, on the advice of several curators, want to include him in an exhibition of Montreal artists for their Toronto gallery. Paintings shown include examples from the *Close Up* and *Diagram of the Multiple Personality* series, and early versions of new *Lifestream* work.

I didn't know who [the Dunkelmans] were. They said they were starting up a gallery and they liked my work and to my utter surprise they bought about five pieces right there on the spot and wrote out the cheque. (III. Teitelbaum interview, 1986)

I had separated from my wife and I was knocking about Montreal changing personnel jobs and trying to paint. I had rented a little house in St-Henri, the working district, and that was a real split. I didn't have much structure to my life. (III. Teitelbaum interview, 1986)

September 6–30: *Art Montreal '67*, Dunkelman Gallery, Toronto, Ontario (Ewen, Ferron, Fournelle, Hurtubise, Lacroix, Molinari, Sager, Saxe, Sullivan, de Tonnancour, Tousignant, Trudeau and Vaillancourt).

July/August: *Panorama of Painters from Quebec*, Musée d'art contemporain de Montréal, Montreal, Quebec, curated by Gilles Hénault.

September 22–October 15: *Ontario Centennial Exhibition*, works from across the country were included, selected by British critic Bryan Robertson. The show was funded by the Ontario Arts Council and travelled to the Art Gallery of Ontario and other centres in Ontario and Quebec.

1968

Summer: As a consequence of the stress of his separation from his family and the loss of his job at RCA Victor, Ewen ends up in Queen Mary Veterans Hospital in Montreal. Six weeks later, he travels to Kitchener, Ontario, to stay with his sister, Marjorie Margesson. Completes a small number of works. Enters Westminster Veterans Hospital, near London, Ontario, for treatment of recurring depression.

July: Five of Ewen's works are included in the National Gallery of Canada's *Seventh Biennial,* chosen by American curator William Seitz. Unusual in format, that year's biennial of 70 artists highlighted only 15 who were represented by multiple works. These artists were: Jack Bush, Paterson Ewen, Brian Fisher, Reg Holmes, Ernest Lindner, Jan Menses, Guido Molinari, Kazuo Nakamura, N.E. Thing Co., Toni Onley, William Perehudoff, Bodo Pfeifer, David Samila, Takao Tanabe and Harold Town.

The stay and the treatment did me a lot of good . . . I came out of there in a state of good physical and mental health. (III. McKaskell interview, 1976)

Autumn: Ewen moves into the York Hotel, London, and later to a studio at 521 Richmond Street. Here, he continues the *Lifestream* work begun in Montreal. These were small in scale and horizontal in format, and consisted of two or more lines broken at various intervals. By early spring of 1969, he has three new *Lifestream* series on the go. In each, acrylic paint was applied with a roller and contained within taped edges. The new series were characterized by a notable freedom of gesture. In the first of the three series, a single line floated through a colour field; in the second, the line was broken at irregular intervals; in the third, a wide band of free-floating stripes were painted across the surface of the canvas. All of the London *Lifestream* works were distanced from hard-edge abstraction by irregular lines floating in undefined space.

November: American critic and curator William Seitz receives *Close Up No. 2* (1967) for the permanent collection of the Rose Art Museum at Brandeis University, Waltham, Massachusetts, as a donation from Ben and Yael Dunkelman.

In recent years my friends in the painting world have been Molinari, Tousignant, Saxe and Hurtubise. From them I have learned the hard-edge technique and applied it in my own way. I don't use a ruler. I have never done a mural. I work from the desire to paint and paint in bursts. To me every painting is a different experience and I do not work from any particular theory. I wish to create rather than produce. In Montreal I have been called "the prospector." I accept this description in the sense that I do wish to continue always to explore. (II. Biographical statement, Dunkelman Gallery papers, 1968)

[Ewen's] purist style that developed stage by stage from free brush painting to arrive at an art of extreme elimination, makes primary abstraction the vessel for a concentrated poetics of existence, mortality and the measured beat of time.
(VI. 1968, Seitz)

March: *Paterson Ewen Retrospective*, Dunkelman Gallery, Toronto, Ontario.*

July/September: *Seventh Biennial of Canadian Painting*, curated by William Seitz, National Gallery of Canada, Ottawa, Ontario.

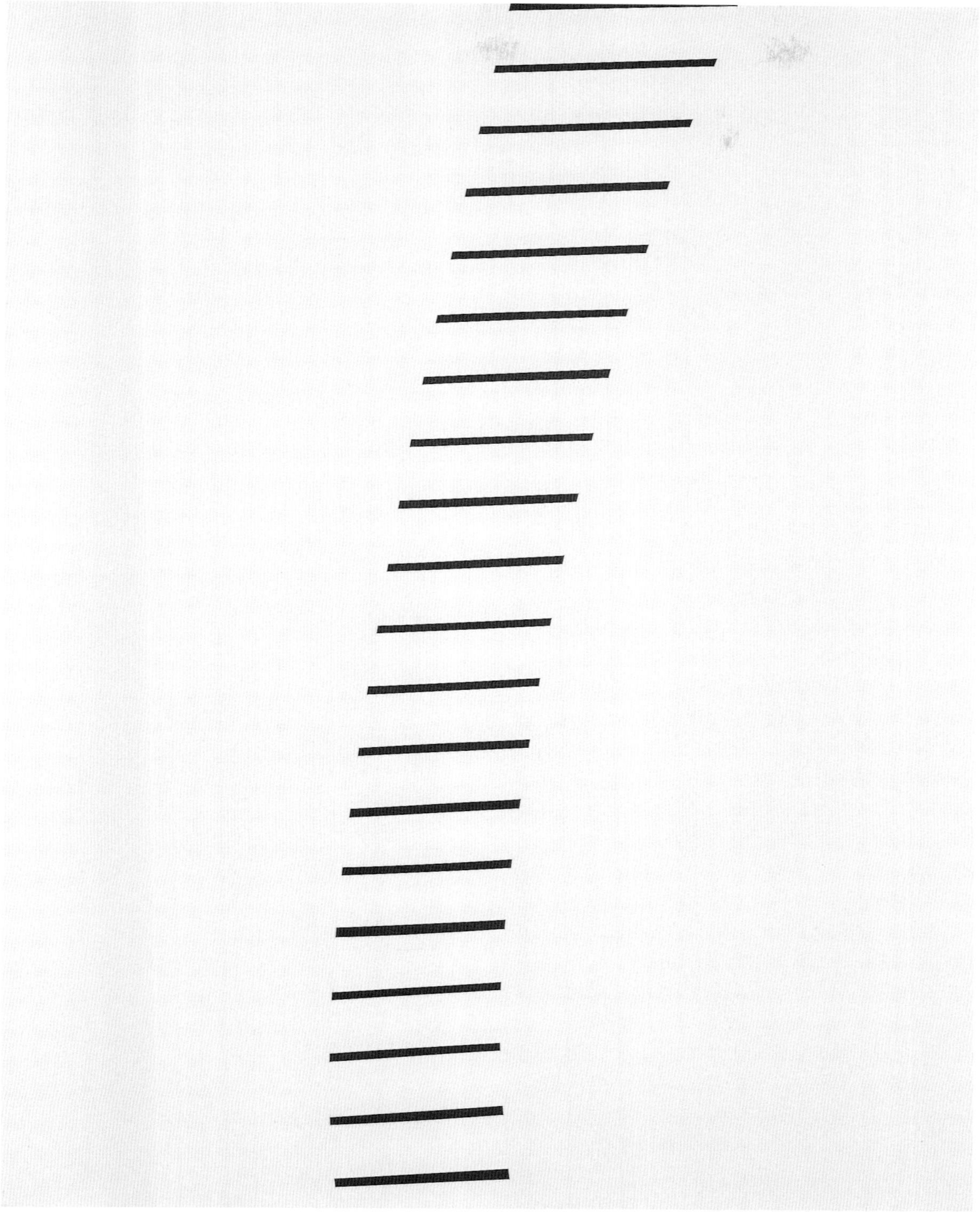

LIFESTREAM 1969
Acrylic on canvas
152.4 x 126.9
Private Collection

Facing page:
LIFESTREAM 1969
Acrylic on canvas
170.2 x 170.4
Art Gallery of Ontario

1969

September: Ewen begins teaching at H. B. Beal Secondary School, where he was hired by Herb Ariss. Don Bonham had introduced Ewen to the faculty at Beal, having invited him to give a talk to the art students. He teaches at Beal until the spring of 1971. Continues work on *Lifestream* paintings. Of his teaching at the time, Ariss recalled:
Pat had a first rate mind and was one of the best art critics I have ever listened to. He quickly instituted weekly art critiques which in the main was his teaching contribution. Naturally his example was a factor that many students tried to emulate. (Herb Ariss, 6 January 1987 letter to Matthew Teitelbaum)

The whole conception of the paintings is the idea of a life stream that goes through everyone's life and universal life—and I've picked a little bit of it for each painting. I feel there is a life force going on somewhere . . . it relates to electronic waves. (VIII. Crawford, 1969)

[In some cases] I would rip off little pieces of tape and put them across, so I would end up with all those little elongated rectangles. (III. Teitelbaum interview, 1986)

Walking into the Carmen Lamanna Gallery right now, for example, he might expect (drawn by advance notice) to see large-format, color-field paintings by the Canadian artist, Paterson Ewen. What he would see, instead, would be large paintings, indeed, one thick color to a canvas, each canvas cut across by a thumb-thick, flat-edged, parabolic line. The line neither cuts the painting into two appealing and/or parts, nor does it address the matter of gesture (of the artist's hand) adequately. The viewer, having coasted in, with his clutch let out, either reverses quickly or stands there until his generator dies. (VIII. Hale, 1969)

The stream articulates not only its own shape, but also that of the field it delimits, and this is a graphic equivalent to the interaction of the colour areas, so that declarative image-making gesture and structural organization of the picture plane are literally accomplished at one consummate, premeditated stroke. Not surprisingly, the paintings are most successful when most absolute. (VIII. Lord, December 1969)

Paterson Ewen's first painting and his last painting in this exhibition at 20/20 Gallery express a mode of both near and far, an all at once spontaneous totality, an immediate apprehension of form and space as a presence. The first painting suggests the parallax phenomenon. If you stand in front of a window and gaze out into the landscape and if you walk backwards from that position, you will notice that the building seems to get larger in its apparent size and seems to move closer to you. Simply because the frame of the window acts as a focal limitation and thereby radically discriminates the rest of the details beyond the presence of the buildings. The window seems to get smaller when you move away from it. Of course this is just a phenomenon. (VIII. Martin, 1970)

I was getting really sick of the static quality of my own hard-edge work and, at the same time, I didn't want to revert to some sort of pure gesture. I still wanted it to be basically abstract in nature . . . [The *Lifestream* paintings] . . . were done by painting a colour field, choosing a second colour very instinctively—just deciding at a certain point that the second colour was a colour I wanted and then standing back and looking at the canvas as if I was playing a football game or something and then attacking it with the tape and running the tape from one end of the canvas to the other as quickly as I could and then running a second piece of tape alongside that one.
(III. 1976, McKaskell interview)

February: *Paterson Ewen Retrospective*, McMaster University, Hamilton, Ontario.*

April 22–May 11: *London Survey,* 20/20 Gallery, London, Ontario (Ariss, Bellamy, Boyle, Bonham, Chambers, Coulter, Curnoe, Dewdney, Ewen, Favro and Fenwick).

August 21–September 16: *Group Exhibition,* Carmen Lamanna Gallery, Toronto, Ontario (Baxter, Berthot, Beveridge, Bolduc, Ewen, Kureau, Macklin, Marden, Martin, Mayensen, Molinari, Piao, Shields, Nova, Ristvedt and Rabinowitch).

September 3–30: *David Rabinowitch, Royden Rabinowitch and Paterson Ewen,* London Public Library and Art Museum, London, Ontario.

September 20–November 1: *London S/W 17,* Rothman's Art Gallery, Stratford, Ontario, (H. Ariss, M. Ariss, Bailey, Boyle, Brown, Chambers, Coulter, Ewen, Fones, Jefferess, Johnson, Kemp, Martin, Redinger, Steinbacher, Urquhart and Zelenak).

October 31–November 18: Carmen Lamanna Gallery, Toronto, Ontario.*

1970

Late Winter: Ewen moves into a studio at 19 King Street, London, Ontario, a building shared, at various times, with Dave Gordon, Murray Favro, Kerry Ferris, and Jamelie Hassan, among others. Here he paints his first "phenomena paintings," *Traces Through Space, Drop of Water on a Hot Surface* and, toward the end of 1970, *Rain Triptych.*

[*Traces Through Space*] was the breakthrough painting. I gave up brushes and everything else. I put gesso on, almost carelessly and dipped this piece of felt [in paint] and then [made] a dotted line. I had bits of felt . . . and I could shape them if I wanted larger dots or smaller dots. [After *Traces Through Space*] I realized I was into phenomenon. I started to collect scientific books, [though] not so scientific that I couldn't understand them. I went to early scientific books about rain [which] . . . I think are pretty sound scientifically. Not that I cared much. It was just like the still life as far as subject matter went. It was all diagrammatical. I did an artesian well, and then I did some lightning pieces . . . I felt the need to do a large [diagrammatical] work about how rain falls. [*Rain Triptych*] was the second to last canvas piece.
(III. Teitelbaum interview, 1986)

I really felt like just playing instead and I thought I was making an anti-art gesture in the formal sense with those last paintings. Daubing rows of dots on plain canvas with felt. But then somehow this turned out feeling like traces of things moving through space and this is what first suggested the idea of phenomena . . . I began reading. I got all kinds of amateur books and old textbooks about phenomena. How rain falls and how lightning works, clouds, eclipses and waves. I began to get the feeling as I read that what we usually call the more simple things are immensely complicated so I just accepted my limitations and put down the parts of these happenings that were for me fun to do. (VIII. Johnson, 1975)

Because of the persons who bought my paintings I have determined never to paint another canvas. I don't know what I'll do. But I'm determined it won't be this sort of thing. (VIII. Crawford, 1970)

As objects, my paintings fit into a category which I reject. (III. 1970, discussion at 20/20 Gallery)

[When Paterson came to London] he had a reputation from his days in Montreal, but [in London] he was showing with unknown artists. He wasn't famous, he wasn't known, didn't have a national reputation. So I think what was great about him was that he was willing to talk to the younger artists on an equal basis. [He wasn't] Harold Town or some famous figure dispensing wisdom. He was just somebody you could share conversation with. He had a lot of friends. Don Bonham, the American, and Greg Curnoe couldn't stand each other—and were sworn enemies. Bonham represented everything that Curnoe loathed and vice-versa [yet] Pat was friends with both of them. The business of the differences with ages just disappeared with him completely. (III. David Gordon interviewed by Teitelbaum, 1995)

Canadian Painters, Man and His World Pavilion, Montreal, Quebec.

30th Annual Western Ontario Exhibition, London, Ontario.

January 6–25: *Paterson Ewen Retrospective 1947–1969,* 20/20 Gallery, London, Ontario.*

May 2–24: *4 in 5, Four Artists in May,* Rothman's Art Gallery, Stratford, Ontario (Bonham, Ewen, C. Wickham Hughes and S. Hughes).

1971

March: Ewen shows his new figurative works for the first time in *Pie in the Sky,* an exhibition held in Toronto, made possible by a grant from the Ontario Arts Council. The exhibition is key for Ewen. Not only is it the first Toronto showing of his new "figurative" works, it is a public statement of his connectedness to a younger generation of London artists not recognized in the 1968 exhibition *Heart of London.* Don Bonham is his age, but the other artists are considerably younger: Dave Gordon, Bryan Maycock, Steve Parzybok and Bob Bozak. The exhibition is held in an abandoned auto showroom on Avenue Road in downtown Toronto. In a report for the Ontario Arts Council, Bob Bozak wrote:

The general concept of this show as well as that of the "Warehouse Co-op" was to collectively provide a self-appointed group the opportunity to show their works at a reasonable cost to those involved and to allow those to maintain complete control of the show. The intentions of the artists were certainly varied but all were dedicated to the idea of making the exhibit a success for the benefit of all. How the participants used their gained exposure is not important because the group's existence is only temporary. It is possible some may use the success towards attracting a dealer. (II. Maycock, 1971)

Ewen wrote the section on the exhibition's purpose and noted:
Purpose: to publicize the show and attract the interested public. I feel that the purpose was attained to a limited degree. As we had a band we attracted young people which is not bad as it was essentially a young group and the work is experimental. I enjoyed the opening as an integration of the visual and the auditory. The band was a bit expensive, however ($200). (II. Maycock, 1971)

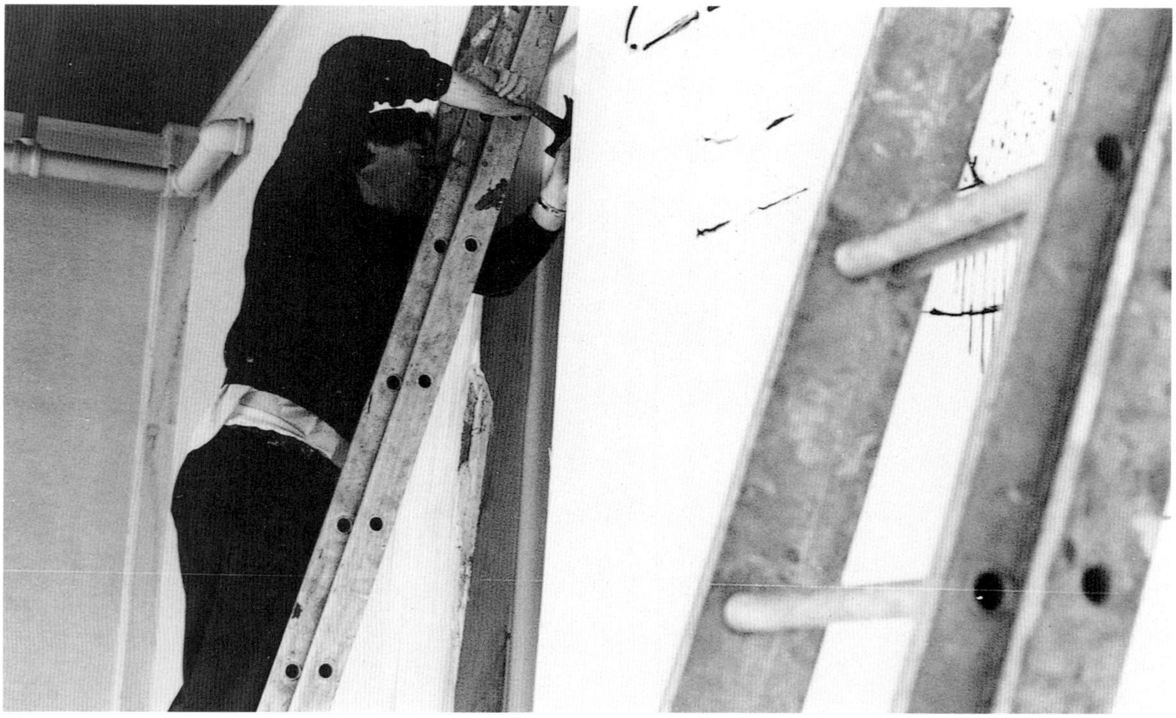

Installation shot of *Pie in the Sky* exhibition, 77 Avenue Road, Toronto, March 1971

Then I moved into phenomena . . . it was like—I saw diagrammatical paintings that had these dotted lines. That was exactly at the same time as Philip Guston moved from his quite good abstract paintings to his excellent crazy paintings, also made up of dotted lines. The fact [is] that Dave Gordon actually came down with an issue of *Art in America* or one of the other art magazines, showed me what Philip Guston was doing . . . and that was quite a laugh. (III. Teitelbaum interview, 1986)

April/May: Ewen completes his first three works incorporating varied material including wood and sheet metal. These works are, in order of realization: *Thunderchain, Rocks Moving in the Current of a Stream,* and *How Lightning Worked in 1925.*

June: Receives a grant of $7,500 (a Senior Fellowship) from The Canada Council. As a result, he takes a leave of absence from his position at H. B. Beal Secondary School and uses the money to move to Toronto and set up a studio; this enables him to be a full-time artist for the first time. Ewen takes with him the unfinished *Thunder Cloud as Generator #I.* Shortly after moving to Toronto, he completes this work and its companion, *Thunder Cloud as Generator #2.* He realizes his first two gouged works on plywood, *Solar Eclipse* and later *Eruptive Prominence.*

Summer: Don Norman, a young Toronto artist, lends Ewen an electric router to replace his hand gouge, allowing him to work on his paintings with greater speed and freedom; soon after, he purchases it from Norman for $50. The first works made with the router are *City Storm with Chain Lightning, Forked Lightning* and *Storm Over the Prairies.*

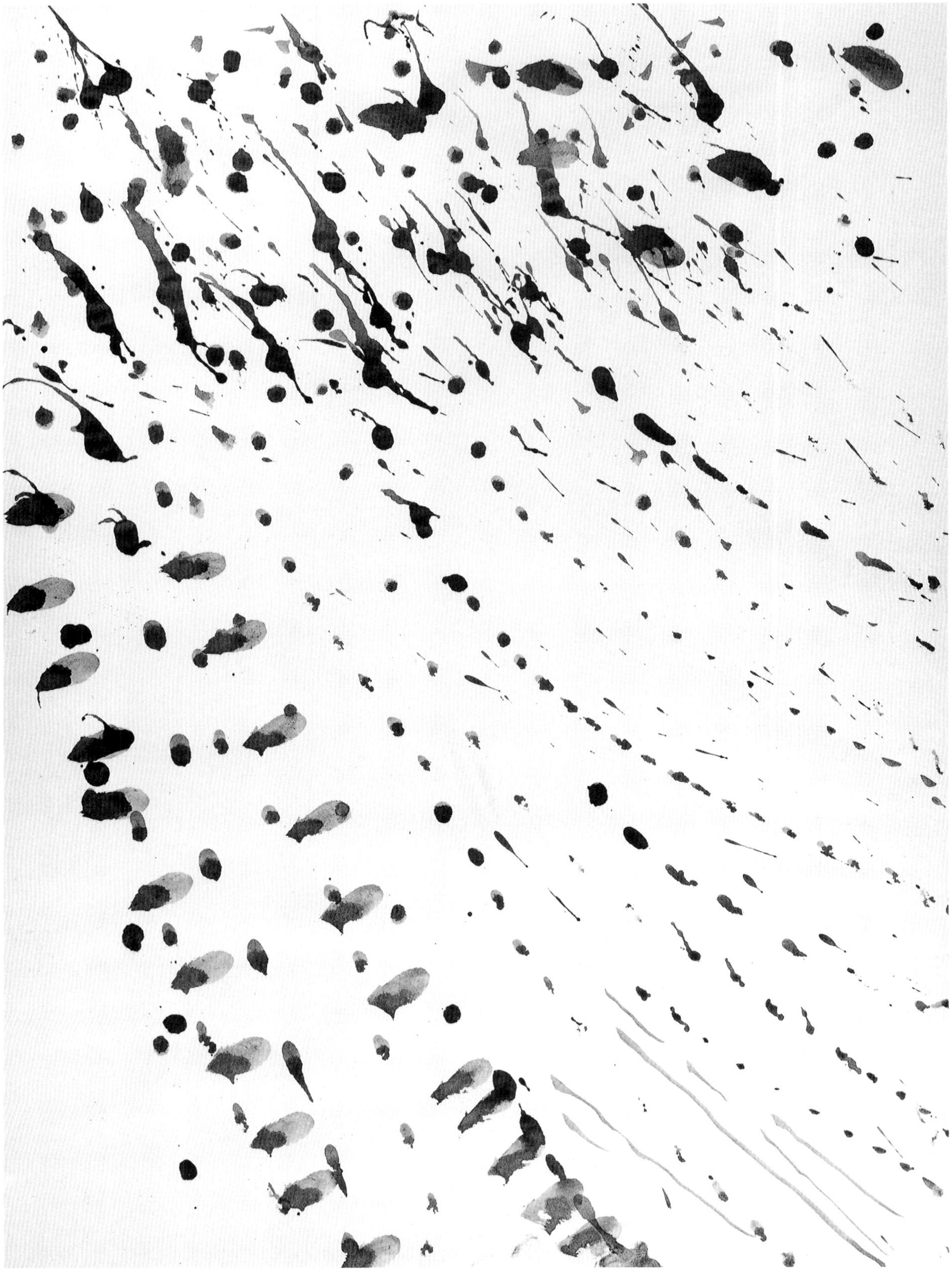

RAIN HIT BY WIND #1
1971
Japanese ink on paper
60.5 x 45.8
Art Gallery of Ontario, promised gift of Alan and Alison Schwartz

Facing page:
RAIN HIT BY WIND #2
1971
Japanese ink on paper
60.5 x 46.0
Art Gallery of Ontario, promised gift of Alan and Alison Schwartz

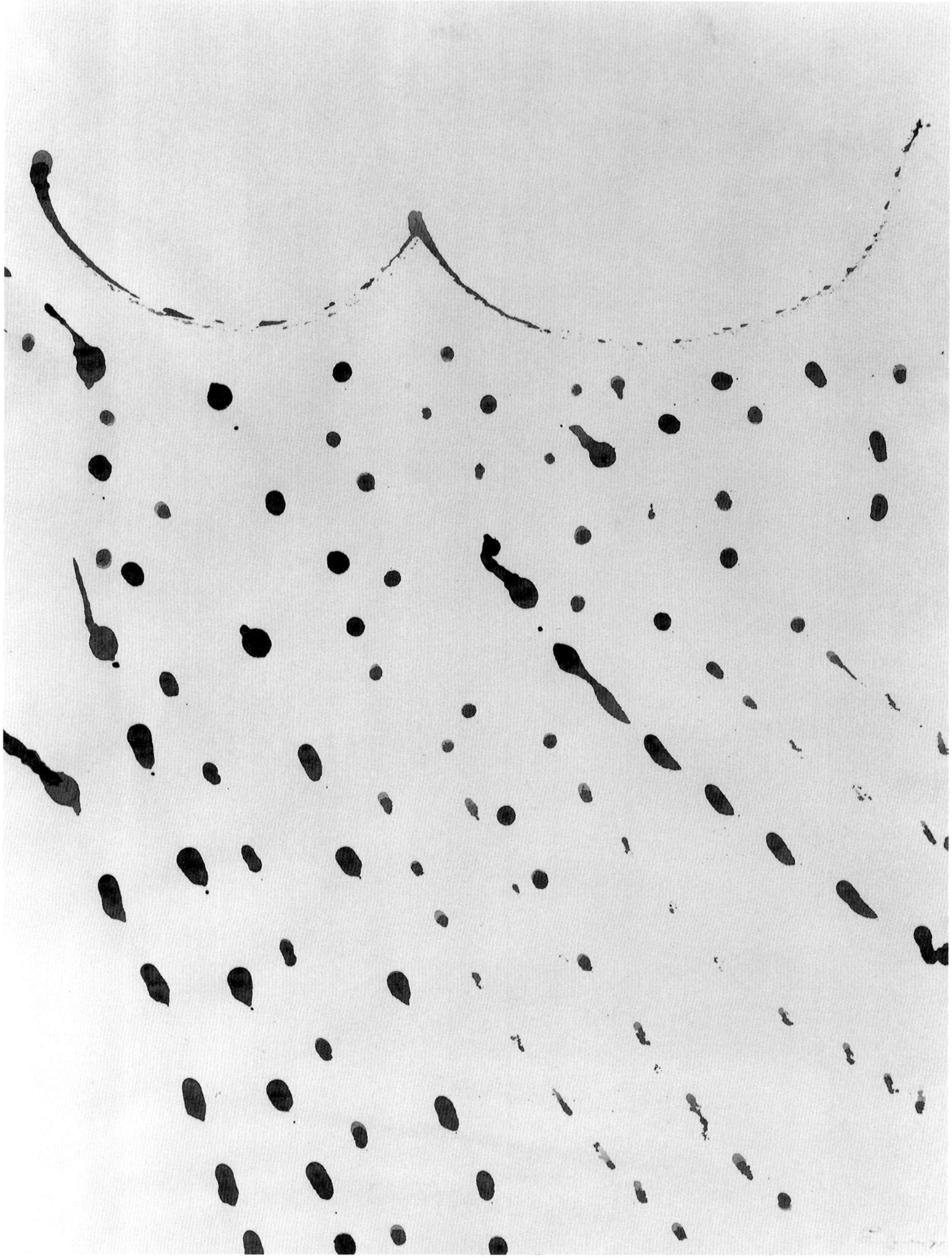

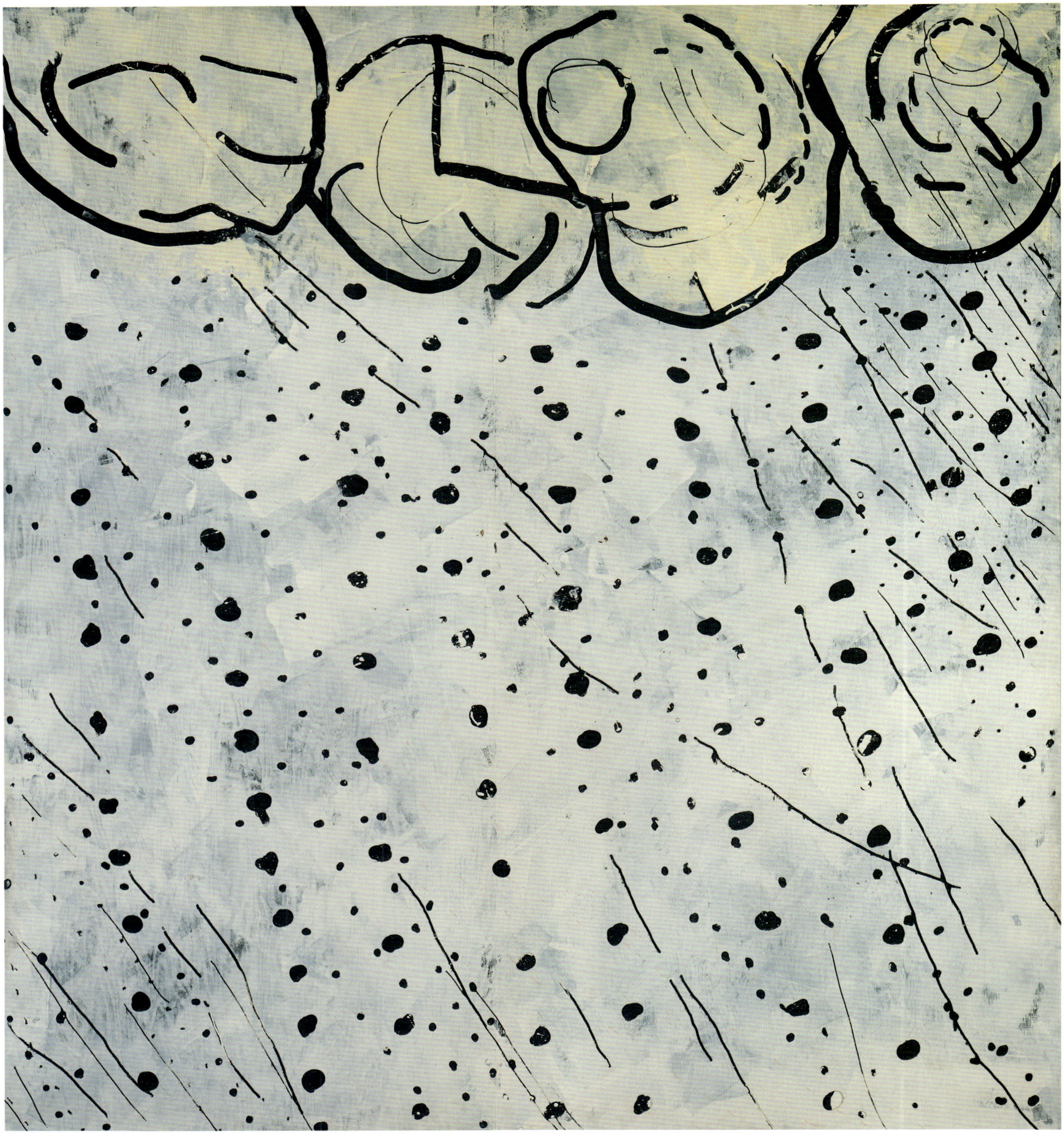

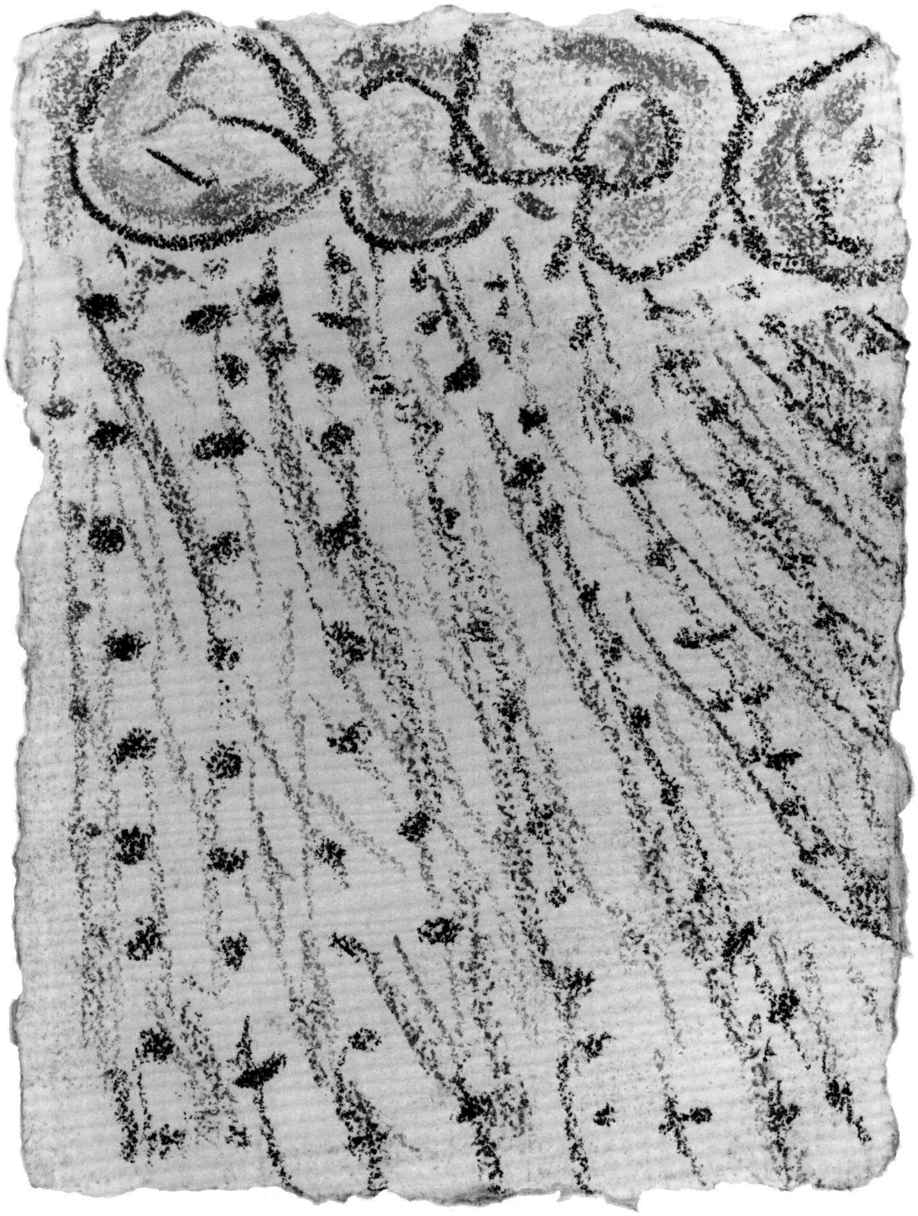

PRECIPITATION 1986
Crayon on handmade paper
25.7 x 19.1
Art Gallery of Ontario

Facing page:
PRECIPITATION 1973
Acrylic on gouged plywood
244.0 x 229.0
Art Gallery of Ontario

All of the pieces in the first exhibition at Carmen's of this more or less ecological work, phenomena pictures, were hand gouged. But then a friend in Toronto said, I have an electrical router and why don't you try that. I was a little suspicious. I still had the old almost academic idea—well, I don't know about machinery you know. But he said borrow my router and try it and if it suits you you can buy it. Which is what happened. As soon as I started to use it I found that by this method of kneeling down with it I could really draw quite freely with it. (VIII. Johnson, 1975)

October: Not yet a "gallery artist" with Carmen Lamanna, Ewen invites Ben Dunkelman to his basement studio in Toronto, 81 A Front Street East, to look at his latest work. Jared Sable, representing Dunkelman Gallery, replies in a letter to Ewen that they are not interested in mounting a show of his work.

NORTHERN LIGHTS 1973
Acrylic, oil, dry pigment on galvanized steel and gouged plywood
167.5 x 244.0
Art Gallery of Ontario

Paterson Ewen's sketches for paintings—Rainfall, Flag Effect *and* Thunder Cloud—*are superb drawings in Japanese ink or Magic Marker. They have the same kind of thoughtful planning and spontaneity which characterize the paintings.* (VII. "Auto Displays . . .", 1971)

March 19–31: *Pie in the Sky,* in a former automobile showroom at 77 Avenue Road, Toronto, Ontario (Don Bonham, Bob Bozak, Dave Gordon, Paterson Ewen, Bryan Maycock and Steve Parzybok).

1972

July: Ewen receives a short-term grant from The Canada Council.

Late Summer: Ewen returns to London. His position at H.B. Beal Secondary School was filled during his absence in Toronto; he is hired as a lecturer in the visual arts department at the University of Western Ontario in London.

When I accepted $7,500 grant, June 1971—I gave up a teaching job at $11,600. I have appreciated the time to work, but now *I am destitute and in debt* for materials, rent, etc. (II. Canada Council application, 1972)

The work became a lot more fun when I was able to start nailing stuff on it—whether it was link fence in the case of *Rain and Fog Lifting from the Mountain* or another piece where I used a piece of fibre matting as grass, or [when] I made a piece with chainlightning and I used a piece of real chain for the lightning. I've been having fun with this thing. And that's very important. It certainly is to me. (III. Kricorissian interview, 1979)

January 5–20: *Phenomena-scapes by Paterson Ewen,* Carmen Lamanna Gallery, Toronto, Ontario.*

1973

October-November: Ewen exhibits at the Carmen Lamanna Gallery in Toronto, his third solo show there. For the first time, he is able to sell all of his paintings; among the purchasers are the National Gallery of Canada, the Art Gallery of Ontario, The Canada Council Art Bank and the Department of External Affairs.

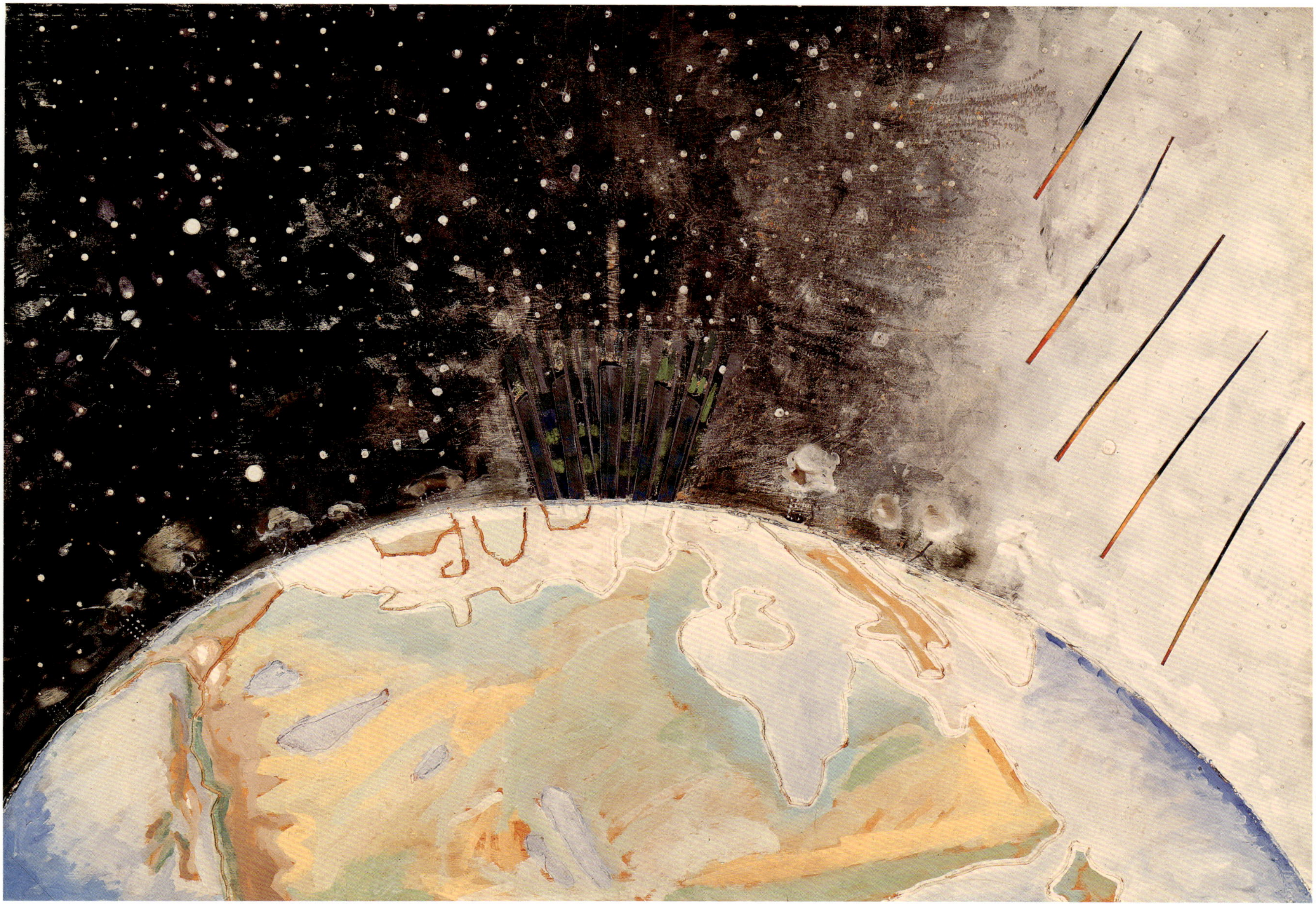

I saw a little bandaged man in an encyclopedia. It was maybe two inches high and it was explaining all the different bandages—foot bandages, knee bandages, etc., etc. It intrigued me so much I thought I would do a bandaged man on a four-by-eight piece of plywood using canvas as the bandage [*Bandaged Man*]. I was a bit of a wreck at the time after my year in Toronto. And as I went along with the bandaged man I began to realize it looked more and more like me. It had my body and it became very scary. When I went to bed at night I used to turn it to the wall. There's no question it is a kind of self-portrait. Maybe it's going too far but I'm not so sure. To say maybe I did that at a time when I was a wreck and needed bandages. (x. Rochon, 1988)

[*Precipitation*] was the last painting I worked on with the plywood upright and it was the only occasion in all of this last work of five years when I've been routing and gouging that I almost injured myself . . . It was just a convention because I was used to working as on an easel painting standing in front . . . and I got up on a ladder with a router . . . using a big bit tearing through plywood at 1/2-inch depth at 25,000 rpm . . . there is a lot of torque and the router started coming toward my face. I can't see this painting without thinking of that hazard but I must say I did get a very vigorous cloud out of it. From this point on I worked on the saw horses, no more ladders. (v. Shadbolt and Johnson, 1977)

To the best of my present memory [*Northern Lights*] is the only work in this series that comes from a direct experience. I was in Algonquin Park on a snow-shoe trip and there was a very exciting aurora borealis and when I got back from the trip I said that's going to be my next painting . . . I used radiation again—strips of galvanized iron with colours of the spectrum on it. (v. Shadbolt and Johnson, 1977)

What matters about these pictures, however, is not only the subject matter itself or its scientific basis, but also the sheer physical vigor of the visual statement. This is neither process nor concept art, but work very frankly concerned with art objects and with pictorial effects. The paintings are executed on single or joined sheets of framed plywood whose original character is not only never lost sight of, but rather tends to be emphasized by the way the plywood is manipulated. The edges of clouds, the lines of force of air currents, raindrops and the direction of their fall, the paths of stars, the contours of a hill are gouged out of the surface of the plywood by hand or with a router, not with any craftsmanly precision, but roughly, almost brutally, as if to emulate the vigor of the natural processes. (vii. Untitled review, *Artscanada*, December 1973)

Paterson Ewen has made art out of a perspective that has only been used in the past by science-fiction illustrators. It has been a daring thing to do because the cliché is so well established. The artist's eye is situated out in space, in a position which is threatened by occasional atmospheric violence. Ewen's paintings are of the weather, the galaxy, the planet . . . Because Ewen takes a gay, almost cartoon view of the world from his outpost in space, and because everything in these paintings looks as though it has been done with vigorous pleasure, he is able to achieve a synthesis, frequently attempted but rarely achieved in painting today. (viii. Homer, 1973)

Art Gallery of Waterloo, Waterloo, Ontario.

Art '74, Beth Tzedec Congregation, Toronto, Ontario.

October 13–November 1: Carmen Lamanna Gallery, Toronto, Ontario.*

1974

I have to put the plywood up on wooden sawhorses. The sheets are so big I can't reach the middle, so I have to climb right up on them and go gouging and painting on all fours. (VIII. Dault, 1974)

[My] new paintings: They are more weather as such. And in terms of materials I think you can write it down mostly to that large sheet of plywood worked upon with the router. Kneeling in the middle of the painting with that gouging machine. It was like an exercise, a physical exercise in almost an oriental position. This being in the center of the work instead of standing up opposite it is so much a part of the process. Although this only struck me after I found myself doing it. (VIII. Johnson, 1975)

All over the whole thing I grooved into the wood with the electrical router, changing the bit as I felt the groove should be larger or smaller . . . I have to put myself in the center of the whole thing that's going on and holding it together. When I move to one side and feel it tipping I must be careful to shift my weight back and stretch out my arms as far as I can. And in this very exciting and very physically demanding process, the machine is very noisy and dangerous at 25 thousand revolutions a minute, I have to be quite careful not to get my clothes caught or gouge the side of my knee. (VIII. Johnson, 1975)

The Great Wave: Homage to Hokusai: I've seen several other artists' versions of Hokusai's *Great Wave* since . . . and it's not so strange . . . what an image! There was van Gogh and then I've seen some other contemporary versions, as a matter of fact I saw it on a quilt by, I think, Larry Bell . . . so certainly it is some kind of prototypical image . . . I don't believe too much in originality . . . you learn art from other art and then looking into somebody's face or landscape is the point of departure to do your work of art. I did the same thing here as with the Galaxy . . . [I] looked at many versions, all reproductions of the print, all differing in colour, paper, ink quality and none that close. I just wanted a big wave and was quite ready to let Hokusai influence me in the making of a great wave . . . all I wanted was sky and water . . . you take what you want and leave out what you want, that is the great luxury of the artist. (V. Shadbolt and Johnson, 1977)

Paterson Ewen has done an extraordinary thing with painting. Ewen paints landscapes. Archetypally Canadian landscapes, full of rain and cold wind, icy clouds, and the deep, black water of northern lakes. In a sense Paterson Ewen is the classical inheritor and possessor of the conventions of the Group of Seven. (VIII. Dault, 1974)

Paterson Ewen's movement from an interest in earthscapes and earth structures into the planets, the stars, and the universe might be read as a return from his earlier interest in physicality to the spiritual, the unearthly. That both aspects exist simultaneously in the works in this exhibition gives them the poignancy of primitive vigour reaching for an expression of ethereality. (VI. Balkind, 1976)

Green Scene, National Museum of Natural Sciences, Ottawa, Ontario.

October 24–November 10: *Present Company: In Pursuit of Recent Art in Ontario*, Art Gallery of Ontario, Toronto, Ontario.

November 30–December 19: Carmen Lamanna Gallery, Toronto, Ontario.*

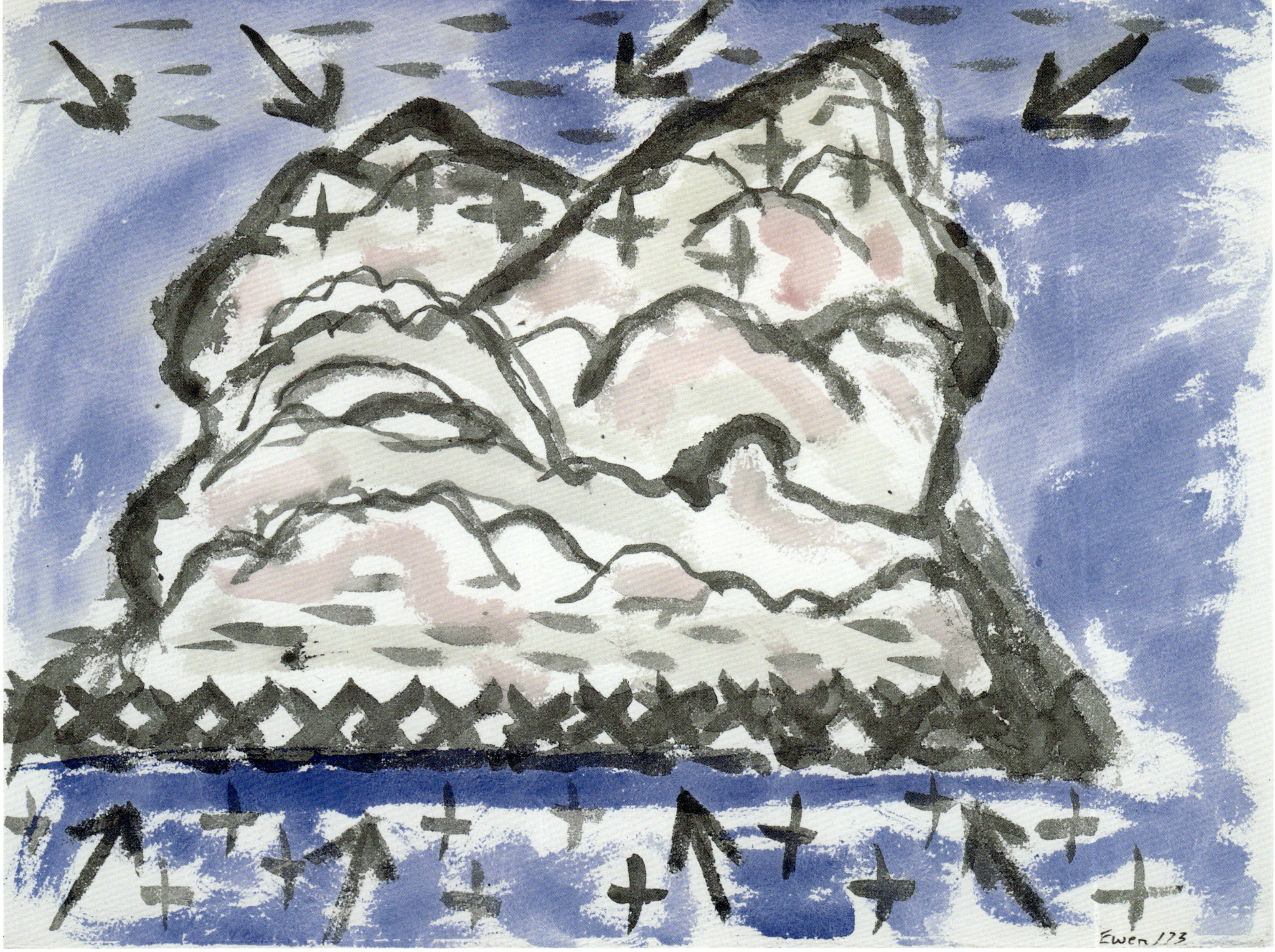
Ewen '73

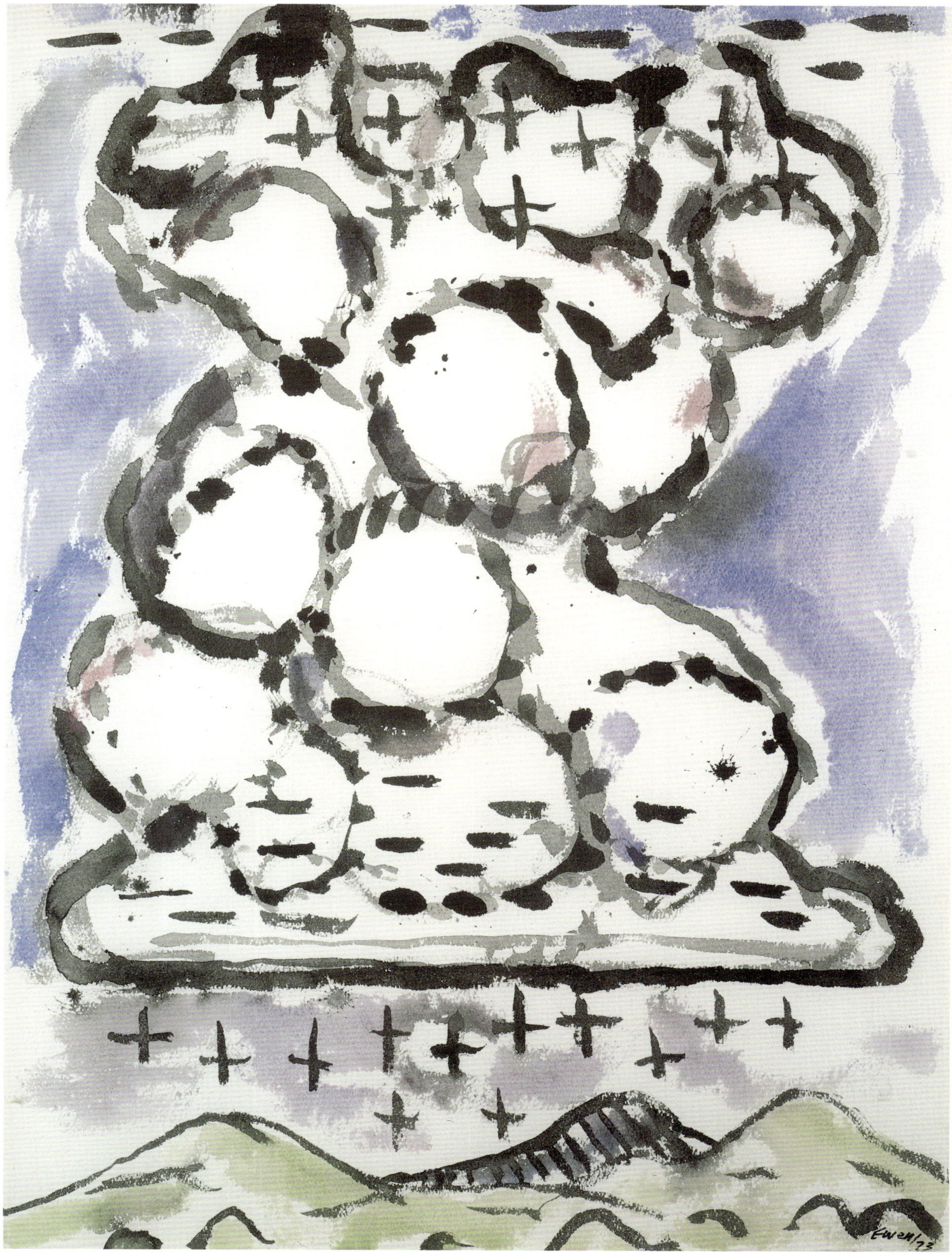

THUNDER CLOUD AS GENERATOR #4 1973
Watercolour on
Arches paper
76.2 x 57.5
Art Gallery of Ontario

Facing page:
THUNDER CLOUD AS GENERATOR #3 1973
Watercolour on
Arches paper
57.5 x 76.2
Art Gallery of Ontario

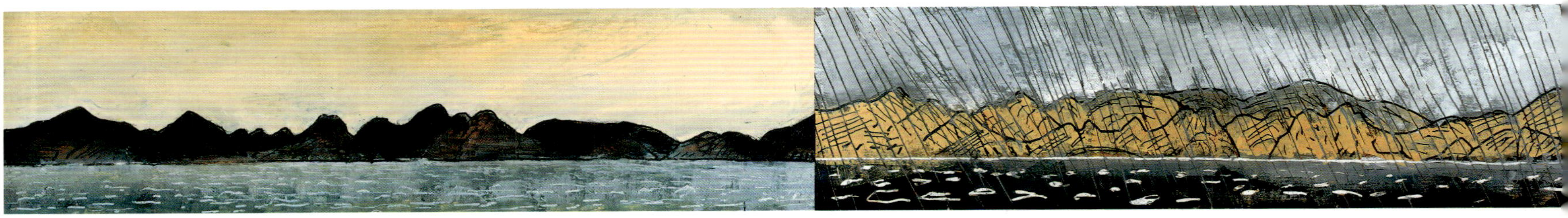

Above:
COASTAL TRIP 1974
Acrylic on plywood with incised line
3 panels, each 61.0 x 243.8
Art Gallery of Ontario

Right:
COASTAL TRIP 1974
Acrylic on plywood with incised line
centre panel, 61.0 x 243.8
Art Gallery of Ontario

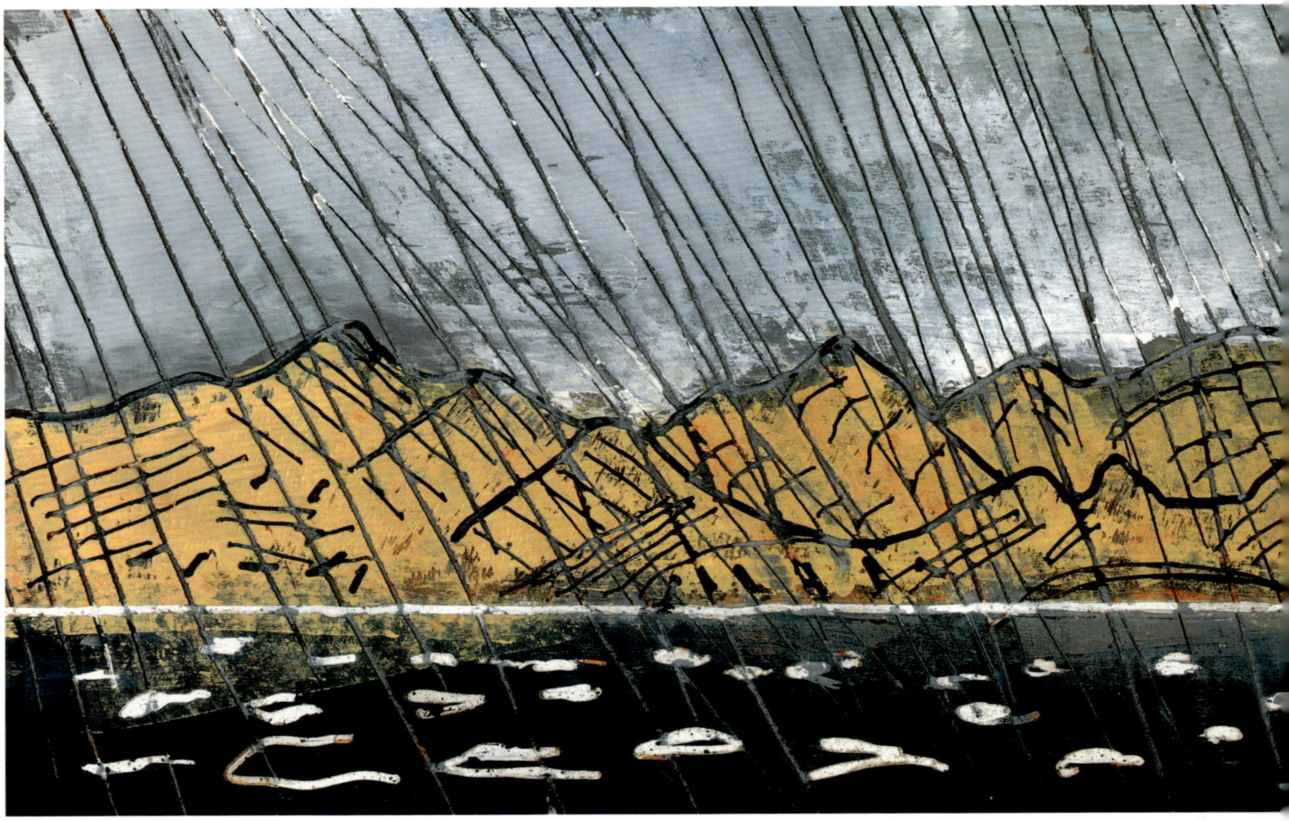

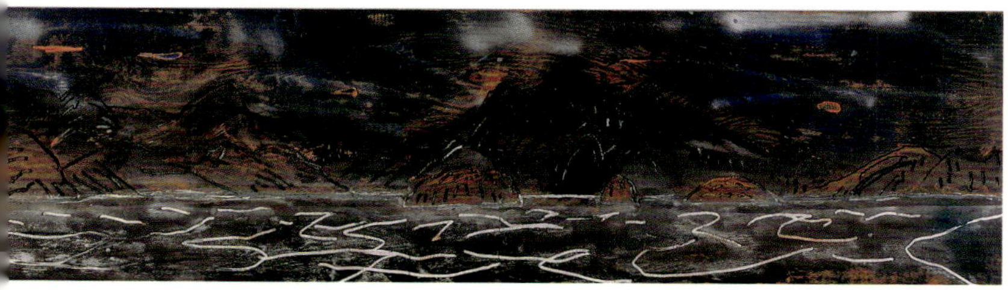

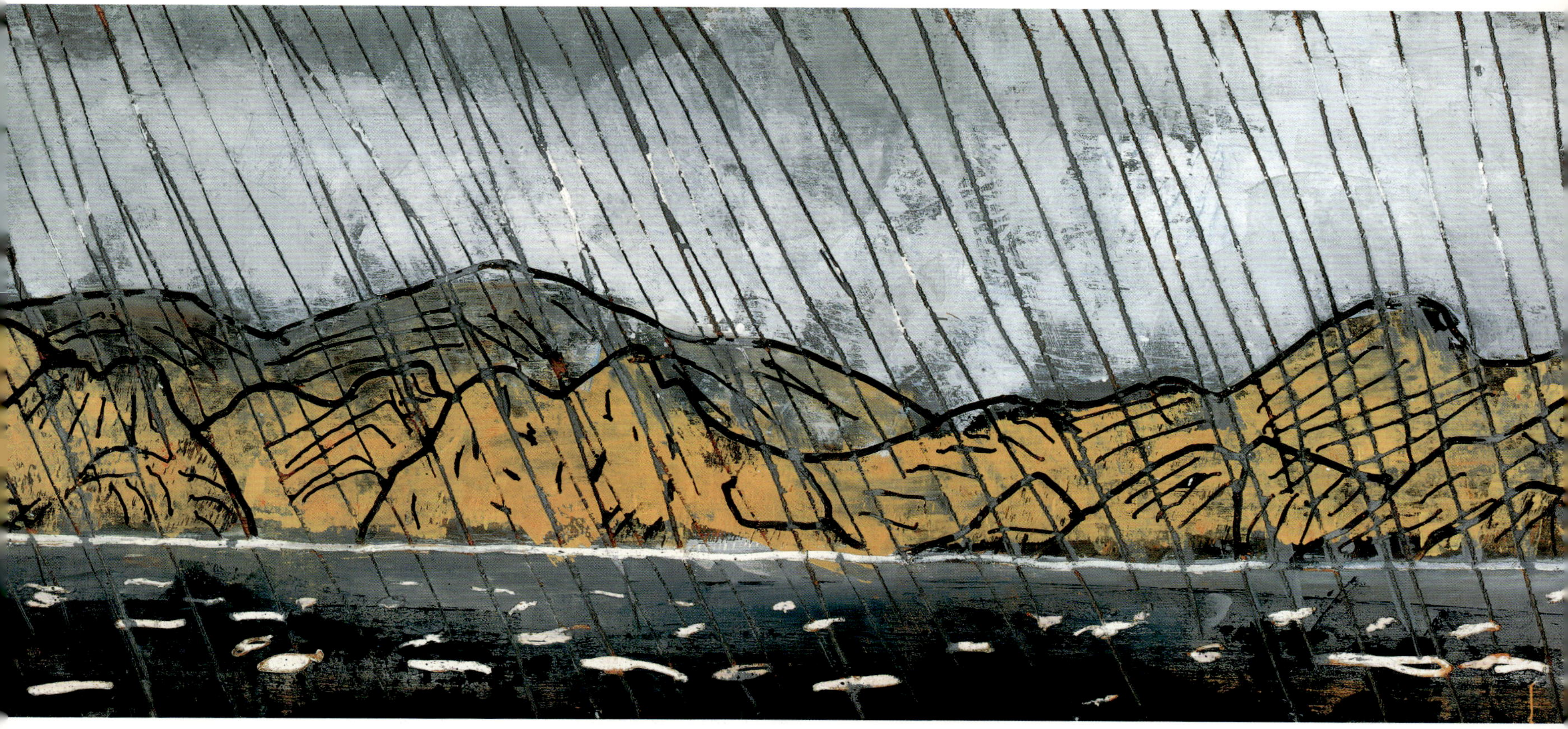

PORTRAIT OF VINCENT

1974

Mixed media on plywood

243.8 x 121.9

Vancouver Art Gallery

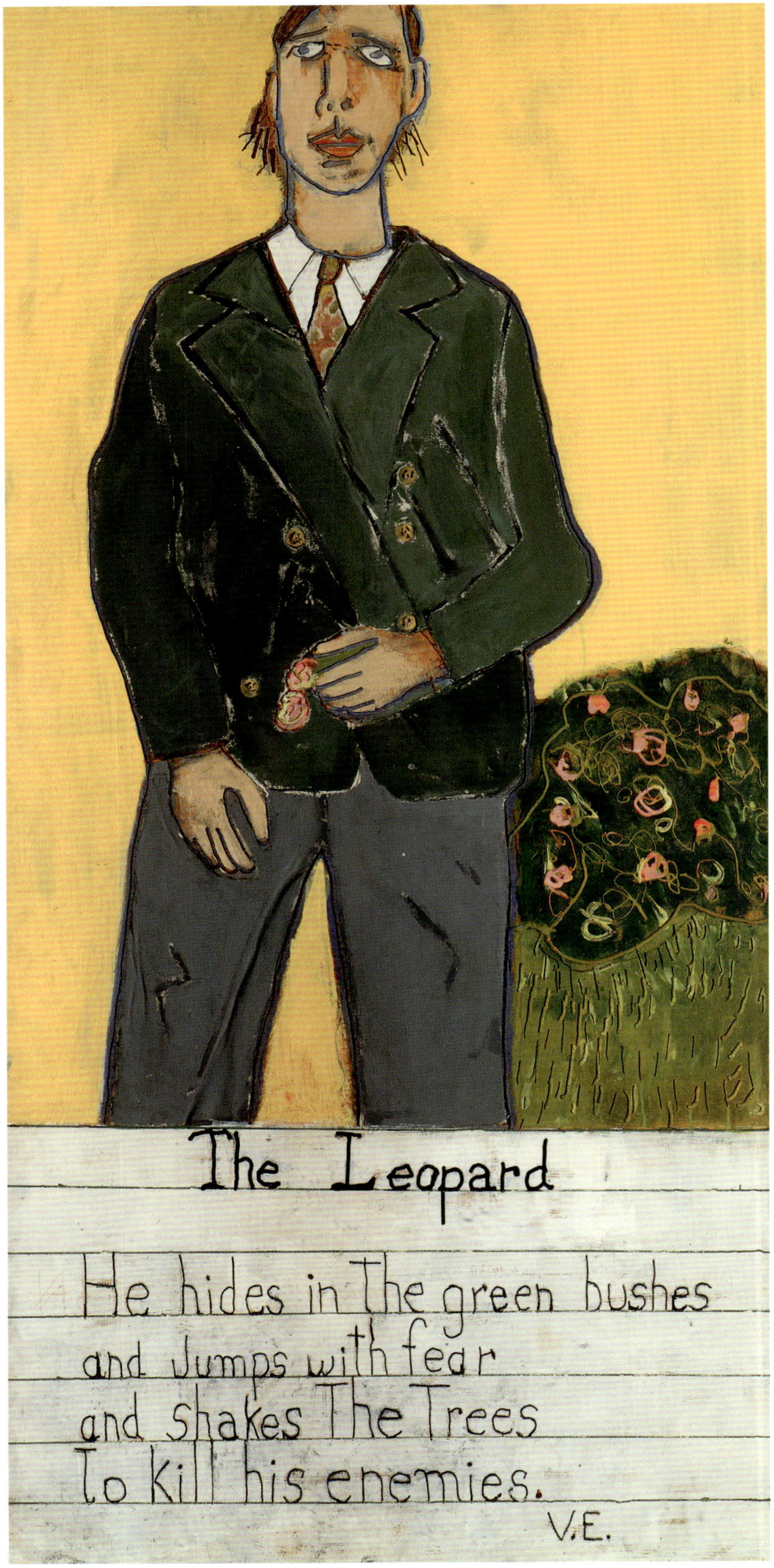

1975

Summer: Ewen learns from University of Western Ontario colleague Helmut Becker how to make his own paper for his watercolours on a paper-making machine in the fine arts department.

Autumn: Ewen serves on the Canada Council Art Bank Advisory Arts Selection Committee.

December: Elected as a member of the Royal Canadian Academy of Arts.

The coastlines of the new paintings I got from a very peculiar book. It is a Japanese marine book and it is tied together with string like shoelaces . . . In fact I have always since I was a boy had a penchant for things Japanese. There was a coincidence. We happened to meet the secretary to the Japanese ambassador one time when he was in Montreal, and he came to dinner at our house. And he brought gifts for each of us . . . he gave me a book on Hiroshige. You know we have different books when we are boys and this one I liked a lot and kept going back on. It deals with coastlines and with islands and with rain. And you know the Japanese artist's method was to go out into the rain or to observe a tree or a bird or a flower or a wave but he would never try to depict it then. He would simply observe it and when he had captured enough of it in all levels of his being, then he would go back and do it. (VIII. Johnson, 1976)

During the early 1970s rumours were circulated about the death of painting by people who could not accept the superficiality of the Modernist aesthetic. In a tremendous burst of energy, Ewen began to play with everything he had learned about painting, developing a strategy for work that allowed "constant decision making; real, intuitive decision making because you come up with more or less random effects that are beautiful in themselves." The surfaces of the paintings on wood are crowded with decisions made. The wood is a material for drawing in with a router and on with paint and felt markers, and a surface for painting on (the image) and over (runs of paint), while the added materials, completing their function as image, are restored to their essence as things. (V. McKaskell, 1976)

January 6–25: *The Carmen Lamanna Gallery at the Owens Art Gallery*, Owens Art Gallery, Mount Allison University, Sackville, New Brunswick.

January 16–February 16: *The Canadian Canvas*, travelling exhibition sponsored by Time Canada Ltd.: Musée d'art contemporain, Montreal, Quebec; Musée du Québec, Quebec; Edmonton Art Gallery, Edmonton, Alberta; Vancouver Art Gallery, Vancouver, British Columbia; Mendel Art Gallery, Saskatoon, Saskatchewan; Art Gallery of Ontario, Toronto, Ontario; Anna Leonowens Gallery and Dalhousie University Art Gallery, Halifax, Nova Scotia; Alberta College of Art, Calgary, Alberta; and Winnipeg Art Gallery, Winnipeg, Alberta.

March 16–April 26: *A Response to the Environment*, Rutgers University Art Gallery, New Brunswick, New Jersey.

September 13–October 1: *Watercolour Retrospective*, Forest City Gallery, London, Ontario.*

1976

June-July: Ewen is invited by Eric Fischl, a painter and faculty member, to visit the Nova Scotia College of Art and Design in Halifax, Nova Scotia, as a guest lecturer. While in Halifax for a month, Ewen works on two lithographs, *Thunder Cloud as Generator* and *Thundercloud as a Generator*.

August: Ewen teaches for a three-week period at the Banff School of Fine Arts in Banff, Alberta.

Ewen, who has read many textbooks on atmospheric conditions, bases much of his recent work on the climactic: In a child-like diagrammatic way he translates raindrops into fragmentary parallel lines and dots; clouds become crude, circular tracings. However, one does not come to these paintings to learn the difference between a cirrus and cumulonimbus cloud. Instead the semi-figurative subject matter, employed as a declaration relinquishing formalism, is a kind of point of departure, an amusing armature from where one takes off and to which one returns with a new perspective. (VIII. Lehmann, 1976)

Ontario Now—A Survey of Contemporary Art in Ontario, Kitchener-Waterloo Art Gallery, Kitchener, Ontario, and Art Gallery of Hamilton, Hamilton, Ontario.

January 9–February 1: *London Painting Now,* London Regional Art Gallery, London, Ontario.

February–March 1977: *Changing Visions: The Canadian Landscape,* organized by the Art Gallery of Ontario and the Edmonton Art Gallery; exhibited at the Art Gallery of Ontario, and ten other centres.

April 3–22: *Exhibition of Drawings: Carr-Harris, Ewen, Janitch, Favro, D. Rabinowitch, Tangredi,* Carmen Lamanna Gallery, Toronto, Ontario.

May 31–July 4: *Seventeen Canadian Artists: A Protean View,* Vancouver Art Gallery, Vancouver, British Columbia.

June 26–July 29: *Carr-Harris/Ewen/General Idea/Janitch/Mackenzie/Martin/David Rabinowitch/Royden Rabinowitch/Tangredi,* Carmen Lamanna Gallery, Toronto, Ontario.

August: *Faculty Exhibition,* Walter Phillips Gallery, Banff, Alberta.

September 23–November 7: *Forum 76,* Montreal Museum of Fine Arts, Montreal, Quebec.

October 9–November 7: *Seven Canadian Painters,* from the collection of The Canada Council Art Bank, Ottawa, exhibited at The Harbourfront Art Gallery, Toronto, Ontario.

November 6–30: *Paterson Ewen Retrospective,* London Regional Art Gallery, London, Ontario.*

December 18–January 16, 1977: *Paterson Ewen,* Galerie B, Montreal, Quebec.*

PEGASUS QUADRANGLE 1975
Watercolour on handmade paper
49.5 x 61.3
Art Gallery of Ontario

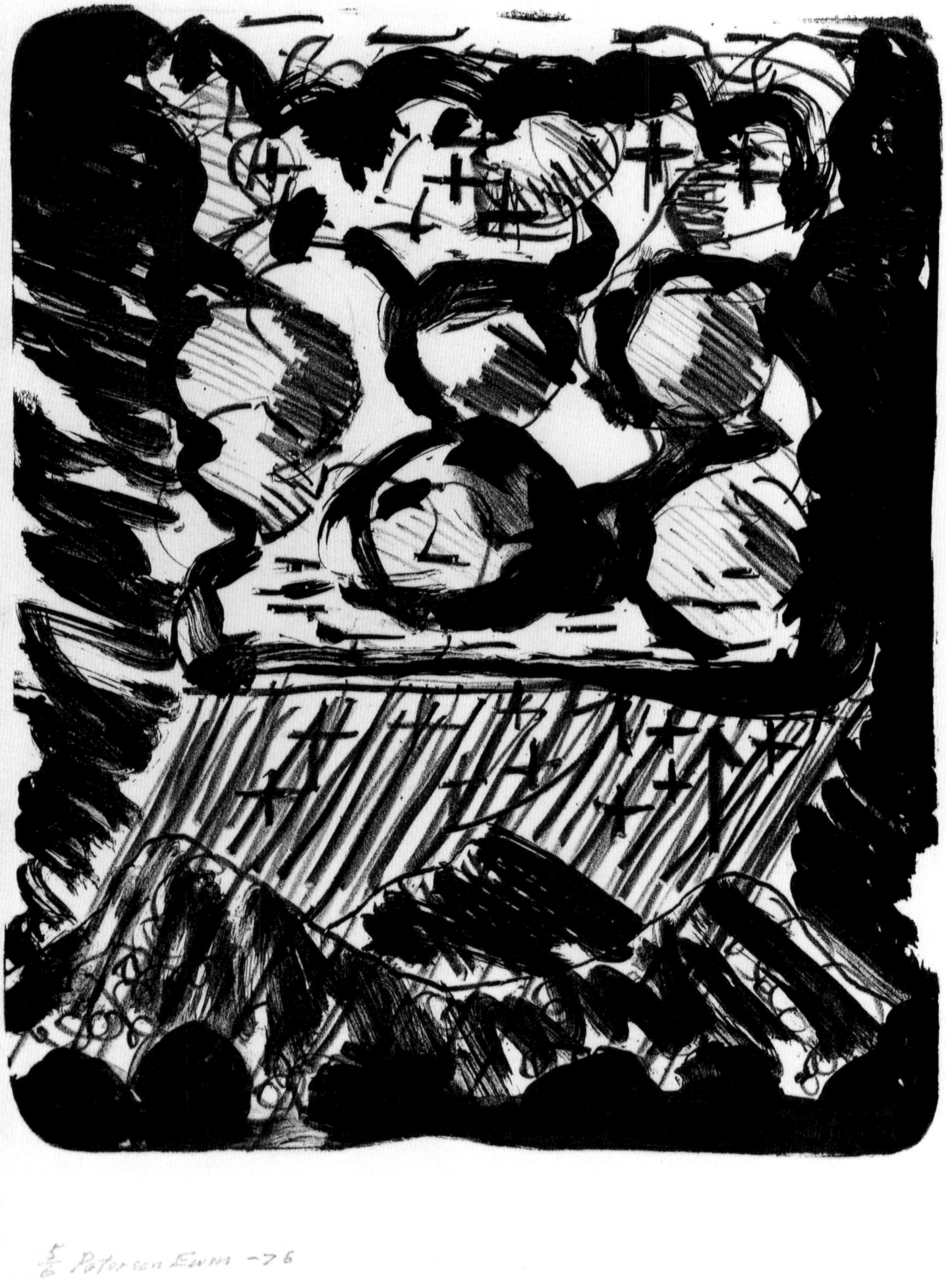
Paterson Ewen -76

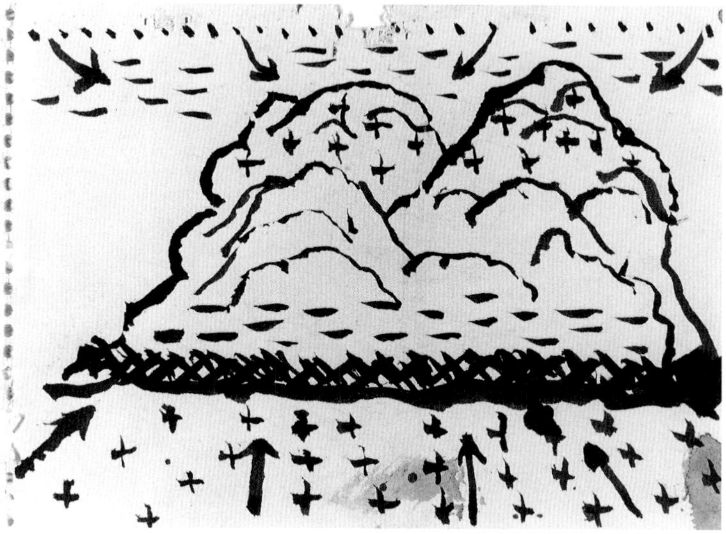

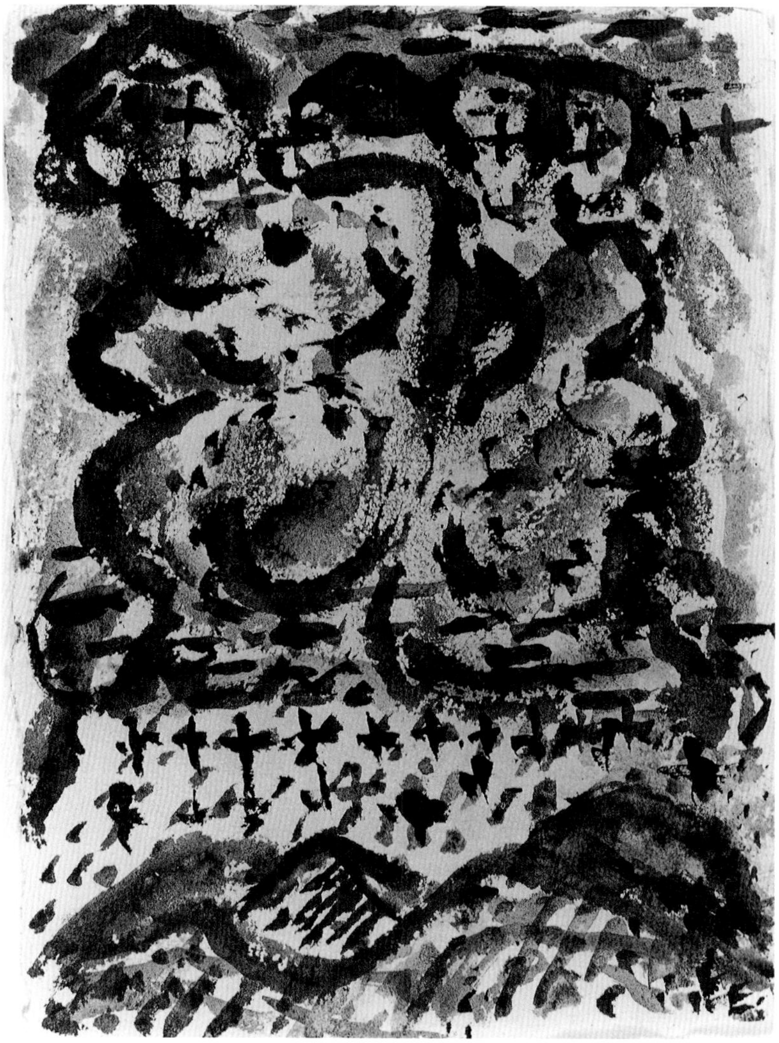

THUNDER CLOUD AS GENERATOR c. 1973
Japanese ink on paper
12.9 x 17.8
Art Gallery of Ontario

CUMULUS CLOUD AS A GENERATOR 1986
Acrylic on handmade paper
25.4 x 18.4
Art Gallery of Ontario

Facing page:
THUNDER CLOUD AS GENERATOR 1976
Lithograph on paper
38.3 x 28.4
Art Gallery of Ontario

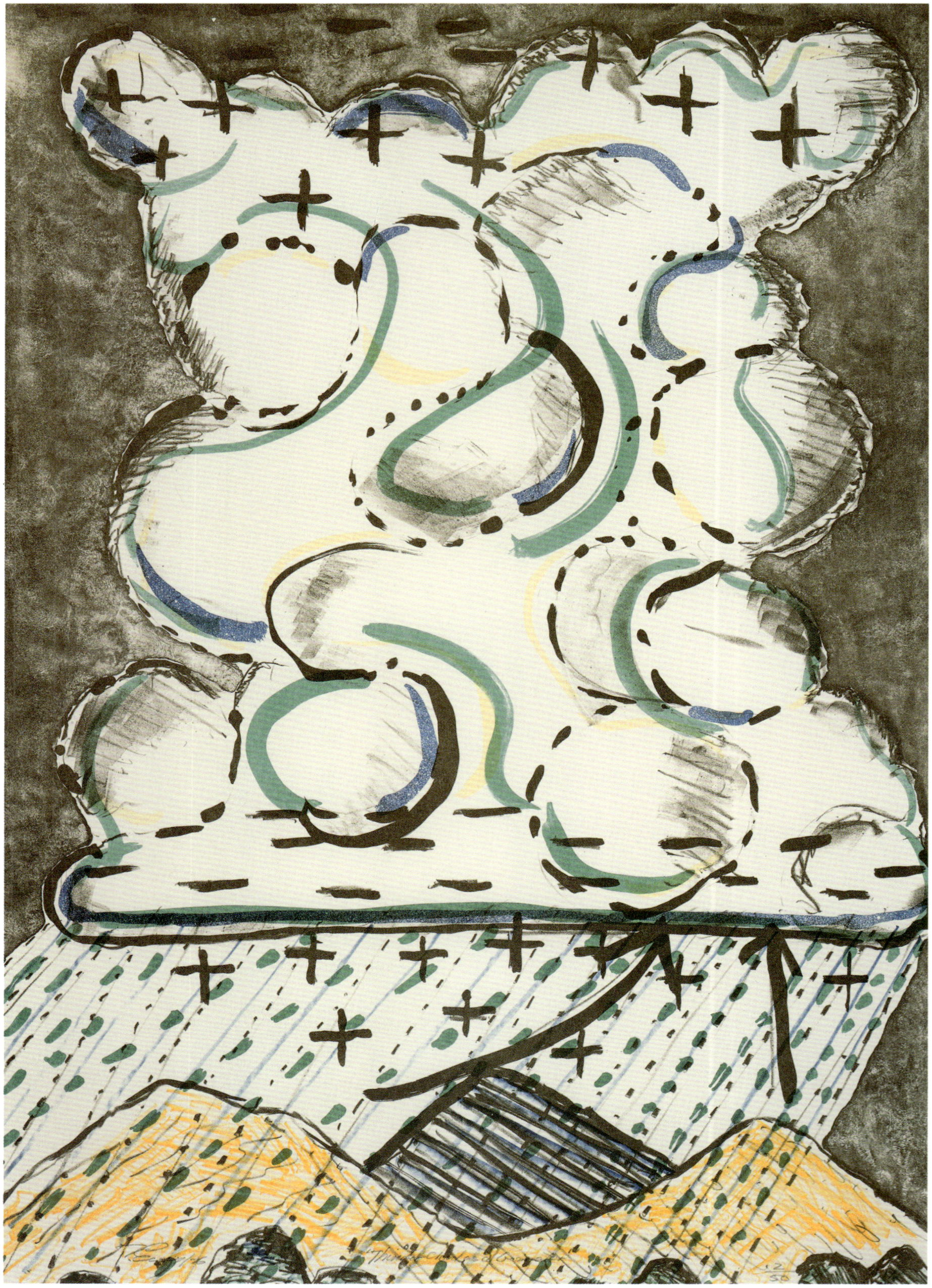

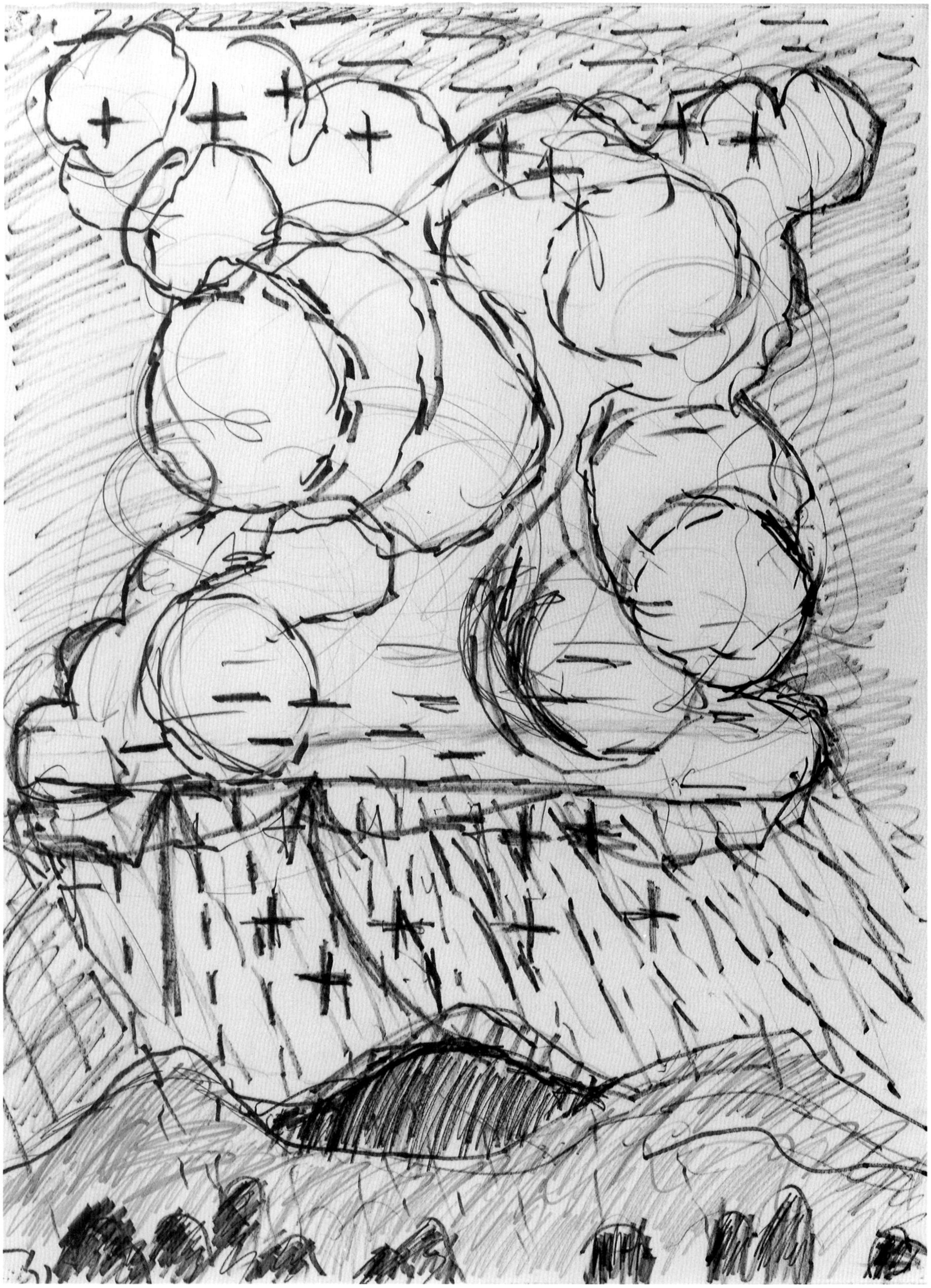

THUNDER CLOUD AS GENERATOR 1976
Felt pen and graphite on BFK Rives paper
75.7 x 55.9
Art Gallery of Ontario

Facing page:
THUNDERCLOUD AS A GENER•TOR 1976
Lithograph on German etching paper
78.7 x 56.6
Art Gallery of Ontario

1977

July–August: Ewen instructs senior-level students at the Nova Scotia College of Art and Design in Halifax, Nova Scotia, for seven weeks.

We almost get the picture of Ewen working like a gleeful alchemist, poring over his books, wielding his wicked router, his glue pot, his spray can—teasing, forcing his ideas through the dense material till finally the elements transmute into the new creation, one would like to imagine with the boom of a thunderclap. (v. Shadbolt and Johnson, 1977)

Carmen Lamanna Gallery, Toronto, Ontario.

McIntosh Gallery, University of Western Ontario, London, Ontario.*

May: *Paterson Ewen: Recent Works* opens at Vancouver Art Gallery, Vancouver, British Columbia; travels to National Gallery of Canada, Ottawa, Ontario; Art Gallery of Nova Scotia, Halifax, Nova Scotia; Southern Alberta Art Gallery, Lethbridge, Alberta; Sir George Williams Art Gallery, Montreal, Quebec; Art Gallery of Windsor, Windsor, Ontario; Winnipeg Art Gallery, Winnipeg, Manitoba.*

October 18–November 1: *Queen's Silver Jubilee Exhibition*, MacDonald Gallery, Queen's Park, Toronto, Ontario.

November 16–December 11: *London•Saskatoon•Exchange*, Mendel Art Gallery, Saskatoon, Saskatchewan (Eric Atkinson, Michael Bidner, Greg Curnoe, Don Dunsmore, Paterson Ewen, Stephen Livick, Gilbert Moll, Patrick Thibert).

1978

I don't mind being compared to Monet at all. I don't see how someone this decade could do landscapes that involved weather and atmosphere and not be connected to the Impressionists. They did say [of the Impressionists] that they painted light. And they did this by dots and dashes. The French call it taché. They said of Constable that he painted the weather. And he has been a very direct influence. When he was painting his clouds over fields, he was, along with the scientists of the time, studying cloud formations. It is interesting that Turner (another one of my great heroes) painted the atmosphere and was a direct influence on the Impressionists. If I am influenced by the Impressionists to some degree, it's quite true. But through that whole line from Constable and Turner to the Impressionists and then I think the Post-Impressionists in the sense that I lay on broader areas of colour than the Impressionists. (III. 1979, Kricorissian interview)

The astonishing thing about Paterson Ewen is that all of his macho hacking and routing and grinding results not in crude, beefy paintings but rather in works of the most delicate, lambent effects. Ewen worries and pummels his plywood sheets into paintings whose nearest sources are Turner and Monet. (VIII. Dault, 1978)

January–February 7: Gallery One, Concordia University, Montreal, Quebec.*

January 7–26: Carmen Lamanna Gallery, Toronto, Ontario.*

January 12–February 7: Sir George Williams Art Galleries, Montreal, Quebec.*

June 11–July 16: *Nine Canadian Artists/Kanadische Kunstler*, Kunsthalle, Basel, Switzerland.

1979

Jacques Ferron publishes *Le Ciel de Québec* (published in English as *The Penniless Redeemer* by Exile Editions, 1984), in which Ewen is a central "fictional" character engaged in conversation with Paul-Émile Borduas.

July–August: Ewen travels to North Bay, Ontario, to teach a painting course titled "Art in Life" at Canadore College.

Art Experience, Canadore College, Thunder Bay, Ontario.

April: Halls Walls, Buffalo, New York.

June: *The Texture of Our Land*, Art Gallery of Peterborough, Peterborough, Ontario.

July 29–September 2: *Creative Flight*, Surrey Art Gallery, Surrey, British Columbia, and Langley Centennial Museum and National Exhibition Centre, Fort Langley, British Columbia.

October 19–December 10: *Compass: Eight Painters*, Harbourfront Art Gallery, Toronto, Ontario (Gerald Ferguson and Garry Neill Kennedy, October 19–30; Gershon Iskowitz and Ron Martin, November 2–14; Gathie Falk and Frank Nulf, November 16–28; David Bolduc and Paterson Ewen, November 30–December 10).

1980

July: Paterson Ewen and his new partner, Mary Handford, travel to Europe, where they visit Paris, Avignon and Barcelona. While in Barcelona, they visit the Picasso Museum.

Up close, the paintings look like old weathered backyard fences. A couple of feet back, however, and they turn into radiant and sometimes downright awesome recreations of natural events and meteorological phenomena. (VIII. Dault, 1980)

Ewen makes his unorthodox "canvases" of huge sheets of plywood, which he scores and gouges with a router, adorns with pieces of metal and roughly paints. They have all the grandeur of elemental forces—the grooves transformed into impressionist crests of waves or windblown trails of sunlit clouds. It is as if Tom Thomson's West Wind *was rerouted through the cosmic scale of Turner.* (VIII. Monk, 1980)

There is a wonderful coincidence between the elemental energy contained in the windstorms, the ocean currents and the movements of bodies in outer space, and the vigour of execution which the surfaces of the plywood sheets show off. They have been gouged and pitted; things have been nailed onto them, and paint has been crudely applied as if to simulate the power of natural forces. But if the handling is vigorous, it also embodies the pleasure with which it was done and the artist's enjoyment of working with the hands for its own sake. The vision may be awestruck, but it is not reverential and is coloured by a mischievous twinkle of the eye at the venerable, if tired, landscape tradition the work suggests that it might want to resurrect. (VI. Nasgaard, 1980)

January 5–24: Carmen Lamanna Gallery, Toronto, Ontario.*

January 5–March 2: *Canadian Painting in the Seventies*, Glenbow Museum, Glenbow-Alberta Institute, Calgary, Alberta.

January 25–March 9: *Reflecting a Rural Consciousness*, Canadian Cultural Centre, Paris, France.

May 7–June 25: *Contemporary Canadian Art* (from the collection of The Canada Council Art Bank), Nabisco World Headquarters, East Hanover, New Jersey.

June 26–July 20: *Dealer's Choice*, Harbourfront Art Gallery, Toronto, Ontario.

July 26–August 21: *Paterson Ewen; Mary Janitch; Colette Whiten; Ron Martin; Robert Fones; Shirley Wiitasalo*, Carmen Lamanna Gallery, Toronto, Ontario.

August 22–September 28: *London and Area Artists Part I*, London Regional Art Gallery, London, Ontario.

September 6–October 19: *10 Canadian Artists in the 1970s*, organized by the Art Gallery of Ontario and exhibited at the Art Gallery of Ontario, Toronto, Ontario; Louisiana Museum of Modern Art, Copenhagen, Denmark; Stadtische Kunsthalle, Recklinghausen, Germany; Musée de l'État, Grand Duche de Luxembourg; Museum van Hedendaagse Kunst, Ghent, Belgium.

1981

June: Ewen travels to the University of Lethbridge in Lethbridge, Alberta, where he is commissioned to create a mural for its Performing Arts Centre. The mural is a depiction of the Alberta landscape. A video is made of Ewen working on the mural.

The landscape around here, the plowed fields and a particular kind of perspective, look a lot like van Gogh's last period at Auvers. One small phenomenon in particular. The clouds constantly change shape because of these gusts of wind that blow in. In the unplowed fields where grass is growing, the wind hits it and makes it sway and flutter in a way that van Gogh related very clearly in a lot of his late work. I was quite thrilled. He's always been a great favorite of mine, among others. (x. Tousley, 1981)

I'd go right to my present work and say that what my tools do is they make grooves which are not unlike the furrows van Gogh painted in. (x. Rochon, 1988)

The Lethbridge commission is a major effort, larger than any work Ewen has made and somewhat different in subject matter. His other landscapes have not dealt with specific places. The cartoon on the work-in-progress, sketched in vividly colored pastels, refers directly to southern Alberta's mercurial sky and rolling topography. (x. Tousley, 1981)

April 3–28: *Recreating the Landscape*, Sarnia Public Library and Art Gallery, Sarnia, Ontario.

May 16–June 18: *Paterson Ewen; Ron Martin; John Scott; Shirley Wiitasalo*, Carmen Lamanna Gallery, Toronto, Ontario.

July 9–October 2: *20th Century Canadian Painting*, organized by the National Gallery of Canada and exhibited in Japan at the National Museum of Modern Art, Tokyo (July 9–August 2); Museum of Modern Art, Hokkaido, Sapporo (August 29–September 20); Oita Prefectural Art Center, Oita (October 1–28).

1982

Ewen is announced by Jessica Bradley, Canadian Commissioner to the Venice Biennale, as Canada's representative at the Venice Biennale in June.

Ewen comes to his new work in an untutored way in our "image-ridden" Guston society, the raw impurities of his work forces continuity and direct response. It is precisely because we are "image-ridden" that these paintings, fragments which mesh into a whole, become "raw miracles" because they make bare certain indwelling features of life that are continuous and vital.
(x. Andreae, 1982)

Its magnificent energies notwithstanding, however, Moon Over Tobermory *is a picture forever teetering on the brink of bathos, its slight subject always in danger of being overcome by a romantic exhilaration too heroic for it. If* Moon Over Tobermory *manages to stave off its tendency to caricature itself (even its title strikes me as a funny flirtation with "Moon Over Miami") it does so finally because Ewen's romanticism is essentially a romanticism of the body, the resulting picture only the slightly cooled-off trackings left by a sound and a fury the viewer is left to reconstruct for himself. This one important step backwards from the painting's subject allows the viewer to swallow Ewen's mystical storminess as if it were private with him—even as it lies cataclysmically before us.* (viii. Dault, 1982)

Ewen has said that he does not have "ideas" for paintings, rather he has images fully formed in his mind, remembered from something seen or experienced. These may germinate for years, months, or days, but he does not begin to work until an image demands that he do so. There are no preliminary drawings because this obsessive engagement with the image is literally lived through the act of inexorably inscribing it into the surface of the work. (v. Bradley, 1982)

January 8–February 21: *Contemporary Canadian Painting* (Greg Curnoe, Paterson Ewen, Gathie Falk, Ron Moppett), Norman Mackenzie Art Gallery, University of Regina, Regina, Saskatchewan; Nickle Arts Museum, University of Calgary, Calgary, Alberta.

January 9–February 4: Carmen Lamanna Gallery, Toronto, Ontario.*

February 13–March 6: 49th Parallel Gallery, New York, New York.*

June 13–September 12: *XL Biennale di Venezia*, Venice, Italy.*

September 12–October 10: *Contemporary Canadian Paintings from the Collection of The University of Western Ontario*, Art Gallery of Windsor, Windsor, Ontario.

October 13–November 2: *Paterson Ewen: Canada's contribution to the 1982 Venice Biennial*, Canada House Cultural Centre Gallery, London, England.*

October 15–November 7: *Painting 82*, Harbourfront Art Gallery, Toronto, Ontario (Bolduc, Coughtry, Ewen, Martin, Molinari, Rayner, Shadbolt).

November 26–January 16, 1983: *Paterson Ewen*, Canadian Cultural Centre, Paris, France.*

1983

February: Ewen travels to the University of Lethbridge in Alberta as a Visiting Artist to lecture and meet with students.

May: Ewen and Mary travel to the northern communities of Frobisher Bay and Resolute Bay for three weeks.

The project grant in question has allowed me to go to Resolute Bay, via Frobisher Bay; to take some photographs and to observe the ice flows from Cornwallis Island, and to go out on the water. (II. Canada Council application, 1983)

I got a lot out of that trip in many ways. Looking at maps to see where my father had been. But most important for me, at that stage in my life, was to see this incredible—I was going to say landscape, but I guess it's a seascape, an icescape, or a waterscape. I don't know. It's just frozen tundra and makes up something like land, and produces one inch flowers at a certain time of the year. Very beautiful. Has some interesting birds—the Ivory Gull [for one]. It's beautiful to see an Ivory Gull land on a crystal white ice flow, where you see the off-white against the ice flow. That was a great trip. I'd like to go again. (III. Teitelbaum interview, 1986)

July 30–September 1: *Paterson Ewen, Ron Martin, John Scott, Shirley Wiitasalo*, Carmen Lamanna Gallery, Toronto, Ontario.

September 9–October 30: *Ontario Landscapes: Selections from the Collection*, London Regional Art Gallery, London, Ontario.

September 14–October 15: *The Non-Figurative Artists' Association of Montreal*, Sir George Williams Art Galleries, Concordia University, Montreal, Quebec, and five other centres.

1984

Fall: Ewen witnesses a tornado from the back door of his house. Five years later, his memory of the experience is transformed into a series of works on paper and a work on plywood, *Tornado* (1989).

It's a proverbial Tornado Alley around here [London]. There was a bad one in the 1970s that ravaged the hamlet of Oxford Centre. There was another one in 1984 that didn't kill anybody but did a whole lot of damage. I had the privilege of seeing that one. I was standing in my driveway and I can tell you I took a real double-take—like in a cartoon. Then all I could think was "Isn't that great" . . . I was in awe, caught up in, as it were, a state of startled wonder. But it took five years to translate that state into a painting. (IV. Campbell, 1989)

Nature isn't just pastoral. It's violent. Sometimes it's beautiful in the almost sentimental sense, and sometimes it's violent and deadly. (VIII. Godley, 1988)

March 8–April 8: *The 7th Dalhousie Drawing Exhibition: Actual Size*, Dalhousie University, Halifax, Nova Scotia.

April 25–May 27: *Wind and Wave: Artist and Engineer*, McIntosh Gallery, University of Western Ontario, London, Ontario.*

May 10–August 26: *Reflections: Contemporary Art Since 1964*, National Gallery of Canada, Ottawa, Ontario.

June 22–August 24: *Vent et eau*, Vieux Port de Québec, Quebec City (Quebec '84 celebration), Quebec.

July 2–August 1: Carmen Lamanna Gallery, Toronto, Ontario (Ewen, Rae Johnson, Ron Martin, Joanne Tod and Shirley Wiitasalo).

October 6–November 1: *Paterson Ewen*, Carmen Lamanna Gallery, Toronto, Ontario.*

1985

January 13–February 8: *L'Impulsion totémique : La tradition continue*, Galerie John A. Schweitzer, Montreal, Quebec.

February 27–August 11: *Works of Art and Scholarship*, McIntosh Gallery, University of Western Ontario, London, Ontario.

June 15–August 11: *The Allegorical Image in Recent Canadian Painting*, Agnes Etherington Art Centre, Kingston, Ontario (John Clark, Pierre Dorion, Ewen, Eric Fischl, Oliver Girling, Betty Goodwin, Will Gorlitz, Renée Van Halm, Lynn Hughes, Andy Patton, Joanne Tod and Shirley Wiitasalo).

September 6–October 27: *The Artists Collect: Frequently forgotten works of art from the collections of London artists*, London Regional Art Gallery, London, Ontario.

October 21–November 14: *The Physicality of the Landscape*, Artspace, Peterborough, Ontario (Marlene Creates, Christo and Ewen).

October 22–November 17: *Atmospheric Synthesis*, Art Gallery of Peterborough, Peterborough, Ontario (David Bierk, Ewen, Gathie Falk and Otto Rogers).

1986

Spring: Ewen paints *Self-Portrait* from photographs taken in the late 1970s. The photographs were taken at the university to record his physiognomy.

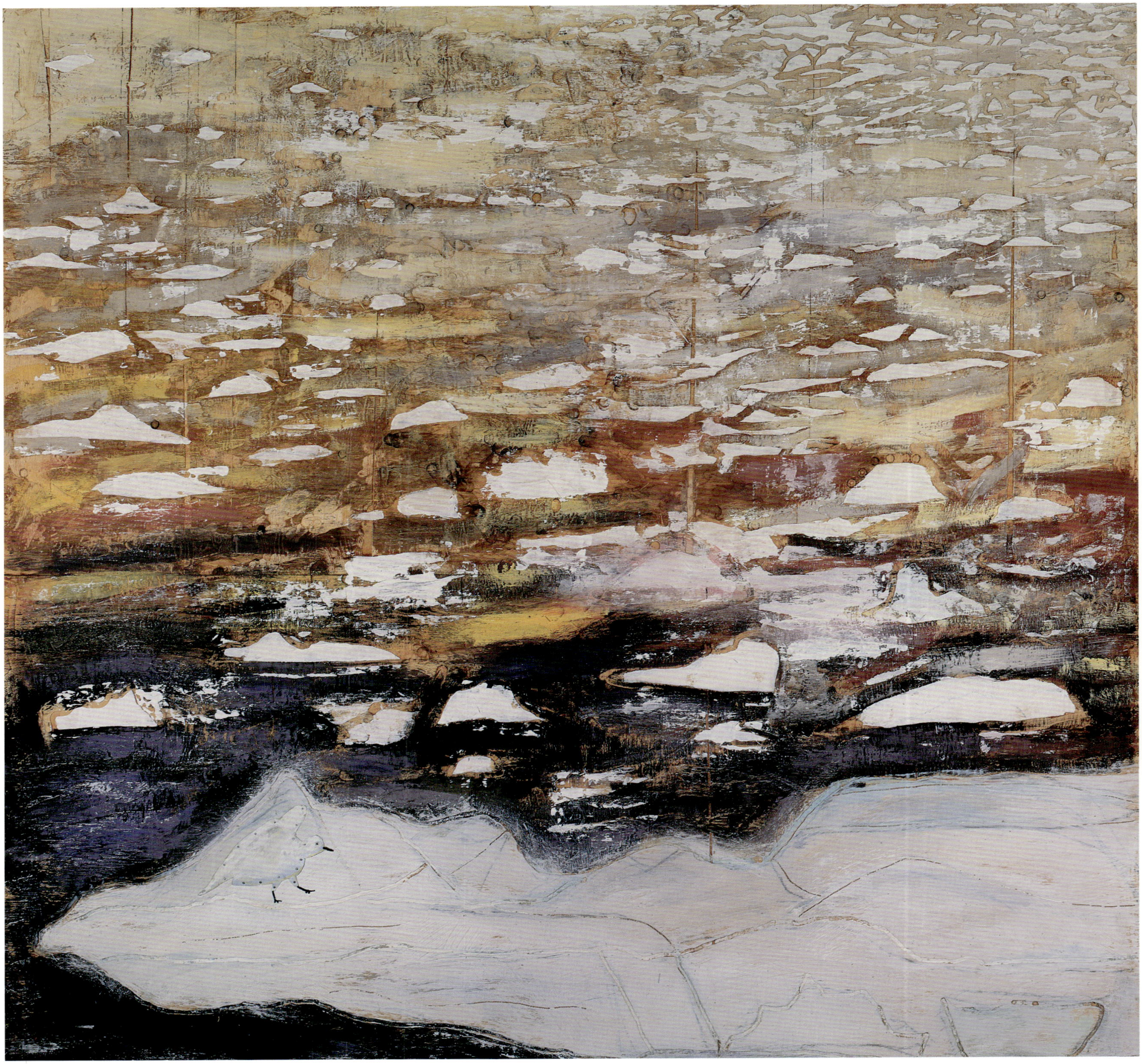

People think of me as a landscape painter because I've done hundreds of landscape images, but my half dozen portraits are my greatest works. (VIII. Hanna, 1989)

July: Ewen and Mary break off their relationship. Ewen sells the house on Maitland Avenue and moves into an industrial space/studio in London's east side.

December: Ewen checks himself into Homewood, an alcohol treatment centre in Guelph, Ontario. The National Gallery of Canada purchases *Self-Portrait.*

April 4–May 18: *How we See—What we Say,* Art Gallery at Harbourfront, Toronto, Ontario.

September 13–October 11: Galerie Chantal Boulanger, Montreal, Quebec.*

November 13–19: *Focus: Canadian Art 1960–1985,* Art Cologne, 20th International Kunstmarkt, Cologne, West Germany (Ian Carr-Harris, Robin Collyer, Ewen, Murray Favro, Robert Fones, Ron Martin, Louise Noguchi and David Rabinowitch).

ICE FLOES WITH IVORY GULL 1984
Acrylic on gouged plywood
228.6 x 243.8
Collection Mr. and Mrs. Jules Loeb

1987

May: After nearly twenty-one years, the Carmen Lamanna Gallery closes its 840 Yonge Street location.

June: Ewen gives up alcohol for good and is discharged from Homewood. He is awarded the Banff School of Fine Arts National Award. The prize, which includes the Donald Cameron Gold medal, a $5000 cash award, and a short residency at the Banff School of Fine Arts, is presented to artists who have made an outstanding contribution to the development of painting and related arts in Canada.

Summer: Ewen has a very prolific period during which the moon becomes a favourite image.

September: Admitted to St. Joseph's Hospital, where he stays until the end of the year.

November: After a six-month closure, the Carmen Lamanna Gallery reopens at its new location, 788 King Street West, with an exhibition of new works by Ewen. Simultaneously, *Paterson Ewen: The Montreal Years,* the first comprehensive exhibition of largely undocumented paintings made prior to 1970, opens at the Mendel Art Gallery in Saskatoon.

There is no sense of pause or absence—space in the astronomical sense—in these paintings, as we might expect in modern depictions of heavenly bodies. At least in his art-making—a literary enterprise despite all the gouging and so forth—he portrays a cosmos densely filled with the strong music of the spheres, made visible with paint and power-tool. What would that music sound like, if Ewen's paintings were scores? The freest jazz imaginable; or, perhaps, a stringent string quartet by Morton Feldman, who also understood the music and space and the cosmos. (VIII. Mays, 1987)

April 25–July 6: *Waterworks,* London Regional Art Gallery, London, Ontario.

November 14–December 17: Carmen Lamanna Gallery, Toronto, Ontario.*

November 20–January 3/1988: *Paterson Ewen: The Montreal Years,* Mendel Art Gallery, Saskatoon, Saskatchewan and four other centres.*

1988

January: *Paterson Ewen: Phenomena Paintings 1971–1987* opens at the Art Gallery of Ontario. In the wake of the opening, Ewen suffers a breakdown and again enters St. Joseph's Hospital, where he remains until early summer.

February: Ewen retires from the University of Western Ontario.

June: Ewen and Mary resume their relationship.

September: Ewen receives the Toronto Arts Award for outstanding contribution to the visual arts.

Ewen is preoccupied with two problematics which seem to haunt him continuously: the destruction and construction of the surface along with the definition of spatial ambiguities located therein; and the seduction of the beautiful, that hint of a notion that persists in undermining art. (VIII. Hornstein-Rabinowitch, 1988)

The material as a means to producing the image that initiated the activity. We come to the most difficult topic in any discussion of Ewen's work: the image and its content. How does one talk about the sun and moon? Ewen paints them, and he paints them again and again. Painting is only part of the construction; there is something functionally significant and signifying about the material that makes it more than painting in what it communicates. (V. Monk, 1988)

January 22–April 3: *Paterson Ewen: Phenomena Paintings 1971–1987,* Art Gallery of Ontario, Toronto, Ontario, and five other centres.*

February 24–May 22: *À propos d'une peinture des années soixante,* Musée d'art contemporain de Montréal, Montreal, Quebec (Ewen, Charles Gagnon, Yves Gaucher, Jacques Hurtubise, Jean McEwen).

May 1–July 2: *Montreal Painting of the 1960s,* Americas Society Art Gallery, New York, New York.

November 12–December 8: Carmen Lamanna Gallery, Toronto, Ontario.*

1989

February: Ewen paints his first tornado image from a book on weather phenomenon, while in Saskatoon, Saskatchewan. Returning to London, he realizes a series of other works on paper using the image (including a number on unique papers made by colleague Helmut Becker) and finally a large plywood work, *Tornado.*

May 26: Ewen receives an honorary Doctor of Laws degree from Concordia University in Montreal, Quebec.

June 7: Ewen receives an honorary Doctor of Letters degree from the University of Western Ontario in London, Ontario.

We understand the world through images we see from our earliest childhood, yet we understand very little of the kinds and structures of such images . . . Formal education should prepare us to make discoveries and do things with our talents; it should give us a discipline with which to express ourselves clearly. (II. Ewen, 1989)

July: Ewen goes to Emma Lake, Saskatchewan, to spend two weeks as artist-in-residence. He leaves after the first week. During the trip to Emma Lake, he begins *Sun Dogs,* but leaves it unfinished when he returns to London. Shortly after returning, he removes most of the surface colour and completes the work.

October: Ewen and Mary buy a house near the University of Western Ontario at the north end of Wellington Street in London, Ontario.

Paterson Ewen's art validates and humanizes that data which is vicariously obtained and abstracted through technological hardware. He confronts us more directly with the immensity of natural events than the clinically graphic images of science that are so often his source. His paintings are powerfully crude to the modern eye, with a directness like art of a simpler time. They somehow validate, not the experience of the phenomena, but our understanding of it. (VIII. Mueller, 1989)

In the context of many of the artists working in London from the sixties to the present, Paterson Ewen, in his large landscape and weather chart based work, must (then) be seen as a painter thoroughly grounded in classic Montreal modernism, turning to the use of non-conventional materials while at the same time returning to a more direct or visceral method of painting developed from his earlier, pre-Plasticien work. (VIII. Curnoe, 1989)

Ewen looks for—and finds—a topography that seems intuitively true to the tactile sense as well as the more stylistic exigencies of the creative imagination. It is a topography, moreover, that transcends the diverse schemata he has assimilated and meaningfully approximates the direct experiences he has had. The artist's hands, working in unison, attempt to gain familiarity with, and then articulate, the fine points of that topography, gliding over the surface of the wood, palms compressed against it, fingers following the most eloquent grains, the most promising knots, the most minute declivities. And all this may take place within the compass of a watchful eye, but touch certainly works its own intimate magic in this particular Ecuador of the senses—a magic that extends right through sight into the unseen aspect of the living body. (IV. Campbell, 1989)

The routing of the wood sheet, the gradual accretion of mixed media on the surface plane, the rubbing in of pigment, the incessant tactile contact, the incubation of vision, and the movements in imaginal space: all these breathe life into the composition, the very sense of which is coaxed slowly out of close familiarity with the wood itself—intuitively, inexorably, with a certain serenity. What remains is never an idealized landscape, depicted with crippling verisimilitude, but the evidence of a journey from the symbol to the thing symbolized, and a supernal register of things seen. (IV. Campbell, 1989)

September 8–30: *Paterson Ewen: Works on Paper: Artist's Choice (1949–1989)*, Forest City Gallery, London, Ontario.*

November 11–December 14: Carmen Lamanna Gallery, Toronto, Ontario (*Startled Wonder: The Phenomenascapes of Paterson Ewen* is released to coincide with this exhibition).*

Page 152:
LANDSCAPE [MIDDLESEX COUNTY, ONTARIO #1] 1988
Watercolour on handmade paper
18.3 x 24.5
Art Gallery of Ontario

Page 153:
LANDSCAPE [MIDDLESEX COUNTY, ONTARIO #2] 1988
Watercolour on handmade paper
17.8 x 24.1
Art Gallery of Ontario

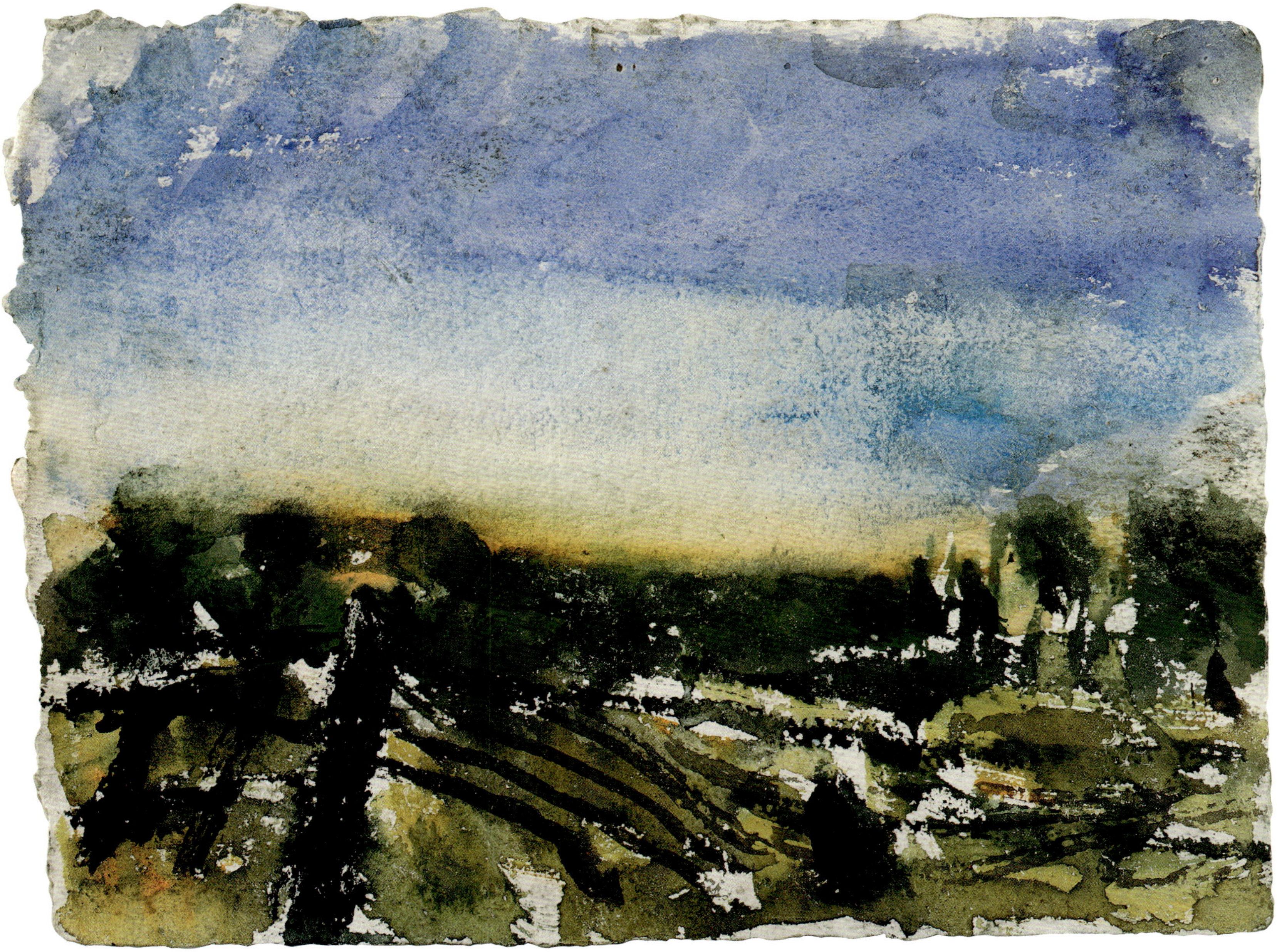

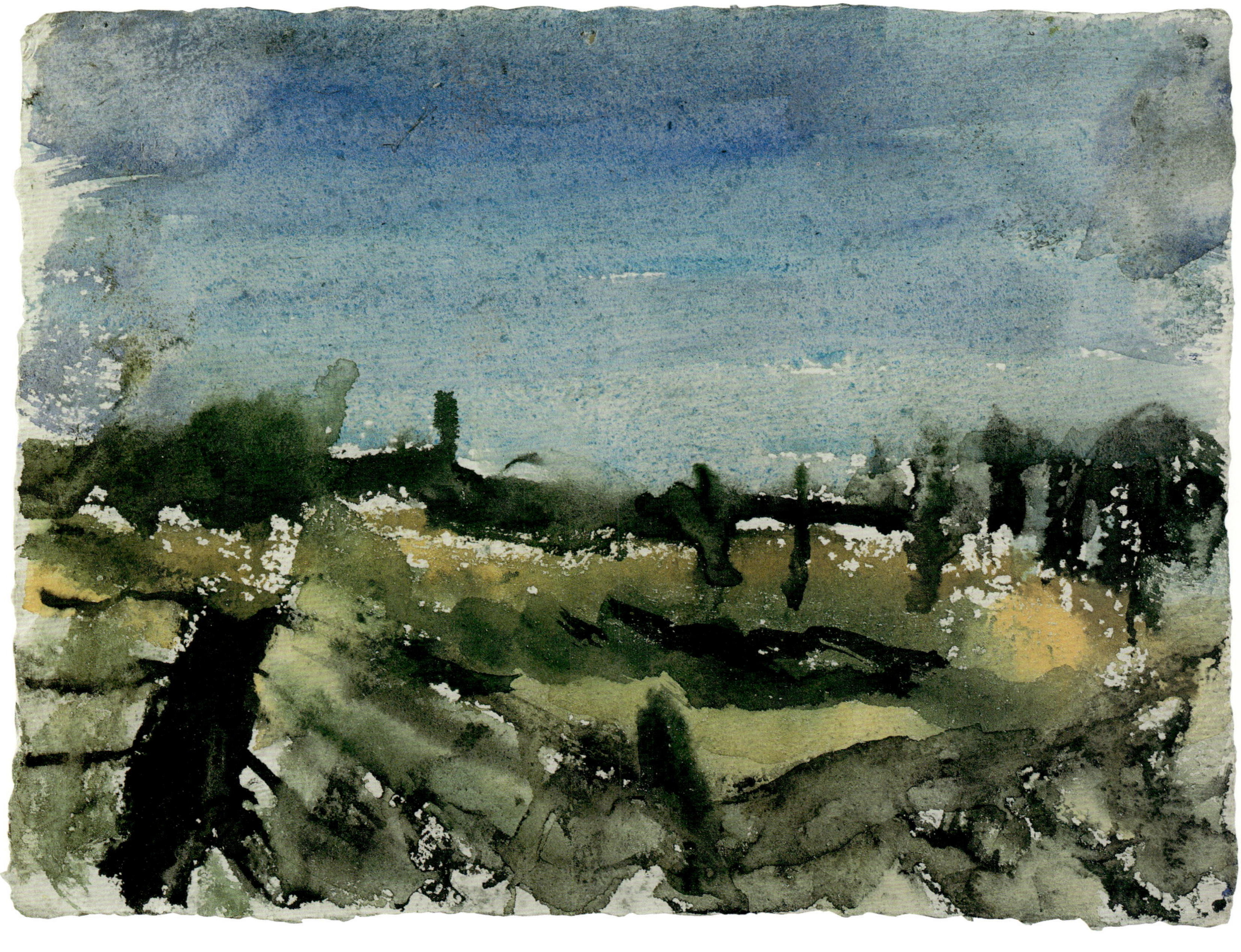

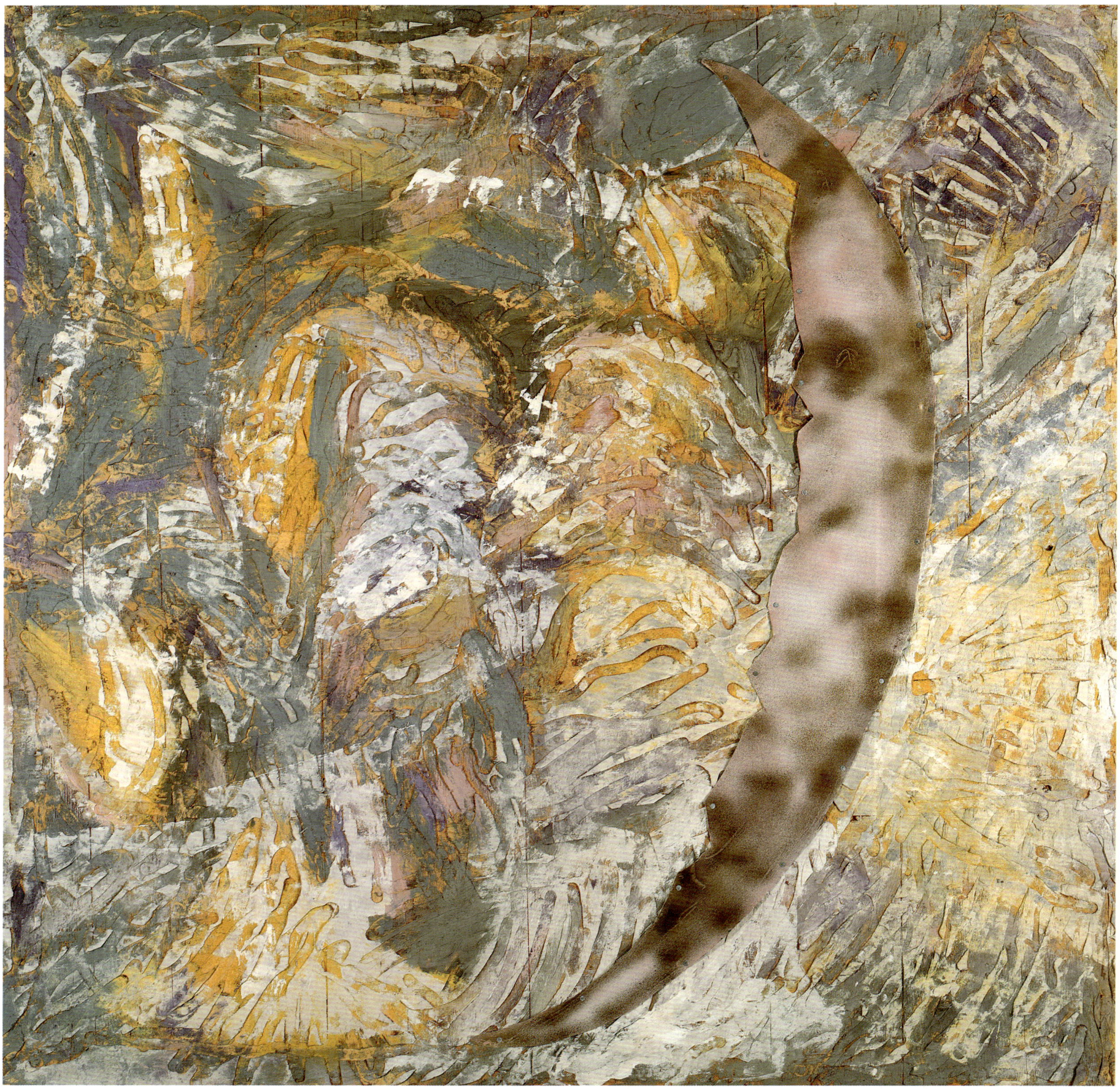

1990

Spring: Ewen and Mary visit Europe to see the centennial exhibitions of van Gogh's work in Holland. They also see the works of J. M. W. Turner and John Constable in England.

In depicting the evanescence of passing universal phenomena, Ewen creates the appearance of material substantiality. The works exist as ritual, as personal incarnations of remembered experience mapped out through the phenomenology of marking. (VIII. Grande, 1990)

August 1–September 1: Carmen Lamanna Gallery, Toronto, Ontario (Iain Baxter, Ian Carr-Harris, Robin Collyer, Ewen, Murray Favro, General Idea, Diane Keaton, Joseph Kosuth and Brice Marden).

November 10–December 13: Carmen Lamanna Gallery, Toronto, Ontario.*

1991

January: After accidently boring a hole in the plywood with the router while working on *Planet Cooling*, Ewen sees the opened plywood as an evolution in his work. He begins to create works which utilize this idea, including *Cross Section of a Cumulus Cloud* and *Satan's Pit*.

May: Carmen Lamanna, Ewen's friend and dealer for twenty-two years, dies after a short illness.

Paterson Ewen's looming painting Eclipse of the Moon *confronts us simultaneously with the sublimity of outer space and the massive weight of an earthbound object. The painting's materiality reminds us that it is more than a surface image; it is the physical site and document of the artist's gestures with a router. It is also the transcription of a phenomenon which many viewers have experienced as a moving image viewed on television or through binoculars, here fixed and made real by its size and concreteness, by the apparentness of the technique of representation. Ultimately more phenomenal than representational, Ewen's paintings are similar to memory in that their actuality or "presentness" has the power to displace that which has purportedly been transcribed.* (VI. Jenkner, 1991)

June 22–September 15: *Site memory: Contemporary Art from Canada: Works by 11 Canadian Artists*, MacDonald Stewart Art Centre, Guelph, Ontario, and later, the Cleveland Center for Contemporary Art (Claude-Philippe Benoit, Stan Deniston, Ewen, Suzanne Giroux, Hugh LeRoy, Al McWilliams, Roland Poulin, Jim Reid, Ron Shuebrook, Michael Snow and Tim Whiten).

September 28: Informal show opens at the home of Donatella and Jay Chiat, 149 East 38th Street, New York.

DECADENT CRESCENT MOON 1990
Acrylic and metallic paint on galvanized steel and gouged plywood
236.3 x 244.0
Art Gallery of Ontario

Page 156:
CROSS SECTION OF A CUMULUS CLOUD 1991
Acrylic on galvanized steel, steel nails and bolts on gouged plywood
147.3 x 190.5
Art Gallery of Ontario

Page 157:
SURFACE OF THE SUN
1993
Acrylic on gouged plywood
226.1 x 228.6
Art Gallery of Ontario

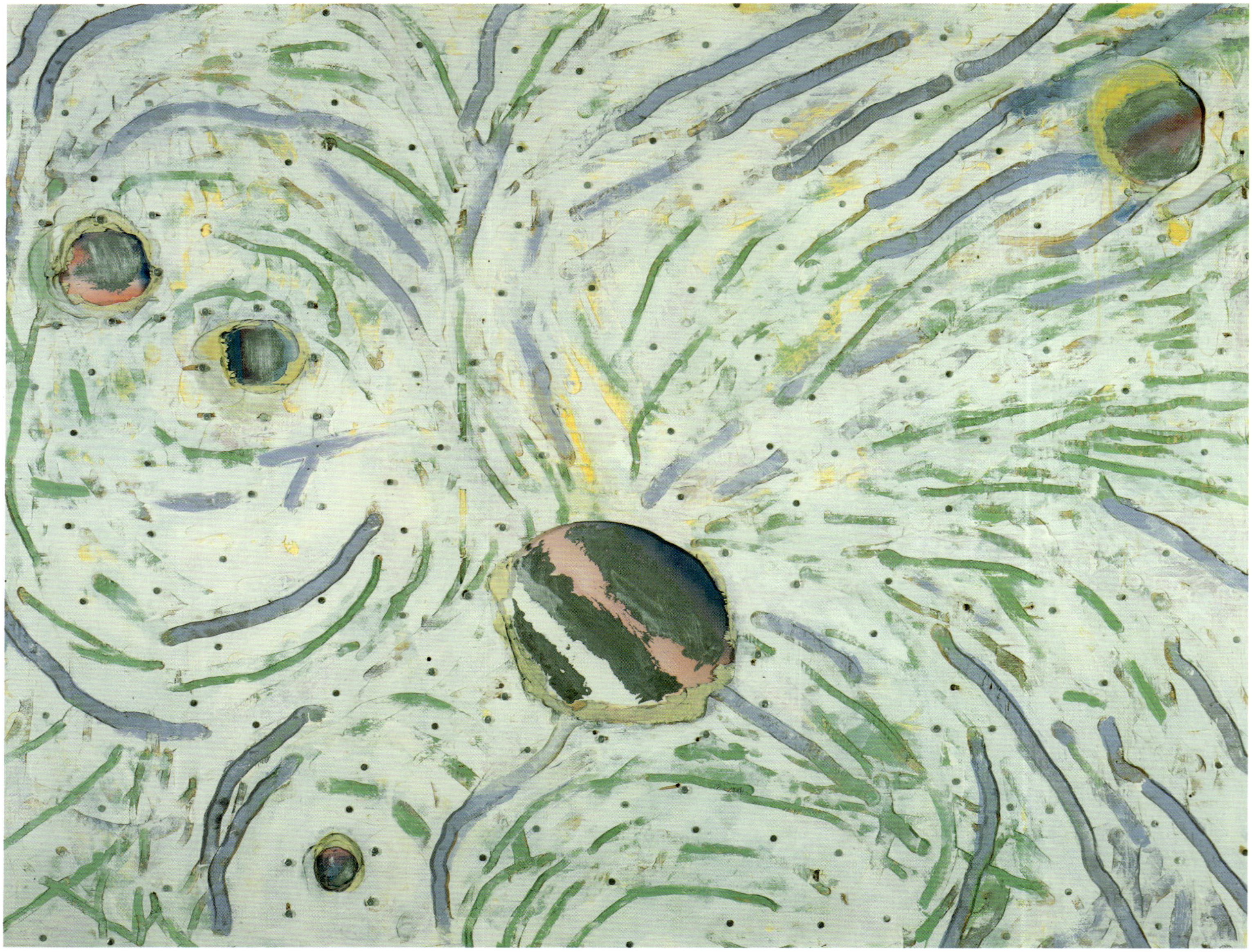

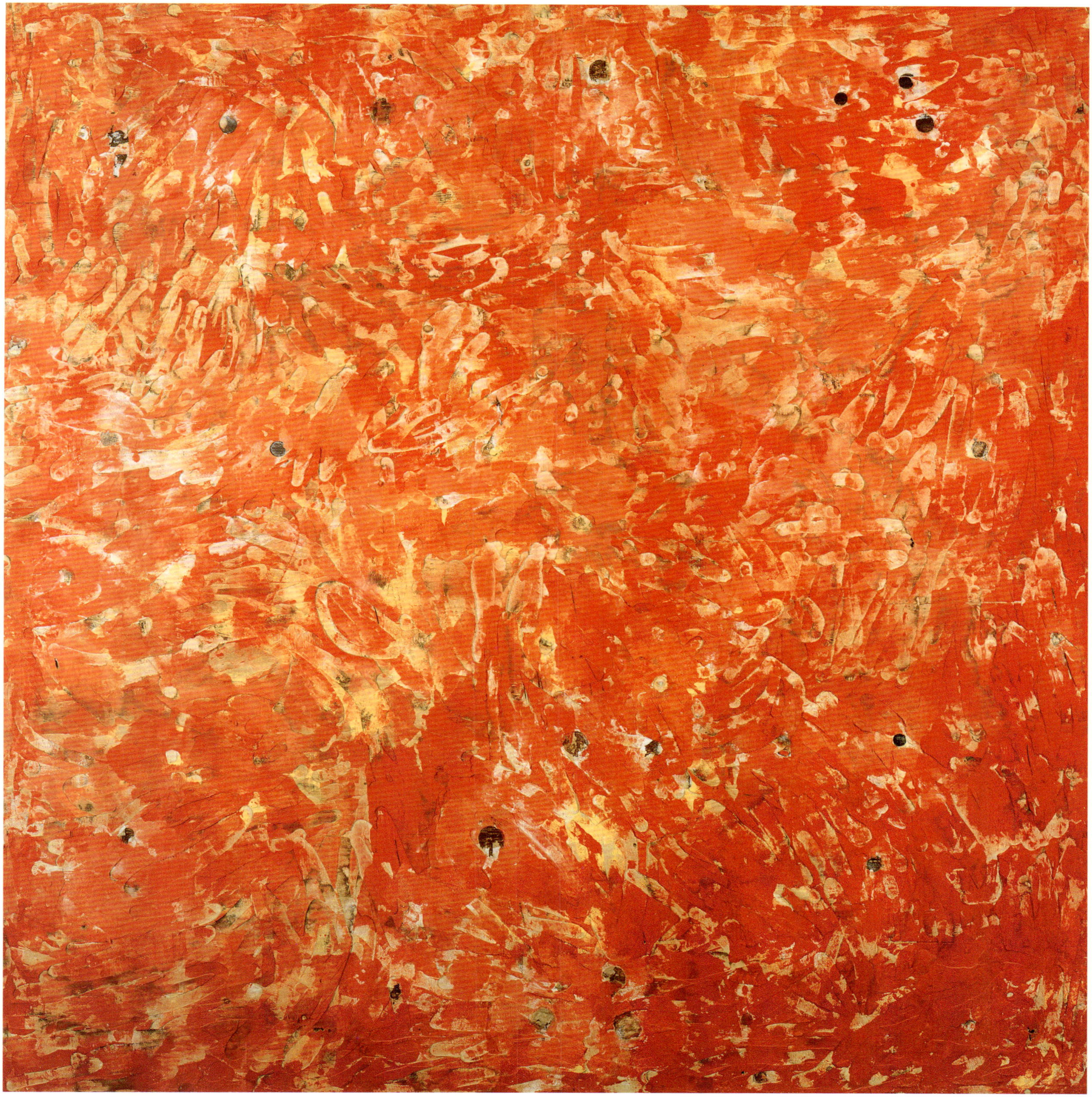

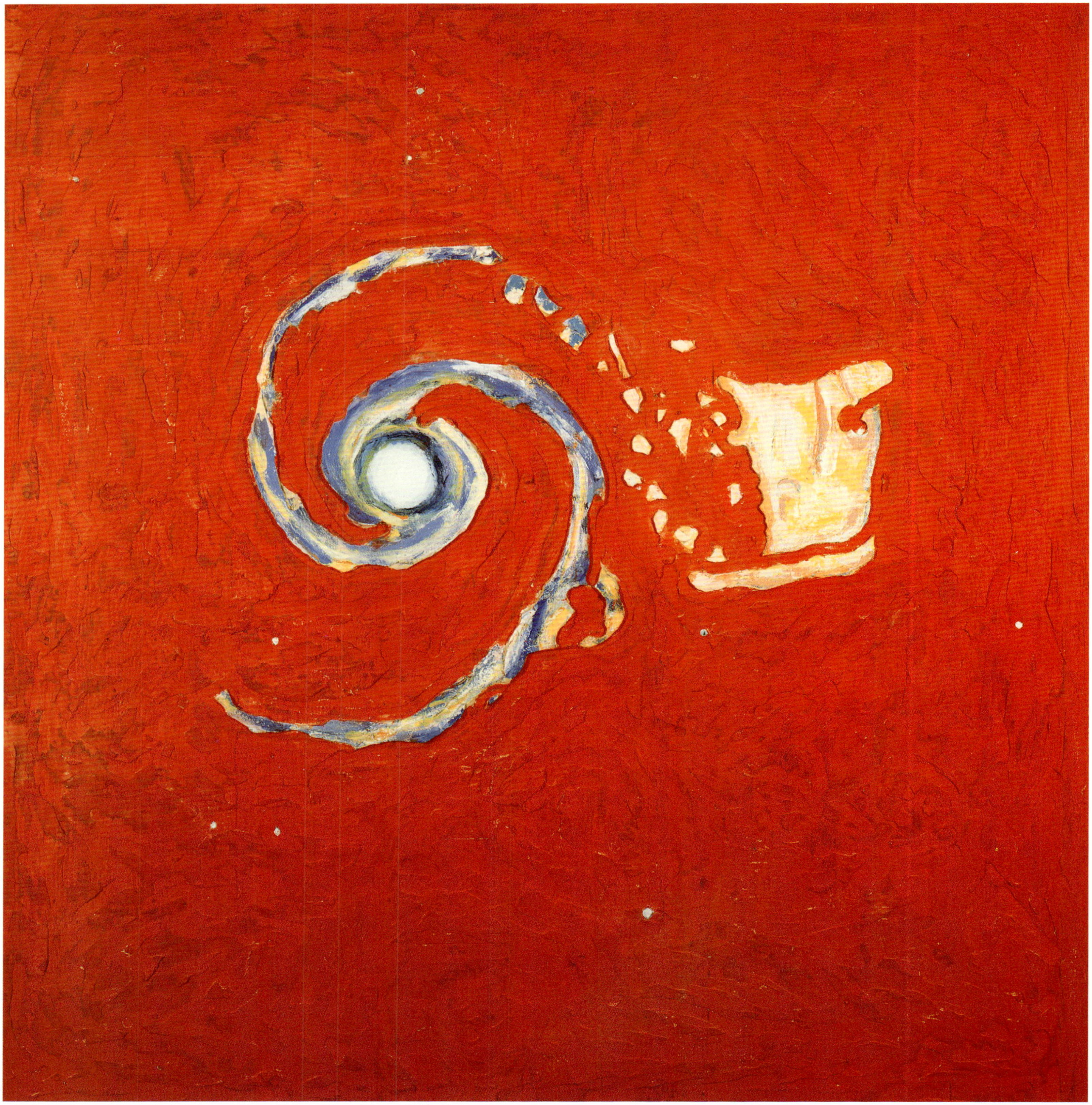

1992

January: Ewen is admitted to St. Joseph's Hospital for an operation; in March, he is transferred to Victoria Hospital, where he remains until mid-August.

October: Ewen travels to the opening of a group show at the Baldacci-Daverio Gallery in New York, and sees *The Great Utopia,* an exhibition of Russian Constructivist work at the Guggenheim.

May 14–August 2: *Montreal, 1942–1992: l'anarchie resplendissante de la peinture,* Galerie de l'Université du Québec à Montréal, Montreal, Quebec (Marcel Barbeau, Luc Béland, Paul-Emile Borduas, Ulysse Comtois, Peter Drausz, Ewen, Marcelle Ferron, Charles Gagnon, Marc Garneau, Yves Gaucher, Pierre Gauvreau, Betty Goodwin, Jacques Hurtubise, Ilana Isehayek, Christian Kiopini, Raymond Lavoie, Fernand Leduc, Serge Lemoyne, Rita Letendre, Richard Mill, Guido Molinari, Jean-Paul Mousseau, Alfred Pellan, Guy Pellerin, Leopold Plotek, Jean-Paul Riopelle, Louise Robert, Marcel Saint-Pierre, Françoise Sullivan, Claude Tousignant and Carol Wainio).

COSMIC CANNIBALISM
1994
Acrylic on gouged plywood
243.5 x 235.9
Art Gallery of Ontario

June 25–September 1: *Paterson Ewen: Critical Works, Works on Paper 1949–92,* Art Gallery of Hamilton, Hamilton, Ontario.*

September 17–October 10: Equinox Gallery, Vancouver, British Columbia.*

October 20–November 14: *As Above/So Below,* Baldacci Daverio Gallery, New York (Raffaele Bueno, Ewen, Ron Moppett and Marco Tirelli).

November 5–December 13: *Collective Efforts: 50 Years of Intentionality,* McIntosh Gallery, University of Western Ontario, London, Ontario.

November 18–January 31/1993: *The Crisis of Abstraction in Canada: The 1950s,* organized by the National Gallery of Canada, exhibited at Musée du Québec, Quebec City, Quebec, and four other centres.

November 28: *Paterson Ewen: 60s Edge,* studio show, London, Ontario.*

December 18–February 28: *Achieving the Modern: Canadian Abstract Painting and Design in the 1950s,* Winnipeg Art Gallery, Winnipeg, Manitoba, and four other centres.

1993

Spring: Inspired by reproductions of works by Georges Seurat in their painted frames, Ewen creates a series of works in which he adheres plywood frames to pieces of metal, and paints, gouges and etches images over both.

May: Ewen's first solo exhibition in New York City since 1958 opens at the Paolo Baldacci Gallery on East 57th Street.

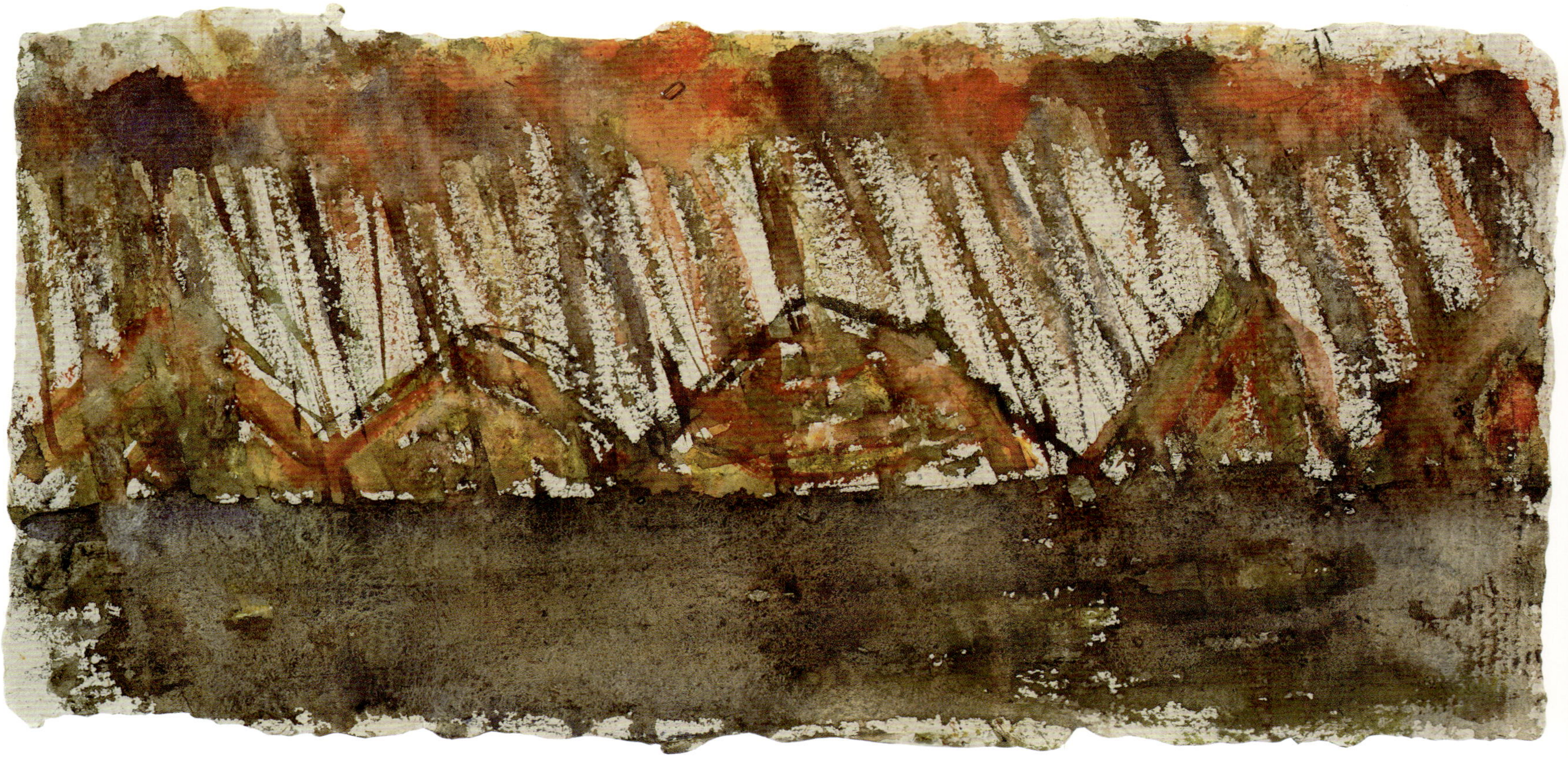

While not fitting the traditional category of landscape, Paterson Ewen's paintings of natural phenomena challenge our perceptions of our physical surroundings. In the past, landscape painting was commonly used to identify a sense of place to prospective colonizers; the land was often represented as commodity, something that was owned or that could be owned, a symbol of material wealth and power. The history and development of landscape painting in Canada are part of the history and development of Canadian identity. Ewen's paintings of natural phenomena are unlike traditional landscape painting, where land is dominated and controlled, or where the natural world exists solely for our visual pleasure. The landscape in Ewen's paintings of natural phenomena does not invite a tranquil interpretation. Unlike early uses of landscape painting in Canada, there is no invitation to buy, settle or tame the places in these paintings. While we would prefer to consider ourselves as being in control of our environment, Ewen's phenomenascapes perhaps show us the bigger picture. (v. Sawchyn, 1993)

January 20–March 15: *Vancouver Collects*, Vancouver Art Gallery, Vancouver, British Columbia.

May 4–June 5: *Paterson Ewen: Recent Paintings*, Paolo Baldacci Gallery, New York, New York.*

July 2–August 30: *Paterson Ewen: Interior Motives*, Mendel Art Gallery, Saskatoon, Saskatchewan.*

September 12–October 24: *Terra Incognita*, Expression Centre d'exposition de Saint-Hyacinthe, Saint-Hyacinthe, Quebec (Daniel Dion, Ewen, Jocelyn Jean, Gilles Mihalcean, Hélène Mugot, Alain Paiement and Su Schnee).

November 5–27: *The Canadian Spirit in Art*, Equinox Gallery, Vancouver, British Columbia (Ewen, Ivan Eyre, E. J. Hughes, Dorothy Knowles, Gordon Smith and Takao Tanabe).

1994

Unlike van Gogh, Ewen does not roil his painted night skies with existential angst. His heavens, rendered in baked enamel on thin steel plates, are matter-of-fact, often invoked by swirls, loops, scratches, scribbles made by a turn of the drill and a few touches of colored paint. The wooden frames are sometimes included in the picture field and painted over with similar motifs; at other times they remain emphatically frames, grooved and painted in mockingly pretty color combinations. (VIII. Lilly Wei, 1994)

June 2–July 29: Paolo Baldacci Gallery, New York, New York (Carlo Carr, Giorgio de Chirico, Paterson Ewen, James Hyde, Medrie McPhee, Giorgio Morandi and Marco Tirelli).

July 1–August 21: *Approaching Terra/Luna*, Art Gallery of Peterborough, Peterborough, Ontario (Philippe Boissonnet, Paterson Ewen and Bill Vazan).

RAIN OVER COASTLINE 1994
Watercolour on Japanese paper
20.1 x 42.1
Art Gallery of Ontario

Page 162:
MANY MOONS II 1994
Acrylic on plywood, galvanized steel livestock fencing
244.0 x 190.0
Art Gallery of Ontario

Page 163:
MANY MOONS 1994
Acrylic on plywood, enamel on galvanized steel
244.0 x 337.5
Art Gallery of Ontario

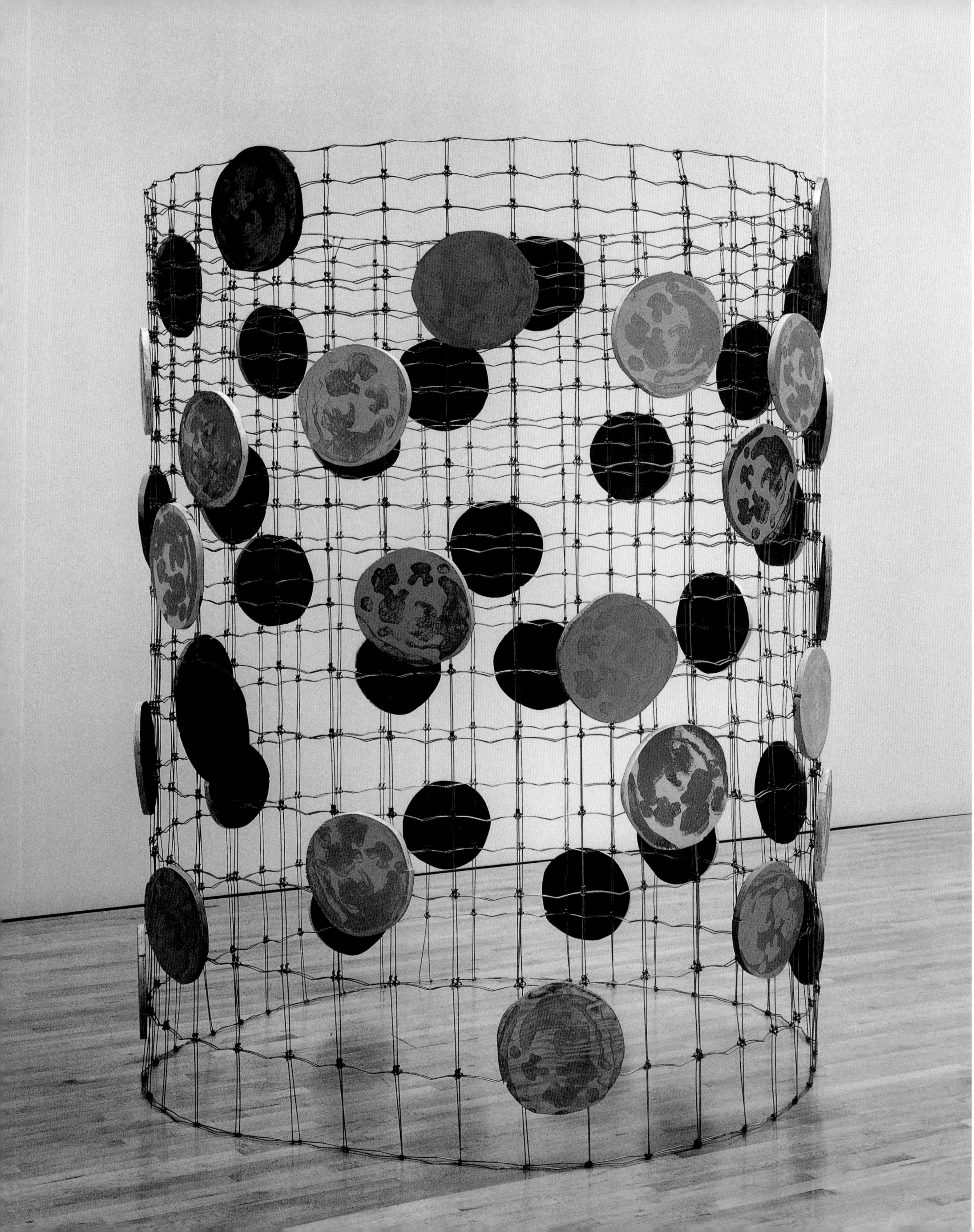

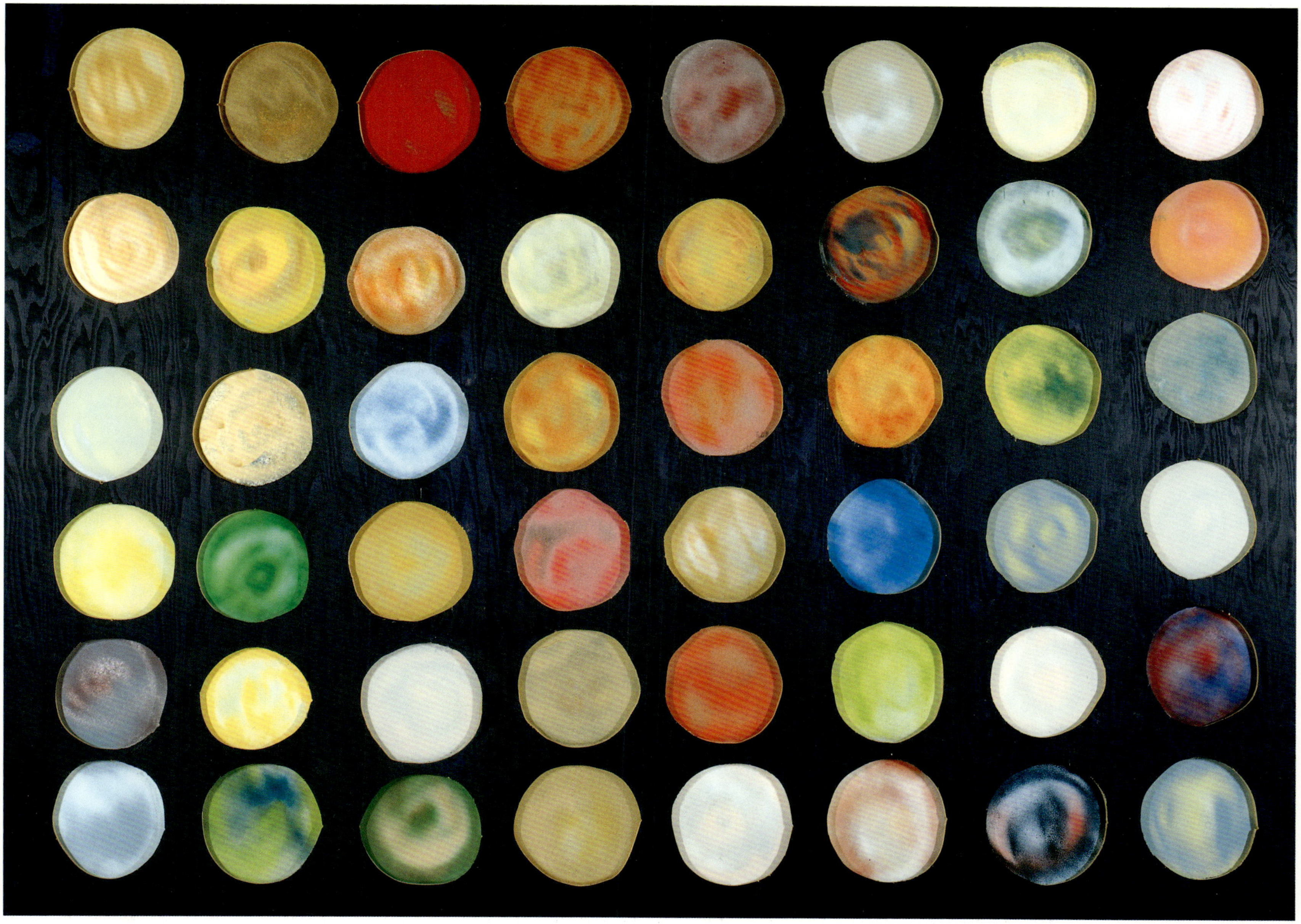

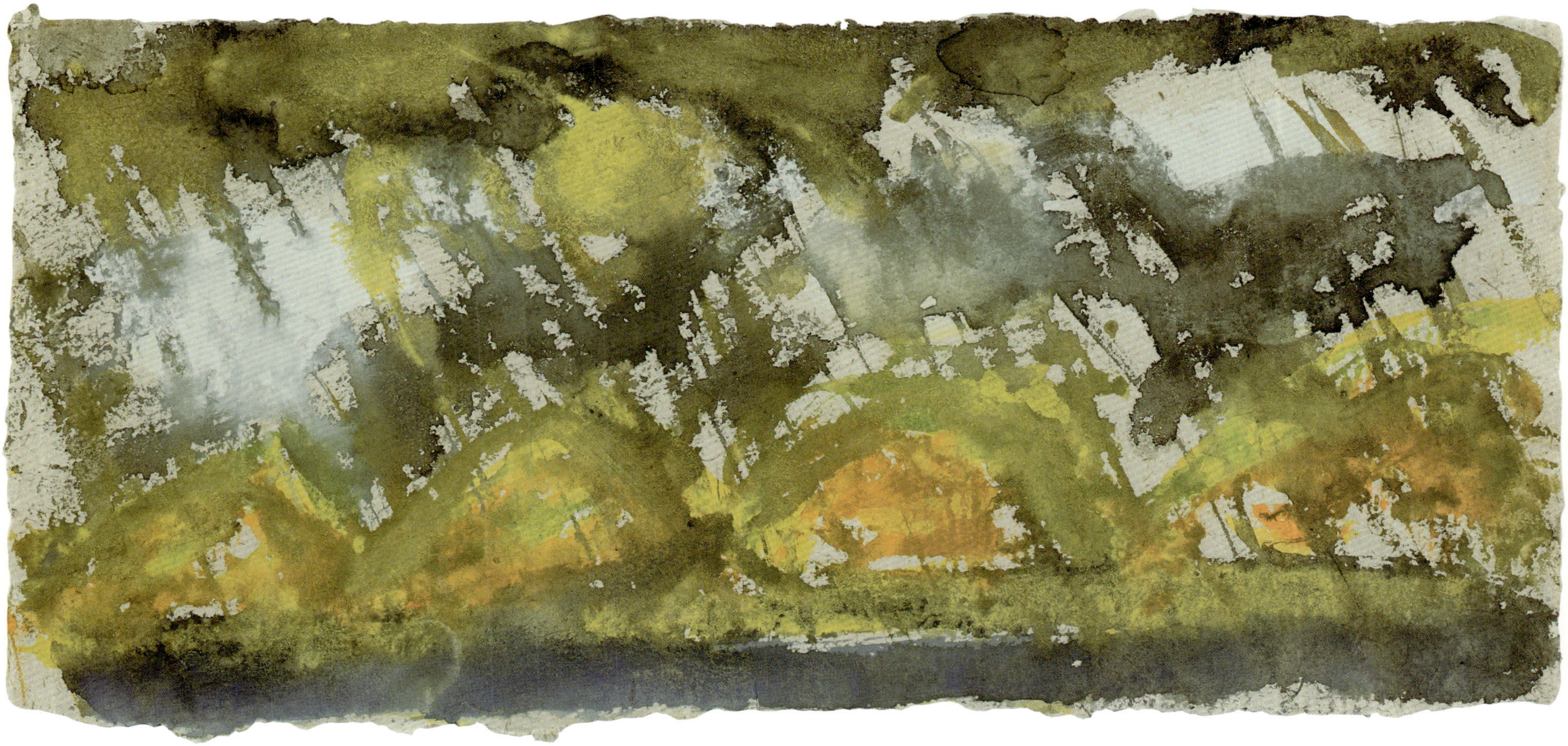

1995

Winter/Spring: Ewen starts applying translucent washes of colour to the plywood surface with his bare hands.

May: Ewen is awarded the Jean A. Chalmers Award for visual arts, which includes a $20,000 cash prize.

I like winning prizes . . . You don't have to compete for them, they're for something you've done and so there's no pressure, and they're delightful. (x. Kelly, 1995)

July: The Art Gallery of Ontario announces two major gifts of Ewen's work, constituting the largest representation of his work in a public collection.

August: Ewen and Mary Handford are married.

Ewen's paintings work the borderlines between art and the physical environment, limits marked by the sublime. The phenomena presented by Ewen—a tornado, a shipwreck, a typhoon—tie his work clearly to the landscape sublime of the early 19th century. (x. Cheetham, 1995)

January 13–February 18: *American Art Today: Night Painting*, Art Museum at Florida International University, Miami, Florida.

March 1–25: Equinox Gallery, Vancouver, British Columbia.*

1996

February: Ewen and Mary travel to Germany (Frankfurt, Bonn, Cologne, Madglabach) to see the work of the Expressionists. A highlight of the trip is seeing Kirchner's *Half-Length Woman with Hat* (1911) and *Five Women* (1913), installed beside each other in the Museum Ludwig in Cologne.

March: Ewen completes his fifth figure painting on plywood—a female nude, inspired in part by the Expressionist works seen in Germany. Earlier figure works include: *Bandaged Man* 1973, *Portrait of Vincent* 1974, *Self-Portrait* 1986, and *Nude* 1990.

February 15–March 17: *The Montreal Connection*, McIntosh Gallery, University of Western Ontario, London, Ontario.

September 20: *Paterson Ewen: Earthly Weathers/Heavenly Skies*, opens at The Art Gallery of Ontario, Toronto, Ontario. Simultaneously, an exhibition of work from 1996 is shown at the Olga Korper Gallery, Toronto, Ontario.

SUN SHOWER 1994
Watercolour on Japanese paper
19.5 x 42.0
Art Gallery of Ontario

Page 166:
SUN DOGS #4 1989
Acrylic on gouged plywood
122.0 x 145.7
Art Gallery of Ontario

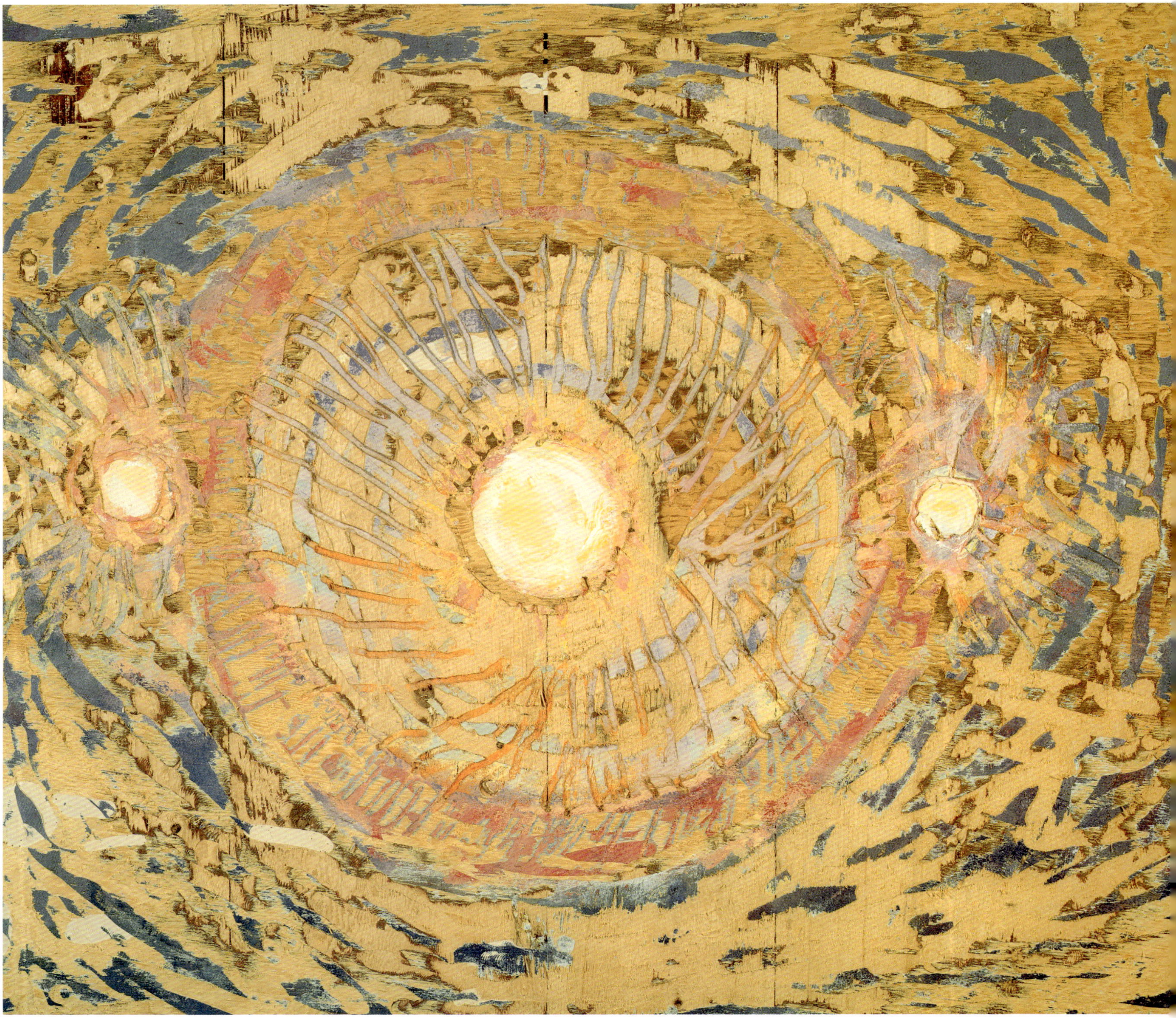

BIBLIOGRAPHY

Compilers' note: This bibliography is as comprehensive as possible. We welcome a record of significant citations that may have been omitted.

I. WRITINGS BY PATERSON EWEN

"About Marian Scott." *20 Cents Magazine* 3, no. 9 (November 1969).

"An Autobiographical Statement: Paterson Ewen." *Brick* 32 (Winter 1988): 23–24.

Untitled article [on Jack Chambers] in *Reflecting a Rural Consciousness*. Peterborough: Artspace, 1980.

II. UNPUBLISHED SOURCES

Biographical statement, 1968. Dunkelman Gallery papers, MG 28 III 110 Vol. 2, National Archives of Canada.

Ewen, Paterson. Acceptance speech at presentation of honorary degree, University of Western Ontario, London, 1989.

Ewen, Paterson. Canada Council art programs applications: 1962, 1964, 1968, 1970, 1971, 1972, 1975, 1983 and 1985.

Fortin, Pierre. *The Critical Development of Patterson [sic] Ewen.* Under-graduate paper, University of Western Ontario, London, Ontario, 1982.

Fraser, Heather A. *Paterson Ewen: The Turn from Non-Figurative to Figurative Painting (1947–1970)*. M.A. Thesis, Queen's University, Kingston, Ontario, 1989.

Handford, Mary. *Paterson Ewen.* Undergraduate paper, University of Western Ontario, London, Ontario, 1979.

Maycock, Bryan, *et al. Pie in the Sky Group*. Typescript summarizing the London Warehouse Co-op exhibition at 77 Avenue Road, Toronto. London, 1971.

III. TAPE-RECORDED INTERVIEWS, PRESENTATIONS AND CONVERSATIONS

1969. Paterson Ewen interview by Greg Curnoe, 18 March 1969.

1970. Discussion at 20/20 Gallery, London, Ontario, 6 January 1970, at the opening of the *Paterson Ewen Retrospective*. Participants: Paterson Ewen, Barry Lord, Robert Millet (panel), and, among others, David Rabinowitch, Royden Rabinowitch, Goldie Rans (audience).

1976. Boardroom presentation by Paterson Ewen at Nova Scotia College of Art and Design, Halifax, March 1976.

1976. Paterson Ewen interview by Robert McKaskell, London, Ontario, spring 1976.

1977. Paterson Ewen interview by Doris Shadbolt at Vancouver Art Gallery, Vancouver, February 1977.

1979. Paterson Ewen interview by Linda Kricorissian at Art Gallery of Ontario, Toronto, 23 April 1979.

1986. Paterson Ewen interview by Matthew Teitelbaum, 6-13 June 1986.

1988. Paterson Ewen interview by Matthew Teitelbaum, 13 June 1988.

1990. Paterson Ewen interview by Matthew Teitelbaum, December 1990.

1995. David Gordon interview by Matthew Teitelbaum, 1 August 1995.

IV. BOOKS

Balkind, Alvin, *et al. Visions: Contemporary Art in Canada*. Vancouver and Toronto: Douglas & McIntyre, 1983.

Burnett, David. *Cineplex Odeon, the First Ten Years: A Celebration of Contemporary Canadian Art*. Toronto: Cineplex Odeon Corporation, 1989.

Burnett, David. *Masterpieces of Canadian Art from the National Gallery of Canada*. Edmonton: Hurtig Publishers, 1990.

Burnett, David, and Marilynn Schiff. *Contemporary Canadian Art*. Edmonton: Hurtig Publishers, 1983.

Campbell, James D. *Startled wonder: the phenomenascapes of Paterson Ewen*. Toronto: Carmen Lamanna Gallery, 1989.

Ferron, Jacques. *The Penniless Redeemer*. Trans. by Ray Ellenwood. Toronto: Exile Editions, 1984. (Originally published in French as *Le Ciel de Québec*. Montréal: VLB Éditeur, 1979.)

Poole, Nancy. *The Art of London, 1830–1980*. London, Ont.: Blackpool Press, 1984.

Robert, Guy. *L'Art au Québec depuis 1940*. Montréal: Éditions La Presse, 1973.

Viau, Guy. *La peinture moderne au Canada français*. Québec: Ministère des Affaires culturelles, 1964.

V. CATALOGUES OF EXHIBITIONS: SOLO SHOWS

Bradley, Jessica. *Paterson Ewen: Biennale di Venezia, 1982: Canada*. Ottawa: National Gallery of Canada for the Corporation of National Museums of Canada, 1982.

Foreman, Brian. *Vancouver Art Gallery Collection: Paterson Ewen*. Vancouver: Vancouver Art Gallery, 1993.

Fraser, Heather A. *Paterson Ewen: Critical Works: Works on Paper, 1949–92*. Hamilton: Art Gallery of Hamilton, 1992.

McKaskell, Robert. *Paterson Ewen Retrospective*. London, Ont.: London Art Gallery, 1976.

Monk, Philip. *Paterson Ewen: Phenomena: Paintings 1971–1987*. Toronto: Art Gallery of Ontario, 1988.

Paterson Ewen: Recent Paintings. New York: Paolo Baldacci [Gallery], 1993.

Sawchyn, Linda. *Paterson Ewen, Interior Motives*. Saskatoon: Mendel Art Gallery, 1993.

Shadbolt, Doris. *Paterson Ewen, Recent Works*. Published as *Journal* no. 24 (1 September 1977). Ottawa: National Gallery of Canada, 1977.

Shadbolt, Doris, and Nick Johnson. *Paterson Ewen, Recent Works*. Vancouver: Vancouver Art Gallery, 1977.

Teitelbaum, Matthew. *Paterson Ewen: The Montreal Years*. Saskatoon: Mendel Art Gallery, 1987.

VI. CATALOGUES OF EXHIBITIONS: GROUP SHOWS

Aarons, Anita. *Painting 82 / Painting 82; an Exhibition in Two Parts*. Toronto: Art Gallery at Harbourfront, 1982.

Amman, Jean-Christophe, *et al. Neun kanadische Künstler*. Basel: Kunsthalle, 1978.

Art Montreal '67; Paintings and Sculptures. Toronto: Dunkelman Gallery, 1967.

Balkind, Alvin. "Ontario" in *The Canadian Canvas; a Travelling Exhibition of 85 Recent Paintings*. [n.p.]: Time Canada Ltd., 1974.

Balkind, Alvin, *et al. Peintres canadiens actuels/The Canadian Canvas*. Montreal: Musée d'art contemporain, 1975.

Balkind, Alvin. *17 Canadian Artists: a Protean View*. Vancouver: Vancouver Art Gallery, 1976.

Bélisle, Josée, and Pierre Landry. *Ewen, Gagnon, Gaucher, Hurtubise, McEwen: à propos d'une peinture des années soixante*. Montréal: Musée d'art contemporain, 1988.

Berlind, Robert. *The Seventh Dalhousie Drawing Exhibition: Actual Size*. Halifax: Dalhousie Art Gallery, Dalhousie University, 1984.

Bierk, David. *Reflecting a Rural Consciousness / Reflexion sur un sentiment rural*. Peterborough, Ont.: Artspace; Paris: Centre Cultural Canadien / Canadian Cultural Centre, 1980.

Carr-Harris, Ian. *How we see What we say*. Toronto: Harbourfront Art Gallery, l986.

Corbeil, Gilles, and Claude Gauvreau. *Espace 55: Exhibition Showing 11 Montreal Painters*. Montreal: Montreal Museum of Fine Arts, 1955.

Daigneault, Gilles. *Montréal 1942–1992: l'anarchie resplendissante de la peinture*. Montréal: Galerie de l'Université de Québec, 1992.

DeGrow, Donald. *London Painting Now (a Survey of London Painting, first in a series of 4 survey exhibitions)*. London: London Art Gallery, 1976.

Delloye, Charles, *et al. La Peinture canadienne moderne*. Quebec: Ministère des Affaires culturelles du Québec, 1962.

80th Annual Spring Exhibition. Montreal: Montreal Museum of Fine Arts, 1963.

Forum 76. Montreal: Montreal Museum of Fine Arts, 1976.

4 in 5: Four Artists in May. Stratford, Ont.: Rothman's Art Gallery, 1970.

Graham, Mayo. *Greg Curnoe, Paterson Ewen, Gathie Falk, Ron Moppett*. Regina, Sask.: Norman Mackenzie Art Gallery, 1982.

Grenville, Bruce. *The Allegorical Image in Recent Canadian Painting*. Kingston: Agnes Etherington Art Centre, 1985.

Hénault, Gilles. *Panorama de la peinture au Québec 1940–1966*. Montréal: Musée d'art contemporain, 1967.

James, Geoffrey. *Contemporary Canadian Painters: an Exhibition of Works from the Canada Council Art Bank, Presented by the Department of External Affairs of Canada*. Paris: Canadian Cultural Centre, 1977.

Jenkner, Ingrid. *Recreating the Landscape*. Sarnia, Ont.: Sarnia Public Library and Art Gallery, 1981.

Jenkner, Ingrid. *Site Memory: Contemporary Art from Canada*. Guelph: Macdonald Stewart Art Centre, 1991.

Lamanna, Carmen. *The Carmen Lamanna Gallery at the Owens Art Gallery [Sackville, N.B.]*. Toronto: Carmen Lamanna Gallery, 1974.

Leclerc, Denise. *The Crisis of Abstraction in Canada: the 1950s*. Ottawa: National Gallery of Canada, 1992.

McWilliams, Allan. *Creative Flight*. Surrey, B.C.: Surrey Art Gallery, 1979.

Moppett, George. *London • Saskatoon • Exchange*. Saskatoon, Sask.: Mendel Art Gallery, 1977.

Nasgaard, Roald. *The Queen's Silver Jubilee Art Collection: a Selection of Contemporary Canadian Art*. Toronto: The Queen's Silver Jubilee Committee, Government of Ontario, 1977.

Nasgaard, Roald. *10 Canadian Artists in the 1970s*. Toronto: Art Gallery of Ontario, 1980.

Nasgaard, Roald, and Karen Wilkin. *Changing Visions: the Canadian Landscape*. Toronto: Art Gallery of Ontario; Edmonton: Edmonton Art Gallery, 1976.

O'Brien, Paddy. *The Heart of London*. London, Ont.: London Regional Art Gallery, 1981.

Paikowsky, Sandra. *The Non-Figurative Artists' Association of Montréal*. Montréal: Sir George Williams Art Galleries, Concordia University, 1983.

Poole, Nancy. *London S/W 17*. Stratford, Ont.: Rothmans Art Gallery, 1970.

Reid, Dennis. *Twentieth Century Canadian Painting*. Tokyo: National Museum of Modern Art, 1981.

Rodger, Judith. *WaterWorks*. London: London Regional Art Gallery, 1987.

Saint-Martin, Fernande. *Trois générations d'art québécois, 1940, 1950, 1960*. Montréal: Musée d'art contemporain, 1976.

Seitz, William. *Seventh Biennial of Canadian Painting*. Ottawa: National Gallery of Canada, 1968.

Seven Canadian Painters Selected from the Canada Council Art Bank. Toronto: Harbourfront Art Gallery, 1976.

78th Annual Spring Exhibition. Montreal: Montreal Museum of Fine Arts, 1961.

79th Annual Spring Exhibition. Montreal: Montreal Museum of Fine Arts, 1962.

Shepherd, Michael. *Canadian Art in Britian*. London: Canada House Cultural Centre Gallery, 1982.

67th Annual Spring Exhibition. Montreal: Montreal Museum of Fine Arts, 1950.

Spalding, Jeffrey. *Aspects of Canadian Painting in the Seventies*. Calgary: Glenbow Museum, 1980.

Tamplin, Illi-Maria. *Atmospheric Synthesis: Paterson Ewen, Otto Rogers, Gathie Falk, David Bierk*. Peterborough, Ont.: Art Gallery of Peterborough, 1985.

The Tenth Winnipeg Show. Winnipeg: Winnipeg Art Gallery 1966.

30th Annual Western Ontario Exhibition. London: London Public Library and Art Museum, 1970.

33rd Annual Western Ontario Exhibition. London: London Public Library and Art Museum, 1973.

Valliant, Lois. *Montreal 1950's & 1960's: Works on Paper: Surrealist/Automatiste/Abstract Cross-Currents*. Montreal: Concordia Art Gallery, 1989.

Walter, John A. *Centennial Exhibition of Quebec and Ontario Contemporary Painters 1967*. Kitchener: Kitchener-Waterloo Art Gallery, 1967.

Wechsler, Jeffrey. *A Response to the Environment*. New Brunswick, N.J.: Rutgers University Art Gallery, 1975.

VII. EXHIBITION REVIEWS: ANONYMOUS

"À New York." *La Presse* [Montréal], 25 février 1956. [Parma Gallery, New York]

"Art: Fine Arts Museum Showing Espace 55." *The Gazette* [Montreal], 12 February 1955. [*Espace 55*, Montreal Museum of Fine Arts]

"Art: Gallery XII Shows Andrew, Ewen Works." *The Gazette* [Montreal], 14 May 1955. [Gallery XII, Montreal Museum of Fine Arts]

"The Art Bank is Coming . . . the Art Bank is Coming!" *Harbourfront News* 2, no. 17 (17 September 1976). [*Seven Canadian Painters Selected from the Canada Council Art Bank*]

"At Galerie Delrue." *Montreal Gazette*, 23 February 1963.

"Au Musée. Les 'Lyriques formalistes' à la galerie de l'Étable." Unidentified newspaper clipping, ca. January 1960. [Galerie de l'Étable, Musée des beaux-arts de Montréal]

"Eine Ausstellug der Kunsthalle Basel betritt Neuland: Erstmals Künstler aus Kanada in der Schweiz." Unidentified newspaper clipping, 1978. [*Neun kanadische Künstler*]

"Auto Displays Replaced by Art." *London Free Press*, 22 March 1971. [London Warehouse Co-op exhibition at 77 Avenue Road, Toronto]

"La coulisse d'une galerie." *Le Devoir* [Montréal], 21 juin 1958). [Galerie Denyse Delrue]

"'Espaces 55' groupera neuf peintres au Musée . . ." *La Presse* [Montréal], 11 janvier 1955. [*Espace 55*, Musée des beaux-arts de Montréal]

"Exhibition of Oils and Watercolors at Parma Gallery." *Art News* 55 (March 1956):54. [Parma Gallery]

"Exposition Paterson Ewen et Armand Vaillancourt." *La Presse* [Montréal], 12 novembre 1959. [Galerie Denyse Delrue]

"The Heady Eccentricity of Paintings by Paterson Ewen." *Montreal Calendar Magazine* (6 January to 2 February 1978). [Paterson Ewen and Ann McCall, Sir George Williams Art Galleries, Concordia University]

"Kanadische Künstler in der Kunsthalle: Suche nach eigenen Wegen." *Basler Volksblatt*, no. 150 (1 Juli 1978). [*Neun kanadische Künstler*]

"Kunsthalle: Kanadische Künstler." *Basler Allgemeine Zeitung*, 26 Juni 1978.

"Montreal Missing out on Magnificent Ewen Show: Powerful Retrospective to Travel Across Canada." *Montreal Gazette*, 26 March 1988, D5. [*Paterson Ewen: Phenomena: Paintings 1971–1987*]

"Neun kanadische Künstler." *Basler Woche*, no. 24, 16 Juni 1978.

"Neun kanadische Künstler in der Kunsthalle Basel." *Luzerner Neueste Nachrichten*, 16 Juni 1978. [*Neun kanadische Künstler*]

"New Art Group [The Formal Lyricists] Plans Exhibition." Unidentified newspaper clipping, ca. January 1960. [Galerie de l'Étable, Montreal Museum of Fine Arts]

"Noises Off: [New York discovers Paterson Ewen]." *Globe and Mail* [Toronto], 4 March 1994, C6. [Paolo Baldacci Gallery, New York]

"Nouvelles des arts: chez Denyse Delrue." *Le Devoir* [Montréal], 9 novembre 1961.

"Pat Ewen chez Denyse Delrue." *La Presse* [Montréal], 18 novembre 1961.

"Paterson et Vaillancourt exposent." *Le Devoir* [Montréal], 11 November 1959. [Galerie Denyse Delrue]

"Patterson [*sic*] Ewen." *Montreal Gazette*, 25 November 1961. [Galerie Denyse Delrue]

"Paterson Ewen: New Paintings & Works on Paper." *Globe and Mail* [Toronto], 17 November 1989, C6. [Carmen Lamanna Gallery]

"Paterson Ewen: Œuvres récentes." *Le Soleil de Colombie* [Vancouver], 28 avril 1977, 7. [*Paterson Ewen: Recent Works*]

"Paterson Ewen at Art Gallery of Hamilton." *Globe and Mail* [Toronto], 25 July 1992, C13. [*Paterson Ewen: Critical Works: Works on Paper, 1949–92*]

"Paterson Ewen at Dalhousie Art Gallery." *Halifax Chronicle Herald*, 28 October 1988, 4E. [*Paterson Ewen: Phenomena: Paintings 1971–1987*]

"Paterson Ewen at Montreal Museum of Fine Arts." *Montreal Gazette*, 7 October 1989, H5. [*Paterson Ewen: Phenomena: Paintings 1971–1987*]

"La Peinture: Ewen et Deziel: Paterson Ewen." *Le Haut Parleur* [St-Hyacinthe], 21 mai 1950. [First one-man exhibition at 1445 Crescent Street, Montreal]

"Peinture abstraite et péril atomique." *La Patrie*, 26 novembre 1961. [Galerie Denyse Delrue]

"Retrospective show." *Montreal Gazette*, 11 June 1960. [Galerie Denyse Delrue]

"Sept peintres contemporains." *Canada d'Aujourd'hui* no. 41 (octobre 1977). [*Seven Canadian Painters Selected from the Canada Council Art Bank*]

"Two New Exhibits Planned." *Halifax Mail Star*, 30 August 1977. [*Paterson Ewen: Recent Works*]

Untitled review. *Artscanada* no. 30 (December 1973):194 ff. [Carmen Lamanna Gallery]

Untitled review. *Artnews* no. 79 (Summer 1980):218 ff. [Carmen Lamanna Gallery]

Untitled review. *Globe and Mail* [Toronto], 20 October 1973. [Carmen Lamanna Gallery]

"Visions of Paterson Ewen." *London Free Press*, 29 April 1988, E1–E[2]. [*Paterson Ewen: Phenomena: Paintings 1971–1987*]

"Yves Trudeau et Paterson Ewen exposent des œuvres récentes." *La Nouvelliste* [Trois-Rivières], 8 novembre 1963. [Galerie XII, Musée des beaux-arts de Montréal]

VIII. EXHIBITION REVIEWS

Andreae, Janice. "At Forest City Gallery: Ewen's Landscapes 'Unique'." *London Free Press*, 29 September 1975. [*Paterson Ewen Watercolours*]

Andreae, Janice. "Paterson Ewen." [Exhibition] *Parachute* 51 (June–August 1988):38–39. [*Paterson Ewen: Phenomena: Paintings 1971–1987*; *Paterson Ewen: the Montreal Years*]

Andreae, Janice. "The Season in Review: London, Ontario: London and Area Artists part 1 at the London Regional Art Gallery." *Artmagazine* (February–March 1981):52–53. [*Heart of London*]

Ashberry, John. "Paterson Ewen." *Art News* 56, no. 9 (January 1958):57. [Parma Gallery]

Ayre, Robert. "Art Notes: Non-Objective Can Be Non-Meaningful." *Montreal Star*, 11 February 1956. [*7 Peintres actuels*, Galerie L'Actuelle, Montreal]

Ayre, Robert. "Clearing Out the Clutter." *Montreal Star*, 15 March 1964. [*Dynamisme '64*, Galerie du Siècle, Montréal]

Ayre, Robert. "The 67th Show: Varied Array is Presented." *Montreal Star*, 18 March 1950. [*Spring Exhibition*, Montreal Museum of Fine Arts]

Baele, Nancy. "'Phenomascapes,' the Paintings on Plywood." *Ottawa Citizen*, 30 January 1988. [*Paterson Ewen: Phenomena: Paintings 1971–1987*]

Baele, Nancy. "A Scientific Approach to Art: National Gallery Exhibit Marries Two Disciplines." *Ottawa Citizen*, 1 April 1989, C1, C12. [*Paterson Ewen: Phenomena: Paintings 1971–1987*]

Bale, Doug. "Paterson Ewen at the London Regional Art & Historical Museum." *London Free Press*, 3 October 1992.

Barnard, Elissa. "'Phenomascapes' Crack, Hiss with Force of Nature." *Halifax Mail Star*, 28 October 1988. [*Paterson Ewen: Phenomena: Paintings 1971–1987*]

Bernier, J.-J. "Paterson Ewen, Betty Goodwin." *Parachute* 45 (décembre–janvier 1986/87):29–30.

Blendell, Peter. "Paterson Ewen at Carmen Lamanna." *Artists Review* no. 8 (30 January 1978).

Bogardi, Georges. "Unlocking the Vault." *Montreal Star*, 27 November 1976. [*Seven Canadian Painters Selected from the Canada Council Art Bank*]

Bowen, Lisa Balfour. "Art: AGO Season-Opener not to be Taken Seriously." *Toronto Star*, 13 September 1980. [*10 Canadian Artists in the 1970s*]

Bowen, Lisa Balfour. "Master Artist Paterson Ewen: . . . and a Few Parallels to van Gogh." *Toronto Sunday Sun*, 24 January 1988, S12–S13. [*Paterson Ewen: Phenomena: Paintings 1971–1987*]

Bowen, Lisa Balfour. "Sculpture Dominates International Art Show." *Globe and Mail* [Toronto], 16 June 1982. [Venice Biennale]

Carroll, Nancy. "Paterson Ewen." *Parachute* 26 (printemps 1982):41. [Carmen Lamanna Gallery]

Carroll, Nancy. "Paterson Ewen: Carmen Lamanna Gallery." *Vanguard* 9, no. 3 (April 1980):22–23.

Chandler, John Noel. "*17 Canadian Artists—A Protean View*: The Vancouver Art Gallery." *Artscanada* 33, no. 3 (October–November 1976):56–60.

Crawford, Lenore. "Ewen Art Works Lauded." *London Free Press*, 7 January 1970. [*Paterson Ewen Retrospective 1947-1969*, 20/20 Gallery, London, Ontario]

Crawford, Lenore. "Ewen's Life Stream Art Work on Display at City Museum." *London Free Press*, 9 September 1969. [*Three Man Show: Rabinowitch, Ewen and Rabinowitch*, London Public Library and Art Museum, London, Ontario]

Cron, Marie-Michèle. "La Rentrée culturelle: Arts visuels: Terre, Terre!" *Le Devoir* [Montréal], 29 août 1993, C24. [*Terra Incognita*, Expression Centre d'exposition de Saint-Hyacinthe]

Curiger, Bice. "Eine anregende bis aufregende Art Kunst zu machen." *Tagesanzeiger* [Zürich], 22 Juni 1978. [*Neun kanadische Künstler*]

Curnoe, Greg. "Paterson Ewen: phenomena paintings 1971–1987: Monk's dream." *Parachute* 55 (juillet–septembre 1989):61–63. [*Paterson Ewen: Phenomena: Paintings 1971–1987*]

Dash, R. Warren. "Paterson Ewen." *Arts* 32, no. 4 (January 1958):60–61. [Parma Gallery]

Dault, Gary Michael. "London Painter Hacks and Grinds Majestic Landscapes on Plywood." *Toronto Star*, 20 January 1978. [Carmen Lamanna Gallery]

Dault, Gary Michael. "Paterson Ewen at Carmen Lamanna." *Vanguard* 11, no. 3 (April 1982):33 [Carmen Lamanna Gallery]

Dault, Gary Michael. "Refreshing Landscapes are Painted on Plywood." *Toronto Star*, 6 December 1974, E12. [Carmen Lamanna Gallery]

Dault, Gary Michael. "Two of the Best Within a Block [Paterson Ewen and Graham Coughtry]." *Toronto Star*, 21 January 1980, F7. [Carmen Lamanna Gallery]

De Repentigny, Françoise. "Un Beau travail de collaboration." *La Presse*, [Montréal] 7 décembre 1957. [Galerie Denyse Delrue,]

De Repentigny, Françoise. "D'Anciennes figures de rêve sous des formes et des couleurs neuves." *La Presse*, [Montréal] 20 mars 1956. [L'île Ste-Hélène, Montréal]

De Repentigny, Françoise. "Le Formel lyrique à l'Étable: 4 peintures, un monde en équilibre." *Le Devoir* [Montréal], 9 janvier 1960. [Galerie de l'Étable, Musée des beaux-arts de Montréal]

De Repentigny, Françoise. "Une galerie adaptée à la peinture." *La Presse* [Montréal], 21 septembre 1957. [Opening of Galerie Denyse Delrue]

Dénéchaud, Jean. "Exposition de Paterson Ewen." *La Presse* [Montréal], 10 mai 1950. [First one-man exhibition at 1445 Crescent Street, Montreal]

Dexter, Gail. "Art." *Toronto Star*, 16 March 1969. [Dunkelman Gallery, Toronto]

Dexter, Gail. "Ewen, Miro, and a Letter from [Dennis Burton]." *Toronto Saturday Star*, 16 March 1968. [Dunkelman Gallery]

Duncan, Ann. "Ewen Exhibition, Brilliant, Even if it's Late, Scaled Down." *Montreal Gazette*, 7 October 1989. [*Paterson Ewen: Phenomena: Paintings 1971–1987*]

Duncan. "Show Explores Early Years of Compelling Artist." *Montreal Gazette*, 15 October 1988, H13. [*Paterson Ewen: The Montreal Years*]

Edmonstone, Wayne. "Amalgam of Images: Artist Ewen at Work." *Vancouver Sun*, 21 May 1977. [*Paterson Ewen, Recent Works*]

Eyre, Janieta. "Ewen's Art Yields Symbolism and More Pedestrian Pleasures." *The Varsity* [University of Toronto], 29 February 1988, 16. [*Paterson Ewen: Phenomena: Paintings 1971–1987*]

Filler, Marion. "The Arts: Show Reveals Sophistication of Canadians." *Daily Record* [Morristown], 25 May 1980. [*Contemporary Canadian Painters: an Exhibition of Works from the Canada Council Art Bank*]

Folch, Jacques. "Paterson Ewen." *Vie des Arts* no. 25 (Winter 1961–62):53.

Friedrichs, Y. "Künstler aus Kanada der 70er Jahre." *Kunstwerk* 34, no. 3 (1981):78.

Gaudet, Éliane. "La passion des phénomènes naturels : Paterson Ewen au Musée des beaux-arts." *Le Droit* [Ottawa-Hull], 25 mars 1989, 11A. [*Paterson Ewen: Phenomena: Paintings 1971–1987*]

Giani, Claudia. "Neun kanadische Künstler in der Kunsthalle Basel." Unidentified newspaper clipping, 1978. [*Neun kanadische Künstler*]

Gladu, Paul. "L'expo des 'formalistes lyriques'." *Le Petit Journal*, 17–24 janvier 1960. [Galerie de l'Étable, Musée des beaux-arts de Montréal]

Godley, Elizabeth. "Nature's Forces: the Big Picture." *Vancouver Sun*, 14 July 1988. [*Paterson Ewen: Phenomena: Paintings 1971–1987*]

Grande, John K. Untitled review. *Artforum* 28 (January 1990):151. [*Paterson Ewen*, Montreal Museum of Fine Arts, Montreal]

Guilbert, Charles. "Paterson Ewen: Notre peintre qui êtes aux cieux." *Voir* [Montréal], 5–11 octobre 1989. [*Paterson Ewen: Phenomena: Paintings 1971–1987*]

Hale, Barry. "Art." *Toronto Daily Star*, 7 November 1969. [Carmen Lamanna Gallery]

Hanna, Deidre. "Ewen's Astonishing Gouged Landscapes." *Now*, 9–15 November 1989, 48. [Carmen Lamanna Gallery]

Hanna, Deidre. "Looking Inside Native culture, City Celebrations, Ewen's Wit." *Now*, 8–14 October 1987. [Carmen Lamanna Gallery]

Hanna, Deidre. "Paterson Ewen at the Carmen Lamanna Gallery." *Now*, 8–14 October 1987.

Hodge, Paul. "Four Artists Featured in Exhibition." *Regina Leader Post*, 15 January 1982. [Greg Curnoe, Paterson Ewen, Gathie Falk, Ron Moppett]

Homer, Merlin. "Paterson Ewen at Carmen Lamanna." *Proof Only* 1, no. 1 (15 November 1973):4.

Hooker, D. "Paterson Ewen." *Arts Review*, pt. 22 (22 October 1982):550. [Venice Biennale selection at Canada House Gallery, London]

Hornstein-Rabinovitch, Shelley. "Aura: Paterson Ewen." *C Magazine* 17 (Spring 1988):50–51. [Carmen Lamanna Gallery]

Hume, Christopher. "Art." *Toronto Star*, 23 November 1990. [Carmen Lamanna Gallery]

Hume, Christopher. "Art: Finding Excitement in Nature." *Toronto Star*, 20 October 1984. [Carmen Lamanna Gallery]

Hume, Christopher. "Router Replaces the Brush in Plywood Lunar Portraits." *Toronto Star*, 19 January 1988, H1. [*Paterson Ewen: Phenomena: Paintings 1971–1987*]

Inglis, Grace. "The Weatherman: The Forecast is Bright for Paterson Ewen's Paintings of Weather." *Hamilton Spectator*, 30 January 1988, D4. [*Paterson Ewen: Phenomena: Paintings 1971–1987*]

James, Geoffrey. "Art: Cosmic Visions from a Driven Creator." *Maclean's*, 8 February 1988, 36–37. [*Paterson Ewen: Phenomena: Paintings 1971–1987*]

Johnson, Nick. "Paterson Ewen: *Rain*," *Artscanada* 32, no. 1 (March 1975):40–45. [Carmen Lamanna Gallery]

Johnson, Nick. "Paterson Ewen: *Rain*." *Artscanada* no. 40 (March 1982):131–32.

Johnson, Nick. "10 Canadian Artists in the 70s." *Artscanada* no. 37 (December 1980–January 1981):44–45.

Klepac, Walter. "Toronto: Paterson Ewen at Carmen Lamanna." *Art in America* 66, no. 4 (July 1978):119.

Kritzwiser, Kay. "At the Galleries: Paterson Ewen." *Globe and Mail* [Toronto], 15 January 1972. [Carmen Lamanna Gallery]

Kritzwiser, Kay. "[Paterson Ewen at] Dunkelman Gallery." *Globe and Mail* [Toronto], 16 March 1968.

Kupper, Hans Jürg. "Metaphysik des Alltäglichen." *Basler Allgemeine Zeitung*, 11 Juni 1978, 6. [*Neun kanadische Künstler*]

Lajoie, Noël. "L'exposition de l'A.A.N.F.M." *Le Devoir* [Montréal], 10 mars 1956. [L'île Ste-Hélène, Montréal]

Lamy, Laurent. "Les Beaux-arts: Pat Ewen." *Le Devoir* [Montréal], 4 juin 1966.

Lamy, Laurent. "La Collection Delloye chez Denyse Delrue." *Le Devoir* [Montréal], 8 fevrier 1962. [Galerie Denyse Delrue]

Lamy, Laurent. "Dans les galeries, Pat Ewen et Françoise Sullivan au Centre Social de l'Association des Architectures." *Le Devoir* [Montréal], 21 juin 1962.

Lamy, Laurent. "La vie des Arts . . . : Pat Ewen, à la Galerie Denyse Delrue." *Le Devoir* [Montréal], 2 mars 1963.

Laurence, Robin. "Roller Coaster Ride into the Cosmos." *Vancouver Sun*, 27 November 1993, D6. [*The Canadian Spirit in Art*, Equinox Gallery, Vancouver]

Lawson, Shelley. "Phenomenascapes Land at National Gallery of Canada. *London Free Press*, 31 March 1989. [*Paterson Ewen: Phenomena: Paintings 1971–1987*]

Lawson, Shelley. "Show Unveils Ewen's Character: The Works Resemble Those of the Group of Seven." *London Free Press*, 9 September 1989. [*Paterson Ewen: Works on Paper*, Forest City Gallery, London, Ontario]

Lehman, Henry. "An Interior Climate." *Montreal Star*, undated clipping, 1976. [Galerie B, Montréal]

Lehman, Henry. "Two Artists, One Subject [Toni Onley and Paterson Ewen]." *Montreal Star*, 21 January 1978. [Sir George Williams Art Galleries, Concordia University, Montreal]

Lord, Barry. "New Work from Montreal," *Art in America* 57, no. 3 (May– June 1969):100. [*20 Year Retrospective*, McMaster University; Dunkelman Gallery]

Lord, Barry. "Ottawa: Seventh Biennial Exhibition of Canadian Painting." *Artscanada* (August 1968):38.

Lord, Barry. "Paterson Ewen." *Artscanada* no. 26 (December 1969): 60–61. [Carmen Lamanna Gallery]

Lowndes, Joan. "A Chance to Catch Proteus and Ask Him how Canada Ranks in Art." *Vancouver Sun*, 5 June 1976. [*17 Canadian Artists: a Protean View*]

Lupien, Jocelyne. "Les phénomènimages de Paterson Ewen." *ETC MONTRÉAL* no. 10 (Winter 1989):36–37. [*Paterson Ewen: Phenomena: Paintings 1971–1987*]

MacDonald, C. G. "Paintings at Local Exhibitions Range from Topical to Victorian." *Montreal Herald*, 9 May 1950. [First one-man exhibition at 1445 Crescent Street, Montreal]

MacKay, Mary. "Ewen's Style Clearly Improved with Age." *Windsor Star*, 15 April 1988. [*Paterson Ewen: The Montreal Years*]

MacWilliam, David. "Art." *Georgia Straight*, 26 May–2 June 1977, 17. [*Paterson Ewen: Recent Works*]

Malone, Judy. "Acclaim Eluded Artist 'til He Quit Courting It." *London Free Press*, 6 November 1976. [*Paterson Ewen Retrospective*]

Marler, Louise. "Paterson Ewen." *Artscanada* no. 234–235 (April–May 1980):38. [Carmen Lamanna Gallery]

Martin, Ron. "Paterson Ewen Retrospective 1947–1969." *20 Cents Magazine* [London, Ont.] 4, no. 2 (February 1970):25–28. [*Paterson Ewen Retrospective 1947–1969*, 20/20 Gallery, London, Ontario]

Martin, Ron. "Three Man Exhibition: David Rabinowitch, Royden Rabinowitch, Paterson Ewen at the London Public Library and Art Museum." *20 Cents Magazine* 3, no. 9 (November 1969).

Matyas, Joe. "A Sip of Ewen Not Nearly Enough." *London Free Press*, undated clipping [1995?], D3.[*The Montreal Connection*, McIntosh Gallery, University of Western Ontario, London]

Mays, John Bentley. "Art: Ewen's Cosmos Intelligent, Original." *Globe and Mail* [Toronto], 30 January 1982. [Carmen Lamanna Gallery]

Mays, John Bentley. "Artist Finds Resonant Images in Weather's Eternal Cycles." *Globe and Mail* [Toronto], 4 February 1988. [*Paterson Ewen: Phenomena: Paintings 1971–1987*]

Mays, John Bentley. "Dangerous Moons in Austere Quarters." *Globe and Mail* [Toronto], 26 November 1987. [Carmen Lamanna Gallery]

Mays, John Bentley. "Dash of Politics in AGO's Art Stew." *Globe and Mail* [Toronto], 6 September 1980. [*10 Canadian Artists in the 1970s*]

Mays, John Bentley. "Ewen Heads for the Top, By Way of Venice." *Globe and Mail* [Toronto], 21 June 1982. [Venice Biennale]

Mays, John Bentley. "Moving Images of Heaven and Earth." *Globe and Mail* [Toronto], 16 November 1990 [Carmen Lamanna Gallery].

Mays, John Bentley. "Paterson Ewen: New Paintings and Works on Paper at Carmen Lamanna." *Globe and Mail* [Toronto], 17 November 1989.

Mays, John Bentley. "World of Wonder." *Globe and Mail* [Toronto], 25 July 1992. [*Paterson Ewen: Critical Works: Works on Paper, 1949–1992*]

Mellow, James R. "In the Galleries: Modern Canadian Painters." *Arts Magazine* 30, no. 12 (September 1956):58. [*Modern Canadian Painters*, Parma Gallery]

Mellow, James R. "Paterson Ewen." *Arts Magazine* 30, no. 6 (March 1956):67. [Parma Gallery]

Mercer, Cydna. "Paterson Ewen: Phenomena, Paintings 1971–1987." *Muse* 7, no. 1 (Spring 1989):62–63.

Mercer, Cydna. "Paterson Ewen: Phenomena, Paintings 1971–1987." *Muse* (French edition) 7, no. 1 (Spring 1989) :64–65.

Miller, Earl. "Paterson Ewen at Carmen Lamanna." *Art Post* 5, no. 3 (Spring 1988):14–15.

Monk, Philip. "Condemned to history (but not invited to lunch): Reply to Greg Curnoe and Andy Patton." *Parachute* 56 (October–December 1989):78–9. [*Paterson Ewen: Phenomena: Paintings 1971–1987*]

Monk, Philip. "A '70s selection for export only." *Maclean's*, 29 September 1980. [*10 Canadian Artists in the 1970s*]

Mueller, Richard. "Paterson Ewen." *ArtsAtlantic* 9, no. 2 (Spring–Summer 1989):53–54. [*Paterson Ewen: the Montreal Years; Paterson Ewen: Phenomena: Paintings 1971–1987*]

Mullen, Rachel. "In the Galleries: Ideas, Color, and Line Given Free Rein at Nabisco's Canadian Exhibit." *Hunterdon Review* [Whitehouse Station, N.J.], 14 May 1980. [*Contemporary Canadian Painters: an Exhibition of Works from the Canada Council Art Bank*]

Munro, Eleanor C. "Paterson Ewen." *Art News* 55, no. 1 (March 1956):54. [Parma Gallery]

Murray, Joan. "*10 Canadian Artists in the 1970s* at the Art Gallery of Ontario." *Artmagazine* 12, no. 51 (November-December 1980):23–25.

Musiol, Marie-Jeanne. "Phénomènes de Paterson Ewen." *Vie des Arts* 34, 136 (automne 1989):66–67. [*Paterson Ewen: Phenomena: Paintings 1971–1987*]

Nasgaard, Roald. "Toronto." *Artscanada* 30, no. 5–6 (December 1973):193–97. [Carmen Lamanna Gallery]

Nemiroff, Diana. "Paterson Ewen et Ann McCall à l'université Concordia." *Vie des Arts* no. 23 (October–November 1977):45–46.

Nixon, Virginia. "Power-Tool Art Produces Exhilarating Canadiana." *Montreal Gazette*, 4 February 1978. [*Paterson Ewen: Recent Works*]

Nixon, Virginia. "Roundup: Weather Work, Art from Holland, Japan." *Montreal Gazette*, 24 December 1976. [Galerie B, Montréal]

Oxorn, Pearl. "Canadian Art Goes on the Road." *Ottawa Journal*, 4 December 1976. [*Seven Canadian Painters*]

P. J. "Paterson Ewen's Phenomenal Attack." *Now*, 11–17 February 1988. [*Paterson Ewen: Phenomena: Paintings 1971–1987*]

Paine, Paula. "Art: Show at AGO." *The Ontarion* [University of Guelph], 16 September 1980. [*10 Canadian Artists in the 1970s*]

Paradis, Andrée. "La Biennale de Venise: l'art comme art." *Vie des Arts* 27, no. 108 (automne 1982):41–42.

Parzybok, Steve. "Ron Martin's New Work and Paterson Ewen's Retrospective Show." *20 Cents Magazine* 4, no. 3 (March 1970):21. [*Paterson Ewen Retrospective 1947–1969*]

Patton, Andy. "History Evaporates: Philip Monk and Paterson Ewen." *Parachute* 55 (juillet–septembre 1989):63–67. [*Paterson Ewen: Phenomena: Paintings 1971–1987*]

Perry, Art. "Ewen Works Rough Edge of Expression." *Vancouver Province*, 28 May 1977. [*Paterson Ewen: Recent Works*]

Pfeiffer, Dorothy. "Art: Gallery XII." *Montreal Gazette*, 9 November 1963. [Gallery XII, Montreal Museum of Fine Arts]

Pfeiffer, Dorothy. "Non-Figurative Galaxy." *Montreal Gazette*, 20 September 1958. [The Non-Figurative Artists' Association of Montreal: Third Annual Show, Montreal Museum of Fine Arts]

Pfeiffer, Dorothy. "Non-Figurative Show." *Montreal Gazette*, 22 February 1958. [Galerie Denyse Delrue]

Pfeiffer, Dorothy. "Patterson [*sic*] Ewen." *Montreal Gazette*, 25 November 1961. [Galerie Denyse Delrue]

Purdie, James. "Art Bank Outshines Outdated Societies." *Globe and Mail* [Toronto], 16 October 1976. [*Seven Canadian Painters Selected from the Canada Council Art Bank*]

Reaney, James. "Art: Prairie Sky on the Inside, Projected Works on the Outside." *London Free Press*, 24 September 1983. [*Ontario Landscapes*]

Reid, Robert. "Exhibition Salutes Ewen's Innovation." *Kitchener-Waterloo Record*, 27 January 1988, D1–D2. [*Paterson Ewen: Phenomena: Paintings 1971–1987*]

Robert, Guy. "Ewen à la Galerie Denyse Delrue." *Le Devoir* [Montréal], 16 novembre 1961.

Robertson, Sheila. "Artist Comes to Terms with Forces of Nature." *Saskatoon Star-Phoenix*, 10 July 1993, D7. [*Paterson Ewen: Interior Motives*]

Robertson, Sheila. "Curator Explores Ewen's Roots." *Saskatoon Star-Phoenix, Sunday Accent*, 12 December 1987, 16. [*Paterson Ewen: The Montreal Years*]

Robitaille, Adrien. "Tempérament vrai : celui de Pat Ewen." *Le Devoir* [Montréal], 13 mai 1950. [First one-man exhibition at 1445 Crescent Street, Montreal]

Rosenberg, Anne. "Vancouver: Three-Part Review of Five Artists." *Artmagazine* 8, no. 34 (August-September 1977):25-28. [*Paterson Ewen, Recent Works*]

Sable, Jared. "A Display of Meagre Efforts." *Toronto Telegram*, 6 September 1969. [*Three Man Show: Rabinowitch, Ewen and Rabinowitch*, London Public Library and Art Museum, London, Ontario]

Sarrazin, Jean. "Paterson Ewen: Alertes et Blackout." *Le Nouveau Journal*, 18 novembre 1961. [Galerie Denyse Delrue]

Sarrazin, Jean. "Sculpter des statues . . . sculpter des hommes [Vaillancourt et Ewen]." Unidentified clipping, octobre/novembre 1959. [Galerie Denyse Delrue]

Schlagheck, Irma. "Kunst in Kanada mit auffallend grossem Anteil an Video-Artisten." *Neue Zürcher Zeitung*, no. 141 (1978):23. [*Neun kanadische Künstler*]

Sewell, Gregory. "If Macaroni Moves You . . ." *The Strand* [Victoria College, University of Toronto], 27 January 1988. [*Paterson Ewen: Phenomena: Paintings 1971–1987*]

Shadbolt, Doris. "Paterson Ewen: Recent Works," *Vanguard* 6, no. 4 (May 1977):12–13. [*Paterson Ewen, Recent Works*]

Shadbolt, Doris. "Paterson Ewen—Œuvres récentes." *Le Soleil de Colombie* [Vancouver], 20 mai 1977.

Shirey, David L. "A Sampling of Canada's Artistic Riches." *New York Times*, 18 May 1980. [*Contemporary Canadian Painters: An Exhibition of Works from the Canada Council Art Bank*]

Tancock, Martha. "Review: Artspace and AGP Host Companion Landscape Shows." *Peterborough Examiner*, 23 October 1985. [*The Physicality of Landscape; Atmospheric Synthesis*]

Taylor, Kate. "Paterson Ewen at Art Gallery of Hamilton." *Canadian Art* 9, no. 2 (Summer 1992):16. [*Paterson Ewen: Critical Works: Works on Paper, 1949–1992*]

Tousley, Nancy. "Canadian Painting: Aspects of the 70s." *Vanguard* 9, no. 5–6 (Summer 1980):30–37. [*Aspects of Canadian Painting in the Seventies*]

Tousley, Nancy. "Paterson Ewen." *Canadian Art* 10, no. 1 (Spring 1993):69, 71. [*The Canadian Spirit in Art*, Equinox Gallery]

Trowell, Ian. "Ewen Capturing Public Imagination." *London Free Press*, 29 January 1988. [*Paterson Ewen: Phenomena: Paintings 1971–1987 Paterson Ewen: The Montreal Years*]

Villeneuve, Paquerette. "Spoleto. Définitive entrée en scène de la peinture canadienne en Europe." *Aujourd'hui* (septembre 1962):46. [*La peinture canadienne moderne; 25 années de peinture au Canada-français*]

Villers, Jean-Pierre de. "Paterson Ewen: les années montréalaises." *Vie des Arts* 33, no. 132 (automne 1988):51–53. [*Paterson Ewen: The Montreal Years*]

Wanless, Tony. "Ewan [*sic*] Changes Plywood into Art." *Windsor Star*, 10 March 1978, 16. [*Paterson Ewen: Recent Works*]

Watkins, Eileen. "Art: Neighborly Visit." *Sunday Star Ledger* [Newark, N.J.], 1 June 1980. [*Contemporary Canadian Painters: an Exhibition of Works from the Canada Council Art Bank*]

Wei, Lilly. Untitled review. *Art in America* 82 (May 1994):117. [*Paterson Ewen: recent paintings*, Paolo Baldacci Gallery]

Weiler, Merike. "Abstract Artist Creates a New Landscape Style." *Toronto Star*, 18 January 1972. [Carmen Lamanna Gallery]

Wilkin, Karen. "Ten Canadians—and How a Controversy Grew." *Artnews* 80, no. 2 (February 1981):104-7. [*10 Canadian Artists in the 1970s*]

Wilkin, Karen. "Toronto [Paterson Ewen]." *Artnews* 79, no. 6 (summer 1980):218–19. [Carmen Lamanna Gallery]

Williams, Judy. "Reviews: Vancouver: Paterson Ewen." *Artscanada* 34, no. 3 (October–November 1977):45–46. [*Paterson Ewen: Recent Works*]

Wylie, Liz. "Rude Magnificence Pervades Ewen show." *The Georgian* [Concordia University], 20 January 1978, 7. [*Paterson Ewen: Recent Works*]

Wylie, Liz. Untitled reviews of *Paterson Ewen: Painting, 1971–1987 Phenomena* [by] Philip Monk; *Paterson Ewen: the Montreal years* [by] Matthew Teitelbaum. *Journal of Canadian Art History* 11, no. 1/2 (1988):139–41.

IX. ARTICLES: ANONYMOUS

"AGO Gains Major Collection of Paterson Ewen Paintings." *Toronto Star*, 7 July 1995, A2.

"AGO to Feature Ewen Paintings: 39 Works Donated for Canadian Show." *Globe and Mail* [Toronto], 7 July 1995, C8.

"The Art of Paterson Ewen." *Wood World* (February 1977):16–17.

"Award Honors Artist." *Edmonton Journal*, 9 July 1987.

"Banff Centre Award Goes to Ewen." *Globe and Mail* [Toronto], 30 June 1987.

"Canada Council Fellowships: Seven City Artists Chosen." *Montreal Star*, 24 February 1964.

"Canada Selects Abstract Artist for Venice Show." *Kitchener Waterloo Record*, 15 April 1982.

"Early Riopelle Acquired for Permanent Collection." *Western News* [University of Western Ontario, London], 10 December 1981.

"Ewen, Bierk Present Art Talks." *North Bay Nugget*, 27 July 1979.

"Ewen Gets Banff Centre Award." *Calgary Herald*, 2 July 1987.

"Ewen's Art 'Realistic'." *London Free Press*, 25 January 1978, D14.

"'Formal Lyricists' New Group to Seek Recognition in Arts." *Montreal Gazette*, 6 January 1960.

"Gallery Receives Works by Paterson Ewen." *Journal* [Art Gallery of Ontario] 3, no. 5 (September/October 1995):7.

". . . mais c'est passablement difficile . . . (Pat Ewen)." Interview, unidentified newspaper clipping, ca. 1960.

"Modern Art Salesmanship." *Toronto York Home News*, 30 December 1958.

"Mural Nears Completion." *Medium* [University of Lethbridge] 3, no. 16 (19 June 1981):1.

"Natural World Absorbs Artist." *Calgary Herald*, 29 December 1989, C1.

"One Drop at a Time." *London Free Press*, 19 July 1995.

"Paterson Ewen." *Globe and Mail* [Toronto], 15 January 1972.

"Paterson Ewen Making Name in Art Circles." *Kenora Miner and News*, 25 August 1950.

"Paterson Ewen Paints Weather." *Chimo!* 1, no. 2 (1978):23–26.

"Paterson Ewen Wins $20,000 Chalmers." *London Free Press*, 17 May 1995.

"Recent Acquisition [*Clouds over water*]." *The Gallery* [Art Gallery of Ontario] 2, no. 7 (September 1980):12.

"Sept peintures contemporaines." *Canada Today/d'aujourd'hui* no. 41 (octobre 1977).

"Seven City Artists Chosen." *Montreal Star*, 24 February 1964.

"Two London Artists Win $7,000 Awards." *London Evening Free Press*, 16 March 1971.

Untitled article [One Canadian talent . . .] *Windsor Star*, 27 December 1980.

X. ARTICLES

Andreae, Janice. "Artist in Profile: Paterson Ewen: Natural Forces Reign Supreme." *This Is London* 35, no. 3 (April 1981):13–15.

Andreae, Janice. "Paterson Ewen: Painting, Image and Allegory." *Parachute* 28 (September/October/November 1982): 22–28

Ayre, Robert. "Paterson Ewen." *Montreal Star*, 15 February 1958.

Ayre, Robert. "Paterson Ewen." *Montreal Star*, 2 March 1963.

Ayre, Robert. "Paterson Ewen." *Montreal Star*, 26 May 1966.

Baker, Kenneth. "A Canadian Painter in the American Tradition." *San Francisco Chronicle*, 6 February 1988.

Bale, Doug. "London Artist Wins Toronto Arts Award." *London Free Press*, 30 September 1988.

Bale, Doug. "Londoner Chosen for Venice Exhibition." *London Free Press*, 23 October 1981.

Bale, Doug. "On View: Of Note [Recent Acquisition, London Regional Art and Historical Museums]." *London Free Press*, 21 March 1992.

Bale, Doug. "Venice Bienale 'Olympics' of Art World." *London Free Press*, 23 April 1982.

Bale, Doug. "Works Begun as 'Anti-Art' Bring Ewen World Recognition." *London Free Press*, 23 April 1982.

Blackadar, Bruce. "Culture Community Saluted with Toronto Arts Awards." *Toronto Star*, 30 September 1988.

Bogardi, George. "Paterson Ewen's 'Phenomenascapes.'" *Chimo!* 5, no. 5 (September 1982):24–[26].

Carr-Harris, Ian. "Standing on the Mezzanine: Ewen, Wiitasalo, Monk and the AGO." *Vanguard* 17, no. 6 (December 1988–January 1989):10–15.

Cheetham, Mark A. "The Sublime Is Now (Again)." *C Magazine* 44 (Winter 1995):24–39.

Chicoine, René. "De la 'Montagne' de Ewen a la 'Rivière' de Zoa-Wa-Ki." *Le Devoir* [Montréal], 15 février 1958.

Chicoine, René. "Formes et Couleurs." *Le Devoir* [Montréal], 15 février 1958.

Chicoine, René. "Formes et Couleurs: syndicat des cadres." *Le Devoir* [Montréal], 14 février 1959.

Crawford, Lenore. "Looking at Art: Beal grads 'with the scene.'" *London Free Press*, 17 January 1970.

Crawford, Lenore. "Paterson Ewen: After 25 Years, He's an Overnight Success." *London Free Press*, 19 July 1975.

Dafoe, Chris. "Toronto Salutes Top Artists." *Globe and Mail* [Toronto], 30 September 1988.

Daigneault, Gilles. "Semaine faste pour la peinture." *Le Devoir* [Montréal], 27 septembre 1986.

Daigneault, Gilles. "Visual Arts in Canada." *Canada Today / d'aujourd'hui* 20, no. 1 (1989):9–10.

De Repentigny, Françoise. "Paterson Ewen." *Le Devoir* [Montréal], 15 février 1958.

De Repentigny, Françoise. "Peintres abstraits: fait concret." *Le Devoir* [Montréal], 29 janvier 1960.

De Repentigny, Rodolphe. "Comment le peintre Pat Ewen passa du paysage lyrique à l'abstraction." *La Presse* [Montréal], 27 janvier 1955.

De Repentigny, Rodolphe. "Hudon, Mousseau, Francis et autres." *La Presse* [Montréal], 4 fevrier 1956.

De Repentigny, Rodolphe. "Pat Ewen." *La Presse* [Montréal], 15 février 1958.

De Repentigny, Rodolphe. "Peintures Canadiennes: Confrontations." *La Presse* [Montréal], 15 avril 1956.

Dellamora, R. "Paterson Ewen's allegories." *Artsmagazine* 13, no. 58-9 (May–July 1982):17–22.

Duncan, Anne. "Township Artists Open Studios for Tours by Public." *Montreal Gazette*, 8 July 1995.

Ferron, Jacques. "Claude Gauvreau, from *Du fond de mon arrière cuisine*." *Exile* 3, no. 2 (1976):20–57.

Folch, Jacques. "Essai de situation." *Vie des Arts* (Christmas 1959):60.

Fraser, Heather C. "Paterson Ewen: the Turn from Non-Figurative to Figurative Painting." *Journal of Canadian Art History* 13, no. 1 (1990):25–52.

Freedman, Adele. "Phenomenology." *Canadian Art* 4, no. 4 (December 1987):60–67.

Greenwood, Michael. "Myth and Landscape." *Artscanada* 35, no. 3 (October/November 1978):1–8.

Hanna, Deirdre. "Paterson Ewen Gift Sparks AGO. Showcase." *Now*, 13–19 July 1995.

Hudson, Andrew. "Phenomenon: Colour Painting in Montreal." *Artscanada* (November/December 1964):358.

Jasmin, Claude. "Paterson Ewen." *La Presse* [Montréal], 2 mars 1963.

Kelly, Deirdre. "Paterson Ewen's Painterly Expression." *Globe and Mail* [Toronto], 19 May 1995, C9.

Kirchhoff, H. J. "Chalmers Winners a Cross Canada Cross-Section." *Globe and Mail* [Toronto], 16 May 1995, C1.

Kritzwiser, Kay. "The Elemental Art of Paterson Ewen." *Globe and Mail* [Toronto], 20 October 1984.

Kritzwiser, Kay. "Paterson Ewen." *Globe and Mail* [Toronto], 20 October 1973.

Lajoie, Noël. "Confrontations picturales." *Le Devoir* [Montréal], 4 février 1956.

Lawson, Shelley. "Ewen Exhibits Set for London." *London Free Press*, 23 January 1988.

Lawson, Shelley. "Visions of Paterson Ewen." *London Free Press*, 29 April 1988.

Leduc, Fernand. "La voie de la solitude." *Le Soleil*, 3 avril 1971.

MacDonald, Max. "An Awesome Dude of an Artist." *The Ontarian* [University of Guelph], 18 September 1990, 24.

MacKay, Gillian. "Profile: Paterson Ewen: Capturing the Universe in Process." *Maclean's*, 28 June 1982, 9–[11].

Mays, John Bentley. "Ewen's Cosmos Intelligent, Original." *Globe and Mail* [Toronto], 30 January 1982.

Mercer, Cydna. "Art: Exploring the Soul of a Changing Land." *London Free Press*, 2 April 1986, A13.

Millet, Robert. "Beaux-Arts: la mémoire." Unidentified newspaper clipping, 31 mars 1962.

Millet, Robert. "Un de ceux que se font voir ailleurs." *Le Magazine Maclean's*, avril 1968.

Monk, Philip. "Phenomena of Light and Space: Paintings by Paterson Ewen." *AGO* [Art Gallery of Ontario] *News* 10, no. 1 (January 1988):1.

Moore, Jacqueline, and Louis Jaques. "Their Objective Is Non-Objective." *Weekend Magazine*, 8 September 1956, 12.

Paikowsky, Sandra. "L'Association des Artistes Non Figuratifs de Montréal." *Vie des Arts* 26, no. 103 (été 1981):29–31, 76–78.

Rennie, Gary. "The Art of Judging." *Windsor Star*, 13 May 1977, 12.

Robillard, Yves. "Ewen : retour à l'école." *La Presse* [Montréal], 21 mai 1966.

Rochon, Lisa. "The Bandaged Man: The Art of Paterson Ewen." *Brick* 32 (Winter 1988):19–22.

Saint-Martin, Fernande. "Le Dynamisme des Plasticiens de Montréal," *Vie des Arts* 44 (automne 1966):44–48, 92–93, 98–99.

Teitelbaum, Matthew. "Exaltation: Paterson Ewen's *Rain* Triptych." *Review: Latin American Literature and Arts* (July-December 1987):46–49.

Tousley, Nancy. "Plywood Painter Makes Major Mural for Lethbridge." *Calgary Herald*, 13 June 1981.

Trowell, Ian. "Total Commitment, Total Artistry." *Christian Science Monitor*, 15 July 1989, 16–17.

Walford, Ursula. "London Artist Carves World-wide Reputation." *London Extra* [University of Western Ontario School of Journalism] 3, no. 3 (15 March 1978).

Bibliography compiled by staff of the E. P. Taylor Research Library and Archives, Art Gallery of Ontario.

PHOTO CREDITS

All photographs are by Carlo Catenazzi, Art Gallery of Ontario, Toronto, with the following exceptions:

Tess Boudreau: p. 21

Courtesy of Paterson Ewen: pp. 6, 8 (top), 8 (bottom), 9, 10, 11, 12, 13, 14, 15, 16, 17, 19, 20, 24, 29, 62 (left)

Dave Gordon: pp. 61, 62 (right)

Holly Hames, Vancouver Art Gallery: p. 69

Mary Handford: pp. 27, 28

Teresa Healy, Vancouver Art Gallery: p. 134

Grant Kernan, Mendel Art Gallery, Saskatoon: pp. 36, 38, 44, 50, 51 (bottom), 52, 55, 104, 110 (left), 110 (right), 117

London Free Press Collection of Photographic Negatives, The D. B. Weldon Library, The University of Western Ontario, London, Ontario: p. 23

London Regional Art Gallery: p. 70

Courtesy of Doris McNab: p. 18

Brian Maycock: p. 121

National Gallery of Canada, Ottawa: p. 92

Larry Ostrom: pp. 2, 66, 67, 76, 77, 127

Rose Art Museum, Brandeis University, Waltham, MA: p. 58

Don Vincent: pp. 31, 32

Additional notes: Goodridge Roberts's *Fourteen Island Lake* and Ewen's work *Untitled (Fourteen Island Lake)* (pages 44 and 45) were painted while working together in the summer of 1949. The images "Waterspout" (page 34) and "Drop of water in a hot frying pan" (page 62) are both drawn from source books in Paterson Ewen's library. *Moore House Comet* (page 88) was one of two paintings that Ewen showed in *The Canadian Canvas* with Eric Fischl. The other was *Portrait of Vincent* (page 134). For more than twenty years, *Midnight over the Prairie* (page 182) has hung in Paterson Ewen's studio. It reminds him, he says, to keep his edge.

Following page:

MIDNIGHT OVER THE PRAIRIE 1972

Tar and coconut matting

25.4 x 45.7

Collection Paterson Ewen

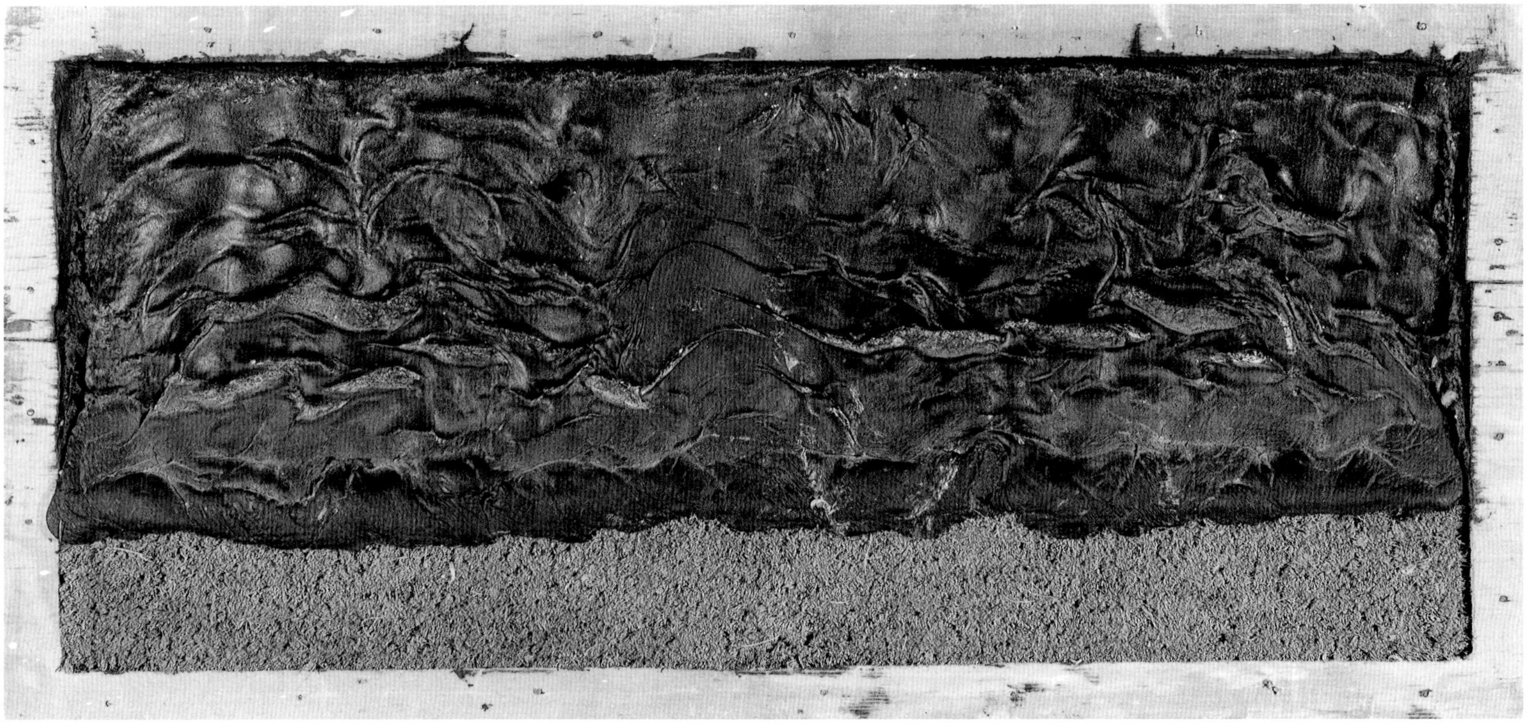